International Business Ethics
Challenges and Approaches

Edited by Georges Enderle

University of Notre Dame Press
Notre Dame   London

International Business Ethics
Copyright © 1999 by
The University of Notre Dame Press
Notre Dame, IN 46556
All rights reserved.

Manufactured in the United States of America

Library of Congress Cataloging-in-Publication Data

International business ethics : challenges and approaches / edited by
    Georges Enderle.
         p.   cm.
    Includes bibliographical references and index.
    ISBN 0-268-01213-X (cloth : alk. paper). — ISBN
0-268-01214-8 (pbk. : alk. paper)
        1. Business ethics. 2. International business enterprises —
Moral and ethical aspects.   I. Enderle, Georges.
HF5387.I58 1998
174'.4 – dc21   98-39116

∞ The paper used in this publication meets the minimum requirements
of the American National Standard for Information Sciences—Perma-
nence of Paper for Printed Materials, ANSI Z39.48-1984.

Contents

An Introduction to International Business Ethics

Georges Enderle

"International business ethics" is a fairly new field of investigation, compared to "business ethics" that already has a history of 25-plus years in North America, and, even more so, to the well-established disciplines of management, economics, and ethics. This new field is emerging not because it has been designed by academics, but primarily because international business itself has dramatically developed since the 1980s. It has brought about plenty of ethical implications and challenges. To a large extent, they affect not only "international" business but also "domestic" business, which are increasingly being interconnected, and reach far beyond the commonly defined "business domain." This process of globalization with multiple dimensions is extremely complex and rather opaque and, therefore, needs a great deal of clarification through thoughtful and courageous business initiatives as well as academic expertise.

This volume attempts to meet these needs. It proposes illuminating perspectives and signposts for this widely uncharted field, and reports about specific ethical commitments of business leaders and organizations. More than three dozens contributors, half of them from non-Western countries, form a truly international group, and paint an extraordinarily rich and fascinating picture of international business ethics as it evolves. They initially presented their views at the First World Congress of Business, Economics, and Ethics in 1996, organized by the International Society of Business, Economics, and Ethics (ISBEE) and hosted by Reitaku University and the Institute of Moralogy in Kashiwa-City near Tokyo. Then, in the light of intense discussions, substantial refinements were made and numerous links between different contributions were established. So it seems fair to say that this volume is a pioneer in international business ethics: it contains outstanding articles from practical as well as multidisciplinary perspectives, and delineates the contours of how international business ethics may develop at the turn of the Millennium.

Challenges

The title points to "challenges" of, and "approaches" to, international business ethics. Before introducing the four topic areas of this volume, I would like to highlight a few general findings. The rhetorics both of globalization and the triumphant advance of capitalism easily lead to the conclusion that we live in a rather homogeneous world, at least with regard to the logic of business and economics. However, as several contributors forcefully argue, this quite simplistic view does not reflect at all today's "real world" in which we live. To presuppose a homogeneous global market place either reveals a substantial lack of knowledge or mirrors an astonishing ethnocentric world view. Hence, even before asking for ethical guidance in international business, it is crucial to become aware of, and familiar with, the resistant *diversity* in space and time that characterizes business environment and business behavior. Such a sense of realism is imperative from two perspectives: the pursuit of long-term business success, and the relevance of ethics that is embedded in, and nurtured by, culture.

Nonetheless, humankind today faces enormous *common* challenges, recognized and reflected in a series of global summits on environment (1992), human rights (1993), population (1994), social development (1995), and women (1995). Ultimately, the substance and process of *development* are at stake, as diverse as the situations in individual – developed as well as developing – countries may be. It seems fair to say that in these conferences, despite many conflicts and opposing views, a certain consensus about major global problems has evolved while deep and far-reaching disagreements about the appropriate solutions still remain. Yet, these advances in common understanding are hardly shared by the majority of international businesses. Their concerns and objectives apparently are, at least, unrelated, if not contradictory, to the world views expressed in the documents prepared from the summits referenced above. In order to bridge this considerable gap, energetic and lasting efforts have to be made in both "camps," and much more interaction and a kind of continuous dialogue are necessary if these challenges are to be met efficiently and effectively. International business ethics should embrace this global perspective with determination and help develop practical ways of implementation.

It goes without saying that the challenges mentioned so far are only one, though a very important, part of what humankind faces at the end of this century. A number of additional questions arise and are addressed by various authors in this volume: violence and the legitimacy of international intervention; information technology in different cultures; the roles and responsibilities of nation states and multinational corporations; the need for a new generation of business leaders; the active participation of the world's religions in coping with global issues; and the prospect of East Asia as a major economic region that is going to considerably shape the whole world of the twenty-first century. There is no question that international business ethics is exposed to all these challenges. But how can, and maybe *should*, it approach them?

Approaches

To give a short answer, I would emphasize five complementary approaches that characterize, by and large, the following chapters. The first approach concerns the *economic analysis* implied in international business ethics. While such analysis is indispensable, it can be carried out in many different ways but it should, at least to some degree, allow for a somewhat differentiated understanding of economic success in multi-cultural settings. As A. Sen points out, this is not the case with the rudimentary but widely applied business principle of profit maximization in standard economic analysis. Already Adam Smith, wrongly implored as the father of this simple assumption, had a fairly sophisticated view. All the more in international business today, this principle has "little empirical support nor much analytical plausibility" (Sen 1999, 27). This criticism is strongly supported by A. Takahashi's studies on developing economies in East Asia. Although commonly applied, the standard Western economic models are unable to grasp the economic processes particularly in those rural areas, because they disregard the non-market and non-economic components and ignore the underlying subsistence ethics essential to survival and economic growth. Also, N. Bowie and P. Vaaler remind the reader that, according to more recent approaches in economic theory, ethical commitments beyond self-interest are not necessarily costs but can enhance the bottom line by helping to solve agency problems, lower transaction costs, and increase trust within and between organizations. To sum up this first point, international business ethics should be vigilant about the economic models and theories to be applied and needs less rudimentary approaches than profit maximization in order to thoroughly understand the economic processes and structures in the different parts of the world.

The second approach relates to the role of *cultures and values* for international business ethics. On the one hand, a number of contributors strongly emphasize the cultural idiosyncracies that should be taken seriously, without directly saying, though, "When in Rome, do as the Romans do." A. Sen notices that moral sentiments are seen by standard economic analysis to be quite complex but having a narrow reach, at least in economic matters. A. Takahashi insists on the relevance of cultural diversity and traditions for international business. E. Chepaitis highlights considerable differences between advanced and emerging economies with respect to information cultures defined as sets of values, beliefs, and behavior regarding information ownership and management. The chapters on China, Korea, the Philippines, and Japan all reflect the cultures' impact on ethical perception and behavior in business.

On the other hand, a search for common ethical values and standards beyond cultural differences can be found in many contributions: H. Küng's urgent plea for a global ethic; S. Webley's report on the Interfaith Declaration; the discussion of the Caux Principles for Business; N. Bowie and P. Vaaler's arguments for universal moral standards; the comparisons between, and synergies of, different ethical traditions discussed by K. Goodpaster, J. White, and T. Abeng. In the light of these reports and considerations, the common ethical ground for international business appears to be broader than one might have expected during the Cold-War era. Still, these common features are of a fairly general nature and many important differences, opposing views, and obstacles remain. This is not necessarily bad in every respect because a common ethical ground is only needed for what a community, be it local, national, or global, does and should do together. Moreover, A. Sen's warning against grand generalizations like "Asian values" versus "Western rationality" might be relevant in this context as well. Nonetheless, given the caveats against superficial harmonization and confrontation, a sound and lasting common ethical ground for international business is vital for humankind as we are moving towards an increasingly interconnected world.

Without doubt, the challenges involved in this process are unprecedented in human history and call for all available material and spiritual resources. Consequently, a third approach to cope with them should include a mobilization of *the world's religions*. For Westerners used to secularized societies, this call might sound strange, reviving old experiences of religious wars. However, the sociological fact is undeniable that a large majority of the world population today adheres to religious beliefs and, as H. Küng puts it, "there is no world peace without religious peace." Moreover, the world's religions do have a common heritage and share a common concern. Therefore, rather than teaching the world, the different religions should actively engage in bringing about mutual respect and understanding at the global scale and use their spiritual resources to help establish "a global ethic." Needless to say, how challenging this perspective is for both religious believers and non-believers alike.

A fair number of contributions substantiates this religious approach to international business ethics in one way or another. H. Küng proposes the fundamental consensus of the world's religions, expressed in the Declaration "Towards a Global Ethic" (1993), as the basis for any business ethics. S. Webley shows what key values business people from the three prophetic religions – Judaism, Christianity, and Islam – have in common and how these similarities are applied to business. S. K. Chakraborty searches for common ground in the Hindu-Vedantic ethos, including Sri Aurobindo, Swami Vivekananda, Rabindranath Tagore, and Mahatma Gandhi. J. White discusses the Buddhist Ethic and the Feminist Ethic, and their implications for ethical comportment of organizations. M. Pava gives strong but critical support to the stakeholder theory of the firm from a Jewish point of view. T. Abeng offers his personal perspective as a Muslim business leader in Indonesia, the country with the largest Muslim population in the world. In sum, these chapters impressively illustrate the richness of religious resources and the varying degrees of concretization in their application to business.

One way of becoming more concrete in business ethics – by now a fairly common practice in the field – is to distinguish (at least) *three levels of human action*: the individual, the organizational, and the systemic. This distinction, characterizing the fourth approach, makes it easier to identify different kinds of actors, be they individuals like managers and employees, organizations like companies and professional associations, or systems like nations, world regions, and even the whole world. Then, ethical values and norms are not just "free floating" ideals and demands but related to identifiable actors. Being both comprehensive and differentiated enough, this multi-level approach is crucial for international business ethics and has proved to be useful (see, for instance, the worldwide survey of business ethics in the special issue of the *Journal of Business Ethics*, October 1997). It is used in the Interfaith Declaration (Webley) and also applies to this volume. While Part I of this book basically deals with issues at the global systemic level, Part II concentrates on the organizational level of business organizations. The focus on business leaders in Part III mainly addresses issues at the individual level. Part IV covers topics at the regional and national systemic levels, and winds up with a global outlook.

One might argue that globalization is causing "the end of the nation state" (Kenichi Ohmae) so that the national systemic level of analysis is becoming irrelevant. However, it seems to me that for historical and sociocultural reasons, the nation states are still fairly strong while undergoing a process of redefining their identities in face of the global community. Several chapters in Part IV would support this view. Moreover, J. Etheredge and C. Erdener demonstrate in their empirical study that national identity can and does override ethnic identity in determining the approach to ethical decision making.

The fifth approach to international business ethics pays particular attention to the organizational level within the multi-level conception and to the *practical initiatives of companies*. Since companies and corporations are the prime movers in international business, they bear corresponding responsibilities and can become prime agents to set up and implement high ethical standards. An outstanding example is the development of the Caux Principles for Business discussed in Chapter 10. Business leaders from Japan, Western Europe, and North America have been working together for nearly ten years and have engaged their corporations to adhere to those Principles guided by the ethical ideals of human dignity and "kyosei," which means "working and living together for the common good." A similarly long process for the Interfaith Declaration has been undertaken by a group of Jewish, Christian, and Muslim business leaders. Although such initiatives are not legion, they express a high degree of ethical awareness and commitment, the process of which is probably more important than the written outcome, and they stimulate further initiatives of, and broader acceptance by, large and less-large business firms.

That companies can, and do, go far beyond the development of ethical codes and principles is exemplified by K. Yamaji, one of the architects of the "kyosei" philosophy for Canon. It is impressive with how much ingenuity and determination this philosophy, spelled out in specific and operationable terms, has been made the key of corporate success and the force to implement the company's globalization through "Sensitivity Conscious Management" and "Ecology Conscious Management." The farsightedness, care for details, and practical sense for implementation exhibited in "kyosei" are at their best. Such an astonishing consistency between corporate philosophy and corporate conduct is highly recommendable, but likely to be the exception rather than the rule. It considerably strengthens the credibility of the company among its internal and external constituencies and significantly facilitates the use and communication of ethics, normative values, and expressions. These are crucial questions for companies committed to higher ethical standards, which are discussed in the contributions of J. Song, H. Park, and J. Polet. Moreover, as G. Ornatowski shows, the utilization of cultural values at the systemic level, specifically of Confucian values in prewar and postwar Japan, greatly matters to the successful economic development of a country. In addition to this, S. Grand and S. Rothlin argue that, beyond utilization, "value creation," or a deep transformation of values, is required when extremely different social and religious groups violently conflict at the national and global level. Yet even at the corporate level, though perhaps less dramatically, "value creation" is crucial if companies go global, as the Canon case demonstrates.

Having highlighted some major challenges for, and approaches to, international business ethics by crisscrossing this volume, I now would like to briefly introduce the contributions in a more linear order. Because of their multiple points of view, they greatly differ in style, ranging from essays of renown scholars and reflections of business leaders, to overview articles, theoretical and conceptual considerations, and empirical and quantitative studies.

Global Context and Ethical Orientations

Part I attempts to set the stage for the whole volume. Despite global rhetorics and telecommunication, the global context is characterized by considerable diversity in space and time, the acknowledgment of which is, as Amartya Sen suggests, the first big step we have to take in departing from the on-going traditions of self-centered economics and self-less ethics. Thus, as for their contents as well as their reaches, business principles and moral sentiments should be treated more symmetrically and include multiple objectives while respecting the limits of grand generalizations. Unquestionably, substantive ethical principles and moral sentiments are being used in business and economic behavior and it greatly matters which ones are in place, as the emergence of organized crime and corruption clearly demonstrates. Regarding the process of globalization, probably all contributors agree with Hans Küng's four basic theses that globalization is unavoidable, ambivalent, and incalculable, and can be controlled rationally. Because it is not a natural phenomenon like an approaching weather front, in the face of which one is powerless, various options to cope with it do exist and, consequently, ethics is at the core of these individual and collective decisions.

Taking up this focus, G. R. S. Rao discusses both the fault lines of social evolution commonly understood and the interwoven destinies and universal concerns, and concludes that human society has to move from the "social" to the ethical phase and plane of its development. However, as Elia Chepaitis, John Etheredge, Carolyn Erdener, Simon Grand, and Stephan Rothlin point out, such a move involves serious difficulties: the differences and conflicts between advanced and emerging economies; the ambivalence of national identities; and the ethical legitimacy of global interference into local situations packed with extreme violence.

The three following contributions disprove the view that no common ethical values exist in today's world. S. K. Chakraborty shows the successful search for common ground in the Hindu-Vedantic ethos in India's recent cultural and religious tradition. Simon Webley informs the reader about the common endeavors of Jewish, Christian, and Muslim business leaders in Western Europe and the Middle East. H. Küng emphasizes an emerging consensus on global values by discussing three recent international documents which not only acknowledge human rights but also speak explicitly of human responsibilities: *Our Global Neighbourhood* (1995) by the Commission on Global Governance; *Our Creative Diversity* (1995) by the World Commission on Culture and Development; and *In Search of Global Ethical Standards* (1996) by the InterAction Council (consisting of former Presidents and Prime Ministers). He then proposes the Declaration of the Parliament of the World's Religions *Toward a Global Ethic* (1993) as a basis for an international business ethic.

Ethical Standards and Sources for International Business Organizations

The contributors in Part II focus on the role of corporations for international business ethics. In the global context – even more than at the domestic level – it appears evident that laws and market forces are necessary but not sufficient guides for corporate conduct. Based on this conviction, the Caux Principles for Business were developed and offer an impressive list of general principles and stakeholder principles. They break the still widespread silence in business to speak about ethical guidelines in public and they attempt to be as general as necessary and as specific as possible, the appropriate balance of which is hard to strike. A critical discussion about these Principles by Henri-Claude de Bettignies, Kenneth Goodpaster, and Toshio Matsuoka opens Part II.

While identifying ethical standards as well as standing for them in public is an important step, it obviously does not suffice. The next question is to ask for the sources that inspire, and the incentives that support, these standards. The contributions by Norman Bowie, Paul Vaaler, Kenneth Goodpaster, Judith White, and Moses Pava present a variety of economic, philosophical, and religious approaches which are directly related, in one way or another, to ethical standards and conduct of companies. While arguing from different perspectives, they support a common cause. This distinction between the contents of standards and the sources supporting them is essential in a global and pluralistic society.

In addition to the identification and justification of values, standards, and norms, the question arises as to how they are used and communicated. As Ji-Hwan Song, Hun-Joon Park, and Jacques Polet show, this is a delicate and risky undertaking because by doing so, companies are tempted to manipulate their audiences and expose themselves to various kinds of misunderstandings and criticism. The only way to overcome this ambiguity is to take a long-term stance that proves the seriousness of their ethical standards by their ethical conduct.

Ethical Challenges for Business Leaders Around the World

After the discussion of broad, global issues and the ethical commitment of business organizations, the emphasis switches to business persons and their leadership role, an equally important perspective for international business ethics. When dealing with systems, structures, organizations, and values, one tends to lose sight of the persons who, despite many constraints, have certain spaces of freedom and corresponding responsibilities. In particular, leaders are supposed to be more than merely willing "executives" of organizations and role players in complex systems. Rather, they are expected to take a proactive stand and be able, along with their followers, to shape "the world." Needless to say that here, too, as at the systemic and organizational levels, diversity greatly matters and thoroughly characterizes the situations and personalities of the leaders.

Part III begins with the voice of a prominent business leader in Indonesia and concludes with the prospects of educating and counseling future leaders in Latin America and South Africa. Tanri Abeng, President

Director & CEO of PT. Bakrie & Brothers, a huge conglomerate of Indonesian companies in telecommunications, banking, and mining, presents the Islamic perspectives for business (see also the Interfaith Declaration) and develops the three basic ingredients a leader must possess: vision, value, and courage. The topic of courage as a central virtue to face, and deal with, uncertainty and risks is taken up by Jack Mahoney and then applied to business firms as well. Joanne Ciulla discusses how information affects the relationship between leaders and followers, and highlights trust as the greatest challenge for business leaders in the information age. Going beyond the common emphasis on multinationals, Richard De George suggests that international business ethics should pay more attention to small business and consider the ethics of local entrepreneurs. Eduardo Schmidt reports about the development of a new and comprehensive pedagogical method, "interactive learning," for the ethical formation of business men and women in Latin America. Finally, Coley Lamprecht and Gedeon Rossouw address the challenge to reorient the "lost generation," the militarized youth in black townships in South Africa, and discuss the role that the career counselor can play in rectifying this problem.

Emerging Business Ethics in East Asia and Japan

The regional focus of this volume, presented in Part IV, reflects the economic dynamism and the increasing global importance of East Asia at the turn of the century and its urgent, and emerging, need for, and growing interest in, business ethics. This emphasis, though discretely handled, was conspicuous at the First World Congress of Business, Economics, and Ethics in Tokyo, and is here explored by a number of contributors, mostly from East Asian countries.

Akira Takahashi introduces the reader into the complex cultural diversity of the region and the relevance of its traditions for international business. Because its economies are composed of market and non-market sectors, due attention to ethics beyond market principles should be given, with particular emphasis on both community as its foundation and the increasing relevance of non-governmental organizations in the process. In a major empirical study, Xinwen Wu reports on how business people in East China perceive ethical issues in China's economy in transition from the planned economy to a "socialist market economy." Jegoo Lee and Hun-Joon Park explore the ethical culture of Korean Chaebols, i.e., large business conglomerates, and Alejo Sison discusses the vital importance of trust in Filipino family business.

The following contributions deal with business ethics in Japan at the national and corporate levels and open onto a global perspective offered by Keizo Yamaji, one of the architects of the "kyosei" initiative at Canon and now Chairman of the Board at Nihon Tetra Pak K. K. Mitsuhiro Umezu criticizes the reductionist explanations of the Japanese miracle, both the myth of the "uniqueness of Japanese culture" and the purely political economic explanation, and advances a multiple-reason approach that includes some ethical foundations of Japanese style capitalism. Gregory Ornatowski continues to pursue this perspective by examining how pre– and post–World War II Japanese industrialists and government officials use the Confucian values of respect for learning, social harmony, loyalty, and familism in order to form a modern Japanese ideology of capitalist economic development. Richard Wokutch and Jon Shepard examine corporate social responsibility in Japan today. They interpret it on the basis of a "micro moral unity" that is closely linked to the society's moral values, but only within carefully circumscribed communities of interest. However, with the maturing of the Japanese economy, the negative consequences of this micro moral unity are now becoming apparent and, as the authors say, a new paradigm will be required to address the new challenges. The "kyosei" initiative is certainly an illuminating and encouraging step in this direction. It was started by a business leader and took shape first in a single company. It also inspired the Caux Principles for Business and now has a definitively global content and reach, thus permeating through the different levels mentioned above.

To conclude, international business ethics faces enormous challenges and needs multiple approaches in practice as well as in theory. As the famous woodblock print by Katsushika Hokusai (ca. 1830) "View of Fuji from Beneath a Wave of the Sea at Kanagawa" illustrates (see the cover of this book), international business is a stormy sea. In order to survive and thrive, it is crucial that everyone "row together" and keep all eye on "Mount Fuji," symbolizing global common ethical guidelines. What this picture can mean in more specific terms is outlined and substantiated by the following contributions in a fascinating variety of ways.

Part I
Global Context and Ethical Orientations

Economics, Business Principles, and Moral Sentiments

Amartya Sen

Abstract

*This essay discusses the place of business principles and of moral senti-
ments in economic success, and examines the role of cultures in influencing norms of business behavior. Two presumptions held in standard
economic analysis are disputed: the rudimentary nature of business
principles (essentially restricted, directly or indirectly, to profit maximization), and the allegedly narrow reach of moral sentiments (often
treated to be irrelevant to business and economics). In contrast, the author argues for the need to recognize the complex structure of business
principles and the extensive reach of moral sentiments by using theoretical considerations, a thorough analysis of Adam Smith's work, and a
careful interpretation of Japan's remarkable economic success. Referring to the economic corruption in Italy and the "grabbing culture"
in Russia, he further shows how deeply the presence or absence of particular features of business ethics can influence the operation of the
economy, and even the nature of the society and its politics. Being an Indian himself, he warns against grand generalizations like the superiority of "Asian values" over traditional Western morals. To conclude, it is
diversity – over space, over time, and between groups – that makes the
study of business principles and moral sentiments a rich source of understanding and explanation.*

Claims and Disclaimers

There is an interesting asymmetry between the treatments of business
principles and moral sentiments in standard economic analysis. Business principles are taken to be very *rudimentary* (essentially restricted,
directly or indirectly, to profit maximization), but with a very *wide
reach* in economic matters (covering effectively all economic transactions). In contrast, moral sentiments are seen to be quite *complex* (involving different types of ethical systems), but it is assumed, that at least
in economic matters, they have a very *narrow reach* (indeed, it is often

presumed that such sentiments have no real influence on economic behavior).

The purpose of this essay is to discuss the place of business principles and of moral sentiments in economic success, and in that context, to examine the role of cultures in influencing norms of business behavior. If this lecture is seen in terms of the theses that I would like to present, then the first two theses consist of disputing the presumptions, respectively, of (1) the rudimentary nature of business principles, and (2) the allegedly narrow reach of moral sentiments.

Business principles cannot escape being influenced by conceptions of "good business behavior," and thus involve the standard complexities connected with multiple goals.[1] Multiple objectives can lead to competing demands made by conflicting goals, which have to be resolved in practice by some kind of compromise. Sometimes the multiplicity of normative demands may not take the explicit form of multiple objectives, but of a combination of objectives and constraints. For example, it may involve the pursuit of some unified objective (may be even maximization of profits), but subject to some self-imposed choice constraints that qualify and restrain the pursuit of that unified objective. Such constraints can reflect rules and conventions of "proper" behavior which the person involved chooses to follow. The restraints that bind the maximization of profits would, then, include not only the "feasibility constraints" that reflect the limits of what one *can* do, but also "self-imposed constraints" that the person *chooses* to obey on moral or conventional or even strategic grounds.

Since moral ideas are among the influences that affect the formulation and operation of objectives and obligations, including the demands of ethical behavior and social convention, they can be quite critical in terms of impact on the world of economics and business. The standard model of simple profit maximization as the dominant (perhaps even *exclusive*) principle covering all economic activities fails to do justice both to the content of business principles, which can be much broader, and to the domain of moral sentiments, which can be quite far-reaching.

However, these general claims must not be confused with two other beliefs which often go with the rejection of the presumption of universally self-seeking behavior. There is a need for "disclaimers" to prevent misunderstandings of what is being claimed here. First, it would be, I would argue, a great mistake to try to replace the hypothesis of universal profit maximization with another hypothesis of similar, unconditional uniformity (such as ubiquitous altruism, or universal human sympathy, or some other form of non-contingent high-mindedness). The connections are dependent on many social, cultural, and interactive considerations, and the resulting behavioral principles would tend to be complex as well as variable with respect to time, place, and group.

Second, a departure from profit maximization need not necessarily be benign, nor need moral sentiments be invariably noble. Some of the worst barbarities in the contemporary world have been committed by self-sacrificing racists – ready to do harm to some people even at great cost or risk to themselves. Indeed, this process continues today with relentless persistence – in Bosnia, Ireland, Rwanda, and many other parts of the world. The rejection of a self-centered life can go with the attempted advancement – sometimes violent promotion – of the perceived interests only of a particular group or community (excluding others), and even with willfully inflicting damages on another group or community.

Just as the reading of business principles has to be raised a notch or two from the gross presumption - standard in much of modern economics – of universal profit maximization, the role of moral sentiments may have to be lowered a notch or two from the lofty presumption – standard in some of contemporary ethics - of universal pursuit of the respective conceptions of "the good."[2] The world in which we live is very mixed, and our sentiments, principles, passions, and irritations come in many shapes and forms. The acknowledgment of diversity is the first big step we have to take in departing from the on-going traditions of self-centered economics and self-less ethics.

The conditional variability of our principles and sentiments often does have a regional component and can be linked with history and culture. In some of the social sciences, insufficient attention is paid to these variations; economics is an obvious example of this, with quite a common use of the assumption of universal profit maximization. It is, in fact, important to take serious note of the contingent and variable nature of our values.

But once again, this thesis must not be confused with the idea that the divisions in the world come in very neat and large categories – with the world population being partitioned into grand classes of followers of big ideas. Rapid generalizations of this kind have, of course, been widely made and used in social analysis, for example in praising the role of "Protestant ethics" (emphasized by many Western scholars, most notably Max Weber), or "Asian values" (much championed lately by some political leaders in Asia). In fact, the variations are more finely contingent, more forcefully local, more dependent on exact history, and much influenced by social, political, and economic experiences of the groups in question. Also, the divisions are not static, and cultural mores do shift and alter over time, sometimes quite rapidly. Once again, the appreciation of diversity is central to a realistic understanding of the varying nature of business principles and of the divergent reach of moral sentiments.

The Assumption of Universal Self-Seeking

To see business behavior exclusively in terms of profit maximization misses out many subtleties of commercial conduct, including the influence of social conventions and mores, and the roles played by dialogue, compromise, and the acceptance of "give and take." Business activities involve social interactions, and despite a possibly strong, continuing interest in making economic gains, the interactions inescapably involve much else.

The standard economic models set the focus on *exchange*, but apply that mainly to the exchange of *commodities*, as opposed to exchange of speech, claims, proposals, and settlements. The focus on "silent traders" is frequently modeled on an often-repeated interpretation of Adam Smith's analysis of exchange of commodities. The model takes off from Smith's argument that it "is not from the benevolence of the butcher, the brewer, or the baker that we expect our dinner, but from their regard to their own interest." (Smith, *Wealth of Nations*, 26–27.) There is not much here for which a complex or a sophisticated value system would be of great use. The butcher, the brewer, and the baker have to determine how much meat, beer, and bread the consumer in question would want, and a clear implicit contract can now emerge between the parties, ending with the exchange of commodities and money. The "business principles" involved in such activities would indeed be rather rudimentary.

What would go wrong in taking this to be the "model of economic behavior" is the limited nature of the particular exercise discussed in Smith's over-quoted passage. Adam Smith himself had not presented this case as being the microcosm of all economic activities, but just as an example of a case of pure exchange of commodities, for which the pursuit of self-interest entirely suffices as a motivation. But many exchanges are not like this; for example, the acceptance of a particular settlement in a wage dispute, or the emergence of agreed terms for a business partnership, can require a lot of negotiation, involving exchange of talks, claims, and concerns.

Furthermore, not all economic activities are matters of exchange. There are issues of production and distribution, in which economic reasoning and business principles may, again, have to take much broader forms. Smith himself had occasion to discuss – both in *The Wealth of Nations* (1776) and in *The Theory of Moral Sentiments* (1759) – the complexity of human relations in economic as well as social matters, and the variety of motivations, principles, and ground rules that may be involved. Indeed, even the general reliability of the exchange mechanism and the use of implicit contracts (including the fact that in an on-going cultural tradition, the butcher or the brewer or the baker can accept the consumer's oral "order" without a written contract) turns ultimately on a rich history of norms, mores, trust, and convention.

Behavior of this kind is much more structured than the simple and silent pursuit of self-interest. Business principles play a central role in influencing the behavior of economic agents, and these principles can extend well beyond the straightforward seeking of individual advantage. This is not to deny that individual advantage may be a crucial motivating concern that helps to drive the engine of economic enterprise, and can also seriously influence the forms and limits of communication and agreement involved in economic and business activities. The "rawness" of the pursuit of self-interest can differ from culture to culture, and the types of principles explicitly invoked or implicitly presumed can also similarly vary. Indeed, the inter-regional and inter-cultural variations in business behavior, which we actually observe, illustrate well the fact that business principles can take much richer – and very diverse – forms, with differently structured multiple objectives. We do not have to deny the importance of self-interest to accept that many business decisions and economic activities are motivationally much more complex than the single and simple pursuit of self-interest alone.

The moral sentiments that last and flourish are, of course, influenced by – and may to a considerable extent be selected by an – evolutionary process. That aspect of the emergence of values and norms is beginning to receive serious attention in evolutionary game theory (see Binmore 1994 and Weibull 1995). This is a useful supplement to the focus on reflective ethics that we find in the works of Immanuel Kant and Adam Smith, among others. Selection by *individual reasoning* and that by *systemic survival* are two routes that can work together, rather than exclude each other. But no matter what the balance of importance is between these two different routes, the end-result is the use of substantive ethical principles and moral sentiments in business and economic behavior. They exist, they are important, they are productive, and we can ignore them only by impoverishing economic analysis and by demeaning the sophistication and breadth of human conduct.

Variations of Norms and Their Significance

Business principles that are taken for granted in one commercial environment may be very far from standard in another. This variability not only is an observed characteristic of the world as we see it, but also it affects the successes and failures – and the strengths and the weaknesses – of different economies. Indeed, the presence or absence of particular features of business ethics can deeply influence the operation of the economy and even the nature of the society and its politics.

One example is the prevalence of economic corruption in some economies, say, Italy. Parts of business ethics that may be standard in the commerce of, say, Switzerland, may be far less common in Italy, or indeed in many other financial environments. In explaining the differences, it is important to see the role played by conventions of good behavior, and how these conventions have emerged and been sustained in different regions and societies.

The issue of corruption relates also to the weakness of mutual trust. Transactions and trade are much facilitated by the trust that people have in each other's words. Confidence in the reliability of offers and promises made by others helps the efficiency of exchanges in a way that relentless self-seeking cannot. In fact, had self-interest been the only determinant of behavior, there would be many occasions in which letting the other side down (for example, by reneging on earlier arrangements) would be sensible enough. Preventing such reneging through legal means (involving suing, convicting, and penalizing) may be both expensive and painfully slow, and much of the work is done by behavioral codes and morals. The force of that code often varies sharply between different commercial environments.

When the sense of mutual trust – and corresponding standards of market ethics – are not yet well established, an outside organization can deal with the breach and provide a socially valued service in the form of strong-armed enforcement. An organization like the Mafia has been able to play an economic role here in parts of Italy, and this can be particularly important in pre-capitalist economies being drawn rapidly into capitalist transactions. Enforcement of this type, through "bandit" organizations, can be, in practice, contingently useful for different parties, even though they have no direct interest at all in corruption or crime. The respective contracting parties may each need the "assurance" that the other economic agents are also doing the appropriate thing.[3]

The flourishing of strong-armed organizations, which guarantee such "assurance," depends on the absence of behavioral codes that would reduce the need for external enforcement. The business function of enforcement through extra-legal organizations would shrink with an increase in trusting and trust-generating behavior. Complementarity between behavioral norms and institutional reform can, thus, be very strong indeed. Even though the Mafia is one of the most detestable organizations in the world (responsible for so much violence and murder), we still have to understand the economic basis of the influence of the Mafia to understand their hold on the society and their surviving power. We have to supplement our recognition of the power of guns and bombs with an understanding of some of the economic activities that make the Mafia a functionally relevant part of the economy. That functional attraction would cease as and when the combined influence of legal enforcement and behavioral development makes the Mafia economically redundant.

There is, thus, a general connection between the limited emergence of business norms and the hold of organized crime. More generally, variations in norms and values can have quite a profound effect on the functioning of the respective economies.[4] The codes of business and professional behavior are parts of the "productive resources" of a society. Variations in these resources can be seen over time as well as between regions – even between localities. Not only is Italy very diverse in terms of the modalities of behavior – indeed the contrast between North Italy and South Italy has received much attention lately – but variations can be seen *within* North Italy itself and also between one region or another *within* the South.

Variations can also be quite sharp and fast over time. A recent example includes the breakdown of law-abiding behavior in Russia as it went for tremendously rapid economic reform and marketization. The process was no doubt helped by the absence, in pre-reform Russia, of institutional patterns of behavior and codes of business ethics that are central to successful capitalism. There was a strong need at the time of institutional reform for the development of an alternative system of codes and conventions with its own logic and loyalties, which would have to play a central role in post-reform Russia. Instead of that, there clearly was quite an outburst of economic opportunism and breathless attempts to "grab the gravy that could be grabbed." Some of the diffi-

culty in bringing about a smooth transition arose from such counter-productive developments in patterns of business behavior. Instead of
a smooth emergence of mainstream business virtues of established capitalism, Russia experienced an intensification of behavioral problems,
fed by the rapid development of a "grabbing culture," which hindered
rather than helped the process of reform.

Also the "grabbing culture" made the emergence of mutual business
trust that much more difficult. The growth of Mafia style operations in
the former Soviet Union has recently received considerable attention,
and it has certainly been a significant development. To place this development in its context, we have to examine its behavioral antecedents,
and the interconnections between (1) the breakdown of law, order, and
economic discipline; (2) the emergence of extra-legal organizations (as
supplements to business activities); and (3) the intensification of behavioral malaise.

The challenge that is faced is not that of policing only. The combined role of business principles and of moral sentiments, in the form of
social conventions and mores, cannot be overemphasized in this context. There are some hopeful indications now that more stable and less
counterproductive behavioral norms are gradually emerging in Russia,
and if this proceeds smoothly, the development of a prosperous business
economy there would be substantially easier.

Similar variations between regions and cultures, and over time, can
be analyzed in the context of many other economic and social concerns,
such as:

- variations in *industrial productivity* (the operation of codes of
  duty and loyalty within the firm can be very important in this);
- differences in the smoothness of *market relations* (basic standards of honesty and trust can play an important role here);
- dissimilar treatments of the *environment* and *industrial and social pollution* (environmental values are nearly absent in some
  communities and quite well-developed in others);
- diversities in the use and abuse of *public goods* (for example, in
  the operational possibilities of urban transport on an "honor system," with little or no checking of tickets).

The importance of economic ethics and of business principles relates
both to their reach and effectiveness, and to their variability over time,
space, and group. They constitute a crucial aspect of inter-regional and

inter-temporal variations in economic performance and social achievement.

Limits of Grand Generalizations:
The Example of Asian Values

While regional variations are extremely important, there is a real danger of over-simplifying the contrasts by concentrating on immense categories such as "Asian values versus Western values," or "Confucian ethics versus Protestant ethics." Generalizations of such heroic simplicity used to come earlier from scholars in the Western tradition (Max Weber's attributions to Protestant ethics was an extremely influential example), but increasingly we now see such generalizations coming from Asia.

The recent emergence of Asia as the most economically dynamic region in the world has prepared the ground for the same kind of value-arrogance that was characteristic of Europe in the nineteenth century. Asian economic growth is now very far in excess of any other region in the world, and the domain of high growth has persistently expanded in Asia, and continues to do so right now. Can these contrasts be explained by the superiority of an Asian value system that has great advantages over traditional Western morals?

I would argue that one must be deeply skeptical of such grand contrasts. Asia is where about 60 per cent of the total world population live. There are no quintessential values that apply to this immensely large and heterogeneous population, which separate them out as a group from people in the rest of the world. The internal diversity of Asia is simply tremendous. Indeed, even *East Asia*, including Japan, China, and Korea, among other countries, has too many different cultural traditions to permit any easy generalization of "east Asian values." The analysis of values has to be much finer than that.

If geography and the largeness of Asia give us one reason to doubt the helpfulness of the concept of "Asian values," the historical instability of the assessment of Asian culture provides another reason. As the balance of economic development has shifted, the reading of "Asian values" has persistently and radically altered.

It was in Europe that the Industrial Revolution occurred first, not in Asia, and even earlier, the developments that constituted the European Renaissance had been changing the face of Europe before similar things were occurring in Asia. This was a time when questions were frequently asked about what made the European values so productive of great social results, in contrast with which Asian values seemed – to Europeans

– to be very primitive. The question that was repeatedly asked, then, was: what values, what knowledge have made Europe go so far ahead of Asia and the rest of the world?[5] The Asians evidently "lacked" something or other that made capitalism work in Europe, but not in Asia, and economists as distinguished as Alfred Marshall speculated on what behavior patterns kept Asian cultures economically down. It was in this context that Max Weber diagnosed that it was the "rational ethic of activity" that was missing in Asia, but plentifully provided by Judeo-Christian heritage in general and Protestant ethics in particular.

This line of reasoning had to be adjusted when things in Asia started moving. There was, first of all, the remarkable economic success and progress of Japan, and its emergence as a major military and financial power. The question now shifted, with remarkable rapidity, to include Japan in the world of privileged values. By the middle of the twentieth century, the contrast took the form of asking why Japan was "the only non-Western country to have become a major industrial nation?" (Moulder 1977, vii.) And more specifically: "Why did modern industrial capitalism arise in one East Asian society (Japan) and not in another (China)?" (Jacobs 1958, ix.) Special norms, traditions, and values of Japan – from the martial Samurai heritage to its family-centered business traditions – began receiving very special attention.

In the second half of the century, east Asian countries and regions *other than* Japan – South Korea, Singapore, Taiwan, Hong Kong – also started doing very well, and the "specialness" story had to be extended to them too. As a result, the Samurai had to give way to shared traditions on the eastern edge of Asia. This has more recently been followed by mainland China itself becoming a country with very fast economic growth and a rapid industrial transformation of its economy. The theses now shifted to special virtues of Confucianism – the cultural tie that binds China and Japan and much of east Asia – and even today this is the dominant story of "Asian values" and its great successes.

Meanwhile, however, Thailand has started forging ahead at remarkable speed, and its cultural background is Buddhist rather than Confucian. Indonesia, too, with an Islamic culture and much Buddhist and Hindu influences in its past, has begun to grow impressively fast. And, then, even more recently, adding to the cacophony, the large economy of India has started to move forward quite rapidly, and right now South Asia as a whole has a substantially faster rate of GNP growth than any other region of the world (including, of course, Europe and America), except for further East. Old explanations of sluggishness based on the debilitating values of these regions are giving way, at this very moment, to explanations of economic dynamism, with identification of other values, connections, and other achievements.

There are, clearly, strong elements of arbitrariness and "ad-hocism" taking Asian values to be particularly favorable to economic growth and rapid progress. Putting the issue somewhat differently, we can ask: if indeed Asian values have been so important in the recent economic success of these regions, a success which is getting increasingly larger in scope and coverage, *what took it so long*? Did Asian values change radically, and if so, why? Value explanations are much easier to give *ex post* than *ex ante*, and the ease of these answers hides the questions that have to be asked to scrutinize the answers critically.

Exposing the weakness of an earlier grand contrast and a big pro-European prejudice was much overdue, and it is good that the glib generalizations about Protestant ethics and "the rational ethic of activity" have, by now, been largely rejected (see Goody 1996). But the disestablishment of an earlier grand contrast must not be confused with the establishment of a new and different grand contrast, with another massive asymmetry of values – this time in favor of Asia, against Europe. There are things to learn from the recent Asian experiences, and at a less grand level, even the values and value changes in particular Asian regions are very worth studying. There are many things to be learned about the role of values from the Japanese experience itself, but the analysis has to be more detailed and richer in information about local history and tradition.

In a negative sense, Japan's remarkable success does point to the need to modify the admiration for exclusive reliance on profit maximization as the "royal road" to economic success (a royal road much explored in contemporary economics). Certainly, there are many non-individualist values – more geared to social norms and loyalties – that play significant parts in Japan's economic performance, and these have to be understood in their full detail, rather than being drowned in some aggregative story of "Asian values." There is quite a literature on this subject, and different commentators have emphasized distinct aspects of Japanese motivational specialness. Michio Morishima has focused on the special characteristics of the "Japanese ethos" as emerging from its particular history of rule-based behavior patterns (Morishima 1982). Ronald Dore has seen the influence of "Confucian ethics" (Dore 1987). Masahiko Aoki has seen cooperation and behavioral codes in terms that are more responsive to strategic reasoning (Aoki 1989). Kotaro

Suzumura has emphasized the combination of commitment with a competitive atmosphere (Suzumura 1995). Eiko Ikegami has stressed the influence of Samurai culture (Ikegami 1995). There are other behavior-based accounts as well. All these need serious attention as well as careful scrutiny, armed with detailed local knowledge about values and their roles. There is an excellent case for probing the role of values, focusing on the particularities rather than over-grand generalities.

There is, of course, a shared element in these stories, to wit, the presence of motives and modes of reasoning that go well beyond narrow profit-maximization in the operation of firms and individual workers and managers. There may, in fact, be some truth even in the apparently puzzlingly claim made on the front page of *The Wall Street Journal* that Japan is "the only communist nation that works." (*Wall Street Journal*, 30 January 1989, 1.) The witticism does stress the importance of non-profit motivations underlying many economic and business activities in Japan. Attention has to be paid to the peculiar fact that what is arguably the most successful capitalist nation in the world flourishes economically with a motivation structure that departs in crucial respects from the pursuit of self interest, which – we had been told – is the bedrock of capitalism.

It is, thus, important to see the role of complex business principles (not just profit maximization) and the influence of shared moral sentiments (rather than treating them to be irrelevant to business and economics), and at the same time, to recognize that value analysis has to be geared to the particular rather than to grand generalities. In fact, even within Japan there are considerable variations, and there have been many exposures lately of lapses from noble business behavior, and even of straightforward corruption. What is needed is not a general praise of Japanese value systems (not to mention sweeping generalizations about the wonders of "Asian values"), but informational rich analysis of various parts of Japanese traditions and conventions, and their respective bearing on the working and performance of the Japanese economy.

Similar remarks can be made about the other, more recent cases of Asian economic success. The recognition of local variability has to be supplemented by an understanding of temporal change. The answer to the question (asked earlier) "what took it so long?" – includes the fact that values in Asian countries are not static and stationary, and we have to consider not merely the nature of the indigenous cultures, but also the influence of Western ideas and organizational thoughts. It is diversity – over space, over time, and between groups – that makes the study of business principles and moral sentiments a rich source of understanding and explanation.

A Concluding Remark

The need to recognize the complex structure of business principles and the extensive reach of moral sentiments has been the motivating theme of this essay. The assumption of universal profit maximization as the only business principle – common in many economic analysis – militates against both. But this assumption has little empirical support, nor much analytical plausibility, and there is a strong case for going beyond that rudimentary structure.

The need to displace profit maximization as the sole business principle does not call for the placing of another simple and uniform rule as an alternative general system, with the same level of universality. Rather, there is a strong case for analyzing more complex structures, involving diverse concerns, and varying over time, space, and culture. A promising – and versatile – framework is that of *multiple objectives*, which can very plausibly include the search for profits as one important objective *among others*. The other objectives can compete with profit maximization in influencing business behavior, and can sometimes work as constraints reflecting established moral codes and social conventions. The force of profit maximization may have to work subject to these constraints.

In understanding the content and operation of social conventions and behavioral constraints, a richer comprehension of particular cultures can be very important. Indeed, cultural differences can have a crucial influence on business behavior. But we must not take the cultural parameters to be static and immutable, nor see them in terms of monumental and magnificent contrasts across very broad regions. These grand generalizations hide more than they reveal.
I have argued for the simultaneous recognition of:

1. the significance of cultural variations;
2. the need to avoid cultural stereotypes and sweeping generalizations;
3. the importance of taking a dynamic rather than a static view of cultures; and
4. the necessity of recognizing heterogeneity within given communities.

The recognition of diversity over time and space – involving local variations as well as historical shifts – can be very important in understanding the practical nature and role of business principles and moral sentiments. This may look a little complex, compared with easy generalizations about "Western rationality" and "Asian values," but that complexity is, I believe, inescapable given the nature of the subject. Simplicity is not, after all, the only virtue.

Endnotes

1. I have tried to discuss these issues in *Resources, Values and Development* (1984), and in *On Economics and Ethics* (1987).

2. An excellent model of a community of persons with each pursuing their "comprehensive conception of the good" has been illuminatingly analyzed by John Rawls, *A Theory of Justice* (1971). Rawls does not claim that actual communities are exactly like this, and a substantial part of modern ethics seems to be primarily concerned with using that presumption to explore the "possibility" of "just social arrangements" (without committing itself on the nature of the observed world).

3. On this, see Stefano Zamagni, ed., *Mercati Illegali e Mafie* (1993), particularly his own paper on the economic circumstances that facilitate the persistence of a Mafia-inclusive equilibrium. See also my "On Corruption and Organized Crime," address to the Italian Parliament's Anti-Mafia Commission, Rome, 1993; Italian translation in Luciano Violante, ed., *Economia e criminalità* (1993).

4. On these issues, see Armando Massarenti and Antonio Da Re, *L'Etica de Applicare*, with an introduction by Angelo Ferro, and comments of Giovanni Agnelli and Salvatore Veca (Milano: Il Sole 24 Ore Libri, 1991).

5. In Samuel Johnson's *Rasselas*, Imlac identifies "the northern and western nations of Europe" as being "in possession of all power and all knowledge, whose armies are irresistible, and whose fleets command the remotest parts of the globe" (Johnson, *Rasselas*, 1759, 47).

References

Aoki, Masahiko, *Information, Incentive and Bargaining in the Japanese Economy* (Cambridge: Cambridge University Press, 1989).

Binmore, Ken, *Playing Fair* (Cambridge, Mass.: MIT Press, 1994).

Dore, Ronald, *Taking Japan Seriously: A Confucian Perspective on Leading Economic Issues* (Stanford: Stanford University Press, 1987).

Goody, Jack, *East in the West* (Cambridge: Cambridge University Press, 1996).

Ikegami, Eiko, *The Taming of the Samurai: Honorific Individualism and the Making of Modern Japan* (Cambridge, MA: Harvard University Press, 1995).

Jacobs, H. Norman, *The Origin of Modern Capitalism and Eastern Asia* (Hong Kong, 1958).

Johnson, Samuel, *Rasselas: The Prince of Abissinia: A Tale* (London: Dodsley, 1759).

Massarenti, Armando, and Da Re, Antonio, *L'Etica de Applicare*, intro. Angelo Ferro, and comments of Giovanni Agnelli and Salvatore Veca (Milano: Il Sole 24 Ore Libri, 1991).

Morishima, Michio, *Why Has Japan "Succeeded'? Western Technology and Japanese Ethos* (Cambridge: Cambridge University Press, 1982).

Moulder, F. V., *Japan. China, and the Modern World Economy: Toward a Reinterpretation of East Asian Development (c. 1600 to c. 1918)* (Cambridge: Cambridge University Press, 1977).

Rawls, John, *A Theory of Justice* (Cambridge, Mass.: Harvard University Press, 1971).

Sen, Amartya, *On Ethics and Economics* (Oxford: Blackwell, 1987).

Sen, Amartya, *Resources, Values and Development* (Oxford: Blackwell, and Cambridge, Mass.: Harvard University Press, 1984).

Sen, Amarya, "On Corruption and Organized Crime," address to the Italian Parliament's AntiMafia Commission, Rome, 1993; Italian translation in Luciano Violante, ed., *Economia e criminalità* (Roma: Camera dei deputati, 1993).

Smith, Adam, *The Theory of Moral Sentiments* (1759, 6th revised edition, 1790; republished, eds. D.D. Raphael and A.L. Macfie, Oxford: Clarendon Press, 1975).

Smith, Adam, *An Inquiry into the Nature and Causes of the Wealth of Nations* (1776; republished, edited by R.H. Campbell and A.S. Skinner, Oxford: Clarendon Press, 1976).

Suzumura, Kotaro, *Competition, Commitment and Welfare* (Oxford: Clarendon Press, 1995).

The Wall Street Journal, 30 January 1989.

Weibull, Jörgen, *Evolutionary Game Theory* (Cambridge, Mass.: MIT Press, 1995).

Zamagni, Stefano, ed., *Mercati Illegali e Mafie* (Bologna: Il Mulino, 1993).

The Ethics Agenda Facing International Business

G. R. S. Rao

Abstract

Conflict of values and, of morality that plague the humanity today in the form of dilemmas of development represent the faultlines of social evolution. Such conflicts, which are conditioned by time and space, can only be resolved through a set of universal normative parameters cutting across the cultural barriers of human civilization. This is what was reflected in the series of global summits on environment, human rights, population, social development, gender justice, and habitat, as ingredients of the Global Agenda-21. Emergence of the "democratic ethic" on a global scale provides an opportunity to correct the faultlines of social evolution. An ethical framework lends qualitative content to the process of globalization of democracy and of economies, and, thus, adds the qualitative character to the progress of humanity.

Globalization impinges the role as well as the efficacy of nation-states. Nation-states and the institutions of global governance are yielding their place to international business as the prime-movers of Agenda-21. In the emerging scenario, multi-national corporations (MNCs) operating across boundaries of states and cultural zones have three distinctive options before themselves:

(a) Take advantage of profitability in the short-term, get sucked away by the maelstrom of conflict of values and of interests in the process, and stand condemned;

(b) Wait for the institutions of governance – global, national, and local – which are themselves caught in a maze of role-conflict to legislate a regulatory framework, or,

(c) Formulate corporate normative guidelines that respond to the demands of multi-national operations and cross-cultural environment, pioneer a framework of Codes of Conduct in the form of an ethics agenda, and thus help the nation-states as well as the human society meet the challenges of Agenda-21.

MNCs have to become Global Business Organizations (GBOs) and aid the progress of human society, while pursuing profits. They have a critical role in shaping and contributing to the Social Agenda of nation-states, and thus providing a turning point to the evolution of a global society.

Faultlines of Social Evolution

At a time when two-thirds people of the world are searching for a meaning of political freedom and democracy and attempting to set out an agenda for development, the "developed" world is experiencing the shocks of social disruption as a consequence of economic growth. Like the Greenwich Mean Time (GMT) which provides a global reference point, economic growth has become the standard reference point of humanity in its pursuit of "development." GMT provides for different time-zones, as "development" provides diverse connotations.

An evolutionary view of human society reveals its ingenuity in an enormous build-up of material culture and resource-centered development. Technological innovations have resulted in mass-production, market economy, capital formation, profits, and the displacement of man. Increases in Gross National Product (GNP) contributed to expanded markets, and competition has grown into political, economic, and social conflict. All this was justified in terms such as per capita income and standard of living, measured almost exclusively in quantitative terms without adequate cognizance of qualitative criteria, at the macro as well as the micro levels.

The differential pace of transfer of resources and of technology and the impact created by competition at the market place reflect the Darwinian postulate of survival of the fittest among corporate organizations, public or private sector, operating as the instruments of economic growth of national communities. As communities organize themselves in order to get the best of terms of trade through measures such as providing explicit or hidden form of subsidies, "tax havens," and selective and unilateral application of "Social Clause," by the very logic, others are exposed to the exploitative equations and collapse of economies as well as markets. The differential impact of market factors are contributing to marginalization of communities within national boundaries, and of nations among the community of nations.

Differential dispositions towards development among the countries categorized as the North versus South, industrial versus agricultural, urban versus the rural/backward communities, and organized versus the unorganized sections of citizens throw up a wide range of issues such as discrimination, preferences, and protectionism. The complexity of the issues of development is compounded by the adverse balance between shrinking resources and the exponentially expanding and artificially created demands on the one hand, and competing priorities, conflicting perceptions of the nature of expectations, and contributions of transnational corporations and management practices to the developmental loop of specific communities and countries on the other.

Corporate policies and practices pursued in various countries have denied large segments of population of their ability and opportunity to participate in and benefit from economic growth. Economic factors have emerged as the critical variable in the polarization of human society. The main cause of hunger proved to be not drought, war, or civil unrest but factors such as politics, public policy, and corporate practices.

Even as the affluent communities of the world have become the "Development – Model" for the Third World, there is a growing consciousness in the North that increases in the per capita income are not necessarily contributing to social equity or quality of life of the community, and that acquisitive culture could aggravate social disparities, degradation, and conflict. This is illustrated by the growing concern for the loss of family-values and the status of family as the basic unit of human civilization. Problems such as unwed-mothers, single-parent-children, drugs, suicides, and violence reflect the expanding spectrum of social degradation. Exploitation of the labour has given way to exploitation by the labour, occasionally reaching proportions of trade-union extremism and terrorism. The pattern of these crises impel human society today to take cognizance of the fall-out of economic development and affluence, and the need for providing correctives so as to ensure that the global economy, while expanding markets and economies, also contributes to Global Human Progress (GHP).

The progression of humanity has to be measured in terms of the positive contribution of material "growth" to human "happiness" and "welfare," and equity between communities as well as between generations, transcending both space and time.

Universal Concerns and Interwoven Destiny

As the national communities passing through different levels and patterns of development are caught in the cross-currents of conflicting values, interests, and identities, the global society has started recognizing the common concerns as reflected in the series of Global Summits on Environment (1992), Human Rights (1993), Population (1994), Social

Development (1995), and Gender Justice (1995), and exploring the normative universals that could protect and promote its interwoven destiny.

Technology and media are breaking the physical barriers and shrinking the human society into a global village, thus contributing to the recognition of interwoven destinies and emergence of earth-citizenship, shared values (universal Human Rights), and common concerns (such as global warming and sustainable development).

The growth of inequities within national communities, partly spurred by the process and the pattern of growth of their economies, are contributing to Gross Social Conflict (GSC), manifesting in forms such as alienation of the youth, discrimination against women, abuse of children on the one hand, and displacement of populations without rehabilitation and resettlement, distress migration, malnutrition, and starvation-deaths on the other. Paradoxically, unemployment is seen either as an opportunity in taking locational decisions, or as an issue of human rights and consequent justification for invoking "Social Clause" and imposing trade barriers. Social agenda is compromised in order to propitiate the Goddess of corporate profit.

As some sections of the humanity seek to pursue their greed for amassment without recognition for minimum human needs and basic human rights of others (e.g., south-bound displacement of millions of toxic wastes), national communities are struggling to cope with the crescendo of disadvantaged sections and their empowerment through affirmative action. This process has been only aggravating the "rights-conflict" both within and across national boundaries. If the market warfare of the twentieth century has faded the territorial conflicts of yester-centuries, social conflicts seem poised to dominate the twenty-first century. Nation-states are found inadequate to promote social integration within political boundaries; often they are also the culprits.

In the face of a market-driven economy of a global order, states are caught in the "Twilight of Sovereignty," and are groping for a redefinition of their roles. The predominance of market over the state is sought to be asserted in forms such as corporate confidentiality and territorial transcendence of MNCs. Even more complex and serious an issue is the emergence and growing nexus between politics and business, often making a menacing partnership with crime and bureaucracy. In almost all the countries, this nexus has eroded the credibility of state and generated alienation of the citizenry, apart from leading to problems of internal turbulence and security in complex patterns.

The credibility of institutions of global governance is also declining, as a consequence of the pursuit of partisan interests rather than the promotion of common concerns. North-South Round Table (1995) brought out the gap between the original vision and present reality of the four pillars of the Bretton Woods Institutions – UN, IMF, WB, and WTO. The debilitation of these institutions is poignantly pointed out thus: that the international institutions have weakened precisely at a time when global interdependence has increased. These institutions are yet to prove their potential in providing economic and social security for most of the worlds' people. The vacuum cannot be allowed to last for long.

Ascendance of Ethics

History of human civilization reveals that the nature and varying degrees of congruence, divergence, and conflict of "values" and "morals" are conditioned by time and space variables. American Independence was seen as a rebellion by the British; widow remarriage was considered a sacrilege in India. While profitability as an acid test of corporate performance was recognized as worthy of a Noble Prize, "profit-alone" was condemned by those who swore by Trusteeship; Western industry that looked around for cheap labour has today become the champion of "Social Clause." Countries that exported labour and those engaged in slave-trade have now become advocates of democracy and human rights, seemingly steering the global society towards a universal value system. Amartya Sen discusses the place of business principles and of moral sentiments in economic success in the chapter of this book entitled "Economics, Business Principles, and Moral Sentiments." Issues of values and morality faced by human civilization emerged before the Global Social Summit in Copenhagen 1995 as issues of "development."

A holistic appreciation of the processes that shape and influence the directional shifts in values and morality warrants a civilizational over-view of mankind, nay, of humankind, going by the contemporary "ideal" of gender equality. Starting from the jungle lords who equated "might" with "right," humankind has witnessed several dominant value-shifts. This evolutionary process has been neither smooth nor complete. The churning process has led to the emergence of democracy "as a higher-order-value" on a global scale, eulogized as though it reflects the acme of human civilization and the final point of evolution.

The ascendance of democracy on a global scale would not, ipso facto, help resolution of the conflict of values and of morality. It would at best help set-up the agenda, within the perspectives of a global civilization. Transcending the trappings of time and space, the democratic ethic could provide a basis for the integration and harmonization of human values and issues of morality into a universal frame of twenty-first century human civilization. Hans Küng in his chapter "A Global Ethic in the Age of Globalization" establishes the logic that there can be no new world-order without a world-ethic.

It is in this context, contrary to the view that the emergence of man represents the finale of the process of evolution, it is now being recognized that after the emergence of man, evolutionary process has taken a turn from the "physical" to the "social," represented by the emergence of social systems and man-made culture, generating, in the process, the conflict of values, interests, and of identities, in turn contributing to the distortions and dilemmas of human civilization. If the human society has to resolve these dilemmas, it has to move from the "social" to the next stage, perhaps the final stage of evolution, the "ethical" plane.

The social organization of man has taken diverse thought processes, belief systems, and patterns of action, aggregated and reflected in the form of man-made (material and non-material) culture. Marriage and family; villages and towns; religion and caste; monarchy, dictatorship, and democracy; communes and corporations; legislatures, judicial institutions, and ombudsmen; barter systems to credit cards; cooperative self-help groups to the World Trade Organization; the League of Nations to the United Nations; monarchies to myriad forms of democracy; socialist to capitalist economies; regulation, deregulation, and self-regulation; the contemporary globalization of democracy and of economies; and the emerging pre-eminence of civil society all represent the human endeavour towards shaping and managing their social order.

With all the wisdom churned out and accumulated by man (measured, one way, by the knowledge explosion and the number of Noble Prizes), social evolution of man has generated many more issues than it sought to resolve. Emergence of the democratic "ethic" on a universal plane, globalization of economies and markets, and the compression of human society into a global village make the ascendance of ethics an imperative for the very survival of human civilization. Harmonization of values and interests between communities, generations of humanity, and the various forms of life on earth represents the ethical core of Agenda-21.

If universal human welfare represents the progression of civilization, it calls for a higher-order integration on the universal or cosmic scale, and the indicators of human development and of quality of life of the human society as a whole. Thus, economic growth has to be integrated with the political process on the one hand, and the demands of social development on the other; imbalances any where have been found to disrupt all the three everywhere. As the Human Development Report pinpoints, the global society has "both an opportunity and a moral imperative to reverse the negative trends of recent times and to reinforce the positive patterns of sustainable human development" (UNDP 1996, iv). Humanist values and ethical rules of conduct cannot be the by-products, but the prime-movers of the process and pattern of development.

Globalization of economies has led to an explosive increase in the flows of capital, technology, trade, and people, even if at varying rates, influencing the values, thought-processes, and action patterns of people organizations, and institutions of national and global governance. An important outcome of the market economy is its dominance over the state in conditioning the social dynamics and development process. The space available for the nation-states, capitalist, socialist, and socialistic alike, in fine-tuning policy in order to meet the needs of situation-specific social development is being increasingly eroded. Ben Boothe (1997, 18) argues that it is not America, China, India, or Japan, but the giant MNCs who will own the twenty-first century, and that the key for governments is to successfully learn how to work with these companies in ways that will help their peoples. Arguing that deregulation causes consolidations, then globalization, then dehumanization, then social and economic destabilization, Ben Boothe explains that it is this process that establishes the "cycle of deregulation" forcing the return to regulation.

The choice between reversibility and irreversibility of the process of globalization is blurred by the aggressive stance of multi-lateral global institutions largely influenced by the economic might and political leverage of "veto-powers." The social-political-economic dynamics of liberalization bring the business organizations face-to-face with the ethical dilemmas of development and conflict of cultures. Liberalization of economies has brought corporate organizations into the centre stage of social development. Consequently, the value-dispositions of corporate managers and of organizations have acquired a critical role in formulating and translating the social agenda of nation-states. Where the states are not in a position to influence corporate organizations, or neglecting their responsibility to do so, the non-governmental and community-based organizations as the instrumentalities of democracies are forcing the corporations to be sensitive to the social agenda.

Religion, ethnicity, race-relations, processes of power, problems of poverty, economic disparities and social stratification, corruption, acquisitive individualism vis-à-vis communitarian values, and a host of social issues such as gender-equality and child labour surface on the agenda of corporate management. In the process of corporate decision-making, managers contribute, consciously or unconsciously, to the shaping of the human society. Mission of industry and business is not merely the maximization of wealth but shaping the human society itself – it is not a choice between profits and ethics, but making profits in an ethically tenable manner.

Economic process tends to over-emphasize maximization of self-interest to the near exclusion of all other criteria. Twentieth-century history testifies to the fact that profit orientation of market economies on the one hand, and public sector monopolies of socialist and socialistic economies on the other, both have contributed their own share of conspiracies, bribery, fraud, and collusion, resulting in the erosion of ethics and confidence of the community in business organizations, including the public sector. A recent study (Zdanowicz, et al., 1995) found significant abnormalities in pricing, under-invoiced exports, and over-invoiced imports leading to the flight of an estimated US$4.4. billions from India to the USA alone during one year (1993), out of a total trade volume of US$7.3 billions. Such distortions also raise issues such as the state's ability to control "global" business, tenability of intervention of states on behalf of their "national" corporate organizations, and unilateral interpretation of multi-lateral agreements between states, backtracking on commitments, apart from placing new demands.

The global society, with five decades of post-war experiences, has succeeded in shifting the focus of the United Nations from the concerns of war and peace between nations to issues of welfare and progress of the worlds' peoples. Liberalization and deregulation imply shifting the onus of development from the state to the business and industry, but not giving up human welfare. Development-thought and experience now recognize that the release of market forces by itself cannot lift a premodern society into modern prosperity; it requires an enabling socio-political environment in which institutions function within an overall atmosphere of transparency and public accountability. Life and social fabric become fragile in a society where morality is brittle. Warren Buffet, an American on being shown the rich material acquisitions of a business magnate, asked, "DON'T TELL HOW HE SPENT IT, TELL US HOW HE MADE IT!"

Contending that statist traditions delay modernization of business groups, Amaury Temporal observes that "some of the most virulent opponents of reform in Brazil are business persons who have ceased to be entrepreneurs and now are running sheltered oligopolies" (Temporal 1995, 27–28). Relating the ethos of business to broader issues of democracy and economy, Amaury pertinently points out that "Brazil's business organizations, which in the past have been a lesser agent of change, can be a valuable partner in shortening the time and cost of transition if they can reach a consensus supporting democracy, market economies, a decent judiciary, institutional change, and accountability." For long, the private sector in the Third World remained a strong opponent of liberalization, and enjoyed monopoly in production along with protection of prices as well as markets. The policy and process of liberalization, initiated since the 1980s, is indeed validated from the standpoint that the socialistic economies with controls, licences, and permits had failed to deliver the mandate of growth for democratic development and social justice.

The Ethics Agenda Before International Business

Globalization of democracy and economies contributes to confluence of cultures. It may result in diversity, if not conflict, of cultures which corporate organizations have to steer through. An environment of cultural diversity within which business organizations operate cannot be allowed to lead to organizational-conflict.

Factors like corruption, bribery, or fair business practices manifest in different cultures influence the ethos of corporate organizations. Multi-national business ventures take cognizance and either internalize the dominant attributes of the "alien" culture where they seek entry or "globalize" their own "native" cultural traits.

Are there any typical differences among nations and regions that have a bearing on the way they deal with growth within their own "national" boundaries and with the process of globalization of economies? Is there any thing such as a distinct personality/ image of corporate organizations which they represent and stand by?

Are there any internationally recognized and universally accepted norms of business ethics? What are the areas of agreement and areas where standards differ? What is the role, if any, of national legislation, global covenants, and conventions, multi-lateral and bilateral agreements, and most important of all, the role of national and international trade associations in promoting a normative framework for navigating ethical issues, especially in transnational business?

Issues of either divergence or conflict of values and morality cover a wide range: (a) options of opening up or continuing on-going operations between nations when political conflict arises and be used as partisans especially in defence related trade and clandestine dealings; (b) playing one government against the other in attempting to obtain the best package of investment opportunities, incentives, and tax holidays; (c) indulging in-corrupt practices in order to promote business interest; (d) use transfer pricing, under/over-invoicing in order to generate "black-money" and evasion of tax burden; (e) pursuit of "native" cultural standards irrespective of ethnic variables in the host country and world-wide profits without regard to what may be best for any individual nation; (f) export pharmaceutical and chemical products deemed hazarduous and banned from the market at home to overseas markets; (g) concentrate most R&D activities at home; (h) transfer obsolete technology to other countries; (j) filling management and technical positions in a host country with nationals from the home country; (k) discrimination in employment and differential norms in personnel policies, practices, and compensation. The possible issues can be enumerated ad nauseam.

Business organizations are realizing that they are the victims of their own success largely because after expanding their horizon from the investors to employees and then on to customers, they have not extended it to encompass the interests of communities and ethics of business which involved not mere longitudinal extension, but the more complex process of inclusion and harmonization of conflicting interests and values. This is a challenge that business organizations alone cannot handle. Many of these conflicts arise as a by-product of the malfunctioning of other societal institutions – political, economic, social, and cultural – operating at the local, national, and global levels.

The process of globalization of business can be facilitated by exploring and resolving conflicting dispositions and disputes through informal problem-solving and negotiation. In the first place, conflicts arise between corporations and the communities at the ethical plane, and when not resolved at that level, they would snow-ball into social and political issues enveloping the state and the formal legal institutions and processes.

Business has been globalized faster than the evolution of a universally recognized and respected normative framework. Corporate organizations should start recognizing that while expanding markets as sources of profit, they have to reckon with the social agenda of national communities. They have to contribute not merely towards growth, but equally towards the pattern of growth.

In the twenty-first century global democracy, possible conflicts between global business interests and local political interests are better resolved by establishing rapport with local communities and institutions of civil society.

Starting well before World War II and culminating in the 1960s and 1970s, the dominant approach to the moral dimension of business was a perspective that came to be known as the corporate neo-classical economics, which held that the sole responsibility of business is to maximize its immediate bottom line subject only to the minimal constraints of the law. Advocates of Corporate Social Responsibility (CSR) argue that ethical management requires more than merely following the dictates of the law or signals of the market, the two institutions that otherwise guide business behaviour. Ethical management represents the third dimension of management, the process of anticipating the other two, i.e., law and the market.

Globalization could be counter-productive, both to business and to the human society, if twentieth century market-economy contributes to the growing perception that Transnational Corporations represent an effective substitute to national armies of yester-years.

Business organizations that follow the new paradigm of global social development are more prosperous than those who refuse to leave the old paradigm. The new paradigm that takes cognizance of global social development encompasses and reflects values such as "community development," "social justice," "sustainability," "profit-sharing," and "participative process." If the advent of "Industrial Revolution" and especially the beginning of twentieth century witnessed communities around the globe welcoming large industrial projects as the harbingers of economic prosperity and social development, the social dispositions have taken a U-turn, condemnation of modern industry and technology as the cause of human misery and deterioration in the quality of life of communities. Industry and business have yet to come to terms with social expectations, as the instruments of the social agenda – both at global and local levels.

In the rich variety of cultural diversity that characterizes human society, globalization of business need not, cannot, and should not move in the direction either of uniformity or conflict of cultures.

References

Boothe, B. B. "Who Will Do the World in Twenty-First Century?" *Span* (September-October, 1997) (New Delhi: USIS).

North-South Round Table. *UN and the Bretton Woods Institutions: New Challenges for the Twenty-First Century.* (New York: St. Martin's Press, 1995).

Temporal, A. "Statist Traditions Delay Modernization of Business Groups," *Economic Reform Today*, Number 2 (1995).

UNDP. *Human Development Report 1996* (New York: Oxford University Press, 1996).

Zdanowicz, J. S., Welch, W. W., Pak, S. J. "Capital Flight from India to the US Through Abnormal Pricing in International Trade," *Finance India* 9, no. 3 (September 1995), 609–627 (Florida International University, Miami, Florida).

Ethics Across Information Cultures

Elia V. Chepaitis

Abstract

Information cultures include beliefs, values, and behaviors regarding information ownership and management which evolve within specific historic, social, and economic contexts. The study of ethics within information systems has been dominated by advanced nations, and primarily focuses on property rights. Responsibility for social and economic impacts of computer usage has been a secondary concern. Furthermore, "information ethics," the moral and equitable use of electronic information, has barely begun. In emerging economies, a rough consensus on information ethics is critical for stability, prosperity, equity, and law. In Russia, consensus is obstructed by a dearth of moral axioms, of veracity, and of trust. Information systems alter relationships and change the nature of power, work, and intellectual life. Although a moral component is ever-present after their introduction, effective ethical arguments percolate slowly, brewed within local information cultures.

Introduction: Information Cultures

Information cultures are sets of values, beliefs, and behaviors related to information ownership and information management. These information cultures develop over time, and include moral positions and foci which evolved within specific historic, social, and economic contexts. Information-handling traditions impact not only the identification of ethical issues in modern information systems, but also the ranking of these issues, modes of ethical discussion and analysis, and the identification of solutions which are considered acceptable and congruent with cherished values.

Contemporary information cultures can be affected by a mix of countervailing influences, by professional groups, religious tradition, the behavior of external partners, and by events which introduce discontinuities and revolutionary alternatives.

This chapter will examine the relationship between information cultures and ethical behavior. Information systems, like all technologies, are inherently neutral only in the abstract. In practice, systems are used within cultures for good or for harm, with multiple impacts and moral evaluations. After all, the two most important components of an information system are not hardware and software, but people and information.

Ethics, Culture, and Information Systems

In advanced nations and mature business organizations, the study of ethics in information systems is an evolving and infant discipline. In surplus economies, nations and groups identify ethical problems within cultural frames of reference which may not be relevant in emerging economies. Within distinctive parameters, moral arguments are shaped by dominant intellectual traditions, widely-held values, local resources, habits of perception, and shared experience (Schiller 1986).

Advanced economies undoubtedly pay insufficient attention to some pressing ethical issues in information systems. In both theory and practice, information ethics in the West focuses primarily on larcenous behavior and employee abuse of computer resources, and property rights (DeJoie, Fowler, and Paradice 1991). Responsibility for the social and economic impacts of computer usage - for ergonomics, job security, and working conditions - has been a secondary concern. Furthermore, the slow migration from computer ethics toward "information," in search of a code of behavior which addresses not only hardware and software issues but also the moral and equitable use of electronic information resources, has barely begun (Johnson 1985).

In advanced economies, falsified, withheld, or delayed information often secures unfair and illegal advantage in portfolio investments. Similarly, corporations shield themselves from litigation and prosecution by withholding or manipulating critical data on product safety or environmental impacts (De George 1993). In the United States, agencies misrepresented data and skewed studies on the use of Agent Orange in Vietnam and, possibly, on the exposure of troops to toxic chemicals in the Gulf war. At the individual level, a common breach of information ethics occurs when unscrupulous careerists take credit for co-workers' or subordinates' ideas and achievements through false documentation.

In the West, business policy and research focuses more often on immediate, ethical problems which affect information consumers and competitive advantage: privacy and security; the theft of software and data; viruses; and the rise of hackers, crackers, and computer highwaymen in cyberspace. Case studies in business schools acquaint students with a range of ethical problems which range from obvious violations of legal codes to ambiguous corporate prerogatives, from breaking and entering to monitoring employees (Kallman and Grillo 1996). Although problems such as the theft of employer time, over-charging, shoddy maintenance, and irresponsible data-handling are widely discussed, it is noticeable that other issues begging for accountability and remediation are seldom discussed. These include antisocial behavior such as the humiliation of novice users and managerial responsibility for increasing stress, isolation, and overwork.

Certainly, the unethical use of information knows no boundaries, although it remains less visible than the misuse of more tangible, material resources. However, the impact of unethical information practices is most severe in emerging countries, where solutions are most elusive (Goldman 1987).

Numerous cultural and systemic differences exist within enormous blocs of nations which scholars used to conveniently (albeit fuzzily) label the Second and Third World (Avgerou 1991). However these blocs often possess similar information cultures: values, beliefs, and behaviors which affect information handling and which differ markedly from characteristics in mature economies.

In former communist nations and in developing economies, problems with information systems are acute, and ethical problems reflect their unique historical traditions and radical economic change (Chepaitis 1990). Ethical issues are prioritized differently than in advanced economies, and are articulated and pondered within the context of past and present information cultures. For example, software piracy is not an issue in Russia, any more than wearing animal furs in Siberia is controversial.

Economic Development and Information Culture in Russia

The author worked as a business consultant in Russia in 1991, 1992, and 1994, and taught international business and information systems in Russia and Morocco on Fulbright fellowships in the 1990s. Although conditions in post-Soviet Russia are unique, examinations of the ethical climate, cultural traditions, and contemporary trends are instructive (Chepaitis 1994). Furthermore, although Russia is urban, industrial, and well-endowed with human and natural resources, its information culture is relevant to the study of ethical problems in developing countries.

In these areas, as in Russia, the emergence of a rough consensus on numerous ethical matters, including those affecting information, and also on the development of an effective legal system, are crucial to stability, prosperity, and equity (Chepaitis 1996a).

In Russia, in addition to the distraction and trauma caused by economic collapse and reconstruction, three cultural legacies shape attitudes toward critical ethical issues, especially in information systems. First, values and beliefs in Russia in the 1990s resemble those in the 1890s, a decade characterized by class antagonism, impatience with reform, and extremist solutions which overwhelmed incremental attempts to establish representative government, a stable economy, a viable infrastructure, and a lifestyle comparable to other Western nations. Second and primarily, ethics is affected by Soviet information culture, shaped by generations of isolation, economic imbalance, deprivation, and mistrust. Third, post-Soviet Russia is and will continue to be profoundly affected by the recent past, by a decade of uncertainty and inequality, by the dominant belief that market economies are inherently corrupt, that economic information should be guarded and controlled, and that most wealth is won through chicanery at one's neighbor's expense (Lebed 1997).

Popular culture is characterized by a dearth of moral axioms, a lack of regard for veracity, and a paucity of trust (Chepaitis 1996). Popular aphorisms such as "We pretend to work and they pretend to pay us" illustrate the legacy of hostile manager-worker relationships, and also a widespread avoidance of accurate accountability and verification. However, this post-Soviet culture is also characterized by unprecedented freedom of the press, tumultuous and open legislative sessions, ardent partisanship and debate on broadcast news, and access to global research networks.

The author finds Russians incredulous about ethics in advanced nations. Undergraduates, faculty, and business associates expressed disbelief and ridiculed references to ethics in both international business and information systems. The widespread belief that unethical behavior is not only epidemic but also endemic in a market economy is pernicious. This attitude can encourage, justify, and mask immoral acts as necessary in a market-driven economy. Furthermore, cynicism about morality in the West also affects the intellectual revolution which will accompany political and socio-economic change in Russia. An ethos of quality and customer satisfaction, of job satisfaction and just reward, or of risk and responsible entrepreneurship is less likely to evolve

Yet information ethics are sorely needed in Russia. Crucial domestic and international partnerships fail because of broken contracts, venal distributors, corrupt bureaucrats, and shoddy quality. When business-men, scholars, and guests are deceived and treated unethically through other means, travelers returning from Russia often advise their organizations to delay investment which might aid economic development, citing widespread unethical behavior. In January, 1997, America Online, a vital component in an emerging economy's information infrastructure, ceased operations in Russia due to widespread bank fraud and the uncontrollable theft of credit card numbers.

It is uncertain how durable the contemporary disregard for information-handling equity and integrity will prove to be. On the one hand, most Russians seem to regard open discussions of information ethics and other moral problems as premature, suspect, fatuous, and embarrassing. On the other hand, in this nation which glorified number-crunching for generations, information technology is prized as a strategic resource, for organizational competitiveness, individual communications, self-aggrandizement, and long-term economic security.

The Criticality of Attention to Ethical Problems in Information Cultures

Ideally, information ethics should be foremost in an assessment of the costs and benefits of information technology in any society. However, in Russia, the lack of primary and secondary data, including sparse public information, presents a serious problem not only for business planners but also for ethicist (Aslund 1995). At present, entrepreneurs in industries ranging from insurance to mining cannot define problems and opportunities because of widespread information scarcities, efficient markets will not be created, and moral business practice cannot be debated effectively.

In the 1990s, well-positioned and self-appointed facilitators often control transport, finance, and, also, information gateways, and charge for access to what should be free services. These extortionists resemble the *tolkachi* of the Soviet period or the corrupt bureaucrats in Gogol's nineteenth century.

Immoral and criminal behavior flourishes in a culture built across three traditions which emphasized the foolhardiness of sharing authentic information. In short, information technology is seen as critical for Russia's competitiveness, but information sharing is resisted. Individual deprivation, persecution, excessive taxation, and cultural displacement are feared if information should become accessible and reliable.

Information Technology, Electronic Information, and the Disruption of Information Cultures

Whether utilized indiscriminately, for self-interest, or for the good of the community, information systems in a developing economy are not only affected by culture, but also threaten established information cultures in radical ways. Information systems alter relationships between people, and change the nature of power, work, and intellectual life. A moral component is ever-present after their introduction, and their impacts on value systems cannot be ignored.

Oral traditions, local bureaucratic checks and balances, face-to-face communications, physical payments and monetary transfers, and traditional supply and distribution channels may be replaced by electronic and distant alternatives, perhaps swiftly and with no regard for cultural congruence or traditional mores.

Furthermore, electronic information resources are also inherently disruptive: they can devalue decision-making traditions, managerial experience, formal education skills, and long-established meritocracies. Electronic information threatens the economic, political, and social status quo. Moreover, in Russia as in many developing countries, information systems may be controversial because of long traditions of information mismanagement in both the imperial and the Soviet past: information hoarding, manipulation, and material shortages resulting from a disregard for popular consumption and demand.

Fearing that adequate information would probably fuel change, and that most change would probably be for the worse, information cultures in developing countries can perpetuate a pervasive distrust of information sharing, data collection, and systems integration.

Emerging nations realize the potential of information systems for optimal restructuring, improved resource management, and enhanced goods and services. However, electronic information also offers new and frequently antisocial means of unprecedented self-aggrandizement and mobility in a society in which information resources were traditionally scarce and unshared. The potential for immoral behavior is enhanced because, in some cultures in which veracity is neither expected nor highly valued, information is more fragile and easily-altered or stolen in electronic form. Furthermore, the widespread lack of means for authentication and authorization adds to the popular distrust that a "wired" economic elite can exploit the less fortunate with impunity.

In contrast with J. Ciulla's chapter "Information and the Ethics of

Business Leaders," in developing economies, pervasive mistrust of leaders endures not because of increased information, but by the enduring aura of mystery surrounding authorities and strategic managers. Secretiveness fuels public fear and cynicism, and enhances the role of gossip and innuendo in information-poor societies. For example, in Russia, the lack of reliable data about leaders and the perennial role of political gossip ("Kremlinology") is pernicious. Rumors of Stalin's death, Krushchev's execution, Brezhnev's dementia, and Yeltsin's incapacitation fueled widespread insecurity and inhibited broad political participation.

Culture-Based Solutions

Culture-based ethics arise from decision patterns shaped by singular national experiences, local values, and ideological traditions. No information culture is identical, although all evolve rapidly after the introduction of electronic information technologies. These cultures do not necessarily become more similar, particularly in economic and political systems which are under stress and in transition.

Numerous studies and recommendations in this book shed light on both the challenge of global culture-based ethics and the uniqueness of the Russian situation. Russia most closely resembles China, where the predominant ethical decision principle is act utilitarianism as seen by John Etheredge and Carol Erdener ("Ethical Decision Patterns in Four Countries"), but Russia lacks China's stability, exposure to business practice, and controlled integration into the global marketplace.

In the short term, a decade of chaos, mistrust and survivalism, and also the absence of existing business principles, of civil order, and of business law, obstruct a rough local consensus on ethical practice which Simon Grand and Stephan Rothlin describe as a positive precondition for value creation ("Value Creation in the Context of Plurality").

Russians poignantly describe themselves as deeply spiritual and predisposed to favor the collective good rather than individual self-enrichment. In the long term, traditional insistence on a moral self-identity, re-rooted gradually in a modern context ("Who are we? What do we stand for now?"), is an asset in the formulation of business ethics and individual accountability. However, in the 1990s, Russians lack any solid common ground like S. K. Chakraborty's Hindu-Vedantic Ethos ("Ego, Ethics, and World-Sustenance"), which would position them to manage change and preserve the social ground.

In the absence of socio-economic order, while the distribution of wealth and opportunity continues to be egregiously inequitable, neither an authoritarian government nor a religious revival can protect Russians from each other in the short term, just as little protected them from the state for the past millennium. It is unlikely that Russian religious leaders, especially the influential Orthodox Church, will join with other Christian, Muslim, and Jewish leaders to formulate common business values, and these are probably as difficult to apply in the crisis economy as in the former command economy. Although Simon Webley's inter-faith ethics ("Values Inherent in the Interfaith Declaration of International Business Ethics") would provide a dynamic forum, ecumenical alliances which include Muslims and Jews are unlikely in the 1990s.

Ironically, the lack of robust information resources exacerbates Russia's ethical malaise. It is difficult to identify alternate choices without sufficient data and business experience. However, in the long term, congruent with Amartya Sen's thesis ("Economics, Business Principles, and Moral Sentiments"), a "local" culture-based ethical consensus will evolve, particularly if Russia achieves a modicum of stability and prosperity. Then, provided with the emergence of G. R. S. Rao's "democratic ethic" ("The Ethics Agenda Facing International Business"), Russia may utilize the full resources of the information age to correct social and political faultlines, to embrace values and behaviors in which Russians can take pride and satisfaction, and to join in the construction of "a global ethic in an age of globalization" (Hans Küng).

Conclusion

Ethical arguments and solutions cannot be imported or imposed. Russia and other emerging economies may have problematic information cultures, but ethical issues and norms will most successfully be examined within those cultures. Moral philosophy, egoistic and deontological theory, moral value and responsibility, and justification must all be debated in the context of the specific culture and the shared experience.

In Russia, a millennium of communalism, the premium placed on consensus, vibrant religious traditions, and emerging professionalism may prove to be seminal resources for ethics in the information age. Increased contacts with Pacific Powers and along with the West, continuing business and religious education, may increase the respect for other intellectual and moral traditions.

The long-term relationships between information cultures and ethical systems are unstructured and fluid. It is certain, however, that information ethics will be increasingly significant in international ethics, in view of ongoing geopolitical and technological paradigm shifts (Tapscott and Caston 1993).

References

Aslund, A. *How Russia Became a Market Economy* (Washington, D.C.: The Brookings Institution, 1995).

Avgerou, C. "Creating an Information Systems Infrastructure for Development Planning," *Proceedings of the Twelfth International Conference on Information Systems* (1991), 251–259.

Chakraborty, S. K., "Ego, Ethics, and World-Sustenance," in this book.

Chepaitis, E. "Cultural Constraints in the Transfer of Computer Technologies." Mtewa, M., ed. *International Science and Technology* (1990), 61–74.

Chepaitis, E. "After the Command Economy: Russia's Informatic Culture and Its Impact on Information Resource Management," *Journal of Global Information Management*, 2, no. 11 (1994), 5–11.

Chepaitis, E. "The Problem of Data Quality in a Developing Economy: Russia in the 1990s," *Global Information Technology and Systems Management* (Nashua, N.H.: Ivy League Press, 1996)., 104–122.

Chepaitis, E. "Ethics at Arms Length in Post-Soviet Russia," *Ethics Today & Critical Thinking Quarterly Journal* 36 (Winter-Spring 1996a), 406–420.

Ciulla, J. B., "Information and the Ethics of Business Leaders," in this book.

De George, R. T. *Competing with Integrity in International Business* (New York: Oxford University Press, 1993).

DeJoie, R. Fowler, G., and Paradice, D., *Ethical Issues in Information Systems* (Boston: Boyd and Fraser, 1991).

Etheredge, J. M., and Erdener, C. B., "Ethical Decision Patterns in Four Countries," in this book.

Goldman, M., *Economic Reform in the Age of High Technology: Gorbachev's Challenge* (New York: W. W. Norton, 1987).

Grand, S., and Rothlin, S., "Value Creation in the Context of Plurality," in this book.

Johnson, D. G. *Computer Ethics* (Upper Saddle River, N.J.: Prentice Hall, 1985).

Kallman, E. A. and Grillo, J. P. *Ethical Decision Making and Information Technology* (New York: McGraw-Hill, 1993).

Kantrow, A., ed., "Why History Matters to Managers," *Harvard Business Review* 86, number 1 (January-February 1986), 81–88.

Küng, H., "A Global Ethic in an Age of Globalization," in this book.

Lebed, A., "What Ails Russia," *Wall Street Journal* (January 28, 1997), A22.

Rao, G. R. S., "The Ethics Agenda Facing International Business," in this book.

Schiller, H. L., *Information and the Crisis Economy* (New York: Oxford University Press, 1986).

Sen, A., "Economics, Business Principles, and Moral Sentiments," in this book.

Tapscott, D. and Caston, C. *Paradigm Shift: The New Promise of Information Technology* (New York: McGraw-Hill, 1993).

Webley, S., "Values Inherent in the Interfaith Declaration of International Business Ethics," in this book.

Ethical Decision Patterns in Four Countries:
Contrasting Theoretical Perspectives

John M. Etheredge and Carolyn B. Erdener

Abstract

Responses to a series of ethical dilemmas were gathered from 503 subjects in China, South Korea, Mexico, and the U.S., including Asian-American and Hispanic-American ethno-cultural sub-groups. The data were examined using a framework in which a non-consequentialist approach to ethical decision making based on human rights and justice was contrasted with orientations toward the principles of rule and act utilitarianism. The results demonstrate that national identity tends to override ethnic identity in determining the approach to ethical decision making, and that the pattern of orientation toward normative positions established in Mexico and the U.S., and possibly emerging in South Korea, is contrasted with a distinctly different pattern in China. The results support the further development of this methodology.

After a long period in which scant attention was paid to international considerations, the field of business ethics has entered a new phase of increasing interest in cross-cultural and comparative studies (De George 1994; Donaldson 1989; Donaldson and Dunfee 1994). Doing business internationally requires an understanding of the relationship between cultural values, managerial values, and business decision making (Adler 1992; Black and Mendenhall 1990; Donaldson 1989; England and Lee 1974; Haire *et al.* 1966; Hoffman *et al.* 1986). One of the most important aspects of this very broad area of concern for international managers are fundamental differences in perceptions of what is right and wrong. This study explores one subset of these differences, focusing on business ethical decision patterns in four different countries. The intent is not only to provide country-specific information but, more importantly, to explore the underlying reasons for the wide variation in business ethical decisions found internationally. Ultimately, the objective of this research is to raise our understanding of international differences in business ethical decisions to a higher level of theoretical understanding.

Background

A small but growing number of empirical studies in business ethics focus on culture. Some examine sub-cultures, including ethnic or professional affiliation (Abratt *et al.* 1992; Burns, 1993; Tsalikis and Nwachukwu 1991). Others compare subjects across countries (Becker and Fritzsche 1987; Robertson and Schlegelmilch 1993; Tsalikis and Nwachukwu 1988; Vitell *et al.* 1993). A few focus on a single foreign country (Hinterhuber 1991; Kelly and Reeser 1973; Lai and Lam 1986). Single-country empirical studies of business ethics have been conducted in Australia (Soutar *et al.* 1994), India (Cyriac and Dharmaraj 1994), Italy (Hinterhuber 1991), and Russia (Kolosov *et al.* 1993). Recent comparative work includes studies of Australian and South African managers (Abratt *et al.* 1992), Israeli and U.S. managers (Izraeli 1988), Swiss and U.S. managers (Ulrich and Thielemann 1993), and Nigerian and U.S. views on bribery and extortion (Tsalikis and Nwachukwu 1991). There has been very little empirical research on business ethics in China, South Korea, or Mexico, however, and none organized so as to permit a comparison across ethno-cultural groupings, e.g. Asian and Hispanic. In recent years, much of the management literature has focused on East Asia, and a similar trend is also evident in business ethics, on a smaller scale. However, neither discipline has systematically studied Hispanic-Americans, Mexicans, or Latin Americans. Studies of business ethics in the U.S. have often included ethnicity as a variable, sometimes as the main variable (Tsalikis and Nwachukwu 1991). Empirical research in management has also focused on ethnicity (Cox 1991; Driskill and Downs 1995; Fernandez 1991; Kelley and Reeser 1973; Larkey and Hecht 1995; O'Mara 1991). With the important exception of Native Americans, ethnic identities in the U.S. are typically associated with major world areas outside the U.S. Therefore, differences in ethical decisions attributed to ethnicity in the U.S. might logically be expected to parallel differences in ethnically similar areas outside the U.S.

The studies identified above have employed a wide variety of survey instruments. Some used original tests designed by the authors themselves (Mitchell *et al.*, 1994; Soutar *et al.*, 1994). Several employed measures that had appeared previously in the business ethics literature (Abratt *et al.* 1992; Becker and Fritzsche 1987; Cyriac and Dharmaraj

1994; Izraeli 1988). Using previously established measures greatly enhances credibility and facilitates the interpretation of results.

Many of these studies have not found significant differences across cultures. This is particularly true for those whose samples shared similar institutional and cultural contexts, even where more than one country was included. Differences have also been identified in a few cases (Becker and Fritzsche 1987; Tsalikis and Nwachukwu 1991).

The Present Study

Findings based on a statistical analysis of survey data collected in 1994 and 1995 in China, South Korea, Mexico, and the U.S. are presented in this study. For further comparison, the U.S. sample is divided into ethno-cultural groups of Caucasian-Americans, Hispanic-Americans, and Asian-Americans. The conceptual framework for this analysis is based on that used by Fritzsche and Becker (1984) in their empirical attempt to link normative ethical theories to management behavior. The original source for this framework was the three moral theories identified by Cavanagh, Moberg, and Velasquez (1981) as the basis from which contemporary work in the field of normative ethics has evolved. These were described as:

> . . . utilitarian theories (which evaluate behavior in terms of its social consequences), theories of rights (which emphasize the entitlements of individuals), and theories of justice (which focus on the distributional effects of actions or policies). (Cavanagh *et al.*1981, 365)

Thus, utilitarianism holds that actions and plans should be judged by their consequences, a theory of rights asserts that human beings have certain fundamental rights that should be respected in all decisions, and a theory of justice requires decision makers to be guided by equity, fairness and impartiality. Fritzsche and Becker (1984) modified this framework by classifying utilitarian theories as being either *act* or *rule* utilitarian.

Shaw (1996) describes act utilitarianism – "the most classic and straightforward form" – as "the moral doctrine that we should always act to produce the greatest possible balance of good over bad for everyone affected by our action." Thus, we have only one moral obligation – the maximization of happiness for everyone concerned – and every action is to be judged according to how well it satisfies this principle. Drawing on the arguments of Richard Brandt (1983), Shaw (1996) distinguishes act from rule utilitarianism by proposing that:

> *Rule utilitarianism* maintains that the utilitarian standard should be applied not to individual actions but to moral codes as a whole. The rule utilitarian asks what moral code (that is what set of moral rules) a society should adopt to maximize happiness. The principles that make up that code would then be the basis for distinguishing right actions from wrong actions. (Shaw 1966, 70)

For Cavanagh *et al.* (1981), "theory of human rights asserts that human beings have certain fundamental rights that should be respected in all decisions." Shaw (1996) states that such fundamental human rights have four important characteristics – they are universal; they are equal rights; they are not transferable; and they are natural rights in the sense that they do not depend on human institutions the way legal rights do. Radically different from the principles of utilitarianism, when moral rights are asserted, the locus of moral judgment becomes the individual, not society (Shaw 1996). While utilitarianism treats individual entitlements as subordinate to the general welfare, the assertion of moral rights is decisively non-consequentialist and places distinct and firm constraints on what actions an organization, or society, can do to fulfill its own ends.

Referring explicitly to Rawls' (1971) theory of justice which, according to Shaw (1996), is "generally thought to be the single most influential work of the postwar period in social and political philosophy," Fritzsche and Becker (1984) propose that this approach calls upon the decision maker to act with equity, fairness, and impartiality. Rawls' approach is presented as a modern alternative to utilitarianism (Shaw 1996). Arguing from a hypothetical-contract position, Rawls (1971, 1975) derives two basic principles of justice. The first states that each person has an equal right to the most extensive scheme of liberties compatible with others having the same liberties. The second principle states that for social and economic inequalities to be justified, they must be (a) to the greatest expected benefit of the least advantaged; and (b) attached to offices and positions open to all under conditions of fair equality of opportunity. Rawls rejects utilitarianism because it might permit an unfair distribution of burdens and benefits, and he contends that society is a cooperative project for mutual benefit and that justice requires the social and economic consequences of arbitrary natural differences among people to be minimized.

In this chapter, this framework of normative ethical theories is simplified by combining the rights and the justice positions, both of which reject utilitarianism's grounds. For simplicity and convenience, this position is described here as a *non-consequentialist* orientation. As Shaw (1996) points out, human rights "derive from the assumption that all human beings, merely by virtue of their being human, have certain entitlements." On the other hand, utilitarianism, whether act or rule, treats all individual entitlements as subordinate to the general welfare. With respect to the nature of justice, Shaw (1996) points out that "a claim that you are being treated unjustly often suggests that your moral *rights* have been violated." Justice also means fair treatment, impartiality, and consistency, although, in addition to equal or impartial treatment, Shaw (1996) believes that individual circumstances make a difference, that justice "also requires that people get what they *deserve*." Thus, justice "generally involves appeals to the overlapping notions of rights, fairness, equality, and desert." Utilitarianism, on the other hand, in maximizing the total well-being of society, would permit an unfair distribution of burdens and benefits. Taking the view that we must exclude the justification of inequalities on the grounds that the disadvantages of those in one position are outweighed by the greater advantages of those in another position, Rawls (1971) states, "each person possesses an inviolability founded on justice that even the welfare of society as a whole cannot override."

This framework has support in Brady's (1985, 1987) "Janus-headed" model of ethical theory which proposed that deontology and utilitarianism are complementary. More recently, the arguments put forward by Brady and Dunn (1995) give further support to the distinction by asserting that "the most defendable theoretical foundation for practical decision making in business ethics is the traditional dichotomy between utilitarianism and Kantian deontology."

Thus, the modified framework of ethical philosophical positions developed from the Fritzsche and Becker (1984) research – the non-consequentialist orientation contrasted in turn with rule and act utilitarianism – is used in this study to examine the patterns of ethical decisions in comparable groups within four countries – China, South Korea, Mexico and the U.S. Within the U.S. sample, however, are three ethnic sub-groups – Asian-American, Hispanic-American, and Caucasian-American. With this approach, it becomes possible to examine the question whether national or ethnic identity is the predominant factor determining the pattern of ethical decision making.

Research Method

The sample consists of 503 subjects in China, South Korea, Mexico, and the U.S. All subjects were either about to enter or had recently entered the work force; a t-test of differences in means showed no significant difference in ethical decision orientations based on work experience. All those in the U.S. sample were citizens of the U.S. Their national and ethnic distribution, by gender, is shown in Table 1.

The questionnaire was based on an instrument that had been used in other comparative ethics studies and had met the necessary tests for reliability. It presents a series of five vignettes chosen to represent a variety of ethical dilemmas commonly faced in business organizations. In comparison with other instruments available, these vignettes have been shown to be effective in highlighting systematic differences in ethical decision patterns across countries (Fritzsche and Becker 1984; Becker and Fritzsche 1987; Premeaux and Mondy 1993).

Table 1: National and Ethnic Distribution of Subjects by Gender

National Identity	Ethnic Identity	Male	Female	Not Stated	Total
U.S.A.	Caucasian-American	34	54	0	88
	Hispanic-American	5	8	0	13
	Asian-American	41	29	0	70
	American (Total)	80	91	0	171
Mexico	Mexican (Hispanic)	77	63	2	142
South Korea	South Korean	3	87	1	91
China	Chinese	44	55	0	99
Total Sample		204	296	3	503

Scenarios are commonly used in business ethics research to overcome ambiguity arising from abstract and limited item information in questionnaires and to make the decision-making situation seem more real (Alexander and Becker 1978). They are especially appropriate for international research, because so much of it is exploratory (Cohen *et al.* 1993; Nyaw and Ng 1994; Reidenbach and Robin 1988, 1990; Tsalikis and Nwachukwu 1988, 1991; Whipple and Swords 1992; White and Rhodeback 1992). Jones (1991) has observed that "human beings may respond differentially to moral issues in a way that is systematically related to characteristics of the issue itself." Therefore, since ethical decisions sometimes reflect the issue at hand, scenarios that represent a number of very different ethical dilemmas were used in this study. The first vignette concerns a bicycle company which must make a payment to a foreign country businessman to gain access to his country's market, estimated at around $5 million in annual profit for the company. The second vignette concerns a new employee who is pressured by his employer to reveal the technological secrets of his former employer. The third vignette concerns a decision on whether or not to use a new technology that will give the company an edge on competitors but violates the legal standard for air pollution. The fourth vignette describes an editor who must decide whether or not to include instructions on how to make an atom bomb in a book he is publishing. In the fifth vignette, a product development manager in an automobile parts supplier must decide whether to inform the buyer firm of a defective automobile part that can result in fatal accidents.

The response format required the subjects to respond to each vignette by indicating, first, what their own decision would be in the situation portrayed. Second, they indicated their reasoning in arriving at this decision by rating a number of possible considerations on a 0 to 10 point Likert scale. There was also an opportunity to add any additional considerations that influenced their decisions.

The vignettes and response items were translated by native speakers of the respective languages (Chinese, Korean, and Spanish) and then back translated into English for comparison with the original (Bhagat and McQuaid 1982; Brislin 1980).

Each subject was given an ethical orientation score based on scales in the instrument. The ethical orientations include rule utilitarianism, act utilitarianism, and a general non-consequentialist orientation (a composite measure created by taking the mean of the justice and rights responses). Apart from this composite measure, the Fritzsche and Becker (1984) response measures have been replicated without modification.

The data were subjected a series of one-way analyses of variance in which each of the three ethical decision approaches was treated as the dependent variable and nationality and ethnic identity were alternatively treated as independent variables. In each analysis, the significance of the variance between groups was determined by computing the F-ratio and the significance between the means of the various sub-samples was assessed conservatively by means of a Scheffé-test using a criterion of $p = 0.05$.

Results

The relative means of each of the three ethical decision orientations are analyzed first by national identity and then by ethnic identity. The ethical decision patterns for each of the four countries and for each of the six ethnic identities are then examined.

National Identity

The results of the analyses of variance for each of the three ethical orientations by national identity are shown in Table 2. For each ethical orientation, Table 2 provides a comparison of the mean response levels for each of the four national sub-samples. The table also shows that each of the three F-ratios departs very significantly from unity, indicating that there is a very highly significant degree of interaction between the independent and dependent variables in each case. For each of the three ethical orientations, the differences between the mean response levels of the four national sub-samples has been compared using the rigorous Scheffé-test.

For both the non-consequentialist and the rule utilitarianism orientations, the means for the U.S. and Mexico, while not significantly different from each other, are both very significantly higher than the means of both China and South Korea. No significant difference was found between the means of China and South Korea on the non-consequentialist orientation but, for rule utilitarianism, the mean for South Korea was significantly higher than that for China. The relative positions on act utilitarianism, however, are less clearly patterned. Mexico has the highest mean, significantly above those of China, the U.S., and South Korea. South Korea has the lowest mean in this case, significantly below those of Mexico, China, and the U.S. The means for China and the U.S. on act utilitarianism, however, are not significantly different.

Table 2: Ethical Orientations by National Identity

National Identity	Non-consequentialist		Rule Utilitarianism		Act Utilitarianism	
	Mean	S.D.	Mean	S.D.	Mean	S.D.
U.S.A.	7.590^{ab}	1.757	6.766^{ab}	1.286	5.357^{bc}	1.524
Mexico	7.573^{ab}	1.912	6.947^{ab}	1.448	6.268^{bc}	1.677
South Korea	5.607	1.627	5.114^{a}	1.314	4.785^{c}	1.420
China	5.316	1.680	4.477	1.292	5.570^{b}	1.313
Total	6.773	2.043	6.068	1.683	5.553	1.594
F-ratio	57.1422***		97.810***		19.337***	

*** $p < 0.001$
Notes:
[a] *Significantly different from China at the $p < 0.05$ level (Scheffé test).*
[b] *Significantly different from South Korea at the $p < 0.05$ level (Scheffé test).*
[c] *Significantly different from Mexico at the $p < 0.05$ level (Scheffé test).*

Ethnic Identity

The results of the analyses of variance for each of the three ethical orientations by ethnic identity are shown in Table 3. For each orientation, Table 3 provides a comparison of the mean response levels for each of the six ethnic sub-samples. It also shows that, again, each of the three F-ratios departs very significantly from unity, indicating that there is a very highly significant degree of interaction between ethnic identity and ethical decision orientation in each case. As above, for each of the three ethical orientations, the differences between the mean response levels of the six ethnic sub-samples has been compared using the rigorous Scheffé-test.

Table 3. Ethical Orientations by Ethnic Identity

Ethnic Identity	Non-consequentialist		Rule Utilitarianism		Act Utilitarianism	
	Mean	S.D.	Mean	S.D.	Mean	S.D.
Caucasian-American	7.536[ab]	1.714	6.756[ab]	1.242	5.301[c]	1.403
Hispanic-American	7.897[ab]	2.043	7.051[ab]	1.536	5.613	1.944
Asian-American	7.599[ab]	1.777	6.725[ab]	1.305	5.381[c]	1.603
Mexican	7.573[ab]	1.912	6.947[ab]	1.448	6.268[b]	1.677
South Korean	5.607	1.627	5.114	1.314	4.785[c]	1.420
Chinese	5.316	1.680	4.477	1.292	5.570[bc]	1.313
Total	6.773	2.043	6.068	1.683	5.553	1.594
F-ratio	34.274***		58.659***		11.670***	

*** $p < 0.001$
Notes:
[a] *Significantly different from China at the $p < 0.05$ level (Scheffé test).*
[b] *Significantly different from South Korea at the $p < 0.05$ level (Scheffé test).*
[c] *Significantly different from Mexico at the $p < 0.05$ level (Scheffé test).*

With respect to both the non-consequentialist and the rule utilitarianism orientations, no significant differences were found among the means for the three ethnic sub-groups within the U.S. sample, and none of these three sub-groups was significantly different from the Mexican sample. All four of these ethnic identities, however, were significantly different from the means of the South Korean and Chinese groups which, themselves, were not significantly different in either case in these analyses.

Again, the relative positions on act utilitarianism are less clearly patterned than in the other two ethical decision orientations. The three American ethnic sub-groups are not significantly different from each other, although the Caucasian-American and Asian-American groups are significantly different from the Mexican group which has the highest mean score. Although closer to the means of the other American sub-groups, the mean of the Hispanic-American sub-group is not significantly different from that of the Mexican group. The mean score for Mexico is also significantly higher than those of China and South Korea. As in the national analysis above, South Korea has the lowest mean for act utilitarianism, significantly below those of Mexico and China.

Ethical Decision Patterns

From Table 3, it can be seen that the pattern formed by the three ethical orientations for each of the three American ethnic sub-groups is very similar – the non-consequentialist orientation is clearly preferred, and act utilitarianism falls well behind rule utilitarianism. Tables 2 and 3 show a similar pattern in both Mexico and South Korea although, in both these countries, the distinction between the three orientations is less marked than in the U.S. Moreover, for South Korea, the pattern formed by the three orientations is well below those of Mexico and the U.S. In China, however, the pattern is entirely different. The preferred orientation is act utilitarianism, closely followed by the non-consequentialist orientation, with rule utilitarianism falling clearly behind the other two ethical decision orientations.

Discussion and Conclusions

Despite the limitations imposed by the measurement technology used in this study, the results emphatically support the view that national identity can and does override ethnic identity in determining the approach to ethical decision making (cf. Erdener 1996). Moreover, there is clear evidence of a consistent pattern of ethical decision making across Mexico and the U.S., and perhaps emerging in South Korea, which is contrasted with a distinctly different pattern evident in China.

Based on the results presented above, there can be little question that the three ethnic sub-groups in the U.S. have the same pattern of approach to ethical decision making. For the Asian-American sub-group, there appears to be no influence attributable to their ethnic source when the pattern is compared with those of South Korea and China. For the Hispanic-American sub-group, the consistent peaking above the other U.S. sub-groups, which, with respect to rule and act utilitarianism, follows the pattern of Mexico, may possibly be attributable to the strong influence of Catholicism in both the Mexican and the Hispanic-American societies.

In all three U.S. sub-groups, however, the importance of human rights and individual justice is clearly paramount. The moral obligation to produce the greatest possible balance of good over bad is of less importance, most particularly when it is applied to individual situations and actions rather than the long term benefit of society. The same pattern is evident in Mexico, although there appears to be somewhat more acceptance of act utilitarianism than in the U.S., and in South Korea, where the pattern is significantly less pronounced, as if it may be emerging and moving toward the pattern established within the two Western societies.

In China, an entirely different pattern was found. The predominant ethical decision principle is that of act utilitarianism – the moral obligation to assess each action according to whether it produces the greatest possible good for those affected. Nonetheless, it is evident that the non-consequentialist orientation, emphasizing human rights and individual justice, is also relatively important, although at a much lower level than in the two Western societies. For China, it is rule utilitarianism – the application of the utilitarian standard to a general moral code – that receives the least support, reversing the relationship found in the other three countries between rule and act utilitarianism.

These different patterns of ethical decision making in Mexico and the U.S. on the one hand, and, to some extent, between South Korea and China on the other hand, suggest a link with these countries' cultural and economic systems. Perhaps the strong capitalist economy that has emerged recently in South Korea is contributing to the development of an ethical decision pattern similar to that of the Western countries, albeit somewhat restrained by the traditions of Eastern cultural values. On the other hand, the strong religious influences within Mexico and within the Hispanic-American community may well be related to the relatively higher levels of both rule and act utilitarianism when compared with the Caucasian-American and Asian-American sub-groups.

As for China, the unusual prominence of act utilitarianism and weakness of rule utilitarianism, relative to the other countries in this study, are attributable to the current transition from central planning to a market economy (Naughton1995). For many people in China, this process has undermined traditional cultural values as well as those of communist socialism (Brahm 1997).[1] Although each country's experience is unique, some aspects of the situation in China are reminiscent of developments in Russia, noted in the chapter by Elia Chepaitis ("Ethics Across Information Cultures") elsewhere in this volume. China also illustrates to some extent the broader pattern of "dilemma of development" noted by G.R.S. Rao's chapter ("The Ethic Agenda Facing International Business"). More extensive analysis of the process of values change and its implications for business ethics in China is clearly needed, with particular attention to the effects of temporal change so well articulated by Amartya Sen in the chapter "Economics, Business Principles, and Moral Sentiments."

Finally, it is important to state that this study is not presented as a definitive description and interpretation of the ethical decision-making preferences and patterns of the nations concerned. The primary objective has been to explore these aspects of ethical orientation and to determine whether the methodology offers promise for further research, by suggesting constructs and relationships that warrant investigation, and for the development of more effective methods of measurement. Perhaps more comprehensive vignettes could be developed around other values, such as those identified in the chapters by Simon Grand and Stephan Rothlin ("Value Creation in the Context of Plurality"), G. R. S. Rao ("The Ethics Agenda Facing International Business"), and Simon Webley ("Values Inherent in the Interfaith Declaration of International Business Ethics") elsewhere in this book. Within the limitations of the study, the results do demonstrate the potential for development of this methodology in the investigation of cross-cultural differences in patterns of ethical decision making, and they do demonstrate the need for further clarification of the patterns of ethical orientation across different cultures, including the often-neglected distinction between act and rule utilitarianism, and the fundamental contrast between consequentialist and non-consequentialist moralities.

Endnote

1. "In the 1980s and early 1990s, Deng pushed breakneck economic growth

with scant regard for politics. Chinese society became as materialistic as any other. There was a crisis in ideology. Unlike many other cultures, religion has never served as the ethical guiding force for Chinese. So China, in entering the modern age at unprecedented speed, is seeking to grasp onto a moral, as opposed to purely political, ideology" (Brahm 1997, 56).

References

Abratt, Russell, Deon Nel, and Nicola S. Higgs, "An Examination of the Ethical Beliefs of Managers Using Selected Scenarios in a Cross-Cultural Environment," *Journal of Business Ethics* 11 (1992), 29–35.

Adler, N., *International Dimensions of Organizational Behavior* (Boston: PWS Kent, 1992).

Alexander, Cheryl S., and Henry Jay Becker, "The Use of Vignettes in Survey Research," *Public Opinion Quarterly* 42 (1978), 93–104.

Becker, H., and D. J. Fritzsche, "A Comparison of the Ethical Behaviour of American, French and German Managers," *Columbia Journal of World Business* (Winter 1987), 87–95.

Bhagat, R. S., and S. J. McQuaid, "Role of Subjective Culture in Organizations," *Journal of Applied Psychology* 67, no. 5 (1982), 653–685.

Black, J. S., and M. Mendenhall, "Cross-Cultural Training Effectiveness: A Review and a Theoretical Framework for Future Research," *Academy of Management Review* 15, no., 1 (1990), 113–136.

Brady, F. N., "A Janus-Headed Model of Ethical Theory: Looking Two Ways at Business/Society Issues," *Academy of Management Review* 10, no. 3 (1985), 568–576.

Brady, F. N., "Rules for Making Exceptions to Rules," *Academy of Management Review* 12, no. 3 (1987), 436–444.

Brady, F. N., and C. P. Dunn, "Business Meta-Ethics: An Analysis of Two Theories," *Business Ethics Quarterly* 5, no. 3 (1995), 385–398.

Brahm, Laurence J., "Reformist Ideology: The Real Meaning of China's 'Spiritual Civilisation,'" *Asiaweek* (January 17, 1997), 56.

Brandt, R. B., "The Real and Alleged Problems of Utilitarianism," *Hastings Centre Report* 38 (April 1983).

Brislin, R. W., "Translation and Content Analysis of Oral and Written Materials," in *Handbook of Cross-Cultural Psychology,* eds., H. C. Triandis and J. W. Berry, Vol. 2: Methodology (Boston: Allyn & Bacon, 1980).

Burns, David J., "Coping with Different Ethical Perceptions in America's Increasingly Diverse Workforce," *Business Forum* 18, nos.1/2 (1993), 41–43.

Cavanagh, Gerald F., Dennis J. Moberg, and Manual Velasquez, "The Ethics of Organizational Politics," *Academy of Management Review* 6, no. 3 (1981), 363–374.

Cohen, Jeffrey R., Laurie W. Pant, and David J. Sharp, "Culture-Based Ethical Conflicts Confronting Multinational Accounting Firms," *Accounting Horizons* 7, no. 3 (1993), 1–13.

Cox, Taylor, Jr., "The Multicultural Organization," *The Academy of Management Executive* 2, no. 2 (1991), 34–47.

Cyriac, K., and R. Dharmaraj, "Machiavellianism in Indian Management," *Journal of Business Ethics* 13, no. 4 (1994), 281–286.

De George, Richard T., "International Business Ethics," *Business Ethics Quarterly* 4, no. 1 (1994), 1–9.

Donaldson, Thomas, *The Ethics of International Business* (New York: Oxford University Press, 1989).

Donaldson, T., and T. W. Dunfee, "Toward a Unified Conception of Business Ethics: Integrative Social Contracts Theory," *Academy of Management Review* 19, no. 2 (1994), 252–284.

Driskill, Gerald W., and Cal W. Downs, "Hidden Differences in Competent Communication: A Case Study of an Organization with Euro-Americans and First Generation Immigrants from India," *International Journal of Intercultural Relations* 19, no. 4 (1995), 505–522.

England, G. W., and R. Lee, "The Relationship between Managerial Values and Managerial Success in the United States, Japan, India, and Australia," *Journal of Applied Psychology* 59 (1974), 411–419.

Erdener, C. B., "Ethnicity, Nationality and Gender: A Cross-Cultural Comparison of Business Ethical Decisions in Four Countries," *International Journal of Human Resource Management* 7, no. 4 (1996), 866–877.

Fernandez, John P., *Managing a Diverse Workforce* (Lexington, Mass.: D. C. Heath, 1991).

Fritzsche, D. J., and Helmut Becker, "Linking Management Behaviour to Ethical Philosophy: An Empirical Investigation," *Academy of Management Journal* 27, no. 1 (1984), 166–175.

Haire, M., E. E. Ghiselli, and L. W. Porter, *Managerial Thinking: An International Study* (New York: Wiley, 1966).

Hinterhuber, H. H., "Die Ethik in der Unternehmung: Probleme, Prinzipien und Einstellungen der italienischen Führungskräfte," in *Unternehmensethik*, eds., H. Steinmann and A. Löhr, 2nd ed. (Stuttgart: Poeschel, 1991), 471–479.

Hoffman, W. M., A. E. Lange, and D. Fedo, eds., *Ethics and the Multinational Enterprise* (Lanham, Md.: University Press of America, 1986).

Izraeli, Dove, "Ethical Beliefs and Behaviour among Managers: A Cross-Cultural Perspective," *Journal of Business Ethics* 7, no. 4 (1988), 263–271.

Jones, Thomas M., "Ethical Decision Making by Individuals in Organizations: An Issue-Contingent Model," *Academy of Management Review* 16, no. 2 (1991), 366–395.

Kelly, L., and C. Reeser, "The Persistence of Culture as a Determinant of Differentiated Attitudes on the Part of American Managers of Japanese Ancestry," *Academy of Management Journal* 16 (1973), 67–76.

Kolosov, Michael A., Deryl W. Martin, and Jeffrey H. Peterson, "Ethics and Behaviour on the Russian Commodity Exchange," *Journal of Business Ethics* 12, no. 9 (1993), 741–744.

Lai, Tze-leung and Yip-wai Lam, "A Study on Work-Related Values of Managers in the People's Republic of China (Part I)," *The Hong Kong Manager* (January, 1986), 23–59.

Larkey, Linda Kathryn, and Michael L. Hecht, "A Comparative Study of African American and European American Ethnic Identity," *International Journal of Intercultural Relations* 19, no. 4 (1995), 483–504.

Mitchell, Austin, Tony Puxty, Prem Sikka, and Hugh Willmott, "Ethical Statements as Smokescreen for Sectional Interests: The Case of the UK Accountancy Profession," *Journal of Business Ethics* 13, no. 1 (1994), 39–51.

Naughton, Barry, *Growing Out of the Plan: Chinese Economic Reform 1978–1993* (Cambridge: Cambridge University Press, 1995).

Nyaw, Mee-Kau, and Ignace Ng, "A Comparative Analysis of Ethical Beliefs: A Four Country Study," *Journal of Business Ethics* 13, no. 7 (1994), 543–555.

O'Mara, Julie, *Managing Workplace 2000* (San Francisco: Jossey-Bass, 1991).

Premeaux, Shane R., and R. Wayne Mondy, "Linking Management Behaviour to Ethical Philosophy," *Journal of Business Ethics* 12 (1993), 349–357.

Rawls, John, *A Theory of Justice* (Cambridge, Mass.: Harvard University Press, 1971).

Rawls, John, "A Kantian Conception of Equality," *Cambridge Review* (February 1975).

Reidenbach, R. Eric, and Robin, Donald P., "Some Initial Steps toward Improving the Measurement of Ethical Evaluations of Marketing Activities," *Journal of Business Ethics* 7 (1988), 871–879.

Reidenbach, R. Eric, and Robin, Donald P., "Toward the Development of a Multidimensional Scale for Improving Evaluations of Business Ethics," *Journal of Business Ethics* 9 (1990), 639–653.

Robertson, Diana C., and Bodo B. Schlegelmilch, "Corporate Institutionalization of Ethics in the United States and Great Britain," *Journal of Business Ethics* 12 (1993), 133–144.

Shaw, William, *Business Ethics,* 2nd ed. (Belmont, Cal.: Wadsworth, 1996).

Soutar, Geoffrey N., Margaret McNeil, and Caron Molster, "The Impact of the Work Environment on Ethical Decision Making: Some Australian Evidence," *Journal of Business Ethics* 13, no. 5 (1994), 327–339.

Tsalikis, John, and Osita Nwachukwu, "Cross-Cultural Business Ethics: Ethical Beliefs Difference between Blacks and Whites," *Journal of Business Ethics* 7, no. 10 (1988), 745–754.

Tsalikis, John, and Osita Nwachukwu, "A Comparison of Nigerian to American Views of Bribery and Extortion in International Commerce," *Journal of Business Ethics* 10, no. 2 (1991), 85–98.

Ulrich, Peter and Ulrich Thielemann, "How Do Managers Think about Market Economics and Morality? Empirical Enquiries into Business Ethical Thinking Patterns," *Journal of Business Ethics* 12 (1993), 879–898.

Vitell, Scott J., Saviour L. Nwachukwu and James H. Barnes, "The Effects of Culture on Ethical Decision-Making: An Application of Hofstede's Typology," *Journal of Business Ethics* 12, no. 10 (1993), 753–760.

Whipple, Thomas W., and Dominic F. Swords, "Business Ethics Judgments: A Cross-Cultural Comparison," *Journal of Business Ethics* 11, no. 9 (1992), 671–678.

White, Louis P., and Melanie J. Rhodeback, "Ethical Dilemmas in Organization Development: A Cross-Cultural Analysis," *Journal of Business Ethics* 11, no. 9 (1992), 663–670.

Value Creation in the Context of Plurality: Philosophical Arguments and the Case of India in Its Global Context

Simon Grand and Stephan Rothlin

Abstract

The recent international conferences on ecology, human rights, poverty, and women make obvious that the international community is aware of the vital importance to advance some fundamental issues of humanity on a global level. There is a broad consensus that the situation is explosive and that some fundamental values are a precondition for further development. At the same time, it is evident the dictatorial imposition of such values is not acceptable. The case of India is of particular interest: the achievement of a global ethic (Hans Küng) requires a deep transformation of values which are intimately linked with the social structure of the caste system in India:

- ☐ The rule of basic equality with respect to existential needs and the concept of reciprocity determine a minimal precondition set, excluding sweeping forms of intervention.
- ☐ Interventions can only be acceptable if: (1) the concerned individuals ask for intervention, (2) if the fundamental characteristics of equality are offended, and (3) if some basic symmetry remains respected. This right, however, includes an obligation of the concerned individuals to take seriously their own responsibilities.
- ☐ The complex interdependence of individual action and political activities presupposes a right to and an obligation for education, a concern for improving their own knowledge situation, as well as a competence in dealing with the unknown and the heterogeneous.
- ☐ This implies, however, that the Western world loosens part of its impact on and control of world development, accepting and even supporting the autonomy of other regions and cultures.

Since the cast system is at the root of social injustice and denial of fundamental values, it has to be abolished.

❐ Because multinational corporations play a crucial role in the global scene, and although they are under enormous competitive pressure, they have to include moral sensitivity in their corporate practices.

Introduction

The recent conferences on ecology in Rio (1992), on human rights in Vienna (1993), on poverty in Copenhagen (1994), and on women in Beijing (1995) make obvious that the international community is characterized by a growing awareness of the vital importance of promoting some fundamental issues of humanity on a global level. This development mirrors political reality, violence against minorities and especially women, and civil wars of incredible cruelty, poverty, nationalism, xenophobia, and fundamentalism.

This chapter relies upon a recent analysis of the situation in India, especially focused on the situation in Mumbai and developments in Bihar with respect to the indigenous people of India, the so-called Adivasi. This focus allows us to investigate some fundamental issues including the tensions between both urban and rural areas and between different religious and cultural groups, as well as violence against women and minorities. The experience in India supports the diagnosis of omnipresent violence and deepens the analysis by questioning some basic notions of the dynamics of development and global change: We found the description by Manganelli (1992) more adequate than the romantic picture of Hesse (1922), as it emphasizes the omnipresent ambivalence in India; cruelty and violence are as present as peace and contemplation, arrogance and selfishness are as true as openness and tolerance. This analysis enriches at the same time the image we have of our own society and of the complex interrelationship between both cultures.

There seems to be a broad consensus that the situation is explosive and that some consensus on fundamental values are a precondition for further development, allowing our world society to benefit from the resources and potentials instead of increasing the destructive tensions and violent confrontations. At the same time, it becomes evident that the dictatorial imposition of some fundamental values and concepts is not acceptable: the memory of colonialism in the nineteenth century has rendered any top-down approach impossible.

As a consequence, we focus on the following questions: What can possibly be a basic line of argument, accepting cultural autonomy and individual responsibility without falling into the traps of relativism and opportunism, while providing, at the same time, a frame of reference for discussions about value creation without assuming a superior rationality? By value creation, we understand a deep transformation of values which is required in the context of extremely different groups and religions within India as well in the plurality of the global context. Only a balanced argumentation will allow the existing value systems to improve and legitimize interventions against injustice without opening the ground for anything goes type strategies (see Feyerabend 1986).

Value Creation and Social Development

The obvious answer, given for decades now, would be to support technological development and economic growth: The narrow minded concept of economic rationality in terms of efficiency and individuality (see Sen 1999, 18f.) seems to represent a conception which is fast becoming the globally accepted logic. At the same time, economic growth increases the social wealth and provides the resources that allow everybody to build his or her own existence. Interestingly, however, recent developments rather contradict such an optimistic diagnosis: The themes of poverty and ecology seem not to find a clear solution in a capitalistic system. In the middle of Western societies, a new poverty emerges in unemployment, tensions between social groups combined with increasing inequalities.

The consequence is the growth of latent and open violence as an evident reaction to uncertainty, ambiguity, and anxiety (see Girard 1972). An analysis of the fundamental argumentation in economics makes clear that economic rationality never systematically leads towards valuable distributions and fair income constellations by itself. Economic rationality rather presupposes some basic values (see Schelling 1960, Elster 1979, 1983), which have to be deduced from political procedures, lying outside the logic of economic reasoning (see Buchanan 1975, 1977, Habermas 1981). Concerning the case of India, we see that only a small minority could have really profited from the market liberalization introduced in 1991 under Prime Minister Narasimah Rao while the gap between the rich and poor widened.

Myrdal concludes that some fundamental problems of order in Asia are related to this basic mechanism: while Europe went through the social and political transformations before the Industrial Revolution, following some orderly patterns of development, Asia is characterized by an economic dynamic which has yet to be framed by some founding values. One could in addition argue with Hirschmann (1977) that the rationale of some basic economic rationale and against the former predominance of emotions and passion had to be achieved, founding the political constellation of Europe at the beginning of the Industrial Revolution.

We are not interested in discussing the empirical adequacy of these theses, but we use the argumentation in order to illuminate some basic intuitions and to structure our further discussion. Following the position of practical relativism (see Feyerabend 1987), we argue in favor of the following position. Individuals, groups, and nations always profit from studying unknown and even opposing cultures – four reasons: first, because a diversity of world views always allows us to understand our own contexts more deeply and often even is a necessary precondition; second, as an enrichment of our lives; third, because it is the precondition and basic characteristic of any global community; and fourth, we would like to check if the vision of a "global ethic" (Küng and Kuschel 1993) is realistic in the case of India.

Decisions about the adequacy and moral status of cultural and individual contexts and world views can only be made if these contexts are known and discussed. The precondition for the discussion is the fundamental orientation in our primary context and basic knowledge about our political embedding in broader communities. We will show how these preconditions – on the cognitive, existential, and political level – have to be situated. It is important to reflect the dependence of our philosophical argumentation on European traditions, without accepting a simplistic cultural relativism, which excludes the possibility of criticizing other cultures or of intervening in particular situations:

> ☐ On the cognitive level, we argue that reflection upon a plurality of world views is needed in order to approach the complexity, heterogeneity, and interconnection of today's social and political constellations (Marty 1990). The development of the World economy and the political system interrelates Europe and India in complex and fundamental ways.
>
> ☐ On the existential level, we argue that beyond a founding orientation in our own social and cultural context, we have to face the permanent potential threat posed by our individual and collective roots, meaning that every position conclusively becomes a minority one in a global context. We had better include this situation in our conceptions because we have to face it anyway.

❒ On the political level, we have to find a constellation of basic values allowing us to live this plurality of individual biographies and social situations. This means that we have to identify an argumentation base for a political philosophy which has a chance of becoming globally acceptable and collectively binding.

Only an argumentation which includes the individual life situations and action contexts has any chance of being relevant for deducing action proposals (see Habermas 1995, 63). We will, therefore, start with some arguments in the tradition of Western political philosophy, but we will have to apply our conclusions to some concrete questions and problems concerning our relations as Europeans with India, probably the most challenging environments for this kind of discussion. There is a risk of following an approach of Euro-centrism here. We will show an alternative which accepts that every argument is rooted in a specific cultural context, which implies however, that all cultures have to be respected with their original contributions.

Political Philosophy of International Order

We will discuss the following questions: Why should we be interested in unknown and foreign cultures like the cultures in India? What are the individual and political preconditions for such an interest to be constructive? What are the consequences for deducing action proposals, including strategies of intervention? We, thereby, focus on the discussion of the political and moral dimension of the problem, because we assume that this dimension is most problematic. At the same time, however, we introduce some intuition with respect to the cognitive and existential dimensions also.

1. The classical question in moral philosophy asks: Why should I be moral? The history of philosophy is the history of possible answers to this question. It becomes increasingly evident however that this question cannot have a generally acceptable answer. Game theoretic models show in addition to individual behavior, opportunistic behavior can always profit from free riding on the moral behavior of others (see Elster 1979, 1983). As a consequence, recent theoretical conceptions revise the question: Why should we be moral? The analysis of moral behavior makes sense only when it is being analyzed as embedded in an inter-subjective, political context.

2. The most general argumentation would rely upon the functional value of some shared moral beliefs, arguing that their value lies in

reducing the uncertainties and ambiguities of social interactions (which is typical for an economic analysis of moral behavior). This gives some basic intuition of the social function of moral (see the sociological tradition following Durkheim or the concept of trust in Luhmann) without however enlightening the possible content of such moral beliefs. It is nevertheless an important argument because it shows the importance of our further discussion on the cost of pluralistic cultural contexts. It is important to understand in which situations this argument is overvalued by the gains of cultural diversity on the cognitive and existential level.

3. Coming to the content of moral beliefs, modern philosophy seems to be forced to detach the argumentation from any metaphysical reference points, including God or transcendence, or their secularized successors like reason, history, and nature. We, therefore, decide to focus on the concrete, situated actions characteristic for human practice in social contexts, providing some basic consequences:

- ☐ The formation of personal individuality (as one precondition of social action) always includes the participation in performed social contexts and the dependence on relationships with other persons. Individual action always happens in the face of somebody else (see the work of E. Levinas and M. Buber for detailed philosophical analysis), providing some sort of existential personal interconnection.

- ☐ Individual action is therefore always linked to a social, cultural, and language context, implying a contingency and relativity of any individuality and social position gained due to some socialization process (see Rorty 1989). We gain, however, only an awareness of this contingency by comparing our view of the world with alternative perspectives, meaning that a plurality of cultures is a cognitive and existential precondition of personal identity.

- ☐ Our personal identity is always more or less related to this existential embedding in some initial situation which we conceptualize as the primary context. Modern societies and the globalization process, however, make it essential to expand towards the secondary contexts of our social and political environment (even Etzioni 1995, 46, supporting this argument), implying that every individual has to establish strategies for living in different cultural contexts.

❑ The growing uncertainty and openness of social reality today, linked with growing globalization and intercultural interdependence, has a fundamental impact on this constellation: an increasing chance of socialization processes failing, an ongoing confrontation with unknown world views (not only when visiting other countries but at the core of our own social reality, especially big cities), and a growing dependence on people not relying upon their own socialization procedures.

Combining these elements of diagnosis, we can deduce some fundamental arguments with an important impact on any debate on political philosophy and social reality:

❑ Our individuality always refers to some constellation of relationships which form our personal world views. They are inevitably contingent, but nevertheless existential on a primary level. A strategy of practical relativism, as we will conceptualize it, therefore includes elements of communitarian argumentation.

❑ Any political order or value constellation intending to structure some common way of living has to guarantee this autonomy by providing, at the same time, some shared values or political procedures organizing the political community. We argue that the growing international dependence, exemplary in the situation of India with its growing impact on the world economy, implies the need to conceptualize the argument for a global community.

❑ Existential and political interdependence make of reciprocity a fundamental concept of political philosophy (Höffe 1995, 20–39): A constellation of symmetric respect and care of individuals is a precondition of successful socialization and social community. We would argue in favor of interventions as being legitimized (even if violating symmetry), if this symmetry is questioned from within and if the people concerned ask for support (see Forum international 1993), which is certainly true for important groups in India, including the confrontation between the indigenous people and some extreme right Hindu parties, or the violence against women, especially related to the dowry problem in Hindu families.

❑ It is, however, important that such interventions have to deal with concrete situations and specific problems. This means that representational arrangements often lack the legitimization

needed to argue in the name of other people. Often the phenomenon of factionalism among the exploited minorities themselves
blocks their struggle for obtaining more rights. Individuals,
companies, or governments that support intervening institutions
have a responsibility for such interdependence.

☐ The growing uncertainty and complexity of global developments make the veil of ignorance an increasingly adequate idea
of social reality. Some elements of justice will be fully legitimate (see Rawls 1971): equality dominates inequality with respect to some fundamental rights of survival and basic securities, not making, however, of equality a totalitarian principle
however (see Sen 1992 on inequality reexamined). Especially in
the context of religious violence, the commitment of the different religious groups toward "a culture of equal rights and partnership between men and women" (Declaration Toward a
Global Ethic, 1993) becomes indeed increasingly urgent.

These arguments are consistent with our basic attempt to realize a program of pragmatic relativism which allows for maximal diversity without endangering the constellation as a whole. The propositions developed so far permits us now to provide some basic arguments concerning
strategies of value creation and intervention.

Conclusion: Strategies of Value Creation

We deduce some points of conclusion in parallel to some general intuitions and political tendencies by relying upon a reflected structure of argumentation which allows us to reconstruct the different statements and
to reconsider problematic steps in further discussions:

1. The fundamental question of political philosophy asks: How can we
    realize a political constellation allowing for peace and happiness?
    We argue that the rule of basic equality with respect to existential
    needs and the concept of reciprocity determine a minimal set of pre-
    conditions. The full reality of politics is mutual recognition of men
    and women among themselves beyond the violence they exert on
    each other. Politics is where groups meet and confront each other
    with their liberty and overcome their mutual violence (Calvez
    1997). Therefore, it is important to distinguish between the primary
    group and the secondary (international) community. The emotional
    priority of the first has to be completed by the political relevance of

the second in a society of global interdependence, making impossible any attempt of sustained isolationism. The analysis of the social situation in India shows clearly how mutual understanding between the castes and the out-castes (Harijans or dalits; Adivasi), and between different religious groups seems to be a priori impossible. It is therefore extremely important that individuals and states share the need to handle individual and cultural diversity.

2. Reciprocity and symmetry, as founding concepts, contradict in several ways the possibility of intervention. What are the additional arguments that are needed to find an appropriate base for intervention? First, if the concerned individuals ask for intervention (see parallel with psychoanalysis); second, if the fundamental characteristics of equality are offended, including the right to life and some basic preconditions of survival (we argue that this includes the right to education and some basic formation); third, if some basic symmetry remains respected. This right, however, includes an obligation of the concerned individuals to take seriously their own responsibility. Concerning the case of India, given the additional three arguments, we must conclude that the abolition of unjust social structures which prevent so many groups from participating actively in the political process and which violate their basic human rights (even in the name of religion) is of uttermost importance.

3. The complexity and interdependence of individual action and political activities presuppose a systematic concern with acquiring information and knowledge. We deduce, therefore, a right and (!) an obligation for education and formation – including a permanent concern for improving the own information and knowledge situation – that should not only be linked to some privileged classes. Interestingly, this same point is a fundamental precondition for every individual to acquire a competence in dealing with the uncertain, the unknown, the heterogeneous, and the foreign, characteristic of global and multicultural constellations.

4. These three arguments are important preconditions when a productive concern with a pluralistic situation becomes probable. Only if the basic needs for survival and security are fulfilled, if the rule of reciprocity is realized, and if the necessary knowledge and information is available, are individuals really entitled to and capable of living their responsibility. This means, on the one hand, that the Western world loosens parts of its impact on and control of world development, accepting and even supporting the autonomy of other

regions and cultures; on the other hand, it may be decisive for exploited minority groups in the struggle for their rights if they are supported by interventions from outside their country.

5. The analysis of the situation in India questions a dogma of modern philosophy concerning the methodology of social theory (see above: Political Philosophy of International Order, point 3) to the extent that any metaphysical and religious reference points are excluded. The religious background in India is so much part of the social reality and is so much at the core of many conflicts that it would be not only narrow minded but misleading to ignore it. We just indicate the necessity of exploring a more adequate approach which would include the link between religious and political factors.

6. International and multinational corporations play a crucial role in the global scene. Our argumentation implies that these corporations have to include moral sensitivity in their specific corporate practices. This is especially problematic, however, when we take into account that they are confronted with an enormous competitive pressure. Nevertheless, we would argue that they will not build up long term relationships and trust, preconditions of business success in today's world, without relying upon reciprocity and symmetry. In addition, managers as individuals have the possibility and responsibility, and frequently even the desire, to discuss about the moral foundation of their economic activities

7. It is evident that power constellations and interest groups maneuver against participation and autonomy because they increase the opposition against existing privileges and advantages. This is of special virulence in India, where Hinduism as the dominant religious culture is building its whole social organization on the caste system, which is mainly based on a logic of difference and inequality. The violence and suppression which results along with the commitment to rights urges an international intervention which would provide the context so that the necessary legal framework could be established and implemented. At the same time, however, due to the role of reciprocity, we have also to accept that individuals or groups of people in India disagree with some values and concepts of Western society. Despite the growing outbreak of religious sectarianism, religions could play an important role in shaping new values which correspond to the local culture. The reflection and analysis of such situations, combined with concrete activities of value creation in India and in Europe, allows to make a further step toward a binding

"global ethic," by enriching at the same time our cognitive and existential situation.

References

Buchanan, James M., *The Limits of Liberty: Between Anarchy and Leviathan* (Chicago, 1975).

Buchanan, James M., *Freedom in Constitutional Contract: Perspectives of a Political Economist* (London, 1977).

Calvez, Jean-Yves, *Politics and University Studies as They Relate to Politics* (Manila:Plenary Lecture at the Ateneo de Manila University, 1997).

Elster, Jon, *Ulysses and the Sirens: Studies in Rationality and Irrationality* (Cambridge/London/New York, 1979).

Elster, Jon, *Sour Grapes: Studies in the Subversion of Rationality* (Cambridge/London/New York, 1983).

Etzioni, Amitai, Interview in *Die Zeit*, 46 (1995): 43 f.

Feyerabend, Paul, *Farewell to Reason* (London, 1987).

Forum international sur l'intervention, *Intervenir? Droits de la personne et raisons d'État*, Académie universelle des cultures (Paris, 1993).

Girard, René, *La violence et le sacré* (Paris, 1972).

Habermas, Jürgen, *Theorie des kommunikativen Handelns*, vols. 1–2 *(Frankfurt am Main, 1982)*.

Habermas, Jürgen, "Wahrheit und Wahrhaftigkeit," *Die Zeit* 50 (1995): 63f.

Hesse, Hermann, *Siddhartha* (Frankfurt a.Main, 1922).

Hirschmann, Albert O., *The Passions and the Interests: Political Arguments for Capitalism before Its Triumph* (Cambridge/London, 1977).

Höffe, Otfried, "Menschenrechte und Tauschgerechtigkeit," in *Freiheit und Gerechtigkeit: Perspektiven Politischer Philosophie,* ed., Fischer, Peter (Leipzig, 1995), 20–39.

Küng, Hans, and Kuschel, Karl-Josef, eds., *A Global Ethic: The Declaration of the Parliament of the World s Religions* (London/New York, 1993).

Manganelli, Giorgio, *Esperimento con l'India* (Milano, 1992).

Marty, François, *La Bénédiction de Babel* (Paris, 1990).

Rawls, John, *A Theory of Justice* (Cambridge, Mass., 1971)

Rorty, Richard, *Contingency, Irony, and Solidarity* (Cambridge, 1989).

Schelling, Thomas, *The Strategy of Conflict* (Cambridge, Mass., 1960).

Sen, Amartya, *Inequality Reexamined* (New York/Oxford, 1992).

Sen, Amartya, "Economics, Business Principles, and Moral Sentiments," in this volume (1999).

Ego, Ethics, and World-Sustenance (Lokasangraha):
Searching for Common Ground in the Hindu-Vedantic Ethos

S. K. Chakraborty

Abstract

The chapter presents some ideas about ethics in the secular-social as well as sacred-cosmic aspects by drawing upon the tradition. The first theme is that of ego-centric, desire-based management of our affairs which is suggested as the mother of all ethic-moral problems. The Vedantic concept of lokasangraha *is offered as an alternative and ethically potent motive for work. The second keynote is that of Vedantic monism,* Oneness. *The feeling of oneness, rather than that of differentiation, is suggested as the ultimate basis of ethicality. The third keynote of the chapter is explaining the nature of* Atman *in Vedantic Psycho-philosophy and suggests that its fundamental nature is that of giving and gifting, instead of grabbing and possessing by the ordinary ego. Giving by its nature is more ethical than grabbing. The last point mentions about the need to cultivate the sensitivity and acceptance of some basic values as always unchangeable. This can become a basis for ethical management of changing.*

Introduction

Theoretically, this chapter is an attempt to throw some light on the link between human perception of ego/self and its impact on the moral aspects of choice and behavior. Practically, it tries to demonstrate how the present feverish thrust in favor of ego/self nurturance works against world-sustenance or *lokasangraha*. Economic and business institutions today symbolize and effectuate this thrust. The chapter tries to present ethics not only along the secular spectrum of inter-personal, inter-organizational, and inter-national aspects, but also in its supra-social, cosmic aspect.

In this effort, I shall rely chiefly upon the writings of Rabindranath Tagore, Swami Vivekananda, Mahatma Gandhi, and Sri Aurobindo. All of them had thorough first hand acquaintance with Occidental civilization and society. And more importantly, they had "lived" Indian thought in their breath and bones. They were gigantic and creative activists in different streams of personal, national, and international events. Except Vivekananda, all the others lived around eighty years, spanning between them the last four and first five decades of the Nineteenth and Twentieth Centuries (1861–1951). Vivekananda lived during 1863–1902,

The kernel of Indian ethos[*] is imbedded in the Hindu-Vedantic world-view. Many offshoots have branched off from this main trunk. And of course there are the Buddhist, Jaina, and Sikh traditions which emerged as later-day modifications/extensions of the unbroken mainstream Hindu-Vedantic world-view.

"Ego was the Helper, Ego is the Bar"

The above caption is an aphorism from Sri Aurobindo (Aurobindo 1973, XVI: 377). Ego as an endowment of Nature is an indispensable nucleus for the formation of a finite personality out of the Infinite impersonality. This finite personality survives on separateness and independence. Yet, within the finite personality the secret impulse towards the Infinite continues to work obscurely. The practical consequences of this urge for self-extension to Infinity, which presently is gross and undisciplined, are like this:

   a. perpetual proliferation of external desires, wants, and artifacts;
   b. craving for physical possession for the sake of self-enlargement;
   c. precedence of subjective preference over objective choices; and
   d. competitive struggles in a world of scarcity.

All our ethico-moral problems, dilemmas, and violations can be embraced within the framework of the above four underlying characteristics of human existence. This is why the initially helping "ego" later on turns effectively into an obstacle, a bar in the way of true human development.

---

* "Indian Ethos" is the invisible foundation of Indian Civilization (like the deep roots of a tree), and comprises all thoughts, philosophies, and practices which have originated in the Indian sub-continent. "Indian Culture," however, is the visible mosaic on the surface (like the branches, leaves, and flowers of a tree) and comprises enriching contributions from Islam, Christianity, and Zoroastrianism from elsewhere.

Bar to which kind of human development? Bar to the feeling of unity and infinity, *even* within the individualized personality. In classical India, in the *tapovans* (forest hermitages), the young pupil's primary education used to begin with the cultivation of this learning and feeling. Sri Aurobindo sums up the principle very well (Aurobindo, June 1991, 5):

> Therefore by transcending ego and realizing the one Self, we possess the whole universe in the one cosmic consciousness, and *do not need to possess physically* (emphasis added).

If we are serious about a theory of ethical regeneration and transformation, then the ultimate (I beg your pardon) answer probably lies in the above statement. The test of ethical maturity for a person could be: how much has she or he been able to outgrow the barrier of separative ego consciousness and enter into the realm of unitive Self consciousness. There is of course no short-cut to this state. Continuous hard work through practical methods is essential. Let us go for some hints.

Alluding to the offer of some donation for his Ashram by a businessman, Sri Aurobindo had made the following observations (Aurobindo, April 1997, 6–7):

> I do not regard business as something evil or tainted, any more than it is regarded in ancient spiritual India. . . . All depends on the spirit in which a thing is done, the principles on which it is built and the use to which it is turned.

The "spirit" referred to here raises the question: is the venture being carried out for selfish, greedy, exploitative, dishonest ego-aggrandizement; or it is being treated as a Self-realization project? We have the following assurance from Sri Aurobindo on this principle (Aurobindo, April 1991, 32):

> Action without desire is possible, action without attachment is possible, action without ego is possible.

The ethical underpinning of Krishna's counseling to Arjuna, the Pandava prince and commander, to engage in the *Mahabharata* war was precisely this principle. Verses 19 and 20 of Chapter 3 in the *Gita* (contained in the *Mahabharata*), as translated by Aurobindo, are reproduced below (Aurobindo 1997, 53–54):

> 19. Therefore without attachment perform ever the work that is to be done (done for the sake of the world, lokasangraha, as is made clear immediately afterward); for by doing work without attachment man attains to the highest.
> 20. It was even by works that Janaka and the rest attained to perfection. Thou shouldst do works regarding also the holding together of the peoples (*lokasangraha*).

Thus, the rule of non-egoistic, non-attached work is a one-stroke reconciliation of both world-sustenance and individual perfection. *Lokasangraha* is an invitation to transcend the imperfections, immaturities, and unethicalities of all conventional motives for action. The motive here is rather to hold together the human race in its cyclic evolution (Aurobindo 1992, 59). The perfection of King Janaka is not one of enormous wealth, power, and fame. They are but an aggregation of finites offering transient satisfactions and breeding recurrent unethicalities. Perfection means unitive Self-consciousness beyond the separative ego-consciousness. The practical attitude of *lokasangraha* promotes the attainment of such perfection as is good for the world and the individual at the same time. *Lokasangraha*, however, cannot be techniqued or programmed. It calls for dedicated emotional culture through an abiding awareness of the inalienable cosmic setting for every individual. The businessman, like the warrior, is no exception to this process.

In respect of politics too Sri Aurobindo does not mince words (Aurobindo 1973, XV: 27).

> ... the modern politician in any part of the world ... does not represent the soul of a people or its aspirations. What he does usually represents all the average pettiness, selfishness, egoism, self-deception that is about him. . . . The disease and falsehood of modern political life is patent in every country of the world and only the hypnotized acquiescence of all . . . in the great organized sham cloaks and prolongs the malady . . .

Since the time Aurobindo had uttered these words nearly eight decades ago, things have worsened. The business-politics alliance now needs a thorough transformational education through the principle and process of de-egoizing *lokasangraha*. Then only may we move towards ethical world-management and moral world-sustenance. For most nations, this alliance is always revealing the worst aspects of nationalistic egos, causing the world incalculable material damage and psychological harm.

For one who has the courage – and the humility – to step with Aurobindo into the Divine space which constitutes the hub of all his philosophical labors, it should be apparent that the warrant of ethicality is not merely the opting for the relative good against the relative bad, but is an entry into the growth of one's Divine nature. The ethical pretensions of the rational ego of man are never a sure foundation. This is inevitable because, caught in the embrace of our secular conditioning, the quest for the Divine/Eternal/Infinite is considered to be an abnormal or luxurious aberration. Such a social milieu may allow a small niche to such notions, but it is not prepared to put its heart into it. The result of this faint-heartedness is summed up by Aurobindo in these apt words (Aurobindo 1992, 145):

> It [society] accepts ethics as a bond and an influence, but it does not live for ethical good; its real gods are vital need and utility and the desires of the body.

Nations which count among the "haves" in this world, individuals who count among the "haves" within the poorer nations of the world – for both the beacon of the consciousness of Divine Self-hood alone – could be the guiding light showing a clear path through the ethical jungle. The prevailing "rational" but muddled temper may be reluctant to lend its ear to the call of the supra-rational. Yet the greatest of ethical personalities in human history, like the Buddha, Jesus, and Lao Tse, have all been seen to forge and demonstrate the saving link between the supra-rational sacred and the rational secular, and they had all subjected their individual egos to the sovereignty of the Universal Self, the Eternal, the Infinite. They could function with infallible, instinctive ethicality whenever they played some part in the secular society they lived in. Theirs is the ideal, the model of *loksangraha* ethics.

Turning therefore to the senior leaders of various global organizations and front-ranking national governments, it appears that unless they set their hearts towards a personal odyssey for transforming the exteriorized, deficit-driven, hungering ego-self to the non-contingent, self-existent satisfaction of the Self, the world as a whole and its various institutions have little hope for ethical sustenance or *lokasangraha*. By all counts such individuals are today far too busy with securing their positions and ensuring their own survival to be able to practice, even minimally, such indispensable transformation. Pulpit orations on ethics and values are usually mere platitudes, just a pretense of conscience. Evidence is endless right across the globe, yet Vedanta assures always that this quest for the Self within, and then putting the ego-self at its command as a disciplined agent, is verily a journey of abiding joy and bliss – *ananda*. The beauty of the idea is that it is at once personal bliss and external ethics. Aurobindo conveys thus the personalized recipe from universal Vedanta (Aurobindo 1973, XIII: 562):

> Arrive at something within you that is *eternal*, ever *unchanged*, calm, unperturbed, equal, impartial to all things and persons and happenings . . . (emphasis added).

"The World is a Grand Moral Gymnasium"

The above metaphorical aphorism comes from Swami Vivekanand (Vivekananda 1962, I: 80). Just as in a body-building gymnasium, I develop and strengthens my physical limbs and muscles, so too the whole world provides me with a grand arena for exercising my ethico-moral and spiritual-Divine sensitivities. This image concretizes a sense of direction for self-management by individuals. The goal of such exercise in self-management is to outgrow separateness and differentiation and approach the realization of Oneness. This is relevant as much to individuals as to whole nations and races.

The philosophical key-note of Vedanta is monism – Oneness. The One, Unlimited Infinite has become the many, multiple finites. "The limited is a mere fiction" (Vivekananda 1962, II: 305), as Vivekananda interprets the Vedantic keynote. This limited, fictional individuality, whether of persons or nations, is an illusion submerging the feeling of Oneness. He squarely refutes the charge that such ideas are impractical speculations. Tracing the origin of such principles he asserts that they have been "practical first, and philosophical next" (Vivekananda 1962, II: 317). He explains further (Vivekananda 1962, II: 317):

> This world *spoke* to the early thinkers. Birds *spoke* to them, animals *spoke* to them, the sun and the moon *spoke* to them; and little by lit-

tle they *realized* things and got into the *heart* of nature. Not by cog-
itation, not by the force of logic, not by picking the brains of others
and making a big book. . . . Its essential method was *practice*. . . . It
is *practice first* and *knowledge afterwards* (emphasis added).

Such then has been the supra-rational genesis of Vedantic monism
or Oneness or *ekatmanubhuti*, in the *ashrams* or hermitages of yore. Silence and solitude constituted their foundations. The silence-solitude
impetus is indispensable for allowing the holistic Self to take the front
seat, pushing the fragmentist ego-self behind and below. Wisdom demands this subjective strategy, as proved by the wise of all times.

The world today is typically not an *ashram* however. It is being
rushed headlong towards becoming an arid and complicated technology
park. In this context, *ashramic* Vedanta may imply a process for
ethico-moral rejuvenation which is apparently a complete mismatch
with the chipped and computerized man-made artificial world. Theoretically, this represents a duel between the true ideal and the apparent
reality. Which side should we vote for? Vivekananda offers us several
complementary insights into this riddle:

(1) There are two tendencies in human nature: one to harmonize
the ideal with the life, and the other to *elevate the life to the
ideal*. It is a great thing to understand this, for the former tendency is the temptation of our lives (II: 293; emphasis added).

(2) . . . Vedanta not only insists that the ideal is practical, but that it
has been so all the time; and this Ideal, *this Reality is our own
nature* (II: 295; emphasis added).

(3) . . . in the Vedanta there is no attempt at reconciling the present
life – the hypnotized life, this false life – with the ideal; . . . this
false life must go, and the real life, which is *always existing*
must manifest itself . . . . (II: 295 emphasis added).

(4) . . . the Vedantic idea is not the destruction of the individual, but
its *real preservation*. We cannot prove the individual by any
other means but by referring to the universal, by proving that
this *individual is really the universal* (II: 333; emphasis added).

(5) . . . the highest ideal of morality and unselfishness goes hand in
hand with the highest metaphysical conception, . . . you need not
lower your conception to get ethics and morality . . .; to reach *a
real basis of morality and ethics* you must have the *highest
philosophical and scientific conceptions* (II: 355; emphasis
added).

(6)Therefore the Vedantist insists upon that *Oneness* (II: 354–355).

The one root temptation – the tendency to scale down the ideal to the level of life-as-it-is (item 1 in the above list) – pointed out by Vivekananda is the correlate of Aurobindo's diagnosis that we want to possess (perhaps often at the cost of others) because of the intrinsic but crude extension-urge in the limited ego. But this is a wrong and destructive mode of search for the unlimited arising from wrong understanding about the true nature and purpose of human life. The sacred, the Divine at the core of human existence is to be sought directly through appropriate psychological principles and methods. Mere aggregation and accumulation of exterior physical finites cannot lead up to this destiny. In fact, this kind of striving only takes us farther and farther away from the true goal. Ethics and morals become a regular casualty as a result. This seems to be a faithful picture of what is besetting the world – between nations, within nations, amongst ethnic groups, amongst business competitors, and so on.

The earlier paragraphs have indicated how the culture of Oneness, which is the same as that of being aware of the one Self in all and all in the one Self, can become the fountainhead of ego-management and of ethico-moral revival. It is equally useful, however, to turn around this sequence and to appreciate how ethics/morals in daily life can gradually cleanse the ego, and finally consummate in the realization of Oneness, Self. I enumerate the following relevant ideas from Satprakashananda, another profound scholar of the same Vedantic persuasion as Vivekananda (Satprakashananda 1997, 42–43, 90, 227, 252):

(1) Morality is the attunement of the individual self to the Self of the universe.
(2) Moral life is closest to spiritual life.
(3) Unselfishness is the prime moral virtue.
(4) Without moral goodness intellect does not develop into insight, but tends to rationalize rather than reason.
(5) To a man of right understanding moral virtue is a value in itself, superior to any other temporal value.
(6) Vedantic teachers all agree that virtues brighten human understanding, whereas vices darken it.

With "unselfishness" as the central moral/ethical virtue (from individual

persons to collective persons like corporations and national governments), the other complementary virtues repeated by Vedanta are kindness, sincerity, charity, justice, truthfulness, humility, and chastity.
They foster fellow-feeling, the feeling of Oneness. The contrary *vices*
which destroy fellow-feeling are anger, jealousy, hatred, pride, false-
hood, fear, lust, and greed. (Of course, these characteristics have been so
contrasted in all classical religions.) Conscious enhancement of the former and reduction of the latter constitutes the essential basis of charac-
ter-building. Vedanta calls the process *chittashuddhi* – purification of
the heart/mind. Mind purification takes precedence over intellect sharp-
ening. In essence it boils down to the reinforcement of healthy, humane,
unifying *emotions*, while simultaneously trying to contain the divisive,
negative *emotions*. Vedanta does not conceive in principle that intellect
or logic can ever displace emotions or feelings. The Vedantic ethical
strategy lies rather in taking the bull by the horn as it were, and recognizing the *prime status of emotions* in the human constitution. Therefore,
instead of futile and impossible attempts to extirpate emotions, they are
taken up for systematic and disciplined transformation towards the
higher and the nobler. It is worth listening to Vivekananda once more on
this theme (Vivekananda 1962, II: 307):

(1) *Feel* like Christ and you will be a Christ; *feel* like Buddha and
    you will be a Buddha. It is *feeling* that is the life, the strength,
    the vitality . . .
(2) . . . one of the most practical things in Vedantic morality . . .
    is the teaching of the Vedanta that you *are* all prophets, and
    all *must be* prophets. The book is not the proof of your con-
    duct, but you are the proof of the book. . . . What is the proof
    of the Christs and Buddhas of the world? That you and I *feel*
    like them (emphasis added).

Thus, by a meticulous strategy to foster virtuous emotions/feelings,
the separative/divisive ego becomes weak. Inner darkness gets dis-
pelled. And the unitive Self begins to climb up the horizon of our consciousness. It has been there always like the sun. Only it is veiled by the
cloud of ego.

Vedanta thus embraces both sides of the coin: from Self to ethics
and morals, and also from morals and ethics to Self. Even though being
anchored in the Self may not be the life-goal for practically all of us now
(it may not be so by the end of the next century!), yet at a more proxi-

mate level we must all agree that true "insight" and clear "understanding" are becoming indispensable for sustainable decision-making and strategy right here and now. So, even if we suspend engagement with Self right away, the case for ethics/morals as the indispensable basis for insight and understanding is beyond challenge. We must realize that a package of deeper and purer subjective qualities or emotions are needed amongst strategists, planners and decision-makers to arrive at wiser and more sustainable choices. Computers, information highways, cybernets, mobile telephones, and what have you will not generate and nourish such qualities. These symbols of our times create more noise and confusion than clarity and understanding. They ceaselessly exteriorize, centrifugalize, and fragment our consciousness. If such things cannot be ruled out, at least the countervailing process of interiorization and centripetalization of consciousness must receive simultaneous attention from leaders who choose, who decide. They might try sincerely to reflect and assimilate the vision of the "world as a grand moral gymnasium," and incorporate the "going within" process in their daily routine – to benefit oneself and the world. This is the only way to access the holy and the sacred within. Otherwise, we shall continue to testify to the century-old warning by Vivekananda: ". . . (in) the modern world excess of knowledge and power, without holiness, makes human beings devils . . . privilege is claimed today as it never has been claimed in the history of the world" (Vivekananda 1962, I: 145). The only major difference now is that the erstwhile colonial occupation of countries has been replaced by commercial invasion.

Another important theoretical clue from Vedanta is its treatment of the concept of "change." The contemporary mood bursts into near-rapture at the one unique discovery: change is the only fact, and also the only truth. This equation of fact with truth is challenged by Vedanta.

The change-theorist is concerned only with the apparent fact of change and transience. Entire models of man and management are constructed on such sensually perceived reality. The practical consequence of this thrust is: everything is relative, there is no eternal; everything is in perpetual flux and motion, there is no immutable and stable foundation. The hypothesis here is that there is a deep though unperceived correlation between the ascendancy of this world-view and the decline in ethico-moral behavior across the globe. For, if there is no ultimate, fixed underpinning for human existence, why then should the "anything-that-works" gospel not be the most sensible one?

Vedantic theory provides the following reconciliation which calls for immediate and serious consideration:

> It is the *unchangeable* that is appearing as the changeable. . . . The
> noumenon is not something different from the phenomena, but it is
> the very *noumenon which has become the phenomena* (Vivekanan-
> da 1962, II: 344).
>   . . . this idea of the *unchangeable* can be established only as re-
> gards the *whole*, but never as regards the part. The very idea of part
> comes from the idea of change or motion . . . the *whole must be un-
> changeable* (Vivekananda 1962, II: 345).

There is a deep and strong connection between the domination of
the fragmentist ego over the last few centuries and its present culmination in deifying change as the sole truth. In the absence of any notion, far
less of any feeling, about the sacred unchanging whole, unethicality is at
a premium in all quarters of world-management, right from the
man-man end of the continuum to the man-Nature end. Unless therefore
all modes of leadership undertake the duty of discovering the feel for the
"unchangeable whole" within, the chances of holistic, sustainable, and
ethical management in the world of manifest differentiation and separateness will remain elusive. Both Vivekananda and Aurobindo emphasize on cultivating the awareness of our unchanging Self.

"The Ego Grabs, the Self Gives"

Rabindranath Tagore had captured the essence of man's ethical problem
in this pithy statement of wisdom (Tagore 1992, 169). If Aurobindo and
Vivekananda appear to be rather stern and no-nonsense interpreters of
Vedantic principles, Tagore, the mystic poet, softens and sweetens
them. The original Sanskrit words used by Tagore are *aham* for ego, and
atman for Self. (The word "soul" is an avoidable sloppy rendering of *atman* in English.)

He, too justifies the role *aham*, but as a loving endowment from the
Creator/God allowing us to carve out a small niche for our selves and
then offer it back to Him. The human being cannot offer unless he/she
first owns something. The function of ego/*aham* is to facilitate this little
bit of owning, but only as a transit point terminating in gifting it back to
the Lord. The flower in the garden blooms for the Lord in any case. But
for me to offer it to Him, I have to make it mine first by plucking it. So
the *aham*/ego element in our personality has a positive practical role
(Tagore 1992, 164).

But the problems arise when the *ego/aham* forgets the fundamental principle of creation-gifting. For Tagore creativity is gifting, and gifting (or giving) is freedom and bliss (Tagore 1992, 162), and for this paper such freedom is the basis of ethics. The Self inherently gifts/gives. The entire Divine plan of the universe rests on gifting out of joy: the sun, the air, the water, the tree are all gifts of joy from the Creator for the created. Therefore the problem of unethicality or immorality does not exist in Nature. Its law-of-the-being is gifting. When we come to humans however, "reflective choice" becomes the crucial differentiating element, and this throws open for us the domain of ethics. The human task is to manifest this universal gifting law-of-the-being in our secular affairs too, without bypassing but firmly managing the grabbing ego/*aham*. The Self in us secretly pines for the bliss of gifting, because the human being is of the same consciousness stuff as the rest of Nature which forever is gifting herself. Let us hear Tagore for an exposition of this mystic insight (Tagore 1992, 169–170):

> The Self (*atman*) gives and the ego (*aham*) acquires – where is the reconciliation between the two . . . ? Gifting by the Self is the very reason why the ego acquires – this indeed is the reconciliation. The ego forgets this; it assumes as if acquisition is for its own enjoyment. The more it clings to this falsehood, the more such falsehood hurts and deceives it. Therefore self-development implies verily that we shall manifest the Self through the ego.

Thus, instead of pitting ego as the arch enemy of Self, Tagore lets us discover a very positive clue for true ethical transformation. The ego-as-a-bar, which Aurobindo has spoken about, is managed in Tagore by turning it into an instrument of the Self and not by suggesting its supersession.

This Vedantic Self-ego theory has been translated into the practical affairs of society through the Epics, the *Puranas*, the *Smritis* and so on. A common outcome of such rendering has been a consistent espousal of the "duty-model," not the "rights-model" in such literature. When duties cease to bind the network of human relationships, the Self is not manifested. Unethicality gets a free run. The clamor for rights then becomes a frustrated and anguished reaction against the absence of the duties-orientation. Slowly this movement assumed predominance. Becoming altogether oblivious of the duties-orientation, rights-orientation acquires the status of the sole engine for social transformation. But ethics and morals are not reinstated as a result. Why? Because rights and ego go together. The ancient seer-sociologists were both practical and farseeing. They had emphasized duties as the basis for moral order in society, for the sense of duty can contain the grabbing ego. Duties done at appropriate levels, in relevant quarters, automatically implies the satisfaction of rights at the corresponding connecting points in the network.

Tagore corroborates Vivekananda and Aurobindo in seizing the unethical implication of personality development in terms of the separative, differentiating, finite ego. He warns (Tagore 1985, 97):

> ... consciousness of personality begins with the feeling of the separateness from all, but has *its culmination* in the feeling of unity with all... the life in which the consciousness of separation takes the first place and of unity the second place, and therefore where the personality is *narrow* and *dim* ... – this is the life of the self (ego).

Clearly, it is the "narrowness," this "dimness" which is the source of all kinds unethicality, from inter-personal jealousies and machinations to man-Nature exploitative games and wars. Education in "Unity," in "Oneness" is then the real response to our ethical concerns.

While expounding an important Vedantic text, the *Isha Upanishad*, Tagore too had dealt with the theme of "change," which, as I have observed earlier, is a notion that fosters panic, fear, apprehension (the other side of greed and competition) thus constituting a potent cause of egotistic unethicality. He speaks thus (Tagore 1985, 59–60):

> It is perfectly evident that the world is movement. (The Sanskrit word for the world means 'the moving one'.) All its forms are transitory, but that is merely its *negative side*. All through its changes it has a *chain of relationship which is eternal*. ... the world through all its changes is not to us a mere runaway evasion, and *because of its movements* it reveals to us *something which is eternal* (emphasis added).

Thus, the universal, transcendental vision of Tagore is able to realize that visible transcience and change are neither the whole nor the true basis of this word. They are only links in the chain of eternity. Of greater and priority importance for *lokasangraha*, then, is to educate ourselves to feel for this eternal. World-sustenance, and its operative condition of ethics, demands this comprehension amongst all of us, especially all of us, especially our leaders. Tagore goes so far as to declare that change by itself is the "negative side." This seems to turn topsy turvy the current apotheosis of change among intellectual persuasions of various breeds.

"Opinions Change, But Not Morality"

This is a conviction which Mahatma Gandhi shares with us (Gandhi 1969, Vol. IV, 17). Gandhi docs not delve directly into the interpretation of Vedanta and offers no conceptual framework as such. He is distinct from the previous three modern Indian seers in that he had tried to practice ethics in the context of a mass political movement he led for a long time. Surely, of coursc, the *Gita* and some of the *Upanishads* (which constitute Vedanta) formed the deepest layers in the design and execution of this movement. It is thus entirely Vedantic of him to warn (Gandhi 1969, Vol. IV, 32):

> . . . we have neither practiced nor known *ethical religion* so long as we do not *feel sympathy for every human being.* Now we know that the *higher morality must be comprehensive*; it must embrace all men (emphasis added).

Thus, Gandhi expresses the earlier ideas of Oneness, Unitive-fceling, all-extending Self in his own simpler vocabulary.

Equality, equity, and egalitarianism are modern verbal approximations of Oneness or *ekatmanubhuti*. But the work *anubhuti* in Sanskrit connotes "feeling." Contemporary social and political processes always pronounce in favor of equality, equity, and the like. Yet they are very little a function of slogans or legislation. Laws do not foster positive feelings. They are negative restraints only. So Gandhi is right in pointing out the psychological core of equality and so on (Gandhi 1969, Vol. IV, 30):

> Equality depends on the state of our mind, and until our mind reaches the state we shall remain backward. . . . If the people in a democratic State are selfish, that State comes to no good.

When equality becomes integral to our emotional fabric, then we need not rush for artificial sameness and uniformity. This trend is as much pronc to a new and unforeseen variety of unethicalities as traditional inequality (ies) is (are). Feeling-level equality can achieve natural harmony amongst unequal uniques. And harmony is pro-ethics. For the high-intellect leaders of the world, therefore, Gandhi's easily expressed notion of the "state of mind" could be a little too simple. Its attainment, or the striving to attain it, may therefore be fortified by the earlier theories of "grabbing ego-giving Self," "ego was a help, ego is a bar."

It is also important to understanding Gandhi's phrase "ethical religion." The Sanskrit word for religion is *dharma*. The etymological root of *dharma* means that which upholds, maintains, and sustains. Such *dharma* is not necessarily denominational religion; rather, it is the *dharma* or religion of universal ethicality. Religious philosophy of the world provides a common ground in that universal brother/sister-hood is really founded upon the spirit of universal children-hood of Lord/God/Almighty/Divine and what have you. Children of the same parents must obviously have natural love and sympathy amongst themselves! This ethical bonding pervades not only human relationships. Vedanta holds it as informing and permeating man-Nature, man-Cosmos relationships as well. That is why the Vedantic *rishis* were *sarvanubhu* or all-feeling, and *sarvamevavishanti* or all-penetrating. Thus, world-sustenance or *lokasangraha* could as well be conceptualized as an ethico-religious venture for the twenty-first century.

This concept of ethical religion has been spelled out by Gandhi for economic and business activities in these words:

(a) Economics that hurts the moral well-being of an individual or a nation is immoral and, therefore sinful! (Vol. VI, 321).

(b) True economics never militates against the highest ethical standard, just as all true ethics to be worth its name must at the same time be also good economical (Vol. VI, 321–332).

(c) . . . the introduction of moral values (is) . . . to be considered in regulating international commerce (Vol. VI, 322).

(d) I venture to think that the scriptures of the world are far safer and sounder treatises on laws of economics than many modern textbooks (Vol. VI, 322).

The frightening speed at which the economics-technology-commerce troika is bulldozing its way into the individual's daily existence, both in and out of home (if a home is left anymore!), is indeed a grave ethico-moral phenomenon. The personal consequences of this economic tornado for man are broken homes, teenage violence, child maternity, mental diseases, sexual licence, unbridled greed, fragile materialistic dependency, increased unemployment, international arms sales, and much else. In the politically uni-polar world of today, all this adds up to an incalculable load of moral responsibility on a few economic super-powers.

Like our previous mentors, Gandhi, too has touched upon, in passing, the principle of the unchangeable "opinions change, not morality." Yes, opinions may *change* across time in the same place. Besides, opinions may also *vary* across places at the same time. Does this mean that the search for a common and enduring ground for ethico-morality is futile? Perhaps not. The unchangeable, common ground exists in a final touch-stone – the definition of being a human being. The universal definition, and the eternal one is *conscious realization and expression of the unitive Self inherent in the individualised human frame.* (The obverse of this is the non-contingent, autonomous nature of Self, the true remedy against greed and rapacity and plunder.) This can serve as the one standard against which all organizational and institutional decisions and choices have to be weighed with sleepless vigil. If business, economics, commerce, technology, and politics, in any of their ramifications, cannot meet the test of facilitating this goal of individual (and hence of society) development, then that must be suspect. Personal ethico-morality at all levels and in all spheres should then be readily seen as the indispensable operational process, the cause, for world-sustenance. This seems to be the import of Gandhi's dictum for *lokasangraha*.

Conclusion: Rational Animal or Supra-Rational Self?

The world today is a witness to the consequences of the untrammeled march of the "rational animal" in man and in nations, especially since the age of enlightenment. The Copernican and other revolutions may have endowed man with "knowledge-is-power." But during this period, man has behaved as an ethical delinquent against Nature and himself. The so-called medieval and dark ages (was the Vedantic period in India dark?) at least cannot be accused of raping mother Earth. Neither perhaps colonial exploitation nor multinational warfare had figured even in their dreams. The current spate of bribery, graft, and corruption in many developing countries should be assessed against this historical backdrop. (Of course no justification is intended.) Commercial rationality, riding on the horse of the grabbing ego is, for instance, generating an ethical problem centering on the patenting of a liquid extracted from *neem*, that particular species of tree which in many ways has been at the center of Indian life from time immemorial. It seems that ruthless grabbing is the key operating value propelling the man-of-commerce, and the man-of-commerce rules the world in the present "age of commerce."

There were earlier times, at least in Indian history, when the society was directed and managed either by the "man-of-wisdom" and/or the "man-of-valor." The "man-of-commerce" was clearly subordinate to either of these categories. The primary operating values of the "man-of-wisdom" were self-abnegation and non-utilitarian learning; those of the "man-of-valor" were self-sacrificing chivalry and honor. The animal in man was reasonably contained within the norms and boundaries set by these two predominant approaches to governance, but with their powers and values on the wane, and society being governed by the commercial class, it is imbibing a highly manipulative and mercenary turn. The "rational" animal is veering towards the diabolical, a state far worse than that of the "irrational" animal of the jungle.

What seems to be unavoidable near the close of the twentieth century is to re-conceptualize the human being in the mold of the supra-rational Self. In this sense, both Buddha and Christ, for example, epitomize the Vedantic model at its best. However, unlike the "sorrow" of Buddhism or the "sin" of Christianity, or the "illusion" of the *Mayavadins*, "bliss," from start to finish, is the refrain of Vedanta. The feeling of Oneness with all, and the realization of the eternal core within are the natural accompaniments of "bliss." However, ego downsizing and ethical living are the two preconditions for becoming the bliss-Self.

Let us hear the voice of Vedanta direct (Gambhirananda 1980, 166–167; verse III.vi.1:G):

> *Anando brahmeti vyajanat.*
> *Anandadhyeva khaliwamani bhutani jayante.*
> *Anandena jatani jivanti.*
> *Anandam prayantya – abhishan – vishantiti.*

> (He knows Bliss as Brahman or the Supreme.
> From Bliss, indeed, all these beings originate.
> Having been born, they are sustained by Bliss.
> They move towards and merge in Bliss.)

If this greatest of inspirations were to move our leaders, ethics in human activities and the resultant *lokasangraha* should then be looking forward to a bright horizon. Vedantic realizations are meant positively for this world, and not merely for the other. Given the grave existential problems we face, the highest principles have to be given *practical* shape. We must at least start by consenting to this effort of accountability, and get on to the right track. Intellectual idealism is proving inadequate. Our task is to stretch forward and upward towards "spiritual realism," as Sri Aurobindo had pleaded long ago (Aurobindo 1992, 228).

Otherwise the balance sheet of our world as on December 31, 1999, is likely to show a "negative net worth," to borrow a jargon from accounting, in respect of ethical capital. "Secular outsights" from the ego inevitably lead to fragmentist choices and decisions. They ought to be placed under the command of "sacred insights" from the Self which are inherently holistic. Holism, holiness, and ethicality need to march together during the twenty-first century and further on.

References

Aurobindo, Sri, *Sri Aurobindo Birth Centenary Library* (Pondicherry: Sri Aurobindo Ashram,1973).

Aurobindo, Sri, *Message of the Gita* (Pondicherry: Sri Aurobindo Ashram, 1977).

Aurobindo, Sri, "Right Attitude in Work," *All India Magazine* (Pondicherry: Sri Aurobindo Ashram, April 1991).

Aurobindo, Sri, "The Uprooting of Desire," *All India Magazine* (Pondicherry: Sri Aurobindo Ashram, June 1991).

Aurobindo, Sri, *The Human Cycle* (Pondicherry: Sri Aurobindo Ashram, 1992).

Gambhirananda, Swami, (transl.) *Taittiriya Upanishad* (Calcutta: Advaita Ashram, 1980).

Gandhi, M. K., *Selected Works*, edited by Shriman Narayan (Ahmedabad: Navjivan, 1969).

Satprakashananda, Swami, *The Goal and The Way: Vedantic Approach to Life's Problems* (Madras: Sri Ramakrishna Math, 1977).

Tagore, Rabindranath, *Personality* (New Delhi: Macmillan, 1985).

Tagore, Rabindranath, *Shantiniketan*, Vol. 1, transl. by S. K. Chakraborty (Calcutta: Vishwabharati, 1992).

Vivekananda, Swami, *Collected Works* (Calcutta: Advaita Ashram, 1962).

Values Inherent in the Interfaith Declaration of International Business Ethics

Simon Webley

Abstract

As international trade and investment accelerate, the day-to-day problems experienced at all levels of corporations involved in cross-cultural business activity increases. A growing number of these are caused because the underlying values, often based on religious differences, vary considerably. This chapter describes a serious attempt by Christian, Muslim, and Jewish business and clerical leaders, with royal patronage, to find common business values which were in harmony with their religious teachings. This endeavour resulted in the production of a code of international business ethics based on the four key values of Justice (just conduct and fairness), Mutual Respect (love and consideration), Stewardship (trusteeship and accountability), and Honesty (truthfulness and reliability). It drew upon the stakeholder model to apply these values to moral issues concerning the place of business in society, the policies of a business, and the conduct of individuals at work.

Introduction

There are major forces operating at the end of the twentieth century which are having the effect of bringing together the nations and people of the earth in an extraordinary and exciting way. Among them are rapidly expanding world trade of goods and services, and increasing flows of capital in the form of foreign direct investment. These phenomena are well documented by the World Trade Organisation[1] (WTO) and the annual United Nations World Investment Reports.[2] This growing integration of world economic activity is being referred to as "globalization." At first, it was used to describe the international financial linkages made possible by electronic data transmission; it now encompass the movement of goods, services, capital, technologies, and people.

When it was first noticed, the process was largely confined to activity between the so called developed countries – members of the OECD.

But it is increasingly being extended to middle-income countries where, for instance, the flow of foreign direct investment reached $70 billion in 1995 out of a total $200 billion.

Among the consequences of the international integration of economic activity is an apprehension that nations and people are losing the ability to control their ways of life. The powerful effect of worldwide competition and the trend toward an interdependent global economy have led to rapid and often abrupt changes in society, which effect the lives of ordinary people in an unpredictable fashion. Bankruptcies, business collapses, and takeovers are becoming everyday events. Few governments are able to resist or even regulate these changes. Indeed, few wish to because among the benefits has been a remarkable rise in prosperity which has affected the less economically advanced nations as well as the richer ones. Enlightened governments have concentrated on trying to see the benefits extend to those who are not immediately involved.

This exponential increase in international economic activity has also resulted in some serious differences in approach to business operations among some of the major participants in the process such as multinational corporations.

To consider these effects and to see what might be done to resolve them, a group of distinguished leaders from business, banking, academia, and religious institutions drawn from the three major monotheistic religions of the world (Muslim, Jewish, and Christian) met between 1989–94 under the auspices of HRH The Duke of Edinburgh, HRH Crown Prince Hassan of Jordan, and Evelyn de Rothschild. Their purpose was to see if it would be possible and useful to draw up a set of guidelines on business ethics which are applicable wherever economic activity involving adherents of their religions takes place. The group met four times and explored, in some depth, the different approaches to behavioural problems arising in business relationships.

The participants exchanged experiences, produced papers, and generally explored a range of business situations which could not be resolved solely by consulting legal texts or by applying strictly business (profit) criteria.

This combination of papers and face-to-face discussion between people whose considerable experience and knowledge was generally recognised by all participants and proved to be a successful way of achieving a common position. The values which underlay the solutions offered to different sets of business dilemmas were then compared to those found in the sacred texts of the three religions wherever they referred to economic activity. (The four key values which were educed by this method are described in more detail later.)

The process was slow and it required an independent and neutral person to evaluate the work, perform the analysis, and produce the draft text which helped to focus the work of the group. This text was subjected to a thorough critique by the leaders of the group as well as the participants.

It was agreed that the purpose of the resulting Interfaith Declaration of International Business Ethics[3] was to provide:

- a moral basis for international business activity;
- some principles of ethical practice to help business people, traders, and investors identify the role they and their organisations perform in the communities in which they operate; and
- guidance in resolving genuine dilemmas which arise in the course of day-to-day business.

The group was conscious that the recent widespread reporting of the rhetoric and activities by extremist adherents (at least in name) of their three religions had produced in the mind of the general public the idea that only disunity and conflict characterised relationships, including business relationships, between those of different religious beliefs. The meetings of the group and the resultant Declaration indicate that whatever their particular insight of the truth may be, and it is acknowledged that there are differences, they, nevertheless, share a common heritage, including a high degree of shared values. This particular group also shared a common ethical basis derived from one book – The Bible – which they considered to be as relevant today as it has been in the past. The need to relate this relevance to contemporary business issues was felt to be particularly important. To do this, they sought to discover the basic values that their respective Faiths has in common which were relevant to economic activity.

Underlying this purpose was their shared concern that at the same time as material prosperity grew in the industrialised world, there is also emerging a value system which is considered to be detrimental to the wholesome development of human beings: selfishness and dishonesty are tending to supplant integrity and generosity. As a result, there is evidence that morality and ethical standards are declining. This is exemplified by the wide reporting of dishonest and corrupt practices. Part of the problem was seen to be an ambivalence concerning what is considered right or wrong, and economic relationships have not escaped its influence. The participants considered that a reiteration of ethical precepts in the form of a Declaration would make a contribution to sustaining and improving the standards of international business behaviour.

It was acknowledged that such a code might be more difficult to apply in some countries than in others because of the different degree of influence that religion has within cultures. Both Muslims and, to a lesser extent Jews, operate within a social atmosphere that is conducive to the influence of their religious precepts being heeded, and where it is normal for moral concerns to be discussed within a religious ethos. Christians in the industrialised countries generally do not enjoy this support and guidance. They are dependent upon personal convictions which often have to be stated in a secular social atmosphere that has little sympathy with them. While the influence of Islamic institutions is more open and obvious, and that of Judaism still strong, the influence of Christianity is largely personal and subsumed.

In the final analysis, the application of ethical principles is a matter of personal judgement rather than rules; a code can only set standards. It follows that the Declaration (or indeed any code of ethics) is not a substitute for corporate or individual morality; it is a set of guidelines for good practice. Its authors hoped that it will contribute to maintaining high standards of business behaviour as well as a better public understanding of the role of business in society.

Method

The method used in producing the Interfaith Declaration was to analyse the content of submissions by group members together with a number of existing guidelines and codes which have been used by international organisations such as the International Chamber of Commerce.[4] Individual company codes of ethics were also used where appropriate.[5] From these sources ethical issues in business were classified under three general headings:

- The morality of the economic system in which business activity takes place;
- The policies and strategies of organisations which engage in business (see Part II of this volume); and
- The behaviour of individual employees in the context of their work (see Part III of this volume).

In the Declaration, the distinction between these categories is recognised, and there may indeed be other levels and sub-categories, but the three selected are those where moral issues most commonly arise.

A second distinction which needs recognition is that while some ethical issues affect all types of industrial and commercial activity, there are others which are distinctive to a particular sector. The outstanding example is that between the provision of financial services (e.g., banking) and the manufacture and trading of products (e.g., industries).

There is a third distinction. The legal framework in which business is conducted is not the same in all countries. For instance, the duties of company directors vary considerably and employment law; e.g., legal notice of dismissal or redundancy is hardly ever the same in any two countries. While recognising that national law applies to a company registered in that country (irrespective of the nationality of its owners and managers), and that it should be scrupulously followed, the laws on the same matter may be less demanding in, say, the country of the parent company. Some areas of business practice which are covered by law in one country may be the subject of self-administered regulation or of voluntary codes of behaviour in another. Therefore, some subjects covered by the Declaration may, in practice, already have the force of law in some countries.

Some Key Principles

Four key ethical concepts were selected and agreed. They recur in the literature of the Faiths as the basis of any human interaction and are relevant and applicable to business relationships. They are: justice (fairness), mutual respect (love and consideration), stewardship (trusteeship), and honesty (truthfulness).

Justice
The first principle is justice which can be defined as just conduct, fairness, and the exercise of authority in maintenance of right. In Muslim teaching, it is seen as a basis of relationship.

The Qur'an, Maida, v.9. states "Stand out firmly for God, as witnesses to fair dealing, and let not the hatred of others to you make you swerve to wrong and depart from justice. Be just: that is next to piety and fear God." It is also a strong theme in Jewish writing. For instance, a passage on the subject in Deuteronomy 16:18–20 concludes with the statement, "Justice, and only justice, you shall follow that you may live and inherit the land which the Lord your God gives you." Jesus, too, suggested that the Jewish teachers of his day neglected the weightier matters of the law: justice and mercy and faith (St Matthew 23:23), and Christians are urged by St Paul to "consider what is just" (Phil 4:8).

Mutual Respect (love)

The second principle, mutual respect or love and consideration for others, is also inherent in the moral teachings of each religion. The statement in Leviticus Chapter 19:18, "Love thy neighbour as thyself," which is reiterated by the Prophet Mohammed as "Love for yourself what you love for others" and by Jesus Christ as "You shall love your neighbour as yourself" (St Matthew 22:39), is a common ethical basis for all interpersonal relationships. The application of this has come to mean that self-interest only has a place in the community in as much as it takes into account the interests of others. My neighbour in the business context can be defined as any person (individual or corporate) with whom the organisation comes into contact in the course of business life. Of paramount importance in this respect is the employee.

The illustration of the Good Samaritan given by Jesus to an enquiry from a Jewish lawyer as to who was his neighbour (St Luke 10:30–37) indicates that one's neighbour is not always of the same ethnic origin or economic status as oneself. Indeed, a neighbour may be much weaker or vulnerable or a different race or religion. A business application of this would be in the case of a small company supplying a large one. The principle of love would suggest that restraint in the use of power by the strong, especially in difficult times, would be ethically correct, and in accord with the written precepts of the three religions. It follows that a large sophisticated company based in a developed country should treat a supplier or customer from a developing nation in the same way it would treat a firm with whom it does business in its home country.

Stewardship

A third principle which the three faiths have in common is that of stewardship (trusteeship) of resources. While this may be readily understood by an owner of a small business or an inheritor of an agricultural holding, the principle is applicable to anyone who is entrusted with the responsibly of managing scarce resources. It applies equally to individual wealth, the long term viability of a business, and the use of renewable resources. Ownership is not seen, therefore, to be absolute. As such, businesses have an obligation to use resources for the benefit of the people in society at large as well as for its stockholders. It also has a responsibility to the past (retired employees) and to the future (survival in the long term).

Muslims point to two Quranic verses on this topic: "And bestow upon them of the wealth of Allah which He has bestowed upon you" Sura (light) No 24.V:33; and "And spend of that whereof He has made you trustees" Sura 57 (iron) V.7.

An authentic saying of the prophet Mohammed confirms this concept of man's responsibility for his wealth. It proclaims that no man will be allowed to proceed to his reward on the day of the judgement unless he first gives account of his deeds which includes how he obtained his wealth and how he used it.

Jews, too, have encompassed the concept of stewardship in their teachings concerning responsibility in society. The patriarch David states, "Who am I, and what is my people, that we should be able thus to offer willingly? For all things come from thee, and of thy own have we given thee" (1 Chron. 29:14).

The New Testament stresses the accountability of Christians for the way they have used resources. Jesus summed this up by stating, "Everyone to whom much is given, of him will much be required" (St Luke 12:48). This principle provides a longer term perspective for business decisions than is likely to be found where the concept of absolute ownership predominates. It also provides the basis for a proper concern for the natural environment on which business activity makes considerable demands. It implies a caring management not a selfish exploitation.

Honesty
The fourth principle inherent to the value system of each of the three faiths is honesty. It incorporates the concepts of truthfulness and reliability and covers all aspects of relationships in human life – thought, word, and action. It is more than just accuracy; it is an attitude which is well summed up in the word "integrity."

Muslims place considerable emphasis on truthfulness in business. For instance, in a Hadith it is stated: "The merchant whose words and transactions are righteous and who is a trusty man will be (resurrected) amongst the martyrs in the day of judgement." [Ibn Mace, Sunan, II/724, No 2139 (Ticaveti)].

Jews, too, constantly stress honesty as the basis for human relationships. Moses in the book of Leviticus is explicit concerning honesty in business, "You shall have true scales, true weights, true measures" (Leviticus 19:36); "All who act dishonestly are an abomination to the Lord"

(Deut 26:16), and regarding truthfulness, the Decalogue states "You should not bear false witness" (Exodus 20:16).

Christians also expect honesty and truthfulness to characterise the lives of believers. Jesus states that doing what is true is a test of obedience to God: "He who does what is true comes to the light that it may be clearly seen that his deeds have been wrought of God" (St John 3:2), and as St Paul urged the Ephesian Christians, "You shall speak the truth in love" (Eph 4:15).

These four principles – justice, love, stewardship, and honesty – form the moral basis of the Declaration that follows.

The Declaration

A. *Business and Political Economy*

All business activity takes place within the context of a political and economic system. It is recognised that:

1. Business is part of the social order. Its primary purpose is to meet human and material needs by producing and distributing goods and services in an efficient manner. How this role is carried out – the means as well as the ends – is important to the whole of society.
2. Competition between businesses has generally been shown to be the most effective way to ensure that resources are not wasted, costs are minimised, and prices fair. The State has a duty to see that markets operate effectively, competition is maintained, and natural monopolies are regulated. Business will not seek to frustrate this.
3. All economic systems have flaws; that based on free and open markets is morally neutral and has great potential for good. Private enterprise, sometimes in partnership with the State, has the potential to make efficient and sustainable use of resources, thereby creating wealth which can be used for the benefit of everyone.
4. There is no basic conflict between good business practice and profit making. Profit is one measure of efficiency and is of paramount importance in the functioning of the system. It provides for the maintenance and growth of business, thus expanding employment opportunities and is the means of a rising living standard for all concerned. It also acts as an incentive to work and be enterprising. It is from the profit of companies that society can reasonably levy taxes to finance its wider needs.
5. Because the free market system, like any other, is open to abuse, it

can be used for selfish or sectional interests, or it can be used for good. The State has an obligation to provide a framework of law in which business can operate honestly and fairly, and business will obey and respect the law of the State in which it operates.

6. As business is a partnership of people of varying gifts, they should never be considered as merely a factor of production. The terms of their employment will be consistent with the highest standards of human dignity.

7. The efficient use of scarce resources will be ensured by the business. Resources employed by corporations include finance (savings), technology (machinery), and land and other natural resources. All are important and most are scarce.

8. Business has a responsibility to future generations to improve the quality of goods and service, not to degrade the natural environment in which it operates, and seek to enrich the lives of those who work within it. Short-term profitability should not be pursued at the expense of long term viability of the business. Neither should business operations disadvantage the wider community.

B. *The Policies of a Business*

Business activity involves human relationships. It is the question of balancing the reasonable interests of those involved in the process, i.e., the stakeholders, that produces moral problems.

The policies of the business will therefore be based on the principles set out in the paragraphs above and in particular:

1. The board of directors will be responsible for seeing that the business operates strictly within the letter and spirit of the laws of nations in which it works. If these laws are rather less rigorous in some parts of the world where the business operates than in others, the higher standards will normally be applied everywhere.

2. The board will issue a written statement concerning the objectives, operating policies of the organisation, and their application. It will set out clearly the obligations of the company towards the different stakeholders involved with a business (employees, shareholders, lenders, customers, suppliers, and the community [local and national government]).

3. The basis of the relationship with the principal stakeholders shall be honesty and fairness, by which is meant integrity, in all relation-

ships, as well as reliability in all commitments made on behalf of the organisation.

4. The business shall maintain a continuing relationship with each of the groups with which it is involved. It will provide effective means to communicate information affecting the stakeholders. This relationship is based on trust.

5. The best practice to be adopted in dealings with six particular stakeholders can be summarised as follows:

Employees

Employees make a unique contribution to an organisation. It follows that in their policies, businesses shall, where appropriate, take notice of trade union positions and provide:

- *Working conditions* that are safe and healthy and conducive to high standards of work;
- *Levels of remuneration* that are fair and just, and that recognise the employees' contribution to the organisation and the performance of the sector of the business in which they work; and
- *A respect for the individual* (whether male or female) in their beliefs, their family responsibility, and their need to grow as human beings. It will provide equal opportunities in training and promotion for all members of the organisation. It will not discriminate in its policies on grounds of race, colour, creed, or gender.

Providers of Finance

A business cannot operate without finance. There is, therefore, a partnership between the provider and the user. The company borrowing money shall give to the lender:

- What has been agreed to be repaid at the due dates;
- Adequate safeguards in using the resources entrusted; and
- Regular information on the operations of the business, and opportunities to raise with directors matters concerning their performance.

Customers

Without customers, a business cannot survive. In selling products or services, a company shall provide for the customer:

- The quality and standard of service which has been agreed;
- After-sales service commensurate with the type of product or service and the price paid;

- Where applicable, a contract written in unambiguous terms; and
- Informative and accurate information regarding the use of the product or service especially where misuse can be dangerous.

Suppliers
Suppliers provide a daily flow of raw materials, products, and services to enable a business to operate. The relationship with suppliers is normally a long term one and must therefore be based on mutual trust. The company shall:
- Undertake to pay its suppliers promptly and in accordance with agreed terms of trade;
- Not use its buying power in an unscrupulous fashion; and
- Require buyers to report offers of gifts or favours of unusual size or questionable purpose.

Community (Local and National Government)
While companies have an obligation to work within the law, they must also take into account the effects of their activities on local and national communities. In particular they shall:
- Ensure that they protect the local environment from harmful emissions from manufacturing plant, excessive noise, and any practice likely to endanger humans, animals, or plant life;
- Consider the social consequences of company decisions, e.g., plant closures, choice of new sites, or expansion of existing ones; and
- Not tolerate any form of bribery, extortion, or other corrupt or corrupting practices in business dealings.

Owners (shareholders)
The shareholders undertake the risks of ownership. The elected directors shall:
- Protect the interests of shareholders;
- See that the company's accounting statements are true and timely; and
- See that shareholders are kept informed of all major happenings affecting the company.

C. Conduct of Individuals at Work

The following are based on best ethical practice for employees in a business. Employees of an organisation shall:

1. Implement the decisions of those to whom he or she is responsible, which are lawful and in accordance with the company's policies, in cooperation with colleagues.
2. Avoid all abuse of power for personal gain, advantage, or prestige, and in particular refuse bribes or other inducements of any sort intended to encourage dishonesty or to break the law.
3. Not use any information acquired in the business for personal gain or for the benefit of relatives or outside associates.
4. Reveal the facts to his superiors whenever his personal business or financial interests become involved with those of the company.
5. Be actively concerned with the difficulties and problems of subordinates, treat them fairly, and lead them effectively, assuring them a right of reasonable access and appeal to those to whom their immediate superior is responsible.
6. Bring to the attention of superiors the likely effects on employees of the company's plans for the future so that such effects can be fully taken into account.

Comparisons

The Declaration is one of a number of codes which have been drawn up to address the problems of international business set out at the start of this chapter. With the exception of the ICC's Code on Extortion and Bribery, they are based on some inherent and explicit values of the group originating them. The Caux Roundtable's Principles for Business set out in Part II of this book were endorsed by business leaders from the US, Europe, and Japan. They are based on two ethical ideals: kyosei (living and working together for the common good) and human dignity (the value of the individual). The Interfaith Code is based on four "key values" derived from the sacred texts of Muslims, Jews, and Christians.

Both use a stakeholder model based on a six category classification. The Interfaith Declaration distinguishes shareholders from suppliers of finance while the Caux Principles incorporate these together and add an extra one – obligations to competitors. Both address the principal issues which are known to cause most concern to international business people.

Others thinkers have helpfully explored a possible basis for incorporating other systems of values, notably Hindu (S. K. Chakraborty) and Hans Küng's seminal work on developing a global ethic based on prophetic, mystical, and wisdom religions of the world. Both are set out elsewhere in this book. Küng's basis for his work is the recognition of human and environmental rights – "the welfare of all humanity and the care of the planet." While this does not go beyond a set of two principles and four directives, it is a useful concept on which to base policies and practices at the macro (systemic), meso (organizational), and micro (individual) levels and will undoubtedly form the basis of future work.

Whether it is possible to incorporate Hindu, Confucian, and Buddhist values into an international code of business ethics remains to be seen. This Declaration gives some encouragement to those who think it is worth striving for.

Endnotes

1. Trade and Foreign Direct Investment (Geneva, WTO, October 1996).

2. United Nations, 1991–1998 World Investment Reports (New York: United Nations, 1991–1998).

3. "An Interfaith Declaration: A Code of Ethics on International Business for Christians, Muslims and Jews." This is reproduced in *Business Ethics – A European Review* 5, no 1 (January 1996).

4. *Extortion and Bribery in International Business Transactions,* International Chamber of Commerce, Paris, 1996.

5. For a survey of these, see Webley, Simon, *Codes of Business Ethics* (London: Institute of Business Ethics, 1993).

A Global Ethic in an Age of Globalization

Hans Küng

Abstract

Starting from four theses that globalization is unavoidable, ambivalent, incalculable, and can be controlled rationally, ethics has an indispensable and important role to play in the process of globalization. Indeed, a number of international documents published in the 1990s not only acknowledge human rights but also speak explicitly of human responsibilities. The author pleads for the primacy of ethics over politics and economics and, in reviewing both the Interfaith Declaration for Jews, Christians, and Muslims, and the Caux Roundtable Principles for Business Conduct, he raises the question about the foundation for the unconditional validity of particular basic ethical values and attitudes. In Küng's view, no universal ethic, but only religion, expressed by the three prophetic religions, the mystical religions of Indian origin, and the wisdom religions of Chinese origin, can provide this foundation. Yet, religion as a spiritual resource intends to influence concrete behavior and decision making. Therefore, the author stresses the importance of a personality culture for business executives and an "ethic of responsibility" to shape business culture and institutions. He then proposes the Declaration of the Parliament of the World's Religions Toward a Global Ethic as a basis to develop a business ethics that can be supported by believers and non-believers alike.

Globalization Calls for a Global Ethic

The problems are extraordinarily complex. So I shall attempt to cope with the mass of material by starting from the macro-level (the questions of the morality of the economic system in itself). I shall then go on to make some comments on the meso-level (the policies and strategies of the organizations concerned), and finally speak about the micro-level (above all about business executives).

I begin with the macro-level. I cannot compete with such a learned international body of specialists in business and business ethics, nor do I want to, but at least here I am sure that I can presuppose four basic theses about globalization, as a consensus, so to speak:

(a) Globalization is unavoidable,
(b) Globalization is ambivalent,
(c) Globalization is incalculable,
(d) Globalization can be controlled rationally.

I shall make a few comments only on the fourth thesis. Globalization is not a natural phenomenon like an approaching weather front, in the face of which one is powerless. The market can fail as a supposedly natural regulatory instrument, so there is a need for politics and the order which it brings. National governments, national banks, and economic communities like the European Community still have considerable room to maneuver. Even the best-known international currency speculator, George Soros (*Der Spiegel*, 1996), is now calling urgently for international market regulations "against excessive speculation" which moves hundreds of billions of dollars a day to and fro, because the markets are "possessed by greed and anxiety" and therefore react "emotionally."

Be this as it may: should the main criterion in the present process of globalization prove to be the maximization of profit, and should that alone prevail, we must be prepared for serious social conflicts and crises. The present strength of capital and the weakness of the trade unions should not mislead us here. For we *cannot* assume that society as a whole would *accept* a lapse into Manchester liberalism (Karl Marx!) and *capitalism without putting up any resistance at all*. Economic tensions cause social tensions, and these in turn cause social conflicts. We might recall that American society already reacted in this way at the beginning of the present century under President Theodore Roosevelt and later once again after the Wall Street Crash of 1929 and the subsequent Great Depression under President Franklin D. Roosevelt.

In principle, we should note here that all these phenomena are not necessary natural processes (as Marx thought) but are also *developments* which – within certain limits – can be *guided*; the questions at issue here are not only economic questions but also *highly political* and ultimately also *ethical questions*, affecting the *whole of society*. Moreover some business decisions turn less on globalization in itself than on the question whether profit, i.e., the maximizing of gain, should be the one and only purpose of a business.

However, the very phenomenon of economic globalization makes it clear that there must also be a globalization in ethics. How can a world with contradictory ethical norms and orders become peaceful and just? There is need for reflection on a minimum of specific ethical values, basic attitudes and standards which are binding on all nations and all classes, on employers and employees. Just as there is a need for a new global law against excessive speculation, so that where there are restrictions those involved do not simply flee to other markets, so there is also a need for an ethical minimum, to guarantee a life together on our globe which is to some degree peaceful. In a word: *globalization calls for a global ethic; world politics and the world economy call for a world ethic.* Is that pure utopia? No. One of the most astonishing and at the same time most welcome phenomena of the last decade of the twentieth century is the almost explosive spread of the notion of a world ethic, not only in theology, philosophy, and education, but also in world politics and the world economy. I would like to tell you about the most important developments.

World Politics Discovers the Global Ethic

When I published the book *Projekt Weltethos (Global Responsibility: In Search of a New World Ethic)* in 1990, there were hardly any documents on a global ethic from world organizations to which I could refer. Of course there were declarations on human rights, above all the 1948 Declaration of the United Nations, but there were no declarations on human responsibilities. However, now, six years later, I can refer to three important international documents which not only acknowledge human rights but also speak explicitly of human responsibilities. Indeed, they programmatically call for a global ethic and even attempt to spell it out in concrete terms.

(a) The International Commission on Global Governance (1995)
The report of the Commission on Global Governance bears the title *Our Global Neighborhood* (The Report of the Commission on Global Governance; hereafter CGG Report). The phenomenon of *globalization* forms the starting point for this four-hundred-page analysis. Here it is striking that before any of the great problem areas (global security, economic interdependence, international law, and reforming the United Nations) are tackled, the question of "values for the global neighborhood" is raised, and in the face of the rise in tensions between neighbors, there is a call for *"neighborhood ethics!"* For without a global ethic, the fric-

tions and tensions in life together in the one world would multiply. "Without leadership (a courageous leadership infused with that ethic at all levels of society) even the best-designed institutions and strategies will fail" (CGG Report 46). There is then the terse comment that "global values must be the cornerstone of global governance" (CGG Report 47). Here the commission believes that "many people world-wide, particularly the young, are more willing to respond to these issues than their governments, for whom the short term in the context of political expediency tends to take preference" (CGG Report 47).

But what basis can be given to an *"ethical dimension of the world political order"*? Here, too, it is worth noting that this document gives the *Golden Rule* as the main basic principle: "People should treat others as they would themselves wish to be treated" (CGG Report 49). On this basis, the basic values of respect for life, freedom, justice, mutual respect, readiness to help, and integrity are developed: "All these values derive in one way or another from the principle, which is in accord with religious teaching around the world, that people should treat others as they would themselves wish to be treated" (CGG Report 49).

Furthermore, there is an explicit call for "these values to be expressed in the form of a *global civic ethic* with specific rights and responsibilities," in which "all citizens, as individuals and as members of different private groups and associations, should accept the obligation to recognize and help protect the rights of others." This ethic should be incorporated into the developing "fabric of international norms" (CGG Report 55 f.). For such a global ethic "would help humanize the impersonal workings of bureaucracies and markets and constrain the competitive and self-serving instincts of individuals and groups" (CGG Report 55). Without this global ethic, the new wider global civil society which is coming into being could "become unfocused and even unruly. . ." (CGG Report 55).

In connection with this a request is made. The authors were presumably unaware that it had already been made in a discussion in the Revolutionary Parliament of 1789, in Paris, but could not be met at that time: *"Rights need to be joined with responsibilities"* (CGG Report 56). For the "tendency to emphasize rights while forgetting responsibilities" has "deleterious consequences" (CGG Report 56). "We therefore urge the international community to unite in support of a global ethic of common rights and shared responsibilities. In our view, such an ethic – reinforcing the fundamental rights that are already part of the fabric of international norms – would provide the moral foundation for constructing a more effective system of global governance" (CGG Report 56).

The international commission expresses the hope that "over time, these principles could be embodied in a more binding international document – a global charter of Civil Society – that could provide a basis for all to agree on rules that should govern the global neighborhood" (*Report* 57).

(b) The World Commission on Culture and Development (1995)
The major report by the World Commission on Culture and Development, which was published in collaboration with the UN and UNESCO under the title *Our Creative Diversity,* is of equal importance (*Report of the World Commission Culture and Development*; hereafter WCCD Report). Here the presupposition is a "commitment to pluralism," but this statement is preceded by a chapter which stresses what is held in common rather than the differences: *"A New Global Ethics," an ethic of humankind, a world ethic.*

But why do we need a global ethic? Because collaboration between people of different cultures and interests could be made easier and their conflicts diminished and limited if all peoples and groups saw themselves "bound and motivated" by "shared commitments." So it is "imperative to look for a core of shared ethical values and principles" (WCCD Report 34).

But what could the *sources of such a global ethic* be? The formulation of a global ethic must be inspired by the cultural resources, the insights, emotional experiences, historical memories, and spiritual orientations of the peoples. Despite all the differences between cultures, there are some themes which appear in almost all cultural traditions and which could serve as the inspiration for a global ethic. The first of these sources are the great *cultural traditions*, especially "the idea of human vulnerability and the attendant ethical impulse to alleviate suffering where such is possible and to provide security to each individual" (WCCD Report 36). Now this is more a Buddhist formulation of the starting point, but it is also acceptable to other religions. And here, too at the same time reference is made above all to the Golden Rule, which has found expression in the traditions of Confucianism, Taoism, Hinduism, Buddhism and Zoroastrianism, Judaism, Christianity, and Islam, and is also implicit in the practices of other faiths, thus pointing to the equal moral worth of all human beings.

Alongside the elements from the great cultural traditions, this commission also attempts to develop elements of an ethic which derive from *"global civic culture"* and which are similarly to be incorporated into a new global ethic. Here the main reference is to human rights.

Yet however much one might support all the demands for human rights, democracy, the protection of minorities, the peaceful resolution of conflicts, and equal treatment in and between the generations, all these principles are more social and political rights and postulates than ethical principles. And for the commission, too, *just how difficult it is to derive a common ethic for humankind from the human rights which are proclaimed* emerges from the fact that human rights are perceived very differently in some non-Western societies. In southern Asia, for example, some human rights activists have had to recognize: (1) that many rights would be regarded only in the context of religion, the family, or other institutions; (2) that people would always talk about their responsibilities before the question of their human rights; and (3) that the human rights as expressed in the UN Declaration are either unknown or very far removed from their own experience.

However, as a person with religious responsibilities, I ask myself why in its welcome plea for a global ethic the World Commission does not speak more energetically and substantively about the great religious and ethical traditions of humankind. Is it for fear of the very word "religion" or for fear of the *reality of the religions*? I suppose that this restraint can be explained in the light of the fatal role which some religions have played in more recent history, and still play – in connection with human rights, democracy, and world peace. But I ask myself: has not the newest era of all, the post-modern era of human history, from Eastern Europe to Latin America and from South Africa to the Philippines, shown that religions can have not only a destructive but also a constructive effect, and can release a quite tremendous dynamic to liberate people from totalitarian systems, to protect human dignity, establish human rights, and preserve world peace?

So I would argue that we should go on the offensive in using the *incomparable resources* of the world religions for establishing and implementing a world ethic. We should do so for three reasons:

1. Time and again over the millennia, the religions have kept demonstrating their inexhaustible power.
2. The religions can speak much more concretely of human responsibilities than some more recent ethical doctrines.

3.   The great leading religious figures of humankind have lived out an
     ethic in an exemplary way.

I have nothing against philosophical and political arguments for a global
ethic: all constructive philosophical and political ideas, notions, and arguments are most welcome. But in a "post-modern" age, we should dis-
card that neglect of the religions so characteristic of modernity (which
was often purely reactionary) in favor of a realistic assessment. That has
happened most recently of all in a third international document which
can support the two other documents while introducing a greater degree
of concreteness and differentiation.

(c) InterAction Council (1996)
The statement by the *InterAction Council*, which consists of former
Presidents and Prime Ministers (Helmut Schmidt of Germany, Pierre
Trudeau of Canada, and Miguel de la Madrid of Mexico, among others),
was approved in Vancouver on 22 May 1996 under the title *In Search of
Global Ethical St*andards. It openly addresses the *negative role* which
the *religions* have often played, and still play, in the world: "The world
is also afflicted by religious extremism and violence preached and practiced in the name of religion" (InterAction Council, no. 2). But the *positive role* of the religions is also noted: "Religious institutions still
command the loyalty of hundreds of millions of people" (InterAction
Council, no. 2), and do so despite all secularization and consumerism.
"The world's religions constitute one of the great traditions of wisdom
for humankind. This repository of wisdom, ancient in its origins, has
never been needed more" (InterAction Council, no. 9). The minimal criteria which make it possible to live together at all are important; without
ethics and self-restraint, humankind would revert to the jungle. "In a
world of unprecedented change humankind has a desperate need of an
ethical base on which to stand" (InterAction Council, no. 8).
     Now follow some statements on *ethics and politics* which are deci-
sive for the problems with which we are concerned: "Ethics should pre-
cede politics and the law, because political action is concerned with
values and choice. Ethics, therefore, must inform and inspire our political leadership" (InterAction Council, no. 9). To respond to the epoch-making change which is coming about, our institutions need a
re-dedication to ethical norms: "We can find the sources of such a
re-dedication in the world's religious and ethical traditions. They have
the spiritual resources to give an ethical lead to the solution of our eth-

nic, national, social, economic, and religious tensions. The world's religions have different doctrines but they all advocate a common ethic of basic standards. What unites the world's faiths is far greater than what divides them" (InterAction Council, no. 10).

This declaration defines much more precisely the core of a global ethic which can also be found in the other declarations. The InterAction Council achieves this precision by taking up the *"Declaration toward a Global Ethic"* passed by the *Parliament of the World's Religions*: "We are therefore grateful that the Parliament of the World's Religions, which assembled in Chicago in 1993, proclaimed a Declaration toward a Global Ethic which we support in principle" (InterAction Council, no. 11). The InterAction Council clearly emphasizes that what the United Nations proclaimed in its Universal Declaration on Human Rights, strengthened by the two Human Rights Covenants, is confirmed and deepened from the perspective of obligations by this Chicago Declaration: the full realization of the intrinsic dignity of the human person, the inalienable freedom and equality of all humans, and the necessary solidarity and interdependence of all humans with each other, both as individuals and as communities.

The *legal and the ethical levels are distinguished* much more clearly here than in the other two documents: "Also we are convinced that a better global order cannot be created or enforced by laws, prescriptions, and conventions alone; that action in favor of rights and freedoms presumes a consciousness of responsibility of duty, and that therefore both the minds and hearts of women and men must be addressed; that rights without obligations cannot long endure, and that there will be no better global order without a global ethic" (InterAction Council, no. 12).

Here the InterAction Council is very well aware that a global ethic is no substitute for the Torah, the Gospels, the Qur'an, the Bhagavadgita, the Discourses of the Buddha, or the Teachings of Confucius and others. A global ethic can only create t*he necessary minimum of common values, standards and basic attitudes*. Here the concept of a global ethic is defined very well, on the basis of the Chicago Declaration: "a minimal basic consensus relating to binding values, irrevocable standards and moral attitudes which can be affirmed by all religions despite their dogmatic differences and can also be supported by non-believers" (InterAction Council, no. 13). The alliance of believers and non-believers (at the same time also that of theologians, philosophers, and scholars in the fields of religion and social science) in the matter of ethics is important. It is even more important that this body of experienced statesmen explicitly takes over as the core of a global ethic what was stated for the first time in the history of religion in the Declaration of the Parliament of the World's Religions as vitally necessary for any individual, social, and political ethic. All this presupposes:

The Primacy of Ethics over Economics and Politics

Even economists cannot dispute the fact that human life does not just consist in economics and that people need more than the market economy for their well-being, contentment, and a good life together. Or to put it positively: even the *market economy* must be *at the service of men and women* and not vice versa. It should enlarge democracy, not replace it or cover it up.

We should remember that the economy (and thus the market) is a *sub-system* of society, alongside and together with which other sub-systems exist, like law, politics, culture, and religion. The economic principle of rationality is justified, but may not be absolutized. However, in economic neo-liberalism, there is a *danger* of elevating the sub-system of the market economy into a *total system*, so that law, politics, culture, and religion are subordinated to the economy. But a *total market economy* would have *devastating consequences:*

The law   instead of being founded on universal human dignity, human rights, and human obligations, would be formulated and manipulated by economic group interests;

Politics   would capitulate to the market and the lobbying of pressure groups and global speculation would be able to shake national currencies;

Culture   would become a contributor to the market and art would degenerate into commerce;

Ethics   would be sacrificed to power and money, and be replaced by what "gives pleasure";

Religion   offered along with much that was para-religious and pseudo-religious as goods in the supermarket of ideas, would be mixed arbitrarily into a syncretistic cocktail for the convenient satisfaction of religious thirst.

Time and again, *de facto constraints* are presented to us by economists as axiomatic *intellectual constraints* without sufficient attention being paid to fundamental alternatives. But what are often presented to us by professional experts as the "laws" of quasi-natural economic "'pressures" are by no means a priori to be accepted by democratically elected politicians and legitimated only after the event. Here some elementary insights must be applied which anyone can easily verify from experience:

- not everything that is, need be;
- not everything that actually happens need be regarded as a norm;
- not everything that functions, functions well;
- not everything that is efficient is also legitimate;
- not everything that seems economically logical leads to general well-being.

To counter the increasing economization of the world in which we live, there are two things which we need not only to reflect on theoretically but also to put into practice:

(1) *the primacy of politics over the economy.* The economy must not function solely in the service of the allegedly rational and strategic self-assertion of *homo oeconomicus,* but must rather serve higher ethical and political ends;
(2) *the primacy of ethics over the economy and politics.* Fundamental though economics and politics are, they are dimensions of the all-embracing world in which men and women live. For the sake of our humanity, they are subject to ethical criteria of humaneness. The much-cited "normative force of facts" needs to be regulated by an ethic which often goes against the facts. So neither the economy nor politics has the primacy, but rather the unassailable dignity of human beings, their basic rights and responsibilities, which are to be preserved in everything.

Principles for a Business Ethic

That a process of rethinking is also underway at the meso-level is demonstrated by two declarations on business ethics which may be known to you (see Webley 1999, de Bettignies et al. 1999, and the text of the Principles for Business in this volume). They indicate that co-operation both between different religions and between believers and non-believers is also possible over quite specific ethical questions:

- *An Interfaith Declaration.* A Code of Ethics on International

Business for Christians, Muslims, and Jews, dating from 1993
(An Interfaith Declaration), and
- *Principles for Business.* The Caux Roundtable, dating from 1994
(*Principles for Business*).

It is significant that neither declaration regards the task of business
solely as providing profit for the *"shareholder."* Business is also responsible for all *"stakeholders,"* all those who have a stake in the business (*Principles for Business* 3 f.). It is, therefore, consistent that both
declarations should have more or less detailed sections on the *obligations* of business *towards all six stakeholders*: the employees, the customers, the suppliers and financiers, the community (local and national
governments), and finally also the owners/shareholders/investors.
These cannot be discussed in detail here. What is important for a global
ethic at a time of globalization is rather *what underlies the individual
ethical requirements,* and both declarations give clear information about
this.

It is most illuminating that already in the foreword to the Caux Declaration, both a "Western" and an "Eastern" *fundamental value* are
shown to underlie the declaration as a whole:

- not only *"human dignity"* and the sacredness or value of each
  person, who must always be an end and not simply a means to
  the fulfilment of others' purposes;
- but also the Japanese concept of *"kyosei,"* which means living
  and working together for the common good, enabling
  co-operation and mutual prosperity to coexist with healthy and
  fair competition (Principles for Business 2).

The Interfaith Declaration mentions some key concepts or basic values
which are universally valid, which have great significance in *Judaism,
Christianity, and Islam,* and for which numerous texts can be cited from
the holy scriptures of these three Abrahamic religions:

- *Justice:* just conduct, fairness, exercise of authority in maintenance of right;
- *Mutual respect:* love and respect for others;
- *Stewardship:* human beings are only "stewards" of natural resources;

- *Honesty:* truthfulness and reliability in all human relationships, in short "integrity." (An Interfaith Declaration [n. 27], 11 ff.)

The Caux Declaration, in which observance of the law and respect for national and international rules are inculcated, also emphasizes that people must "rise above the letter of the law towards a *spirit of trust*" (*Principles for Business* [n. 28], 4). This calls for sincerity, candor, truthfulness, the keeping of promises and transparency – everything that contributes not only towards the credibility and stability of business transactions, but also to their smoothness and efficiency.

It should also be pointed out that the Caux Declaration openly addresses the particularly tricky point of the *"avoidance of illicit operations"*: "A business should not participate in or condone bribery, money laundering, or other corrupt practices; indeed it should seek co-operation with others to eliminate them. It should not trade in arms or other materials used for terrorist activities, drug traffic or other organized crime" (Principles for Business [n. 28], 5).

But since corruption is spreading like a cancer even in countries which formerly had a largely honest civil service and medical profession, and there is an increase in organized crime and criminality among young people, the question of the foundation for basic values and basic attitudes arises even more clearly than before. It poses itself in a novel way especially in the market economy. Why should I unconditionally keep to particular rules, moral standards, and ethical norms?

The Depth-Dimension of Ethics

Ethics should be not only hypothetically unconditional (if it corresponds with my interests) but also categorically unconditional (which was Kant's view). But what are the foundations for the *unconditional validity* of particular basic ethical values and attitudes? For the authors of the Interfaith Declaration, they clearly come from the religion of those concerned, whether they be Jewish, Christian, or Muslim. But the Caux Declaration manifestly presupposes that the basic values and attitudes which it calls for are also accessible to non-believers and doubters, agnostics, and atheists. However, on the other hand, a purely secular argument for particular values and attitudes – as has been demonstrated at length elsewhere (Küng 1991) – easily gets into difficulties over its foundation.

Slowly, even secular critics of the time are noting that *modernization* has been leading to the establishment not only of an unavoidable *secularization* but largely also a by no means unavoidable ideological *secularism,* in which anything that is transcendent, trans-empirical, authoritative, and, indeed, normative, seems to have been banished from life. Each person is his or her own standard.

But how, one asks, are individual or groups to be given standards *if the human being himself or herself is "the measure of all things,"* not ethically bound in the originally Greek sense of the word, but independent in the modern libertinistic sense.

Can standards ultimately be demonstrated as irrevocable for human beings if human beings want to be wholly their own norms, and do not recognize any norms for themselves, any normative authority which transcends them?

Does it make people happier if they know neither norm nor purpose and then, because they want something with all their hearts, they prescribe for themselves a modern pseudo-religion instead of a true religion, of the kind that is expressed in the "Singapore Dream" (which to be truthful is not dreamed only in Singapore), so that

- The five age-old Cs of true religion – Creed, Cult, Code, Conduct, and Community – are replaced by
- The five new Cs of pseudo-religion: Cash, Credit Card, Car, Condominium, and Country Club?

In time will not such unconcealed materialism and selfishness, even in the Asian country which so far is most free from corruption, similarly lead to an unfair, polarized, split society of privileged and disadvantaged, and so in the long run become a danger to democracy, as is being indicated in the most recent controversies in Singapore?

I am convinced that in an age without standards or goals, which at the same time is on the lookout for rules, norms of conduct, and ethical maxims, religion has *a basic function which cannot be performed by ethics alone.* This function can be described briefly in a way which applies not only to the three prophetic religions (Judaism, Christianity, and Islam) but largely also to the mystical religions of Indian origin (Hinduism and Buddhism) and to the wisdom religions of Chinese origin (Confucianism and Taoism). It is not a later relativization of a common global ethic, but something which *deepens* it and gives it a foundation. Why? Here are four perspectives:

❏ No universal ethic, but only religion can provide an unconditional guarantee for unconditional norms, deepest motivations, and highest ideals, and at the same time give them concrete form. In other words: religion can offer an answer to the ultimate "Why?" and "What for?" of our responsibility.

❑ No universal ethic, but only religion can provide a basis for protest and resistance against unjust conditions, even when such protest and resistance seems to be unsuccessful, or frustration has already set in. In other words, religion is an expression of a *longing for the "wholly other"* which is already at work now and cannot be silenced within the world.

❑ No universal ethic, but only religion can through shared symbols and rituals create a home of trust, security, and hope. In other words, religion can offer an ultimate *spiritual community and home.*

❑ No universal ethic, but only religion can communicate a specific depth dimension, a comprehensive horizon of interpretation even in the face of suffering, injustice, guilt, and meaninglessness, and provide an ultimate meaning for life even in the face of death. In other words: religion can offer an answer to the question of the *mysterious whence and whither of our existence.*

So there is a dialectical relationship between religion and ethics, and religious people in particular should not play off the one against the other. What I find most convincing are a religion which obligates people to a *humane* ethic and an ethic which is *open* to the *religious* dimension, indeed which is ultimately supported and motivated by religion. But I need to be rather more concrete, above all for the "elites." This brings us to the micro-level.

No Business Culture Without a Personality Culture

It is quite clear that today much is expected of *executives* in business, administration, and politics. They need to show a capacity for analysis, but at the same time also to be decisive and concerned to implement decisions. Thorough training is as much a prerequisite as long years of experience. Executives need to set clear goals for themselves and others, to employ colleagues and resources with determination, and often analyze complex situations in the briefest time and make the right decisions. In a word, *strong* leadership is called for. But where does it come from?

We may be agreed that strong and effective leadership does not have to do only with actions and strategies but also with a*ttitude, character, and personality.* It needs to be personal leadership with both the head and the heart. Now attitude, character, and personality at the same time also have to do with *integrity, morality, and ethos*! Not just ethics = theory, but *ethos = attitude, an inner moral attitude.* And ethos has to do with value orientations, patterns of interpretation, and criteria for action, and thus most of all – directly or indirectly – also with religious convictions, with religious education, which can be positive or negative religious experiences.

Business culture has always been important, but today it is of almost strategic relevance. Ultimately it consists in a combination of decisiveness with the values, criteria, norms, and modes of behavior of executives and their colleagues in a business. A business consists primarily of people, so business culture presupposes *personality culture.*

Hence my very direct questions:

First, is it not necessary for *executives themselves* to become aware of their own moral and religious values and thus to have a more precise grasp of the moral and religious aspects of the reality of leadership? So the question is: who, what, how are you – as a human being, a person, a character?

Second, is it not also important for *colleagues* not only to know their superiors from the outside as boss, chief executive, director, manager, but also to see something of what moves their heads and hearts, their invisible yet very effective ethos? So the question is, where are people with you?

Third, in a time when the credibility of public institutions and representatives has suffered severely (in a time when people are tired of politics, politicians, and political parties), does it not also need to become clearer to the *public* as well what are the supreme values, universally binding moral standards, norms, and normative authorities, to which our executives in business administration and politics, and indeed also in education and science, feel committed? To put the question in quite personal terms: What do you hold to at all events? What is unconditionally categorical for you, without any ifs and buts (Kant's question)?

Instead of an Ethic of Success or an Ethic of Conviction, an Ethic of Responsibility

No mere ethic of success can have a future. Action for which the end hallows all the means and for which what functions, brings profit, power, or enjoyment, is good can lead to crass libertinism and Machiavellianism. No, such an ethic can have no future. Basically it is not an ethic at all, but a technique, a technique of selfish behaviour.

No mere ethic of conviction can have a future either. Oriented on an idea of value seen more or less in isolation (justice, love, truth), it is concerned only with the pure internal motivation of the person who acts, with no concern for the consequences of a decision or action, the concrete situation, or its demands and effects. On closer inspection this is often not ethic but romanticism, more or less pious wishful thinking.

By contrast, only the kind of *ethic of responsibility* proposed by the great sociologist *Max Weber* in the revolutionary winter of 1918/19 would seem to have any future. Even according to Weber, such an ethic is not "without convictions," but it does always ask realistically about the predictable consequences of our actions and takes responsibility for them: "To this degree an ethic of conviction and an ethic of responsibility are not absolute opposites, but supplement each other. Together they make the authentic person who *can* have the vocation to politics" (Weber 1958, 559.) So what is needed is an ethic of responsibility grounded in an ethic of conviction.

- Without an ethic of conviction, an ethic of responsibility would degenerate into an ethic of success without any conviction, for which any means is right because of the consequences.
- Without an ethic of responsibility, an ethic of conviction would degenerate into a cultivation of self-righteous inwardness.

Of course there are *no religious patent solutions* for coping with the world problems of today and the difficulties associated with them. There is no religious substitute for business competence, professional knowledge, and common sense. But it is also true that religion can help once again to find that basic social consensus about *what is ultimately valid,* without which modern pluralism proves destructive (and who does not think here of the Ten Commandments of the Jewish-Christian and indeed the Islamic tradition, which are so scorned!).

*Religion has an indirect effe*ct on the individual, as it were *from the foundations upwards,* though this effect also extends to the topical questions of the day and technical questions of detail. It does so by bringing into play basic convictions, basic attitudes, and basic values, and providing ultimate grounds, motivations, and norms for concrete behaviour and decisions. To this degree, therefore, economics and religion cannot be completely separated, but relate constructively to each other. And for executives this means that to this degree business and political leadership and ethical and religious leadership are interdependent.

Indeed, to be a *"big business person,"* less than ever today, is it enough just to have a capital of millions or to have hundreds of contacts or dozens of mandates from boards of directors? No. To be a "big business person," in addition to a capacity for analysis, decisiveness, and a will to implement decisions, one needs a view of reality as a whole which goes beyond trade knowledge and professional competence, an understanding of the overall context, a sense for basic human questions and ethical convictions which are deeply rooted and have been well reflected on.

A Fundamental Consensus of the Religions as the Basis for Any Business Ethic

The Declaration of the Parliament of the World's Religions' "Toward a Global Ethic" (1993) (Küng and Kuschel 1993) has been accepted by the InterAction Council as a solid ethical basis for politics. The same Declaration could also be a basis for a business ethic, as it is not only put forward by the various religions but can also be supported by believers and non-believers alike.

The Declaration begins from two basic principles which have to apply to all groups, classes, and nations:

- Every human being must be treated humanely!
- What you do not wish done to yourself, do not do to others!

Or, in positive terms: What you wish done to yourself, do to others. This should be the irrevocable, unconditional norm for all areas of life, for families and communities, and for all races, nations, and religions.

On the basis of these two principles, *four irrevocable directives* are then affirmed, on which all religions agree. These are also supported by the InterAction Council. They can simply be cited here by title, without further explanation:

- Commitment to a culture of non-violence and respect for life (the age-old directive "You shall not kill!," or in positive terms, "Have respect for life!");
- Commitment to a culture of solidarity and a just economic order (the age-old directive, "You shall not steal!", or in positive terms, "Deal honestly and fairly!");
- Commitment to a culture of tolerance and a life of truthfulness (the age-old directive "You shall not lie!," or in positive terms, "Speak and act truthfully!");

- Commitment to a culture of equal rights and partnership between men and women (the age-old directive, "You shall not commit sexual immorality!" or in positive terms, "Respect and love one another!").

I would like to end with the section of the Declaration toward a Global Ethic about commitment to a culture of solidarity and a just social order:

> Numberless men and women of all regions and religions strive to live their lives in solidarity with one another and to work for authentic fulfilment of their vocations. Nevertheless, all over the world we find endless hunger, deficiency, and need. Not only individuals, but especially unjust institutions and structures are responsible for these tragedies. Millions of people are without work; millions are exploited by poor wages, forced to the edges of society, with their possibilities for the future destroyed. In many lands the gap between the poor and the rich, between the powerful and the powerless is immense. We live in a world in which totalitarian state socialism as well as unbridled capitalism have hollowed out and destroyed many ethical and spiritual values. A materialistic mentality breeds greed for unlimited profit and a grasping for endless plunder. These demands claim more and more of the community's resources without obliging the individual to contribute more. The cancerous social evil of corruption thrives in the developing countries and in the developed countries alike.
>
> (a) In the great ancient religious and ethical traditions of humankind we find the directive: *You shall not steal!* Or in positive terms: *Deal honestly and fairly!* Let us reflect anew on the consequences of this ancient directive: No one has the right to rob or dispossess in any way whatsoever any other person or the commonweal. Further, no one has the right to use her or his possessions without concern for the needs of society and Earth.
>
> (b) Where extreme poverty reigns, helplessness and despair spread, and theft occurs again and again for the sake of survival. Where power and wealth are accumulated ruthlessly, feelings of envy, resentment, and deadly hatred and rebellion inevitably well up in the disadvantaged and marginalized. This leads to a vicious circle of violence and counter-violence. Let no one be deceived: There is no global peace without global justice!

(c) Young people must learn at home and in school that property, limited though it may be, carries with it an obligation, and that its uses should at the same time serve the common good. Only thus can a *just economic order* be built up.

(d) If the plight of the poorest billions of humans on this planet, particularly women and children, is to be improved, the world economy must be structured more justly. Individual good deeds, and assistance projects, indispensable though they be, are insufficient. The participation of all states and the authority of international organizations are needed to build just economic institutions.

A solution which can be supported by all sides must be sought for the debt crisis and the poverty of the dissolving Second World, and even more the Third World. Of course conflicts of interest are unavoidable. In the developed countries, a distinction must be made between necessary and limitless consumption, between socially beneficial and non-benefi- cial uses of property, between justified and unjustified uses of natural resources, and between a profit-only and a socially beneficial and ecologically oriented market economy. Even the developing nations must search their national consciences.

Wherever those ruling threaten to repress those ruled, wherever institutions threaten persons, and wherever might oppresses right, we have an obligation to resist whenever possible non-violently.

(e) To be authentically human in the spirit of our great religious and ethical traditions means the following:

We must use economic and political power for *service to humanity* instead of misusing it in ruthless battles for domination. We must develop a spirit of compassion with those who suffer, with special care for the children, the aged, the poor, the disabled, the refugees, and the lonely.

We must cultivate *mutual respect* and consideration, so as to reach a reasonable balance of interests, instead of thinking only of unlimited power and unavoidable competitive struggles.

We must value *a sense of moderation and modesty* instead of an unquenchable greed for money, prestige, and consumption! In greed humans lose their "soul", their freedom, their composure, their inner peace, and thus that which makes them human (Küng and Kuschel 1993, 26–29).

References

Commission on Global Governance. *Our Global Neighborhood: The Report of the Commission on Global Governance*, Oxford, 1995.

de Bettignies, H.-C., Goodpaster, K. E., Matsuoka, T., "The Caux Roundtable Principles for Business: Presentation and Discussion," in this volume.

Der Spiegel (Interview), "Ich bin kein Spieler." Super-Spekulant George Soros über Milliardengier und seine Angst vor einem Crash des Weltfinanzsytems, Number 24 (1996).

InterAction Council, *In Search of Global Ethical Standards*, 1996, no.2.

An Interfaith Declaration: A Code of Ethics on International Business for Christians, Muslims and Jews, London 1993.

Küng, H., Global Responsibility, London and New York, 1991.

Küng, H. and Kuschel, K. J., eds., *A Global Ethic: The Declaration of the Parliament of the World's Religions*, London and New York, 1993.

Principles for Business, Caux Roundtable, The Hague, 1994. See H.-C. de Bettignies, et al., "The Caux Roundtable Principles for Business: Presentation and Discussion" and the text of Principles in this volume.

Weber, M., "Politik als Beruf," in *Gesammelte politische Schriften*, Tübingen. 1958, 505–560.

Webley, S., "Values Inherent in the Interfaith Declaration of International Business," in this volume.

World Commission on Culture and Development, *Report of the World Commission on Culture and Development: Our Creative Diversity*, Paris, 1995.

Part II
Ethical Standards and Sources for International Business Organizations

The Caux Roundtable Principles for Business: Presentation and Discussion

Henri-Claude de Bettignies, Kenneth E. Goodpaster, and Toshio Matsuoka

The Caux Roundtable Principles are not simply a document; they are part of a dynamic process with a most interesting narrative as well as conceptual history, and with a likely significant future. Professor Toshio Matsuoka has firsthand knowledge of the concept of "kyosei," an important Japanese contribution to the evolution of the Caux Roundtable Principles. Professor Henri-Claude de Bettignies shares his very valuable knowledge in the European, particularly in the French, perspective on the Caux Roundtable and the history of the dialogue around the Caux Principles. Professor Kenneth Goodpaster shares the history of the Minnesota Principles and their development into the Caux Roundtable Principles.

Toshio Matsuoka

In July 1985, a friend of mine came to visit my office and brought a copy of a Dutch newspaper. Because it was written in Dutch, I could not understand a single word but at the bottom of this newspaper, there was a color cartoon illustration. It showed a samurai wearing armor with a sword and cutting the earth. Red blood was coming out of the earth, forming the shape of Japan. That was a shocking picture. Of course, we could imagine what the article was likely to say. The title read: "Japan's Deceptive Smile." According to the Philips Corporation's research in the Netherlands, there was collusion between the Japanese Minister of International Trade and Industry (MITI) and Japanese industry, which tried to control the European and American electronics industries. This was the jest of the article. Former President and Chairman of the Philips Corporation, Dr. Philips, sent me a copy of the newspaper article and told me that Japanese business managers did not know that this negative, though false image of Japan existed among Europeans. Historical experiences show, he warned, that economic frictions could lead to actual war. Therefore, Dr. Philips and Dr. Olivier Giscard d'Estaing, the younger brother of the former French President, launched an initiative to hold a frank discussion among business leaders of Japan, the United States, and Europe. In charge of submitting names, I was wondering whom to invite to this new kind of business leader forum. After consultation with Mr. Kaku, the President of Canon, we organized the first meeting and invited: Mr. Kaku; Mr. Yamashda, the former President of Matsushita Electric; Mr. Ogusarawa, the Chairman of Japan Times; and some other Japanese participants. So in August 1986, the first Caux Round Table was held, including thirty people from Japan, the United States, and Europe.

By the way, the name Caux stems from a small village in Switzerland, located on a terrace between the high mountains of the Alps and Lake Geneva below. Caux is a beautiful place, like a paradise on earth, but once this first meeting started, it turned out to be a severe Japan-bashing conference. Japanese participants, including myself, felt like we wanted to leave the conference because it was so critical of Japan. However, this place Caux had a special significance in the 1930s when the world was engaged in military expansion. Then Dr. Frank Buchman, pleading that the countries should arm themselves with morality instead of weapons, launched the Moral Re-Armament (MRA) Movement. After World War II, Caux served as a historic place for the reconciliation between France and Germany, and hosted the first post-war conference with Japan. The underlying motivation for these activities was a strong moral and spiritual force with a number of teachings. One is to concentrate on *what* is correct and right rather than on *who* is correct and right. Another important teaching asks each person in the dialogue group to re-question his or her own righteousness. When you point to another person with your forefinger, blaming her for being wrong, three fingers remain folded pointing back to you, which means that three times more forces are against yourself.

These teachings were not really stipulated and explained during the first day. But on the second day, the atmosphere suddenly changed. Even the American and European participants started to speak differently by acknowledging some wrong criticisms. Then a very frank, honest, and full discussion began. So this first three-day meeting was very useful and productive. Dr. Philips, Dr. Giscard d'Estaing, and President Kaku of Canon served as central figures in the Caux meetings every summer. In addition to summer meetings in Caux, every spring a meeting was held in different cities of the United States, Japan, China, India, and Taiwan. In 1992, a suggestion was made to compile the principles for business. After two years of preparation, these principles were announced and published in 1994.

The inspiration came from Mr. Kaku who introduced the concept of "kyosei" and its application to management. But the concept of "kyosei" was, of course, not invented by Mr. Kaku because in 1991 Keidanren, the Japanese Federation of Economic Organizations, launched the concept of "kyosei" as a fundamental principle, and two hundred presidents of major corporations compiled a book together titled *Kyosei* (which was published by Keidanren).

The word "kyosei" has a long history. Over one hundred and twenty years ago in 1879, a German writer and doctor discovered the concept of "kyosei." In English, it is called "symbiosis," which means "different creatures live together." That is translated into the Japanese word "kyosei." In Buddhism, there is another word called "tomoiki," which stands for symbiosis or living together. An important tradition of "kyosei" in business goes back to Matsushita Electric Company, for which I worked over twenty years, and its founder Mr. Konosuke Matsushita, whom I had firsthand experience to serve during eleven of those years. Mr. Matsushita personally launched his management principles in 1929. He said we have to give due consideration to harmony between profit and social justice, and two years later in 1931 he already used the words "co-existence" and "co-prosperity." When I was working at Matsushita Electric, there was always a poster in the office, written personally by Mr. Matsushita, indicating the importance of co-existence and co-prosperity.

A great interest in the concepts of "tomoiki," "kyosei" or "symbiosis," was also shown by Dr. Chokrokoa, a famous Japanese architect with a Buddhist educational background. In 1980, he decided that the main theme of the World Design Conference in Yokohama should be "The Era of Symbiosis." He recently wrote a book of several hundred pages, entitled "Philosophy of Symbiosis," and set up a homepage on the Internet, which is frequently read, sometimes by as many as two thousand people per day.

While the word "kyosei" in Japanese only means "living together," it has been given a deeper meaning by Mr. Kaku, and it is now often translated into English as "living and working together for the common good." There is no doubt that Mr. Kaku's deep insight has been influenced by a number of crucial events in his life. As a child, he lived in Manchuria, in the North of China, and experienced the political turmoil there. When the atomic bomb was dropped over Nagasaki, he lived in that city and witnessed that tens of thousands of people were killed instantly and tragically, while also being very much concerned about the nuclear exposure of a huge number of people who survived. He became President of Canon when the company was making a big deficit. Although he was extremely busy in his leadership position, he was a very ardent reader of books and documents and read over ten thousand pages per year.

Of course, the word "kyosei" was not clearly defined by the academic experts, and Mr. Kaku broadened and deepened the meaning of this word. First, "kyosei" was applied to the relationship between Japan, Europe and the United States, then to the relations between developed and developing countries. Now, "kyosei" concerns also the relationship among rival corporations, between labor and management, business partners, and local and regional communities, and it extends to the global environment and future generations. In other words, it means to accept the existence of others and try to make the best use of each other's merit. So one plus one is not just two, but there are always synergies, and one really creates three or four or one hundred. That is the true value of "kyosei."

Henri-Claude de Bettignies

When the Roundtable was founded in 1986, I was very involved in the creation and development of another type of institution (also a "Forum"): the *Euro-Asia Centre,* at INSEAD, and though I was approached by one of the Founders of the Caux Roundtable, Oliver Giscard d'Estaing, I was too busy building linkages between the European and the Asia-Pacific business communities to answer positively to the invitation.

However, I was very interested in the Caux project. It was also a pioneering venture, one aiming at reaching an objective I was very concerned with: *to influence and change the mindset of top executives.* It was also an initiative with a *"global"* intention.

My interest was kept alive by frequent reminders from Oliver Giscard d'Estaing, and Ryuzaburo Kaku to participate in the Caux meetings. As I have not yet been able to manage my time well to participate in the Roundtable, my view is the one of an outsider, one who knows several members of the Roundtable and has been pushed to join by European as well as Japanese friends (e.g. Ogasawara Toshiaki, Kawai Saburo). Members of the Roundtable are keen to enlarge their network! Though I have not been to Caux, I am trying to contribute to one of the objectives of the Caux Roundtable: to enhance decision makers' commitment to their *responsibilities* and *actions* toward building a better *global* environment.

So the following comments are not from an "expert" on codes of conduct or even from a "member" of the Caux Roundtable. I will mention here my positive comments about the Caux Roundtable, my questions, and conclude with some remarks toward the future.

1. A Positive Assessment

1.1 The context

The Timing
The founders and early believers of the Caux Roundtable must be given credit for the timing of their creation: the mid 1980s. It was just *before* the "Ethics Boom" which occurred during the late 1980s (during the "go-go" years of Wall Street, before the Drexell-Boesky-Salomon Brothers adventures in ethics). Ethics was not yet fashionable.

The Vision
The scope was from the beginning a *global* one. It was already concerned by the consequences of the "globalization" process, and some of its negative consequences.

The Group
It was from the start a *"tri-lateral"* perspective, bringing together North Americans, Japanese and Europeans. Trilateralism was "à la mode" during that period. It was concerned with top executives, essentially with *business* leaders. Its purpose was to bring together *"decision makers."* People who can make a difference.

The Objective
"Action" was the objective (I believe): to be committed to a small number of principles, and to build commitment around them through a *"forum for discussion."* A platform for debate had to be created, hence the concept of "Roundtable" (with no privileged position). Only commitment could create ownership of the principles and lead to implementation, to action.

1.2 The content

The Preamble
I cannot but subscribe to the observation, today so obvious, of the globalization process, and I am also convinced that organizations will find

neither in the *law* nor in the *market* the solutions to their moral dilemmas, the "guide for conduct." The use of the "stakeholder" concept was more original in 1985 than it is today, but indeed it is the framework which should guide the behavior of decision makers. I also appreciate the emphasis on *shared values* among leaders from different cultures, and religious groups, or even with non-religious individuals or communities. The necessity to engage in a *"dialogue"* among (probably) the most important *change agents* is a necessity to which I cannot but subscribe, and more so when the cornerstone of the dialogue is the moral values behind the decision-making process.

The "General Principles" – On those, views can be more nuanced

- *Regarding Principle #1:* What is new here is that CEOs use the stakeholder concept as a base for their code of conduct.
- *Regarding Principle #2:* I happen to believe that business should produce employment in most countries, contribute to education of the local staff, be willing to share innovation, and enhance the capacity to innovate worldwide, though I would be more nuanced on the pressure for "human rights."
- I have also questions about the use of "free and fair competition," etc., but will come back to this later.
- *Regarding Principle #3:* If we call for truthfulness, keeping promises, and transparency, etc., one wonders if we do not move too much in the wonderful, lofty aims which remind us how good is "motherhood." Clearly if more transparency was implemented in global corporations, corruption would not have the golden years it is enjoying today, and that information technology will enhance further.
- *Regarding Principle #4:* This principle ("Respect for Rules") is potentially the most contentious one. It is "to promote freer trade, to avoid trade frictions" that fair and equitable treatment should be implemented through "international" rules. Who decides on the "international" rules, in terms of labor law, labor rights, minimum wages, child labor, and union acceptance?
- Today, the debate is very hot on those issues in the ASEAN region, or in China. What is the legitimacy of the Europeans, or the West, or the "rich," to impose their "fair" treatment concept? Who decides what is fair? It is the debate on the "social clause."
- *Regarding Principle #5:* Support GATT and WTO. Many would agree, but the Caux Roundtable free-trade Gospel does not turn ev-

eryone on, in today's "global" environment. Here we see the political ideology, the political choice to be very explicit, and mixed with sound moral proposals. Don't we run the risk of turning away potential supporters of the Caux Roundtable in making such an explicit linkage between good corporate behavior and the free trade neo-liberal ideology?

- *Regarding Principle #6:* None would challenge preaching respect for the environment, and the avoidance of the waste (particularly in the rich countries, that others are trying to emulate).
- *Regarding Principle #7:* Very lofty, and here "motherhood" is around the corner! No arms trade, for example, but beyond "arms," where to draw the line? Can we trade frozen embryos? Could it become linked to "terrorist activities?" Where is the limit in what can be traded or not (in the free-trade Gospel)?

The Stakeholder Principles
I will leave Professor Goodpaster to comment on those. It is enough to say that they indicate the broad lines dominant "today," for some of the most talked about stakeholders. Some stakeholders are perhaps given a back seat (e.g. the "birds"), while others would have gained to receive the attention of more *specific* principles.

2. Some "Tentative" Conclusions
The Caux Roundtable deserves attention:

- It brings together CEOs for a dialogue, a conversation so much needed. It is a platform for debate, to fertilize reflection. What we have heard at the First World Congress of Business, Economics, and Ethics indicates, if necessary, how much reflection and debate is needed in so many countries (including Japan).
- It created a "forum," a cross-cultural exchange so much needed at a time when we hear the danger of so many potential "clashes."
- It has brought "visibility" to those issues, and they need to receive much more, particularly among decision makers.
- It has formalized a code, and can be used as a tool to debate, to discuss, to reflect, and to explore. In ethics, it is this debate among us and *within* us which is so necessary.

But,
- The code tends to be broader that perhaps it should be.
- The Caux Roundtable blends a political agenda (free trade) with a

moral approach, and if the two are necessary, they should be more clearly differentiated.

- It is still too much a group of Japanese, Americans, and Europeans: the world is not trilateral. Newly industrialized countries and developing countries should be more represented. The solutions to our global problems will not be found by OECD countries, by "the North," or by the "rich."
- The Caux Roundtable should gain more supporters among decision makers from the *global* environment, and enlarge its diversity in including more policy makers, and participants from the scientific community.
- Whistle blowers should be invited to join the debate, and the "Principles for Business" will gain from an enriched debate. It will further its effectiveness, and contribute further to achieve its ambitious objectives.

Kenneth Goodpaster

Shortly after I arrived at the University of St. Thomas and began to function in the Koch Chair of Business Ethics, I got into contact with the Minnesota Center for Corporate Responsibility which has been around for many years. It was started in 1975 and has been a beacon of corporate responsibility activities within the United States, something of which Minnesota is very proud. That organization (MCCR) hosted a meeting of executives of international corporations in the Twin Cities area including companies headquartered there such as 3M, Honeywell, Cargill, H. B. Fuller, and a number of others. The meeting was called by the executives from the companies who are represented in MCCR because they were experiencing increasing frustration of a very practical kind. The frustration came from doing business away from the United States and coming into contact with cultural differences of various kinds and not knowing sometimes whether there were different ethical standards in other countries. Their managers were getting confused about or whether these were differences of basic ethical values or simply differences of culture that had an underlying similarity when it came to ethical values. So the idea was for us to sit down and discuss whether or not there were any transcultural ethical values. Could such values be articulated in any meaningful way or would they have to remain tacit and in the background? After months of discussions with the groups of executives, we made an effort to articulate the results of those discussions in a document which came to be called Minnesota Principles. In 1991, the

Minnesota Principles became a discussion document among corporations in Minnesota and in some other parts of the United States.

The Minnesota Principles as they existed then have since become incorporated into what are now called the Caux Roundtable Principles. One of the members of the MCCR was invited to participate in the Caux Roundtable discussions just at the time, as Professor Matsuoka explained, that the Caux Roundtable was itself beginning to think it needed to try to articulate some of its convictions. These were convictions that came from the dialogues that they had been having annually (at that time for six years in Caux, Switzerland). So the time was apparently right as a member of the Minnesota delegation presented the Minnesota Principles to the Caux group. There was some enthusiasm in the context of Mr. Kaku's discussions of "kyosei" and his recognition that in the Minnesota Principles there was a more explicit and analytical expression of some of the fundamental ideas of "kyosei." It was clear that common cause and common ground were beginning to emerge. I was involved with the initial articulation of the Minnesota Principles and then I became involved with the dialogue that took place between the Caux Roundtable members and the MCCR. There was a lot of back and forth. There was a meeting where Japanese, European, and American business people came to the University of St. Thomas in downtown Minneapolis, and we had some wonderful discussions and these discussions were not without emotion. There were times during the meetings when some people in the discussions felt that their contributions were not being sufficiently heard. There was a lot of debate about the precise formulation of the final product. If I go back to my computer, I can find multiple version and I remember running back and forth between my computer and the group, trying to come up with new formulations that were answering the needs of the different parties to the discussion. There was an intense moment, I remember, when Jean Loup Dherse from the European delegation and our Japanese friends got into a debate about "kyosei" and human dignity – whether there was enough emphasis within the concept of "kyosei," on the sacredness and dignity of the individual person, or whether it was too collective a concept. As we talked about it, we began to understand more about the meaning of "kyosei," especially the meaning that Mr. Kaku was adding to the concept as it was evolving. We were able to get over the impasse and to see the concepts as at the very least complementary. I have since come to believe that the concept of "kyosei" is very similar in its structural underpinnings to the concept of what moral philosophers in the West have called the "moral point of view." (This is explicitly discussed in my chapter in this book.)

But to get back to our narrative. We hammered out in January 1994 what is essentially before you now, the Caux Roundtable Principles, which incorporated in a large measure the Minnesota Principles but with added new dimensions. The Preamble and the Stakeholder Principles are inherited very much from the Minnesota Principles. The General Principles in the middle were hammered out in the dialogue that we had in January 1994. Eventually they were presented in Berlin and then in Caux, Switzerland in July 1994. They were received and welcomed by the Caux Roundtable and officially adopted as a document that the Caux Roundtable would refer to in the future as the Caux Principles for Business Conduct. In a certain sense, the Minnesota Principles ceased to exist, to the delight of those of us in Minnesota hoped they would take on a much larger, less local meaning.

I believe that there are three fundamental moral values that underlie the Caux Principles for Business Conduct. Besides the philosophy of "kyosei" and the respect for the dignity of the individual which are guiding ideals, there are three values that those ideals give rise to and, it seems to me, are worth our notice. The first value is the pursuit of happiness, or if you prefer, *prosperity*, or the wealth of a nation. This is often seen as business's central agenda – not the distribution of wealth, but the production of wealth in the first place so that it can be distributed. The pursuit of prosperity or at least the material wealth of a society is one of the guiding values of the Caux Principles. But alongside that value is a second which I will call *justice*, but essentially it is the value of making sure that the distribution of that wealth is fair and respectful of the rights of individuals in a society. The third leg of this value stool is *community*. Community is something distinguishable from enhancing the wealth of individuals or protecting the rights of individuals, something that affirms the whole being more than the sum of its parts. Prosperity, justice, and community are the three values that lie behind the Caux Principles; they are the moral philosophy, if you will, behind the Caux Principles.

The pragmatic motivation was a set of business leaders who wanted very much to have a shared set of values on the basis of which to do business across cultural borders. Ambitious as it may have been and flawed as it may be, the Caux document represents an initiative taken not by academics, but by thoughtful business practitioners to seek a better world, guided not solely by market principles and not solely by government regulation and law. Instead, they were guided by a shared spirit of conscience, and that shared spirit of conscience as embodied in this document is something that is truly exciting.

I won't go into the details of the principles, there is not time for that. I just want to say something about the future, which relates to an observation made by Professor de Bettignies. My perception of the Caux Roundtable at this stage in its history is that it is poised for two kinds of broadening. One is the broadening from a very inwardly-focused discussion group to a group that seeks to share the results of those discussions with a much wider audience. This represents a cultural change within the Caux Roundtable. There were some serious debates in my presence a year ago about whether or not it was the business of the Caux Roundtable to be preaching to the world, and there were some members of the Roundtable who felt that it was simply inappropriate. The majority, however, prevailed and not only prevailed as the majority, but actually persuaded the minority. Keeping "under a bushel" the values that were being discussed at Caux and the fact that they were being discussed by business leaders from Japan, Europe, and from North America was seen as a mistake. So there is a broadening going on in the communication of these principles. That is one reason why you are hearing about them here at the World Congress of Business, Economics, and Ethics.

There is another kind of broadening going on. That is the realization, something Professor de Bettignies pointed out at the end of his remarks, that this is not a tripartite world we live in and that the three groups that were represented in the fashioning of these principles, Japan, Western Europe, and the United States do not comprise the whole world community as we know it. The Caux Roundtable has got to recognize that fact in its own constitution and in the people that it brings to Switzerland to participate in its conversations. And that broadening is beginning to occur. So I am very optimistic about that particular aspect of the future of the Caux Roundtable.

My final remark is that if conscience in the business world is to survive, then it must be able to defend itself against two possible ways to kill it. One way comes from within. When the values, articulated by a business organization, are not in fact implemented internally in the organization, they become window dressing, they become essentially hypocrisy. That is, by the way, why the Ethics Officers Association is working to try to develop internal procedures by which companies can make their value convictions, as they are articulated, real. That is one way to avoid killing conscience. We avoid killing it by making it live within the habits and practices of the organization.

There is another way to avoid killing conscience. Organizations that want to live in a more idealistic, value-affirming way have got to have company. It is not enough to be a solo ethical company in a world in which those values are not shared or supported. One can become an economic martyr in the process. I am not suggesting that martyrdom is always bad! Sometimes it can be very effective we have seen many examples of it in the history of both Eastern and Western civilization. Nevertheless, it would be nice if martyrdom were not a prerequisite for business ethics, and I think that will be a less prerequisite if there are more companies willing to step up and identify with a commitment to moral values beyond what are required of them by the market and by law. The mutual support of such companies and the recognition that other companies have so signed on to the spirit of those moral values leads to *encouragement*, and *encouragement* seems to be essential for the development of moral virtues by organizations in a global environment. Then it becomes less plausible to say, "Well, the competition is going to devastate me if I practice these principles." If there are more and more companies stepping forward to say, "We will practice these principles," the outliers become those who refuse to practice them. So it seems to me that if we want to make the world safe for the kind of thing this conference is about, we have to look inside the corporation to make sure its conscience is alive from within. We also have to look outside and create networks of like-minded corporations. I think the Caux Roundtable Principles offer us an opportunity to do that. Maybe someday the International Society of Business, Economics, and Ethics will be affiliated in some constructive ways with the Caux Roundtable.

The Caux Roundtable Principles for Business Conduct

THE CAUX PRINCIPLES

Business Behavior for a Better World

Introduction. This document has been developed by the Caux Roundtable, an international group of business executives from Japan, Europe, and the United States who meet each year in Caux, Switzerland, and who believe that the world business community should play an important role in improving economic and social conditions. As a statement of aspirations, it is not meant to mirror reality but to express a world standard against which corporate performance can be held accountable. In the end, members seek to begin a process that identifies shared values and reconciles differing values so we may move toward developing a shared perspective on business behavior that is acceptable to and honored by all.

These principles are rooted in two basic ethical ideals: the Japanese concept of "kyosei" and the more Western concept of "human dignity." "Kyosei" means living and working together for the common good, in a way that enables cooperation and mutual prosperity to coexist with healthy and fair competition. "Human dignity" refers to the sacredness or value of each human person as an end, not simply as a means to others' purposes or even, in the case of basic human rights, majority prescription. The intermediate General Principles in Section 2 help to clarify the spirit of "kyosei" and "human dignity," while the more specific Stakeholder Principles in Section 3 represent a practical way to apply the ideals of kyosei and human dignity.

Business behavior can affect relationships among nations and the prosperity and well-being of us all. Business is often the first contact between nations and, by the way in which it causes social and economic changes, has a significant impact on the level of fear as well as confidence felt by people worldwide. Members of the Caux Roundtable place their first emphasis on putting one's own house in order, seeking what is right not who is right.

Section 1. PREAMBLE

The mobility of employment and capital is making business increasingly global in its transactions and its effects. Laws and market forces in such a context are necessary but insufficient guides for conduct.

Responsibility for a corporation's actions and policies and respect for the dignity and interests of its stakeholders are fundamental. And shared values, including a commitment to shared prosperity, are as important for a global community as for communities of smaller scale. For all of the above reasons, and because business can be a powerful agent of positive social change, we offer the following principles as a foundation for dialogue and action by business leaders in search of corporate responsibility. In so doing, we affirm the legitimacy and centrality of moral values in economic decision making because, without them, stable business relationships and a sustainable world community are impossible.

Section 2. GENERAL PRINCIPLES

Principle 1. The Responsibilities of Corporations: Beyond Shareholders toward Stakeholders

The role of a corporation is to create wealth and employment, and to provide marketable products and services to consumers at a reasonable price commensurate with quality. To play this role, the corporation must maintain its own economic health and viability, but its own survival is not an end in itself. The corporation also has a role to play in improving the lives of all of its customers, employees, and shareholders by sharing with them the wealth it has created. Suppliers and competitors as well should expect businesses to honor their obligations in a spirit of honesty and fairness. And as responsible citizens of the local, national, regional, and global communities in which they operate, corporations share a part in shaping the future of those communities.

Principle 2. The Economic and Social Impact of Corporations: Toward Innovation, Justice and World Community

Corporations established in foreign countries to develop, produce, or sell should also contribute to the social advancement of those countries by creating jobs and helping to raise their purchasing power. They should also give attention to and contribute to human rights, education, and welfare, the vitalization of communities in the countries in which they operate. Moreover, through innovation, effective and prudent use of resources, and free and fair competition, corporations should contribute to the economic and social development of the world community at large, not only the countries in which they operate. New technology, production, products, marketing, and communication are all means to this broader contribution.

Principle 3. Corporate Behavior: Beyond the Letter of Law toward a Spirit of Trust

With the exception of legitimate trade secrets, a corporation should recognize that sincerity, candor, truthfulness, the keeping of promises, and transparency contribute not only to the credit and stability of business activities but also to the smoothness and efficiency of business transactions, particularly on the international level.

Principle 4. Respect for Rules: Beyond Trade Friction toward Cooperation

To avoid trade frictions and promote freer trade, equal business opportunity, and fair and equitable treatment for all participants, corporations should respect international and domestic rules. In addition, they should recognize that their own behavior, although legal, may still have adverse consequences.

Principle 5. Support for Multilateral Trade: Beyond Isolation toward World Community

Corporations should support the multilateral trade system of GATT/World Trade Organization and similar international agreements. They should cooperate in efforts to promote the judicious liberalization of trade, and to relax those domestic measures that unreasonably hinder global commerce.

Principle 6. Respect for the Environment: Beyond Protection toward Enhancement

A corporation should protect, and where possible, improve the environment, promote sustainable development, and prevent the wasteful use of natural resources.

Principle 7. Avoidance of Illicit Operations: Beyond Profit toward Peace

A corporation should not participate in or condone bribery, money laundering, and other corrupt practices. It should not trade in arms or materials used for terrorist activities, drug traffic, or other organized crime.

Section 3. STAKEHOLDER PRINCIPLES

CUSTOMERS. We believe in treating all customers with dignity and that our customers are not only those who directly purchase our products and services but also those who acquire them through authorized market channels. In cases where those who use our products and services do not purchase them directly from us, we will make our best effort to select marketing and assembly/manufacturing channels that accept and follow the standards of business conduct articulated here. We have a responsibility:

* to provide our customers with the highest quality products and services consistent with their requirements;
* to treat our customers fairly in all aspects of our business transactions, including a high level of service and remedies for customer dissatisfaction;
* to make every effort to ensure that the health and safety (including environmental quality) of our customers will be sustained or enhanced by our products or services;
* to avoid disrespect for human dignity in products offered, marketing, and advertising; and
* to respect the integrity of the cultures of our customers.

EMPLOYEES. We believe in the dignity of every employee and we, therefore, have a responsibility:

* to provide jobs and compensation that improve and uplift workers' circumstances in life;
* to provide working conditions that respect employees' health and dignity;
* to be honest in communications with employees and open in sharing information, limited only by legal and competitive constraints;
* to be accessible to employee input, ideas, complaints, and requests;
* to engage in good faith negotiations when conflict arises;
* to avoid discriminatory practices and to guarantee equal

treatment and opportunity in areas such as gender, age, race, and religion;

* to promote in the corporation itself the employment of handicapped and other disadvantaged people in places of work where they can be genuinely useful;
* to protect employees from avoidable injury and illness in the workplace.;
* to be sensitive to the serious unemployment problems frequently associated with business decisions and to work with governments and other agencies in addressing these dislocations.

OWNERS/INVESTORS. We believe in honoring the trust our investors place in us. We, therefore, have a responsibility:

* to apply professional and diligent management in order to secure a fair and competitive return on our owners' investment;
* to disclose relevant information to owners/investors subject only to legal and competitive constraints;
* to conserve and protect the owners/investors' assets; and
* to respect owner/investor' requests, suggestions, complaints, and formal resolutions.

SUPPLIERS. We begin with the conviction that our relationship with suppliers and subcontractors, like a partnership, must be based on mutual respect. As a result, we have a responsibility:

* to seek fairness in all our activities including pricing, licensing, and rights to sell;
* to ensure that our business activities are free from coercion and unnecessary litigation, thus promoting fair competition;
* to foster long-term stability in the supplier relationship in return for value, quality, and reliability;
* to share information with suppliers and integrate them into our planning processes in order to achieve stable relationships;
* to pay suppliers on time and in accordance with agreed terms of trade; and

✳ to seek, encourage, and prefer suppliers and subcontractors whose employment practices respect human dignity.

COMPETITORS. We believe that fair economic competition is one of the basic requirements for increasing the wealth of nations and ultimately for making possible the just distribution of goods and services. We, therefore, have responsibilities:

✳ to foster open markets for trade and investment;
✳ to promote competitive behavior that is socially and environmentally beneficial, and demonstrates mutual respect among competitors;
✳ to refrain from either seeking or participating in questionable payments or favors to secure competitive advantages;
✳ to respect both material and intellectual property rights; and
✳ to refuse to acquire commercial information by dishonest or unethical means, such as industrial espionage.

COMMUNITIES. We believe that as global corporate citizens we can contribute, even to a small extent, to such forces of reform and human rights as are at work in the communities in which we operate. We, therefore, have responsibilities in the communities in which we do business:

✳ to respect human rights and democratic institutions, and to promote them wherever practical;
✳ to recognize government's legitimate obligation to the society at large, and to support public policies and practices that promote human development through harmonious relations between business and other segments of society;
✳ to collaborate in countries and areas which struggle in their economic development with those forces which are dedicated to raising standards of health, education, and workplace safety;
✳ to promote and stimulate sustainable development;
✳ to play a lead role in preserving the physical environment and conserving the earth's resources;
✳ to support peace, security, and diversity in local communities;
✳ to respect the integrity of local cultures; and

✳ to be a good citizen by supporting the communities in which it operates; this can be done through such actions and activities as charitable donations, educational and cultural contributions, and employee participation in community and civic affairs.

Bridging East and West in Management Ethics:
Kyosei and the Moral Point of View

Kenneth E. Goodpaster

Abstract

In this article, I examine two broad ideals, or "umbrella" concepts, in management ethics, one Eastern and one Western, with an eye toward explaining their fundamental similarities. Beyond questions of meaning and conceptual analysis, however, are questions of implementation. Institutionalizing an ethical orientation – Eastern or Western – is the theme of the last part of the chapter. Different approaches to institutionalization are discussed and a strategy is suggested for making the "umbrella" concepts part of the operating systems of organizations.

My objective in this discussion is to highlight what I believe is a conceptual bridge between Eastern and Western ethical thinking, with a view to facilitating a second bridge, between these basic ideals and their application in organizational decision making. I will begin with the Japanese concept of *Kyosei* and then examine the Western idea of the *"Moral Point of View,"* before turning to application questions.

The Concept of *Kyosei*

The Chairman of Canon, Inc., Ryuzaburo Kaku, has proposed a unifying concept that he believes can serve as a core for the development of business ethics as we enter the twenty-first century. The concept is *kyosei*, symbolized by the two Kanji characters 'kyo' (working together) and 'sei' (life). *Kyosei* can best be defined using several excerpts from Mr. Kaku's recent speeches:

- ❑ "What must be done to ensure happiness for humankind is an eternal question. Kyosei is the answer to this question."
- ❑ "Kyosei provides the concept of living together as we learn to tolerate diverse cultures and to accept their differences."

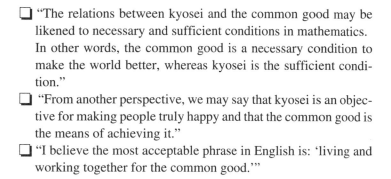

❑ "The relations between kyosei and the common good may be
likened to necessary and sufficient conditions in mathematics.
In other words, the common good is a necessary condition to
make the world better, whereas kyosei is the sufficient condition."

❑ "From another perspective, we may say that kyosei is an objective for making people truly happy and that the common good is
the means of achieving it."

❑ "I believe the most acceptable phrase in English is: 'living and
working together for the common good.'"

These observations about *kyosei* illustrate the subtle complexity of the
concept. Consider the strands of meaning presented. One connotation of
kyosei is the notion of a social *goal*, true happiness or the common good.
Another connotation is a kind of respect or tolerance for cultural differences and diversity (*fairness*). Yet a third strand of meaning is a valuing
of *community,* illustrated in the references to "living and working together."[1]

Kyosei takes us beyond conventional business thinking (markets
and laws) to a comprehensive aspiration for happiness, justice, and cooperation. In practice, we must assume, this means tempering individual, organizational, and even national self-interest by concern for more
embracing "common goods," and tempering the assertion of narrower
entitlements by a concern for more basic rights (e.g., liberty and equality) in a just society. Market forces and government regulations are important disciplines for corporate decision making, but they are not
enough.

We should notice, however, that *kyosei* is an integrative concept in
two ways. Firstly, it seeks to integrate the three strands of meaning mentioned above. But secondly, it has application across several *levels* of
analysis as well – to global society as a whole, to the more local (national, regional) society surrounding the corporation, to the organization
itself as a micro society, or even to subgroups within the organization.
Like the triad of "prosperity, justice, and community," *kyosei* ramifies
and can manifest itself on levels ranging from humanity as a whole to
"wherever two or three are gathered together." As an imperative for
business philosophy, *kyosei* represents what Kaku describes as a fourth
stage of evolution, beyond the first three stages of pure self-interest,

concern for employees, and concern for relatively local stakeholders, respectively.[2]

Kyosei and the *Moral Point of View*

Western moral philosophy in the modern period can be seen as a search for the meaning and justification of *morality*, the *moral point of view*. Harvard philosopher Josiah Royce described the foundation of the moral point of view, what he called *the moral insight,* in his book *The Religious Aspect of Philosophy* (1905):

> The moral insight is the realization of one's neighbor, in the full sense of the word realization; the resolution to treat him unselfishly. But this resolution expresses and belongs to the moment of insight. Passion may cloud the insight after no very long time. It is as impossible for us to avoid the illusion of selfishness in our daily lives, as to escape seeing through the illusion at the moment of insight. We see the reality of our neighbor, that is, we determine to treat him as we do ourselves. But then we go back to daily action, and we feel the heat of hereditary passions, and we straightway forget what we have seen. Our neighbor becomes obscured. He is once more a foreign power. He is unreal. We are again deluded and selfish. This conflict goes on and will go on as long as we live after the manner of men. Moments of insight, with their accompanying resolutions; long stretches of delusion and selfishness: That is our life.

This quotation reminds us that a theme of Western moral philosophy has been an emotional and intellectual escape from the "illusion" of egocentrism or selfishness. Indeed, one way to read modern ethical theory in the West is as a series of challenges to the basic proposition that the governing force in human conduct is self-interest.

Eighteenth-century British philosopher Thomas Hobbes argued in *Leviathan* that self-interest was both motivationally and ethically the supreme principle of conduct, and that because of this principle, men come together to form a powerful state to protect themselves from the "war of all against all." Without such a sovereign power, the life of man would be "solitary, poor, nasty, brutish, and short."

Three major challenges to this ethical principle have been presented over the last few centuries, each mindful that the motivational significance of self-interest is not to be understated, but each convinced also that it is not overriding. The driving force behind these challenges has been a conviction that the dictates of conscience in human life ask more of us than the dictates of the other principles in question. One consequence of these philosophical debates has been a "shaping" of the Western idea of the *moral point of view*. As we shall see, the resulting contours of this "shaping" relate directly to the idea of *kyosei*.

The first challenge to self-interest came from those who argued that *interests* were indeed the correct touchstones of morality, but that the *self*, even in the longer run, provided too narrow a measure of which interests to care about. This challenge has taken several forms, depending on the extension of the class of ethically significant interests. The interests might extend to the family or the clan or the tribe, leaving "outsiders" out of consideration. Some defended the nation state or the region as the boundary of significant interests. The utilitarians in the nineteenth century went further, insisting that *all* human beings, not just some, be considered. Indeed, some went further still, to include all *sentient* beings, creatures capable of experiencing pleasure or pain. The main point to be made in this connection is that one of the dynamics of moral theory consisted in expanding the class of *interests* to be considered in decision making.

But there was another dynamic at work simultaneously, as the "interest-based" philosophers were having their debates over expansion. This dynamic challenged the adequacy of interests themselves, no matter how narrowly or widely conceived, as the foundation for ethical thought. Oversimplifying somewhat, and attributing this challenge to German philosopher Immanuel Kant, we can say that the second wave of criticism focused on the dignity of the individual person and the rights and liberties to which that dignity gave rise.

Simply basing one's ethical choices on interests, *even universal interests,* these critics argued, might permit the greater good of the many to excuse atrocities directed at the few. Some basic principle of justice or fairness was required in order to assert the legitimate claims of the individual person against the will of the many, even in democratic societies.

Such thinking gave rise in the American constitutional debate to the "Bill of Rights" as a protection against certain possible abuses of majority power. The core insight of this second wave of moral theorizing was that *expansion of interests considered* was not sufficient to capture the moral point of view. A second dynamic was called for, what we might call the impulse to *expand the claims of the individual* in the face of the claims of the majority.

A third wave of criticism was born of the first two waves by calling into question what both of them had in common – a strong focus on the individual (either by way of interests or by way of rights) as the principal bearer of value.[3] In the work of philosophers F. H. Bradley (British) and Josiah Royce (American) at the turn of the twentieth century, we see a clear emphasis on the community as a whole, rather than the individual, as the locus of value. Bradley built his ethical theory on *"My Station and Its Duties,"* while Royce made *loyalty* the central principle of his moral philosophy.[4]

Expanding the *interests considered* was the impulse of the "interest-based" moralists and expanding the *rights protected* was the impulse of the "rights-based" moralists. The new wave of ethical critique had as its source an impulse toward expanding the *communities served*, toward shared communal goods which are more than sums of the individual fortunes that participate in them. It was "duty-based."[5]

This third wave, it should be mentioned, was a critique not only of interests and rights as the sole bases of ethical thought, but it was a caution about the adequacy of "stakeholder" thinking in general. Since contemporary business ethics is often characterized as "stakeholder" ethics, this point might lead us to explore the territory "beyond" stakeholder thinking.[6]

What can we learn from this brief review of the search for *meaning* and *justification* in Western ethics? Two things, I believe. First, that definition has proved itself to be *elusive* – perhaps as some have argued[7] – impossible. Second, that the impulse of ethical reflection, even if it is not easy to define, is toward *expansion or inclusiveness along several dimensions: interests, rights, and communities.*

Bridging Ideals: Congruence between East and West

Recalling the three strands of meaning that we found in the Japanese concept of *kyosei* (the pursuit of happiness or prosperity, the concern for justice or fairness, and the affirmation of community), it is clear that the Western search for the *moral point of view* includes very similar elements in its history. This congruence in the "deep structure" of the two concepts makes the metaphor of a bridge seem appropriate. It is implausible to suggest that Eastern and Western ethical ideas are so culturally alien that ethical dialogue is impossible, that traffic between them cannot lead to practical consensus.

It may be that as Eastern moral thought seeks to recover the individual in its traditional affirmation of the common good or the social whole,

Western moral thought seeks to recover the social whole in its traditional affirmation of the individual. The basis for bridge-building lies precisely in this complementarity.[8]

As we reflect on the meaning of *kyosei* in the context of global business organizations, we might benefit from noticing the patterns in the West that have preceded it on the scene, and we might be mindful of some of the *partial* interpretations that might be substituted for it. For if *kyosei* is understood to mean an expanded attention to *interests*, then it will need to confront those who would charge that it is inattentive to *rights*. If it is understood to mean an expansion of attention to rights, then it will need to confront those who would charge that it is inattentive to larger duties of loyalty to a whole community.

As I understand it, *kyosei* (like the *moral point of view*) is not to be identified with any one of these logics of moral thinking, but with some kind of balanced blend of all three. I find these attractive ideals, but ideals that make precise *definition* a problem and, therefore, rigorous *application* difficult.[9]

A Different Bridge: From Ethical Ideals to Action

Concurrent with the pursuit of meaning and justification in ethics (Eastern and Western), there has been a second pursuit to find ways of taking moral ideals and values from the realm of *aspiration* to the realms of *policy, practice, and behavior*. Whatever the outcome of the philosophical dialogue over the basic ideals of human conduct, there has always been this second challenge of bringing ideals (whatever they may be) into action.

Some examples of arenas within which the ideals of *kyosei* and the *moral point of view* might be expected to manifest themselves in the decision making of the organization are:

* Unemployment and retraining of employees whose jobs are made redundant by technological and competitive pressures;
* Environmental impacts of corporate production including pollution, conservation of resources, and preservation of biological species;
* Work and family issues, including the impact of work demands on marriage relationships, the education of children, physical and mental health, and social harmony;
* The efficiency of wealth production alongside the justice of

    wealth distribution in local, national, regional, and international communities; and

    * The use of advertising messages to mislead or misinform potential customers who are vulnerable in various ways, especially in less developed countries.

Historically, there have been several strategies for building a bridge from ideals to action, but let us here focus on three: *dictation, surrogation*, and *institutionalization*.[10]

The first strategy consists of an authority figure dictating a set of rules, along with some guidelines for interpretation. Fascism is one extreme example of such a view, but so is the "dictatorship of the proletariat" in Marx, at least in Communist practice. Penalties for disobedience or noncompliance are enforced firmly, and behavior (often because of fear) is influenced. In effect, the bridge between ethics and practice becomes the will of the one in power, the will of the strongest.[11]

A second strategy consists in identifying *systemic substitutes* for our moral ideals *(kyosei* or the *moral point of view)* different from the will of any individual authority figure. Adam Smith looked for such a substitute in what he called the "invisible hand" of the free market system. Locke and Rousseau found a substitute in the "visible hand" of the government, whether in the executive, legislative, or judicial branches.

What all of these strategies have in common is reliance upon a *process*, either economic or political, to act as a *surrogate* for the realization of our moral principles and ideals. It is as if they do not trust the leadership of organizations or the insights of ordinary people with the capacity to build the bridge to action; or to shift the metaphor: it is as if they insist that flying the airplane of morality cannot be trusted to the captain, it must be governed by a surrogate captain – an autopilot.

The third strategy I will call *institutionalization*. It is the one I believe is the most acceptable. There are two types: *macro*-institutionalization and *micro*-institutionalization. *Macro*-institutionlization means creating support systems between and among organizations willing to self-impose *kyosei,* or *moral* principles. Association among such organizations may be essential if the risks of unilateral adoption of such ideals are to be minimized. The Caux Roundtable Principles of Business Conduct and the support system implicit among organizations endorsing these principles are an example of macro-institutionalization in action.[12]

By *micro*-institutionalization, I mean the creation of an organizational analogue to personal discipline and learning. I mean a sequence of activities designed:

* to articulate a corporate philosophy,
* to assign special responsibility for transforming it into action,
* to educate employees about its meaning,
* to audit operations with attention to conflicts between the corporate philosophy and other organizational incentives that undermine it,
* to report on difficult cases to the corporate leadership, so that finally
* re-integration and clear communication can be restored.

The essential nature of this process is that it involves ethical "flying," consciously, not simply by automatic pilot. This approach acknowledges the authority of leadership, the importance of market signals, and the validity of governmental regulation. But it goes further. It seeks to carry ideals into action and to sustain their presence as guiding influences by creating an organizational cycle of communication – *articulating, educating, listening, reflecting,* and, if necessary, *revising* espoused values in view of the realities of the decision-making environment.

These measures foster a *living conversation* between employees and executives, and if we reflect on the ideals of *kyosei* and the *moral point of view* – living and working together for the common good – we may be persuaded that the best way to apply ideals lies not in dictation or surrogation, but in institutionalization. The challenge for corporations that would build this bridge is to undertake alliances (externally) and foster moral conversation (internally). These are the principal defenses against competitive forces (outside) and hypocrisy (inside) that might lead a company to abandon its ethical ideals.

In summary, *kyosei* and the *moral point of view* offer broad ethical ideals that are congruent with one another in their deep structure. Each seems to be anchored in three avenues of ethical reflection: interest-based, rights-based, and duty-based thinking. Each also finds application on multiple levels, e.g., family, group, organization, state, region, and globe. When we bridge from these ideals to *action*, the most promising path lies not in dictating or relying on surrogates, but in what we have called *institutionalization* (internal as well as external). Let us hope that this broad foundation for dialogue between Eastern and Western thought can lead to improved business and government behavior in the twenty-first century.

Table below illustrates the ideals and applications discussed in the chapter.

	KYOSEI and the MORAL POINT OF VIEW	*Meaning and Justification of Ethical Ideals*		
		Interest-based *(Prosperity)*	Rights-based *(Fairness)*	Duty-based *(Community)*
Applying	Dictation			
	Surrogation			
Ethical	Institutionalization			
Principles	*Macro . . .* *and* *Micro . . .*			

Endotes

1. As characterized by Kaku, *kyosei* includes the core values of: (1) social well-being or prosperity, (2) respect for diversity or justice, and (3) community. It calls not only for working toward prosperity, but also the fair distribution of resources in a society, and the realization of community or social cohesion.

2. Kaku's fourth stage corresponds rather directly to the "Type 3" mind-set described in Kenneth E. Goodpaster's "Ethical Imperatives and Corporate Leadership," reprinted in *Ethics in Practice,* Kenneth Andrews, editor, Harvard Business School Press (1991), 212–222.

3. To be sure, interest-based and rights-based ethical thinking sought to extend and universalize beyond attention solely to the self, but in the end, ethical reflection was *atomic* in its approach to making ethical decisions. Morality was a function solely of the benefits or harms to the interests and rights of individuals.

4. Royce was introduced above in connection with the "moral insight." Bradley, writing in 1876, made his point in the language of community: "To the assertion . . . that selves are 'individual' in the sense of exclusive of other selves, we oppose the (equally justified) assertion that this is a mere fancy. We say that, out of theory, no such individual men exist; and we will try to show from fact that what we call an individual man is what he is because of and by virtue of

community, and that communities are thus not mere names but something real..."

5. We might recall in this context John F. Kennedy's inaugural address: "Ask not what America can do for you, my fellow Americans, but what you can do for America." Even though it is clothed in somewhat nationalistic garments, this exhortation goes beyond interests and rights.

6. Note that this is also a Western source of what we saw earlier in the *kyosei* concept as another kind of integration – ethical attention to nested *levels* of community.

7. For example, British philosopher G.E. Moore in his classic work *Principia Ethica*.

8. Such an interpretation of the Eastern and Western ethical mind-sets certainly fits with this author's experience in helping negotiate the operating philosophy behind the Caux Roundtable Principles for Business Conduct. *"Kyosei"* from the Japanese side was eventually joined with personal *"dignity"* from the European side to form the foundation of the principles.

9. I believe I understood Mr. Kaku to be suggesting this interpretation in October, 1994 in Washington, D.C. at a conference sponsored by the Center for Strategic and International Studies (CSIS).

10. Philip Selznick, in his classic book on leadership, wrote in 1959 that: "There is a close relation between 'infusion with value' and 'self-maintenance.' As an organization acquires a self, a distinctive identity, it becomes an institution. This involves the taking on of values, ways of acting and believing that are deemed important for their own sake. From then on self-maintenance becomes more than bare organizational survival; it becomes a struggle to preserve the uniqueness of the group in the face of new problems and altered circumstances." *(Leadership in Administration* [1959], 21–22)

11. The cover story in *Business Week* (October 9, 1995) was entitled "Blind Ambition," and it described the problems currently being faced by *Bausch & Lombe* because its Chief Executive Officer dictated commands without checking out their concrete implications in the world of work. In many ways, this story parallels that of the H.J. Heinz company written a decade or more ago. Both involve fixation, rationalization, and eventual indifference to the lives of subordinates caught in this kind of trap.

12. The work of the Caux Roundtable – in particular its development of the Principles for Business Conduct – is an important step in the direction of identifying arenas in which corporate ideals most need to be carried into action. The Caux Roundtable Principles are reprinted in the previous chapter.

Some Arguments for Universal Moral Standards

Norman Bowie and Paul Vaaler

Abstract

This chapter provides an economic rationale for the observed fact that many multinational corporations adopt the same ethical standards in host countries as they adhere to in home countries. But are these standards really ethical? Using the notion of market morality, the authors argue that certain moral norms will tend to be adopted due to the competitive forces generated by private and public individuals participating in national and global markets. The chapter concludes by considering various objections to the analysis and by providing some qualifications.

Introduction

Perhaps the most controversial issue in international business ethics focuses on the following question: When in Rome do you do as the Romans do? One expedient and perhaps "politically correct" response is to say that multinational corporations (MNCs) should be respectful of host country moral norms and act consistently with them. After all, an MNC should not be a cultural imperialist, should it?

In this chapter, the authors argue that certain common standards of ethical conduct ought to be adopted by an MNC and, in fact, will be adopted by the MNC. The argument is laid out in two steps. The first step of the argument is to show that, contrary to what might be expected, an MNC will seek to impose its own standards of ethical conduct on the overseas operations it owns or controls. If that argument is successful, it will be shown that for many MNCs, when in Rome, one ought not to do as the Romans do. The next step in the argument is to show how such universal moral standards are derived and applied in several instances. If successful, it will be shown in this second step how an MNC identifies those ethical standards to apply in Rome irrespective of what the Romans do.

At the core of the argument about universal standards is the concept of a "market morality": a set of generally observed norms practiced by MNCs in the global economy. The set of norms suggests how issues of right and wrong, and good and bad, are to be assessed by the MNC independent of the locale where it is transacting business. This set of norms serves as the fundamental basis for an MNC to decide when in Rome or anywhere else, what is appropriate ethical practice. But almost surely the Romans and other critics of our universalist view will raise objections. The authors conclude the article by trying to anticipate some of their objections and by replying to them in advance. The aim of this paper is not simply to articulate an argument contrary to those who might counsel MNCs to follow local ethical standards – let's call the alternative to our universalist view a "cultural relativist" view. This contribution is also meant to provoke discussion among business ethicists and managers about alternative ways to connect MNC value-judgments and ethical practices with MNC survival and profitability in an increasingly global economy.

Why Universal Moral Standards Emerge in the MNCs

The first step concerns the rationale for the emergence of a universal ethical practice within the MNC. The rationale for refraining from cultural relativism and setting a single set of standards in the MNC follows this logic:

1. Certain ethical commitments are believed by management of an MNC to provide the MNC with competitive advantages.
2. Those ethical commitments providing durable competitive advantages abroad tend to be knowledge-based, to be embodied in employees or in MNC routines, and tend to be utilized in transactions with high "asset specificity."
3. Highly specific assets associated with high returns from transactions abroad should not be diluted.
4. Ethical commitments are such assets and therefore should not be diluted.
5. When ethical commitments vary among operations owned or controlled by the MNC, such assets will be diluted due to the phenomenon of cognitive dissonance.
6. Therefore, the MNC should have common ethical commitments in all of the operations it owns or controls.

Ethical Standards and Competitive Advantage

For too often the ethical commitments of an MNC are viewed as costs when in fact many such commitments enhance the bottom line. To demonstrate this point and, by implication, Premise 1 of our argument, we first need to define what is meant by a commitment. We have in mind Ghemawat's (1991) notion of commitment as irreversible investment. Think, for instance, of investments in individual employee training, accommodation, and personal growth. The MNC often makes such investments with knowledge that such individuals could "walk away" with this value-added to another firm. In terms of benefits from ethical commitments, we have in mind investments that, for instance, help to solve agency problems, lower transaction costs, and increase trust within and between organizations.

Agency problems result when a principal cannot effectively monitor an agent to ensure that the agent puts the interests of the principal before the agent's. Identifying and hiring trustworthy agents lowers the costs of monitoring. Transaction costs include such items as lawyers, security systems, and credit checks. Entering transactions with trustworthy agents obviously lowers transaction costs since fewer protective systems will be needed. There is something like a reciprocal relationship between honesty and trust. Honesty among stakeholders of the MNC promotes trust and increasing trust reinforces honesty in a kind of virtuous circle. Indeed, building trustworthy relationships will enhance firm profitability. For example, if MNC stakeholders have sufficient trust that all parties are truthful, there will be less budget inflation as divisions seek capital. Less budget inflation means less negotiation with a resulting reduction in transaction costs. Even academics know how wasteful the annual department budget negotiations with deans can be. More honesty cuts waste in any organization.

In an era when international production is frequently conducted within multi-firm strategic alliances, honesty and trust take on even greater importance. Trusting relationships among allies allow them to, for instance, specialize in joint research and development efforts and raise the overall quality of their products and services. General Motors (GM) did not seem to understand this fundamental point when in the early 1990s they brought in Jose Ignacio Lopez to oversee relationships with GM's various suppliers. Lopez intended to lower GM's costs by breaking supplier contracts and sharing their proprietary information with competitors. Lopez continued his opportunistic behavior with stakeholders when he left GM for Volkswagen and allegedly took several cartons of proprietary GM information. Of course, bad faith and misappropriation do not go unpunished. By 1997, Lopez has left Volkswagen, the German automaker is paying a legal settlement to GM of approximately $100 million, and GM was recently ranked worst by suppliers among the big three U.S. automakers (*Wall Street Journal* 1993a, 1993b, 1993c, 1996). In this type of environment, what incentives do suppliers or other potential allies have to work cooperatively with a manufacturer to improve quality?

Ethical Standards and Tacit Knowledge

Premise 2 of our argument points out that the ethical commitments of the MNC, what we might call collectively the MNC's ethical climate, tend to be knowledge-based and embodied in individual employees or in organizational routines. As a result, the ethical climate is rather difficult to replicate and thus a source of durable competitive advantage. One way to illustrate this point is by distinguishing between ethical codes as written and as actually practiced. A written code of ethics may be easily copied and communicated to rival firms, but offering another firm's written code of ethics to an MNC with a poor ethical climate may avail the recipient very little. It is extremely difficult for one organization to recreate the environment of moral reflection and behavior that another organization was able to employ on an earlier occasion. We can see this point in comparing the behavior of Ashland Oil to Exxon with respect to oil spills. The responsiveness and candor of Ashland Oil in dealing with the 1988 oil spill at Floreffe, Pennsylvania[1] contrasts sharply with the failure of Exxon to respond quickly and candidly to the Exxon Valdez oil spill in Cook Inlet, Alaska later that same year. Apparently, Exxon learned nothing from the public relations success of Ashland.

Our distinction between written codes and actual behavior should suggest the tacit nature of ethical climate within the MNC. This important asset is found in the heads of MNC personnel and in organizational routines. As a knowledge-based asset, ethical climate has special qualities that a firm must consider when attempting to exploit it in competition with other firms abroad. Ethical climate cannot easily be sold or traded abroad with another firm. It is hard to reduce the nature of the asset to writing. Even if it were possible to describe the asset, it might be difficult to convey to a foreign buyer with adequate confidence the full value of the asset. In short, attempts to sell or trade ethical climate among firms frequently falls victim to market failure.

Add to this problem an additional complication: opportunism. Assets like ethical climate may provide the basis for cooperative arrangements among firms. Think again about strategic alliances where one firm enters a foreign market based on the reputation of its partner. But the partner may be tempted to "waste" this reputation, by selling substandard goods. In these situations, customers can hold *both* members of the alliance liable for this deception. Because of problems of market failure and opportunism, we frequently observe firms with a favorable ethical climate choosing to enter a foreign market in modes that give it greater control over the operation; that means entering foreign markets with wholly-owned subsidiaries and majority-owned joint ventures. By going abroad through these "internal" modes, the MNC can control assets that are highly specific to the intended business transactions (Hennart 1988).

Ethical Standards and Dissonance

We have described the economic rationale for internalized operations abroad: market failure and opportunism associated with transactions utilizing the MNC's ethical climate. These factors would otherwise dilute the value of the MNC's valuable asset. Even with internalized modes of expansion abroad, the MNC could dilute the value of an ethical climate by allowing it to vary across operations. This claim takes us to Premises 4 and 5 of our argument above. Cognitive dissonance provides one explanation for this second threat of dilution. This well established psychological phenomenon suggests that if the MNC has one set of ethical standards in the home country and different standards in host countries, MNC stakeholders will not know which values, beliefs, and behaviors really represent the organization. The ethical climate of the MNC will become confused and the competitive advantage it confers will weaken.

The problem of varying standards becomes acute as employees within the organization move about the host country operations more frequently. Service in law, accounting, and management consulting provide paradigmatic examples of "knowledge-intensive" firms relying on the ability to move people and know-how rapidly, effectively, and globally. Consider how a policy of cultural relativism might frustrate transfers of know-how embodied in individual members and teams. When an MNC operates in a host country that discriminates against women, it frustrates the organization's ability to transfer tacit know-how there if embodied in a female lawyer, accountant, or management consultant. The dissonance in values such a policy produces may also frustrate the MNC's ability to train and retain female employees in other locales. To prevent the negative consequences of cognitive dissonance, the ethical climate of the MNC should include standards that are applied universally, that is, in both the home and host country operations. If the MNC does not tolerate discrimination of women at home, then it will not anywhere abroad as well.

Ethical Standards and Strategic Implications

We realize that this analysis may seem counter-intuitive. Suppose the home country norms vary widely from host country norms. Wouldn't the MNC be likely to fail if it practiced home country norms that were at wide variance with those in the host country? Quite possibly. Customers may not buy their product. When such situations occur, the MNC must consider how important its ethical climate really is. If this asset is truly vital, then it would be better for the MNC not to do business in that country than to weaken itself.

Although many MNCs do not behave this way, probably because they do not value their ethical climate assets so highly, some do. Levi-Strauss provides one example. Conventional wisdom might consider Levi-Strauss's decision to exit China and Myanmar (Burma) because of human rights violations there to be foolish. After all, the firm is leaving one of the major markets of the world. We disagree with the conventional wisdom. Levi-Strauss recognizes that it cannot maintain a commitment to basic human rights and thereby to its basic moral integrity while simultaneously doing business in a country that commits human rights violations. Levi-Strauss places a high value on its reputation as socially responsible MNC (Haas 1994).

The first part of our argument is complete. We have shown that good business reasons often indicate that an MNC should have the same ethical climate abroad as it has at home. Its reputation as a socially responsible MNC is a valuable asset and should not be lightly given up.

What Universal Moral Standards Will Emerge in the MNCs

A critic of our approach could point out that the universalism we defend is rather limited. It counsels only consistency in standards without saying anything about the substantive nature of such standards. This "firm-specific" universalism would be satisfied if, say, an MNC consistently discriminated against women in all of its operations. A broader, "philosophical" universalism might not tolerate this outcome, since it also implies the existence of certain substantive values for the MNC to uphold.

How then can we ensure that MNCs adopt a moral climate with the appropriate set of standards? To answer this question, we appeal to the concept of a market morality. It is the set of ethical norms that the vast majority of MNCs would attempt to practice because, other things being equal, adopting such moral practices are either necessary for economic survival or confer advantages that enhance the MNC's prospects for success.

The position we will take below can be outlined in the three additional points below:

7. Certain ethical commitments are either necessary for the MNCs economic success or provide it with a competitive advantage.
8. Other things being equal, market forces will compel MNCs to adopt these ethical commitments in order to enhance prospects for continued survival and profitability.
9. Other things being equal, market forces will promote the development of a common core of ethical standards. All MNCs will tend to adopt a set of identical ethical standards (although this does not preclude MNCs from adopting ethical standards that exceed the core standards common to all MNCs).

Substantive Standards I: Bribery

Let us examine how and why two ethical proscriptions will emerge in an MNC subject to market forces: bribery and discrimination. First, we'll examine the case of bribery, which is something different from extortion payments and facilitating payments. The chief difference between bribery and extortion is who does the initiating of the act. A corporation pays a bribe when it offers to pay or provide favors to a person or persons of trust to influence the latter's judgment. A corporation pays extortion money when it yields to a demand for money in order to have accomplished what it has a legal right to accomplish without the payment. The difference between extortion and a facilitating payment is in many respects a matter of degree. Facilitating payments are not made to obtain or retain business but rather to expedite business activity by a rather low-level government employee. The argument here applies only to bribery. Bribery is always economically inefficient. When bribery influences a transaction, the decision is not based on grounds of quality and/or price. The MNC offering a bribe cannot compete on either ground; if it could, there would be no point to offering the bribe. Thus on strictly economic terms, other things being equal, a firm offering bribes will eventually be forced to exit. A company or public organization accepting a bribe is being paid to purchase products that are inferior on grounds of quality and or price. The consumer gets lower quality, higher prices, and in the long run she should reject such products. Other things being equal, a company taking bribes will perform persistently below those firms that do not take bribes, and in the long term, persistently poor performing firms will exit.

For MNCs, a common issue is how to behave in countries where bribery is the norm. If this practice were common, our argument above breaks down. If nearly everyone accepts and pays bribes in a given country, no firm will be able to find a niche as a "non-briber." Indeed, bribing firms and governmental organizations will find it difficult to do business with a non-briber. This set of relationships will not promote efficient intra-country trade. In making a decision regarding how to deal with bribery, MNCs will realize that as the frequency of bribery increases, the terms of trade worsen there. At the extreme, MNCs may decide to forgo operations in a country where such practices are practiced. On the other hand, in instances short of the extreme, the MNC may be in a position to encourage changes in such norms.

Take the example of Italy and MNCs operating there as an illustration. *Business Week* (1993) pointed out how corruption inflated Italy's outstanding government debt in 1993 by 15%, or approximately $200 billion. As a result of the country's crackdown on corruption, bids for public works projects are coming in at 40% below initial cost estimates. MNCs with large shares of certain global industries usually want bribery curtailed. General Electric and Boeing Company provide financial support for Transparency International, an organization dedicated to uprooting corruption in international business transactions. It is probably no accident that MNC ethical codes always include an anti-bribery clause. As information about product prices, quality, and producers becomes more transparent, bribery decreases within a country. And MNCs are not necessarily passive agents in such developments (*Business Week* 1993).

Substantive Standards II: Discrimination

Another substantive standard of ethical practice concerns discrimination, particularly with respect to women. It is allegedly a fact of life in parts of the Mideast, Asia, and Latin America. But the discrimination makes little economic sense, a point made more than 35 years ago by Nobel Laureate economist Milton Friedman:

> There is an economic incentive in a free market to separate economic efficiency from other characteristics of the individual. A businessman or an entrepreneur who expresses preferences in his business activities that are not related to productive efficiency is at a disadvantage compared to other individuals who do not. Such an individual is in effect imposing higher costs on himself than are other individuals who do not have such preferences. Hence in a free market they will tend to drive him out.... The man who objects to buying from or working alongside a Negro, for example, thereby limits his range of choice. He will generally have to pay a higher price for what he buys or receive a lower return for his work. Or, put another way, those who regard color of skin or religion as irrelevant can buy some things more cheaply as a result (Friedman 1960: 109–110).

If Friedman is right, discrimination against women or other groups of individuals puts those countries and the firms it harbors at a competitive disadvantage. But perhaps Friedman's argument is too simple a rationale for proscribing discrimination. It works fine against discrimination based on taste alone. Think again, here, of employers who will not hire women or members of minority groups. Such employers provide no credible economic rationale for this practice. They have no factual basis for claiming that an aspiring employee will be less productive because of her gender, race, religion, or other status, and they consequently operate at a disadvantage relative to others who do not share such tastes.

Suppose, however, that it were true that individuals with blue eyes were less productive than others. In this hypothetical situation, there is, say, a factual statistical basis for the conclusion that blue-eyed individuals are lazy. Here, Friedman's argument will not work as easily. It may not pay to hire blue-eyed people at the same rate as others, or even to hire them at all. Discrimination would pay.

There is certainly a surplus of apocrypha about undesirable traits related to gender, race, religion, and other status distinctions. In some societies, discrimination is not based on individual taste but on widely-held beliefs about the productive strengths and weaknesses of certain groups. What then? In part, the issue turns on whether the belief is true. If false, competitive forces, both public and private in nature, will tend to show that it is false. Consider again, the unfounded basis of discrimination against women, this time in the professions. For years, few American women were physicians, while in the former Soviet Union women constituted a majority of practicing physicians. Public initiatives in the U.S. were, no doubt, partially responsible for subsequent increases in the percentage of female health-care professionals. But private players in the market competing for qualified professionals also played and continue to play an important part. As breakthroughs in transportation, communication, and technology extend the reach of health-care professionals and their firms, the same grinding logic of the market will tend to undercut discrimination overseas as well.

If globalization of industries and the search for higher quality people and products by MNCs engender a common market morality, how soon will this morality emerge? Isolated instances of discrimination abroad persist to date even in the most knowledge-intensive service industries we listed earlier. Will societies tolerating discrimination have a competitive advantage? If other things were equal, perhaps. But other things are not equal. Discrimination carries with it an implicit social cost in terms of tension and even unrest. That cost can, and probably will, swamp any local gains made from discrimination, even forms of discrimination with factual bases. Linkages among national markets made by enterprising governments and enterprising MNCs will promote a consensus against many forms of discriminatory behavior.

Similar arguments could show that keeping contracts and honesty in business relations among MNC stakeholders is also part of the market morality we have begun to articulate. But this article is only a beginning. A larger project of international business ethics is to identify the nature of this market morality in greater detail and assess the direction of its evolution over time. For now, we have chosen to identify elements related to bribery and discrimination to illustrate the type of standards that will emerge in MNCs and the forces promoting that emergence. In demonstrating this, and by implication, demonstrating the three premises at the outset of this section, we have also bridged the gap from claiming that the MNC will exhibit firm-specific universalism – mere consistency in standards without any claim to their substantive nature – to philosophical universalism based on market morality.

Varieties of Capitalism

Capitalism is not a monolith structure. There are a variety of capitalisms including a U.S. Version, a German version, and a Japanese version among others. Is there a market morality for all these versions of capitalism? The authors think the answer to that question is in the affirmative.

Yes, all forms of capitalism are, or will eventually embrace, the norms that encourage or forbid the specific activities described above. Of course, the existence of a market morality leaves room for different norms as well. For example, there is no economic or moral reason for the Germans to change their practice of having union officials on Boards of Directors. Further research will be required before we know if each version of capitalism has its own set of required norms in addition to the norms of the market morality in general.

Objections and Replies

Exceeding the Market Morality

Having attacked the position of cultural relativism in international business ethics, and having tried to establish instead a universalist view based on market morality, let us now turn to some of the critical questions our view may draw. The first such question may concern questions of minima and maxima. Does our identification of a market morality to which MNCs will adhere limit them from exceeding basic imperatives? There are certainly MNCs that adopt standards of ethical conduct that exceed the minimum requirements of the moral minimum. U.S. MNCs may be like the St. Paul, Minnesota-based, specialty chemicals and adhesives manufacturer, H.B. Fuller, which requires their foreign operations to adopt environmental standards that *exceed* those required by local law. Even if there is a minimal floor or a minimal core of norms constituting the market morality, some MNCs will go further.

At first glance, there seems to be no harm in having MNCs exceed moral minima and provide leadership to others participating in a local market. Indeed, as MNCs provide this leadership, local standards stand to improve. Again, when an H.B. Fuller shows that an MNC can be competitively successful and still subscribe to higher principles of environmental protection, the local communities in which it operates will tend to follow. Why would that happen? Every country wants a cleaner environment if it can afford it. MNCs like H.B. Fuller provide a model for how the bill for a cleaner environment can be paid.

Conversely, there is a tendency for socially responsible MNCs to raise their standards to the level of local standards when those local standards are ethically superior. Consider the establishment of Japanese subsidiaries in the U.S. With respect to process innovation on assembly lines, the Japanese transferred organizational technologies to enhance productivity. With respect to corporate social responsibility, the Japanese brought with them a heritage that puts less emphasis on philanthropic giving to address social problems. Once the Japanese began manufacturing in the U.S, however, they also began contributing to non-profit agencies and supported local community initiatives, thus mimicking their U.S. domestic counterparts. The Japanese choose to follow the U.S. norm when in the U.S. Romans take note. Being seen as a socially responsible corporation is an asset in its own right.

The fact that any MNC adopts standards that exceed the core of a commonly held market morality causes neither theoretical nor practical difficulties. Theory allows ethical commitments to exceed the minimum, and even engenders some such commitments. In practice, where local norms exceed the moral minimum, local norms will be competitively attractive. It is interesting to think about how occasional improvements in local ethical norms will contribute to a gradual drift upward in the overall global market morality. Such differences may encourage a competitive "race to the top" of standards observed by the most ethically rigorous MNCs.

The Adequacy of Capitalism

A second objection to the position advocated here points out that there are some moral issues that may not be resolved by reference to a capitalist market morality. They may point to some of the purported excesses of capitalist systems, particularly those in developing countries. There is, for example, nothing to ensure that some MNCs in some countries will not use child labor or pay abysmally low wages in order to gain cost advantages. Critics invoke this sort of argument to show that some MNCs will exploit weak local laws and gain an advantage in the global marketplace to boot. For every H. B. Fuller that exceeds the local standard, there will be another MNC with operations abroad intended to subvert such standards. This scenario reminds us of the enduring need for public as well as private actors. The market morality we have begun to identify will need buttressing with political agreements among nations to prohibit certain types of abuse. Negotiated agreements concerning minimum environmental standards, work conditions, and product as well as process quality will support the development of the market morality.

The Consistency of Our Overall Argument

Our reply to the second objection leads to a third objection, the reply to which concludes this article. Isn't there an inconsistency in our argument for universal standards of ethical conduct in the MNC? In the first section, the authors argued that an individual MNC would apply moral norms universally in its overseas operations due in part to the nature of ethical climate as a competitive asset that is difficult to sell or otherwise transfer to others. In the next section, it is argued that market pressures would engender the adoption of a common core of identical commitments, and that among those commitments, proscriptions against forms of bribery and discrimination would be part. Here's the purported inconsistency: a hard-to-transfer standard for an individual MNC is nonetheless indicative of a global standard around which all MNCs will converge.

We think this criticism is misplaced. The ethical climate enjoyed by one MNC may be replicated. It is simply difficult to do this quickly by means of buying it from another firm. The set of standards that guide the value judgments of MNCs will have to be developed internally and incrementally. This development is measured in terms of investments in employee training rather in terms of acquisitions of or alliances with other firms. Market morality will highlight the importance of this internal investment and introspection.

Conclusion

We consider this analysis to be the first step in a larger research project. We do not think we have exhausted the specifications of a substantive morality of the market. We do think that we have shown that there are sound business reasons as well as ethical reasons for certain MNCs to adopt uniform moral codes. And we would expect the market morality to shape the content of those codes. In this way, we hope we have provided some reasons to think that there are at least some universal moral standards for the practice of international business, and as a result we should sometimes do as the Romans do only when what the Romans do conforms to universal standards.

Endnote

1.   Details about the oil spill at Floreffe and Ashland Oil's response are available in the case, 'Ashland Oil, Inc.: Trouble at Floreffe' (Matthews, et al., 1991).

References

Business Week, "The Destructive Costs of Greasing Palms" (December 6, 1993), 136–138.

Friedman, M., *Capitalism and Freedom* (New York: The Free Press, 1960).

Ghemawat, P., *Commitment: The Dynamic of Strategy* (New York: The Free Press, 1991).

Haas, R., "Risking Something of Value," *Business Ethics Resource*, Vol. 8, (1994), 1, 3–6.

Hennart, J., *The Nature of the Transnational Firm* (London: Routledge, 1991).

Matthews, J., K. Goodpaster, and L. Nash, "Ashland Oil, Inc.: Trouble at," *Policies and Persons: A Casebook in Business Ethics.* 2nd ed. (New York: McGraw-Hill, Inc., 1991), 456–468.

Wall Street Journal (1993a). "General Motors Fight with VW on Lopez Picks up Some Speed" (April 2, 1993), A3.

Wall Street Journal (1993b). "Germany Finds Documents that Bolster Gm Unit's Position in Dispute with VW" (July 6, 1993), A4.

Wall Street Journal (1993c). "Boxes of GM Papers Tied to Shipment for Lopez" (August 12, 1993), A4.

Wall Street Journal (1996). "GM-VW Dispute Is Still Far from Over" (December 2, 1996), A3, A6.

The Ethic of Care and
the Buddhist Ethic of Compassion:
Implications for Ethical Comportment in Organizations

Judith White

Abstract

The feminist ethic of care and the Buddhist ethic of compassion share some similar values and characteristics that can be applied directly to individual and organizational behavior. These characteristics include an emphasis on not harming others, seeing oneself in relationship with the other, being sensitive to and respectful of the needs of others, and always considering the larger context surrounding the particular situation. Ethical comportment is the practice of these values and characteristics in one's daily interpersonal interactions, integrating one's thoughts, feelings, perceptions, and behaviors.

Introduction

This chapter highlights the similarities between the ethic of care and the Buddhist ethic of compassion, suggesting implications for individual ethical comportment in organizations. Ethical comportment is behavior and reasoning at the individual and interpersonal level that draws upon the ethics of care and the Buddhist ethic of compassion. The ethic of compassion stems from at least 500 B.C., while the contemporary ethic of care comes from more recent developmental psychology and moral development (Gilligan 1982; Gilligan and Attanucci 1988; Jack and Jack 1989; Miller 1976; Noddings 1984; Tronto 1993). Awareness or consciousness of a connection to others and the intention not to harm others are common to both ethical traditions.

Compassion, fundamental to Buddhism, is defined in The Eightfold Path, a Buddhist guide to an ethical life (Conze 1959; Katagiri 1988; Kornfield 1993; Rahula 1979; Snelling 1990). We discuss four steps on The Eightfold Path, showing the similarities with the ethics of care.

Ethical comportment that embodies care and compassion has implications for organizational structural and policy that are detailed in White 1999.

The Buddhist Ethic of Compassion

"You must help others. If not, you should not harm others," from the *Bodhisattva* scriptures, the Great Vehicle (*Mahayana*), and the Low Vehicle (*Hinayana*).

The Dalai Lama, *A Policy of Kindness*

Buddhism began about 2500 B.C. in India, and today is practiced throughout the world. The Buddhist practices of compassion and ethical conduct are presented here.

Compassion, common to all Buddhist traditions, is detailed in traditional scriptures and guidelines for monastic and lay practice. Compassion implies an opening of the heart to others, acting upon an authentic deep caring for others, stemming from a sense of an undoubtable connectedness to all living beings (Chang 1983; Conze 1959; Feldman 1988; Goldstein and Kornfield 1987; Kapleau 1965; Kornfield 1993; Macy 1991; Rahula 1974; Sivaraksa 1988; and Snelling 1990).

In the Western business world, the terms empathy and understanding for others are used rather than compassion. While compassion may have a rational or cognitive element to it, initially it stems from the heart, from a sense of serenity, generosity, caring, and concern. Though compassion does not require giving up the self while attending to the other, the self may be suspended in service of the other. Compassion is developed through selflessness by attending to the needs of the other and lack of attachment to one's own desires and thoughts.

Buddhist compassion involves feeling and action, reaching out and giving to the other, sharing in another's grief or suffering. Similar to empathy, it includes the ability to identify with another on a direct emotional level (McCormick 1994). Compassion differs from social objectivity, (Boyatzis 1982) or perspective taking, more cognitively oriented appraisals of how others perceive themselves, their situation, and their emotions (McCormick 1994). Compassion is more heartfelt and directed toward a specific person or group.

Four stages in the Eightfold Path are particularly relevant to developing compassion for ethical comportment in the workplace.

Right Understanding, Right Thought, Right Effort, and Right Mindfulness

In Buddhism, Right Understanding requires that we see life just as it is, with its inevitable impermanence, suffering, and emptiness. It involves a clear understanding of moral law, the nature of existence, and the elements that make up the conditioned realm of life.

Right Thought, also known as right intention (Aitken 1982; Chang 1983; Conze 1959; Cleary trans. 1994 of *The Dhammapada*; Katagiri 1988; Rahula 1959; Saddhatissa 1987; and Snelling 1990), means one's mind is pure and free from ill-will, cruelty, lust, and similar harmful mind states.

Right Effort means one acquires and fosters noble qualities while avoiding and rejecting ignoble qualities. This has four parts: 1) The effort to prevent the arising of evil which has not yet presented itself; 2) The effort to expel evil which is already present; 3) The effort to induce good which has not yet presented itself, and 4) The effort to cultivate that good which is already present.

Right Mindfulness is a state of constant awareness of one's body, feelings, mind, and thoughts, the culmination of the intellectual process which connects with intuition or direct insight into how things truly are. Thoughts enable the mind to diagnose the truth more clearly as things make themselves evident. In Buddhism, one transcends the intellectual mind to realize the true significance and relationship of all things.

Compassion and Its Implications for Ethical Comportment in Organizations

Individuals bring various intentions and motivations to organizations including motivations to achieve, accomplish goals, fulfill ambitions, or gain status (McClelland 1961). Others need affiliation, to make friends, and develop social contacts. Others are motivated to gain power and influence over others, through manipulating resources or advancing in the organization. In each group, the individual's needs, intentions, and consciousness are directed toward the self rather than the work group or organization.

Applying Right Thought, Right Understanding, Right Effort, and Right Mindfulness to organizations requires shifting intention and awareness to include all others, in time and space. As the Iroquois Native Americans consider the future seven generations, right thought, understanding, effort, and mindfulness heightens awareness and clarifies one's intentions towards all persons. Ethical comportment involves acting with an awareness of the impact of one's behaviors on persons in other places, societies, and time, and includes generosity, kindness, gentleness, nurturance, and a willingness to face and attend to the suffering of others.

In the West, these characteristics are associated with the feminine, whether in men or women (Jung 1971). Jung recommended integrating the feminine and masculine aspects of human nature to create a wholesome and balanced society. In the West, aggression, competition, autonomy, vertical power structures, and a goal orientation are associated with masculinity (Eisler 1987; Ferguson 1984; Kanter 1977; Maier 1992; Miller 1976; Powell and Butterfield 1989; and Tannen 1990).

Most businesses emphasize efficiency, productivity, and bottom-line results by increasing profits and decreasing costs. Current emphasis on technology and automation eliminates jobs (Rifkin 1995). Companies that downsize and lay off workers while increasing profits and executive compensation might investigate their intentions in relationship to stakeholders.

Decision-making itself is a mode of ethical comportment. A company conveys respect for the others' contributions by including them in decisions that directly impact them. In contrast, top-down, unilateral decision-making communicates paternalism, protecting and doing for others presumably less capable. The former's intention is caring and inclusion while the latter excludes others.

An example of the cost of top-down, exclusionary, unilateral decision-making is a situation from the corporate agricultural industry in California's Salinas Valley. One of the country's largest growers designed a broccoli trimming machine to be used in the fields by broccoli trimmers, *after* cutting. Soon afterwards, significant numbers of trimmers had medical problems associated with carpal tunnel syndrome. Many workers filed workers' compensation claims and the company paid medical and vocational rehabilitation benefits to disabled workers, originally believing this was less expensive than redesigning the trimming machine. This example, along with others including RJR Nabisco, Imperial Food Products, Thai garment sweatshops in Los Angeles, pesticide use in agriculture, Firestone Brakes, and Nike in Indonesia highlight some corporations' priorities of profits before the health and safety of people.

An organization's structures, systems, and processes represent its ethical intentions *vis-à-vis* the individuals that work within it. By organizing structures and systems for workers' health and safety, autonomy, skill development, and team work, management demonstrates the ethics of care and compassion. As mentioned earlier, while the design of organizational structures and policies to reflect the values of care and compassion is a very important topic, this chapter limits itself to a focus on individual behavior.

Underlying right thought, right understanding, right effort, and right mindfulness is the assumption that all persons are connected with each other, sharing hopes for a good life for themselves and their children, and a healthy habitat, the earth. Building community within organizations requires ethical comportment: practicing awareness and consideration of others, kindness, truthfulness, and compassion through mindfulness and attention to intrapersonal and interpersonal processes.

The Ethic of Care

The ethic of care, initially considered in the context of domestic relationships (Gilligan 1982; Lyons 1982; Noddings 1984) is now relevant to business ethics. Caring relationships in organizations include active listening, respecting others, and demonstrating empathy towards others (Jack and Jack 1989; Manning 1992; Raugust 1992; Tronto 1993). Caring emphasizes not harming others, valuing relationships with others, and maintaining or repairing relationships (Gilligan 1982; Lyons 1982). Caring may involve self-sacrifice, and an accounting of the other's physical or psychological needs (Manning 1992). Human relationships require continuous caring involving three components: "being receptive to the other, being accepting of the other, and being on-call for the other when s/he is in need" (p. 48).

Caring in the workplace reinforces feminist ethics of cooperation, relationship, and interdependent nurturance, acknowledging the other's reality as his/her own while not precluding extending oneself to the other. Understanding that everyone is different *and* everyone is connected, caring honors the differences while simultaneously *feeling* the connection through emotion, of the need for care and compassion.

Caring leads to inquiry rather than assuming homogeneity of values and needs. The carer asks questions, enriches his/her knowledge of the other's context, and attempts to understand the other from the other's point of view (Jack and Jack 1989; Miller 1991, 1976; Lyons 1983; Noddings 1984; and Tronto 1993). The carer listens and learns while the other shares of him/herself, allowing the caring person to develop in the process of caring for another. Organizational relationships, situations, and circumstances provide many opportunities to care.

Care in the Workplace

In her article, "Feminist Ethics and Workplace Values," Raugust (1992) claims the prevailing ethic in the workplace is patriarchal, with the hegemonic values of autonomy, rights, and individualistic justice. Under this influence, employees relate to each other in terms of the ways "work products are measured and esteemed" (p. 125). Feminist ethics, in contrast, are based on cooperation, relationship, and interdependent nurturance, values more comfortable for women employees. Raugust outlines six tenets of organizational ethics:

1. A caring relationship with others, rather than declaration, defense, and the exercise of individual rights, is the primary priority of ethical enactment.
2. The giving and receiving of care, appropriate to specific persons and situations, is the principal outcome for ethically determined behavior.
3. Interdependence rather than individualism is emphasized, along with the mutuality of giving and receiving more than entitlements to receiving nurturing from others.
4. The focus is on the particular "other" in contrast to the "other" as generalized, faceless, and impersonal.
5. Decisions are founded in context and responsive to the particularities of the individual case, not through formulaic and deductive processes.
6. Interpersonal processes are circular rather than linear, a-temporal rather than time-bound, and accepting rather than transformative.
7. Virtue is the highest good, taking precedence over justice. Exploitation and harm are to be avoided. At work primary tasks are emphasized, while power relations over others is de-emphasized.

These principles embody the core values of both the ethic of care with its importance of relationship with the specific other, and the central emphasis in Buddhism on the interconnection of all living things.

Implications for Organizational Life

At the foundation of both the Buddhist ethic of compassion and the ethic of care (see Figure 1) is a sense of self in relation to others, a sense of "we" in addition to "me" rather than "me" instead of "we." Organization members often feel a sense of connection with others within their organization, but extended organizational boundaries and an expanded, global set of organizational stakeholders suggest a heightened awareness of others and a more inclusive sense of "us." Individuals can envision themselves part of a global community rather than a individual organizational.

Figure 1 The Ethic of Care and the Buddhist Ethic of Compassion

Ethic of Care	Ethic of Compassion
Importance of maintaining and human repairing relationships.	All beings are entitled to kindness and compassion.
Cause no harm to others.	Never harm another.
Self is interdependent with others.	Self is part of an interdependent network of all others beings.
Situational context is essential for understanding and care.	All things are subjects of conditioning.
Feelings and emotions are legitimate and valuable.	Feelings, sensations, emotions, and thoughts are an integrated whole and transitory.
Motivation leads to actions.	Thoughts and intentions are equally important as actions.
Intellect and intuition are both valued.	Intellectual process is linked to intuitive process.

Ethical comportment is the enactment of care and compassion by valuing relationships, speaking truthfully, demonstrating concern for others, intending to be part of the solution rather than part of the problem, and not harming others through one's thoughts, speech, and actions. These, along with attentiveness, responsibility, competence, and responsiveness, discussed below, suggest a shift in intention as well as consciousness, from quantity to quality of processes and products.

Practicing ethical comportment may require training in human relations, in how to treat others with care and kindness, particularly in tough work situations. Additionally, because of increasing diversity in organizations, while a common standard of care and kindness for all persons would seem practical, in fact we need to take into account the fact that each person has different sensibilities as to what constitutes care and kindness, and there are cultural differences as well. Training includes cultural relativity in communication, conflict resolution, decision making, problem solving, team building, coaching, and supervising. Paradoxically, while organizations are working at an accelerated pace, caring takes patience. Organizations reinforce ethical comportment by explicitly stating in their mission, vision, and values the importance of caring. Employees are to be treated like customers, with respect, courtesy, and kindness.

Underlying a change in priorities from efficiency and productivity to care, compassion, and ethical behavior, is a shift from an individualistic culture to a more middle-of-the road position between individualism and collectivism. While individual rights and freedom traditionally have been honored and revered, to live more harmoniously in community requires balancing the needs of the community with those of the individual. This is middle path, somewhat of a communitarian approach (Etzioni 1991/92), involves integrating complex cognitive, affective, perceptual, and behavioral skills (Kolb 1984).

Ethical comportment in organizations requires sensitivity to the needs of others. Caring as a practice requires specific moral qualities and a "general habit of mind" that should inform all aspects of a practitioner's moral life rather than a set of rules or principles (Tronto 1993, 127). Enacting an ethic of care involves four elements: attentiveness, responsibility, competence, and responsiveness.

Attentiveness is the recognition of a need to be cared about, being attentive to the needs of others, instead of succumbing to "the temptations to ignore others, to shut others out, and to focus our concerns solely upon ourselves" (Tronto 1993, 127). Weil describes caring through attention as an absence of will, the need to suspend one's own goals, ambitions, and concerns in order to recognize and be attentive to others. In Buddhism, attention is mindfulness, being present with full attention to the sensory, cognitive, and affective occurrences in this moment. To be fully present in the moment, mindful and attentive to another, is caring, kindness, and compassion. Socrates and Hume both spoke of the importance of a willingness to listen, to be able to suspend one's own concerns and be attentive to the plight of others.

Responsibility, or taking care of, fulfills an obligation arising out of a promise, and is "embedded in a set of implicit cultural practices rather than a set of formal rules or series of promises" (Tronto 1993, 132). Responsibility is an element of individual psychology as well as political motivation. In the context of work one asks what responsibilities does the individual have for the welfare of others, and what responsibilities are those of the individual and those of the firm. Gender and socioeconomic status add complexity to these questions.

The Buddhist ethic of compassion for all living beings implies a practice of taking responsibility for others. To turn one's back on another in need is to turn one's back on a part of oneself because, in the Buddhist belief system, all persons are connected to all other persons, through the sense of spirit, time, history, and biology. Practicing mindfulness is being responsible and attentive. Organizational whistle-blowers can be seen as demonstrating responsibility and care for others, including workers, the environment, taxpayers, and consumers.

Care-giving implies *competence*, the third dimension of an ethic of care. To act competently is to act within one's capabilities. The intention to care in a competent manner is important, while obstacles beyond one's control may interfere with the provision of competent care. In organizations, an individual may intend to be attentive, responsible, and compassionate, but a heavy workload may impede competent performance. An example is a secretary who, because of the work structure and excessive workload, has too many demands and is no longer caring, considerate, or attentive to anyone. The structure impedes caring.

Responsiveness of the care-receiver to the care-giver is the fourth dimension. Care may involve vulnerability and inequality, a dependence of the care-receiver upon the care-giver. The manager depends on the secretary for messages, and is vulnerable to the consequences of how the task is accomplished. The vulnerability and interdependence of all persons is embedded in feminist and Buddhist psychology.

Ethical comportment embodies the essence of the ethic of care with its relationship with the other, and the central emphases in Buddhism on the interconnection of all living things, compassion, and not harming others. Together these core values can address the complex problems of an increasingly diverse organization.

Practical Conclusions

While care and compassion may be intuitive and natural for some, it may require a major shift of heart and mind for others. We believe that almost everyone is capable of responding in a caring and compassionate manner even in the most difficult of circumstances, and that this capability is deeply embedded in one's sense of self-esteem and place in relationship to the world. When one feels secure, content, confident, and free of fear, one is able to extend generosity towards others. When one feels fearful, insecure, and uncomfortable, one is less trusting of others and less likely to extend an open heart to others. Unfortunately, most of us are not entirely aware of our feelings at all times. We may act out of fear without knowing it. The fear may be deep seeded in such a way that we have developed personality characteristics, a world view, and set of behaviors that, perhaps without awareness, we enact daily. Practically, this suggests developing a deeper awareness of one's thoughts, feelings, emotions, and behaviors. This is a Buddhist prescription for freedom and greater peace of mind.

As educators, we can be a catalyst for the development of ethical comportment in our students. Part of our challenge is to facilitate the development of the whole person, though many of us have had little if any training in developmental or counseling psychology. If we are truly interested in the future of the world and the success of our students in the twenty-first century, we might take it upon ourselves to become more concerned about their self-esteem and self-confidence, encouraging, supporting, and caring about their intellectual, physical, and emotional development. We might find ourselves enacting rather than merely espousing our values of caring and compassion towards others. This in turn implies redefining ourselves as facilitators of learning and development rather than imparters of information, ideas, and knowledge.

The concept and practice of ethical comportment lend themselves well to empirical research, using both qualitative and quantitative forms of investigation at the intrapersonal, interpersonal, group, and intergroup levels in organizations. Using Critical Incident Interviews (Flanagan 1954), individuals can recall everyday work experiences and incidents where they felt attended to and cared for, and when they felt ignored, deceived, manipulated, or discriminated against in some way. Another option is for the interviewee to describe a situation when he or she made a decision that involved an act of caring for another person instead of taking a pragmatic approach, or describe a situation when he or she felt pressured to act unethically because of fear, greed, anger, or environmental pressures. An empirical model of ethical comportment can be built from a significant amount of data from interviews, and the model, with behavioral indicators, can then be used to assess and train others.

For another approach, interviews and participant-observation methods can be used to detect the emotional tone of a work environment, whether it is a nursing station on a hospital ward, a crew meeting in a manufacturing plant, or a meeting in an executive team on mahogany row. One can sense an ambiance of friendliness, warmth, humor, consideration, and care for others, or uncomfortable feelings of coldness, resentment, withdrawal, disrespectful gossiping, and fear. Many work environments have some combination of these, the particular constellation dependent on the contextual circumstances, intentions of individual actors, or particular events.

A more specific example of a source of research data: if layoffs are impending, the atmosphere can be tense, with a feeling of "each man [*sic*] for himself [*sic*]." When a merger or downsizing is expected and middle managers anticipate that their own jobs are in jeopardy, rumors and harmful speech may be prevalent, fear may seize the otherwise better intentions of individuals and work groups, and organization members may resort to rules and policies to maintain the *assemblance* of control. Immediately following the earthquake in Los Angeles in January 1994, individuals anecdotally reported that the atmosphere in organizations was more caring than usual, with more people demonstrating care, concern, and compassion for fellow workers than under ordinary circumstances. Behavioral indicators included an increase in carpooling, flextime, shared phones, food, childcare, and extending favors and friendship to people previously considered strangers or acquaintances.

Data from interviews, observations, and surveys can be collected and analyzed using indicators of an ethic of care, developed from Lyons (1982) and White (1994), and incorporating Tronto's model, as well as empirically developing indicators of right speech and right thought or intention from Buddhist literature.

We offer a model ethical comportment, the ethical aspect of everyday interpersonal interactions in organizational life, drawing on the similarities between the ethic of care and the Buddhist ethic of compassion. We advocate enacting care and compassion through right thought, right understanding, right effort, right mindfulness, and overall, caring and consideration of others.

References

Ajahn Sumedho, *The Four Noble Truths* (Hertfordshire, England: Amaravati Publications, 1992).

Boyatzis, R. E., *The Competent Manager* (New York: John Wiley & Sons, 1982).

Chang, G.C.C., ed., "On the Paramita of Ingenuity" in *A Treasury of*

Mahayana Sutras (University Park, Pa.: Pennsylvania State University Press. 1983).

Conze, E., *Buddhist Scriptures* (New York: Penguin, 1959).

Cleary, T., transl., *Dhammada: The Sayings of the Buddha* (New York: Bantam. Books, 1994).

Dalai Lama, *The Policy of Kindness* (Ithaca, N.Y.: Snow Lion, 1990).

Eisler, R., *The Chalice and the Blade* (New York: Harper-Collins, 1987).

Etzioni, A., "The Responsive Communitarian Platform" in *The Response Community, Rights and Responsibilities*, ed., A. Etzioni, vol. 2 (Washington, D.C.: Center for Policy Research, 1991/1992).

Feldman, C., "Nurturing Compassion" in *The Path of Compassion, Writings on Socially Engaged Buddhism,* ed., F. Eppsteiner (Berkeley, Cal.: Parallax Press, 1988).

Ferguson, K., *The Feminist Case Against Bureaucracy* (Philadelphia: Temple, 1984).

Flanagan, J. C., "The Critical Incident Technique," *Psychological Bulletin* 4 (1954), 327–358.

Gilligan, C., *In a Different Voice* (Cambridge, Mass.: Harvard University Press, 1982).

Gilligan, C. and J. Attanucci, "Two Moral Orientations: Gender Differences and Similarities," *Merrill-Palmer Quarterly* 343 (1988), 223–237.

Goldstein, J. and J. Kornfield, *Seeking the Heart of Wisdom* (Boston: Shambhala, 1987).

Hagberg, J., *Real Power: Stages of Personal Power in Organizations* (Salem, Wisc.: Sheffield Publishing, 1994).

Jack, R. and D. C. Jack, *Moral Vision and Professional Decisions* (New York: Cambridge University Press, 1989).

Jung, C. G., *Psychological Types* (Princeton, N.J.: Princeton University Press, 1971).

Katagiri, Dainin, *Returning to Silence. Zen Practice in Daily Life* (Boston: Shambhala, 1988).

Kapleau, P., *The Three Pillars of Zen* (Boston: Beacon Press, 1965).

Kolb, D. A., *Experiential Learning* (Englewood Cliffs, N.J.: Prentice-Hall, 1984).

Kornfield, J., *Teaching of the Buddha* (Boston: Shambhala, 1993).

Lyons, N., "Conceptions of Self and Morality and Models of Moral Choice: Identifying Justice and Care in Judgments of Actual Moral Dilemmas." Doctoral dissertation, School of Education, Harvard University, 1982.

Macy, J., *World as Lover, World as Self* (Berkeley, Cal.: Parallax Press, 1991).

Maier, M., "Revisiting (and Resolving?) the Androgyny/Masculinity Debate in Management," *Journal of Men* (1992).

McClelland, D., *The Achieving Society* (Princeton, N.J.: Princeton University Press, 1961).

McCormick, D., "Spirituality and Management," *Journal of Managerial Psychology* 9, no. 6 (1994), 5–8.

Miller, J. B., "The Development of Women's Sense of Self" in *Women's Growth in Connection: Writings from the Stone Center*, eds., Jordan, Kaplan, Miller, Stiver, and Surrey (New York: The Guilford Press, 1991).

Miller, J. B., *Toward a New Psychology of Women* (Boston: Beacon Press, 1976).

Manning, R., "Just Caring" in *Explorations in Feminist Ethics, Theory and Practice,* eds., Coile, E. B., and S. Coultrap-McQuin (Bloomington, Ind.: Indiana University Press, 1992).

Noddings, N., *Caring. A Feminist Approach to Ethics and Moral Education* (Berkeley: University of California Press, 1984).

Powell, G.N., and D. A. Butterfield, "The 'Good Manager:' Did Androgyny Fare Better in the 1980s?" *Group and Organization Studies* 14 (1989), 216–233.

Rahula, W., *What the Buddha Taught* (New York: Grove Press, 1974).

Raugust, M. C., "Feminist Ethics and Workplace Values" in *Explorations in Feminist Ethics: Theory and Practice,* eds., Coile, E. B., and S. Coultrap-McQuin (Bloomington, Ind.: Indiana University Press, 1992).

Rifkin, J., "What's a Worker Worth in a Workless World?" *Los Angeles Times* (October 11, 1995).

Saddhatissa, H., *Buddhist Ethics* (London: Wisdom Publications, 1997).

Sivaraksa, S., "Buddhism in a World of Change" in *The Path of Compassion. Writings on Socially Engaged Buddhism,* ed., F. Eppsteiner (Berkeley, Cal.: Parallax Press, 1988).

Snelling, J., *The Elements of Buddhism* (Dorset, UK: Element Books, 1990).

Tannen, D., *You Just Don't Understand: Women and Men in Conversation* (New York: William Morrow, 1990).

Tronto, J., *Moral Boundaries* (New York: Routledge, 1993).

White, J., "Individual Characteristics and Social Knowledge in Ethical Reasoning," *Psychological Reports* 75 (1994), 627–649.

White, J., "Ethical Comportment in Organizations: A Synthesis of the Feminist Ethic of Care and the Buddhist Ethic of Companion," *International Journal of Value-Based Management* (1999).

Two Cheers for Stakeholder Theory:
A Critique from a Religious Perspective

Moses L. Pava

Abstract

The specific purpose of this chapter is to both describe and critique, from a Jewish perspective, an important area of business ethics known as stakeholder theory. To date, there are more than a hundred academic articles and a dozen books on the topic (Donaldson and Preston 1995). My conclusion, hinted at in the title of this chapter, is that on the one hand, stakeholder theory represents an important advance over competing theories of how business should be conducted. By clearly invoking the language of ethics and responsibility as a foundation of modern business, stakeholder theory reminds us of the predominant biblical vision that "man does not live by bread alone, but by everything that proceedeth out of the mouth of the Lord doth man live" (Deuteronomy 8:3). Stakeholder theory provides strong and persuasive arguments against the traditional view of business which asserts that the sole goal of the corporation is to maximize profits. On the other hand, care must be taken to distance ourselves from some of the most recent and much more radical pronouncements of a minority of stakeholder theorists. In spite of this last point, on balance, stakeholder theory is a positive and ethically significant development.

What is the Stakeholder Theory of the Firm?

The first task of this chapter is to provide a clear description of the theory. The chore is made more difficult because of a lack of consensus among business ethicists on this basic issue. Perhaps, the best place to begin the discussion of stakeholder theory is not with the academic literature at all, but with a document found hanging on the office walls of corporate executives at Johnson & Johnson. In its corporate credo, Johnson & Johnson clearly articulates its belief that the corporation has responsibilities to meet the needs of many different groups of people. These groups which "have a stake in or claim on the firm" (Evan and Freeman 1988, 146) are called stakeholders. Johnson & Johnson explicitly includes the following groups among its stakeholders: customers, suppliers, employees, managers, local and world communities, and stockholders. The twin themes of "fairness" and "responsibility" permeate the document. In an important review paper, Donaldson and Preston (1995) have carefully noted that stakeholder theory can serve three distinct (although usually consistent) purposes. According to the authors, stakeholder theory has been variously invoked as a *"descriptive,"* as an *"instrumental,"* and as a *"normative"* theory. Their thesis correctly suggests that care must be taken to distinguish among the uses of the theory.

Stakeholder Theory as Descriptive

Donaldson and Preston write, "The stakeholder theory is unarguably *descriptive*. It presents a model describing what the corporation is" (p. 66). Johnson & Johnson's credo is also unarguably descriptive and illustrates Donaldson and Preston's first point nicely. The first purpose of the credo is to describe the nature of the corporation known as Johnson & Johnson. The credo comes to answer the question "What is the corporation?" By explicitly recognizing the corporation's responsibilities to its various stakeholders, the corporation itself suggests that it is to be defined through its numerous relationships. Further, Johnson & Johnson's credo is an attempt to specify with some degree of precision the exact nature of these relationships. Thus, for example, the document states that the corporation has responsibilities: 1) to produce "high quality" products; 2) to insure suppliers "make a fair profit"; 3) to create an environment where employees "have a sense of security in their jobs"; 4) to protect the environment; and 5) to earn a "sound profit" or a "fair return." Ultimately, Johnson & Johnson is defined by the special relationships among the diverse groups which participate in and are affected by the activities of the corporation.

Stakeholder Theory as Instrumental

The purpose of stakeholder theory is not merely to describe impartially. The theory also suggests that firms which carefully follow the advice of stakeholder strategists will outperform (in terms of financial measures) other firms which are managed under more traditional views. The Johnson & Johnson credo also captures this second aspect of the theory. The very last line explicitly links "principles" to profits.

Stakeholder Theory as Normative

After describing stakeholder theory as both descriptive and instrumental, Donaldson and Preston (1995) conclude that the fundamental basis (of stakeholder theory) is *normative* and involves acceptance of the following ideas:

> (a) Stakeholders are persons or groups with legitimate interests in procedural and/or substantive aspects of corporate activity. Stakeholders are identified by *their* interests in the corporation, whether the corporation has any corresponding functional interest in *them*; and
>
> (b) The interests of all stakeholders are of *intrinsic value* (p. 67).

In other words, stakeholder theory not only describes the corporations as it exists, but provides guidelines as to what the corporation potentially could and *should* be.

Unlike the instrumental aspect of the theory, rules are prescribed not because they necessarily enhance financial performance, but because the rules are inherently "right." Johnson & Johnson's credo and its explicit use of such terms as "just" and "ethical" clearly and unambiguously invokes a normative stance. Its professed responsibilities to suppliers to earn a "fair profit," to employees to help them fulfill their "family responsibilities," and to local communities to support charities, will often require justification beyond increased profits to shareholders.

What the Stakeholder Theory of the Firm is Not: The Austere Theory

It is this last aspect of stakeholder theory, its normative aspirations, which make the theory important, controversial, and interesting. To more fully understand stakeholder theory, it is necessary to compare it to its main competitor, what Clarence Walton (1967) terms the "austere" theory of the firm.

Milton Friedman is most closely associated with this more traditional view of the corporation (see Friedman 1962 and 1970, and Friedman and Friedman 1980). His position can be summarized as follows: Business managers have a responsibility to stockholders, the owners of the corporation, to maximize firm value. Managers, acting as agents of the stockholders, have no mandate to embark on socially responsible projects that do not enhance the income generating ability of the firm. In addition, managers should not refrain from profitable investments which satisfy all legal constraints but do not conform to managers' own personal social agenda. Rather, as Friedman put it, "The social responsibility of business is to increase profits." He further emphasized "few trends would so thoroughly undermine the very foundations of our free society as the acceptance by corporate officials of a social responsibility other than to make as much money for their stockholders as they possibly can. This is a fundamentally subversive doctrine" (1962, 133).

According to Clarence Walton (1967), himself a critic of the theory, the traditional view is predicated on the following four factors: 1) large numbers of owners who are willing to commit their resources in risk-taking ventures for profit; 2) competitive markets for all products; 3) ability to substitute one resource for another when the competitively set cost-price equation makes another form of resource combination more profitable; and 4) acceptance by all of the owners of the principle of self-interest as the motivating force in all economic activity (p. 128).

Each of the four elements which justify the traditional view have been subject to severe scrutiny. For the present purposes, the single most important element of the austere theory is Walton's fourth factor. Walton suggests that the austere theory ultimately rests upon one particular view of human decision making. James March (1994) has recently described this view of human decision making as the "rational" model.

In his comprehensive coverage of the topic, March suggests that standard theories of choice in economic thought always assume decision processes are both *consequential* and *preference-based*. Actions, taken today, are dependent on the anticipated consequences of those actions. Decision processes are preference-based in the sense that anticipated consequences are always valued exclusively in terms of personal preferences. Alternatives actions are judged in terms of the extent to which their expected future consequences are perceived to serve the preferences of the decision maker.

Walton's linking of the austere theory of the firm with the rational model of decision making is worth consideration, especially from the perspective of a religiously grounded business ethics. He is not alone in his suggestion that the rational model provides one of the necessary foundations for the austere theory. (See for example, Christopher Stone 1975, 145.)

Supporters of the austere theory are often just as likely to make the connection. In spite of Friedman's use of the term "ethical custom," I believe one is still justified in entertaining a lingering doubt as to whether he is using the term in its traditional sense. And even if Friedman himself is somewhat less than pellucid on this critical issue, more recent advocates of the austere theory are crystal clear. Jensen and

Meckling are nothing if not "pure" rationalists. With no detectable irony whatsoever, Jensen and Meckling (1994) unveil a "set of characteristics that captures the essence of human nature, but no more" (p. 4). They label their model of human behavior REMM: the Resourceful, Evaluative, Maximizing Model. The most important implication of REMM for our purposes is the following:

> Like it or not, individual are willing to sacrifice a little of almost anything we care to name, even reputation or morality, for a sufficiently large quantity of other desired things, and these things do not have to be money or even material goods...(p. 7).

It thus follows that referring to human needs, or one might add, responsibilities, is simply "semantic trickery." Therefore, the authors boldly and unabashedly conclude that there really are no housing, education, food, or energy needs. Rather needs should be exposed for what they are human desires.

If the critics (Walton and Stone) and the friends (Friedman, Jensen, and Meckling) of the austere theory are correct, we can now identify a fundamental distinction between the stakeholder and austere theories. While the austere theory is linked to the rational model of decision making, the stakeholder theory necessarily entails an alternative model of human decision making for support. March calls this alternative the model of appropriateness.

An Alternative Vision: The Logic of Appropriateness

According to March, the logic of appropriateness can be summarized by a set of questions:

> Decision makers are imagined to ask (explicitly or implicitly) three questions:
> 1. The question of *recognition*: What kind of situation is this?
> 2. The question of *identity*. What kind of a person am I? Or what kind of organization is this?
> 3. The question of *rules:* What does a person such as I, or an organization such as this, do in a situation such as this? (p. 58)

The essence of the logic of appropriateness is the notion that decision making is ultimately not only about promoting one's immediate self-interest, but is better envisaged as understanding, interpreting, and accepting ethical principles or rules of behavior. For example, the Caux "Principles for Business," authored by the Caux Roundtable (1994), explicitly acknowledges that the law and market forces are insufficient guides for conduct. Consistent with the logic of appropriateness the principles conclude, "Shared values... are as important for a global community as for communities of smaller scale." (Section 1. Preamble). This perspective asserts that it is meaningful to talk about behavior as if behavior is meaningful (independent of personal preferences).

To be sure, a logic of appropriateness recognizes that some behavior is dictated by individual self-interest, but the domain where self-interest commands jurisdiction is ultimately bounded by rules of appropriateness. According to the model of appropriateness, principles trump self-interest. The Johnson & Johnson credo, and stakeholder theory more generally, must necessarily be grounded in this alternative vision of human decision making. For example, advocates of the rational model have no vocabulary by which to explain Johnson & Johnson's use of terms such as "responsibility," "fairness," and human "dignity" other than explaining them as a cynical attempt by management to manipulate and fool its constituencies for its own personal gain. To understand these terms as an honest attempt to communicate corporate and management "ideals," one must abandon the rational model as the single model of human decision making in favor of something like the logic of appropriateness. In fact, the Johnson & Johnson credo reads as if it is a literal attempt to answer March's last two questions concerning identity and rules.

With respect to stakeholder theorists, Evan and Freeman (1988) and Bowie (1991a and 1991b) have attempted to justify the theory in terms closest to the model of appropriateness. For example, stakeholder theory makes sense, according to Bowie, only to the extent that the model of appropriateness has validity. It thus seems that one of the most important distinctions between the stakeholder and austere theories is the very different models of decision making, which ultimately justify the two theories. The austere theory is inextricably linked to the rational model, while the stakeholder theory is justified through the model of appropriateness. If this is true, a fundamental question for a Jewish business ethics emerges. Can we critically distinguish between the rational model and the model of appropriateness? Is one model somehow "more correct" than the other? An answer to this question would provide an important key in distinguishing between the stakeholder and austere theories of the firm.

March suggests that the question of which view of decision making is ultimately primary and which is derivative is an empirical question. If so, he is correct in finally maintaining an agnostic position on this important question. However, for a business ethics grounded in traditional Jewish sources, the question is more appropriately thought of not as an empirical one, but as a question of faith. The thesis of this chapter is that from a religious perspective, particularly a perspective founded on Jewish sources, the model of appropriateness *must* subsume the rational model. One way of restating this point is as follows: From a Jewish perspective, decision makers not only can choose from among a complete set of known acts, but decision makers can choose between alternative modes of decision making. If so, the religious perspective is consistent with the stakeholder theory, and must necessarily reject the austere theory.

A Jewish Perspective on Stakeholder Theory

True proponents of self-interest believe that ultimately the model of appropriateness can be folded back into the rational model. George Akerlof (1983), for example, suggests that if parents could teach children to feign honesty at a low cost, rational parents would choose to do so.

It is precisely here that religiously-grounded views contrast sharply with the self-interest model. From a religious perspective, in the final analysis, ethics (although consistent with the rational model) can not be fully explained through the rational model. Although choosing to live an ethical life often promotes material interests, the reason for choosing ethics is not self-interest. Rather the choice is ultimately made in attempt to understand life as meaningful beyond the satisfaction of material comforts. In answering March's questions, one must find a place for one's own preferences, but one must also be able to critique and alter those very same preferences. It is beyond dispute that from the Jewish perspective, the acceptance of ethical principles by the individual or community is ideally not motivated through the calculus of material self-interest.

Religious views begin with the model of appropriateness as axiomatic, and it is rationality which is derivative. An important and fundamental articulation of this view is the following rabbinic midrash where, before God gives the Torah to Israel, He approaches every tribe and nation:

He appeared to the children of Esau the wicked and said to them: Will you accept the Torah? They said to Him: What is written in it? He said to them: "Thou shalt not murder." They said to Him: The very heritage which our father left us was: "And by thy sword shalt thou live." He then appeared to the children of Amon and Moab. He said to them: Will you accept the Torah? They said to Him: What is written in it? He said to them: "Thou shalt not commit adultery." They, however, said to Him that they were all of them children of adulterers, as it is said: "Thus were both the daughters of Lot with child by their father." Then He appeared to the children of Ishmael. He said to them: Will you accept the Torah? They said to Him: What is written in it? He said to them: "Thou shalt not steal." They said to Him: The very blessing that had been pronounced upon our father was: "And he shall be as a wild ass of a man: his hand shall be upon everything."...But when He came to the Israelites and: "At His right hand was a fiery law unto them," they all opened their mouths and said: "All that the Lord hath spoken will we do and obey (*na'aseh v'nishma*)." (Mekilta de-Rabbi Ishmael, 1961, 234– 35.)

In this rabbinic embellishment, the rabbis expand on the strange phrasing at Exodus 24:7. This biblical verse, on which the midrash is based, quotes the children of Israel at the foot of Mount Sinai. As the entire nation enters into and accepts the Divine covenant, the people promise to God – "*na'aseh v'nishma*" – which literally translated means we will do and we will hear. The priority of *doing* the commandments over *hearing* the commandments deeply puzzled the rabbis and required explanation. Logically, of course, one must hear the commandments before one can do them. In the above quoted midrash, the seemingly strange and impossible promise of the children of Israel is imaginatively compared to other hypothetical answers to God's invitation. The common feature to each of the other responses is the insistence on viewing the decision to accept the covenant as an opportunity to promote self-interest. The other nations are given the specific content of a commandment and respond to God that the distinctive content of the commandment is inconsistent with their own pre-conceived preferences and identity. The children of Israel, by contrast, at the crucial moment of the founding of the nation, recognize that their identity from that point on is defined through their acceptance of the Divine commandments. According to the rabbinic imagination, it would make no sense whatsoever for the Israelites to ask about and evaluate the specific contents of the Divine revelation before their acceptance. The general promise of the existence of the 613 commandments is sufficient. In this *midrash*, the rabbis recognized that the search for meaning as exemplified in faith (*na'aseh*) must come before its actual discovery (*nishmah*). Returning to the language of this chapter, we can restate this observation as follows: from a religious perspective, the logic of appropriateness must subsume the logic of self-interest. We can summarize this discussion by simply noting that economists are correct to point out that it would often pay to purchase a conscience, but what they have failed to notice is the obvious fact that consciences are not for sale.

A Jewish business ethics is therefore inconsistent with the traditional theory of the firm. As argued above, even advocates of the austere model ultimately justify it by invoking the rational model of decision making. The stakeholder theory, by contrast, is justified through an alternative vision of human decision making, a vision consistent with a religious world-view. Hence, two cheers for stakeholder theory.

Why Withhold the Third Cheer?

In spite of the fact that Jewish sources are more consistent with the stakeholder than the austere view, the endorsement here is only partial. In part, some of the traditional opposition to stakeholder theory has grown out of a healthy and intuitive fear of a perceived risk inherent in the stakeholder approach. The fear is that as the list of stakeholders continually grows to include groups more and more tangential to the core economic mission of the corporation, the entire notion of moral responsibility becomes blurred. There is clearly a kernel of truth to Andrew Singer's question, "Can a Company Be Too Ethical?" (1993). If managers have a direct responsibility to everyone and everything (animals and even the inanimate earth), then the notion of responsibility becomes so diluted that in essence the corporation retains responsibilities to no one. Corporations become like the humanitarian who proclaims a love to all men and women, but in reality is incapable of loving particular men and women. I think this fear is implicit, for example, in Levine's rejection of corporate philanthropy on Jewish legal reasoning (1994), and is more explicit in Goodpaster's (1991 and 1994) critique of stakeholder theory.

The fear has proven well warranted. Freeman (1994), who is usually acknowledged as a leading spokesperson for stakeholder theory, now writes:

> Seeing the stakeholder idea as replacing some shopworn metaphors
> of business with new ones – such as stakeholders for stockholders,
> humans as moral beings for humans as economic beings, and the
> Doctrine of Fair Contracts for the current panoply of corporate
> chartering laws is to give up the role of finding some moral bedrock
> for business. Finding such bedrock... is especially fruitless on prag-
> matist grounds for there are no foundations for either business or
> ethics. All we have is our own history, culture, institutions, and our
> imaginations. For the pragmatist it is "just us" rather than "justice"
> or "justification" in any sense of foundational bedrock. The cash
> value of our metaphors and narratives just is how they enable us to
> live, and the proof is in the living. (p. 418)

Stakeholder theory which began as an attempt to understand corporate behavior in terms of accepted moral principles is now to be judged
solely by "the cash value of our metaphors," as there "are no foundations
for either business or ethics" (see also Wicks, Gilbert, and Freeman,
1994). A theory which originally rejected the rational model as the fundamental model of decision making is now understood by one of its
leading thinkers in terms perilously close to Friedman, Jensen, and
Meckling. The thrust of the stakeholder theory, and its appeal from a religious perspective, has been, and will continue to be, its insistence that
there exist interpretive methods to judge business other than in terms of
the "cash value."

If Freeman's new stakeholder theory was the last word on this topic,
there would be no way (or desire) to integrate the theory with traditional
Jewish sources. Kenneth Goodpaster reminds us, however, that the original stakeholder theory, which insists on the model of appropriateness as
fundamental, is still alive and well. Goodpaster's more moderate stance,
which underscores the primacy of the principal-agent relationship, reflects a deep concern with the problem of moral relativism which is now
fully explicit in Freeman's view. He has recently articulated his position
more fully (1994). Consider the following somewhat paradoxical description of stakeholder theory:

> It may appear that management both does and does not have pri-
> mary (noninstrumental) obligations to stakeholders other than
> shareholders and the corporation. But this appearance is seen to be
> misleading when we understand that *nonfiduciary* obligations are
> owed to some and *fiduciary* obligations to others... Directors and

officers must see themselves as both trusted servants of the corporation and its shareholders (a kind of partiality) *and* as members of a wider community also inhabited by the corporation, its shareholders, and many other stockholder groups. (p. 428)

Goodpaster's stakeholder theory reflects the healthy skepticism that a pure "multi-fiduciary" stakeholder approach tends to lead eventually to moral relativism. Goodpaster concludes, "we believe that the paradox is best left to directors and officers who are experienced enough in both private and public life to understand it – and wise enough to manage it." (p. 429) Thus, in the end, stakeholder theory (or at least one version of the theory) puts corporations in a familiar position. On the one hand, corporate executives possess the freedom to choose appropriate business goals, but on the other hand, the freedom entails social and moral responsibilities as traditionally understood.

Conclusion

Stakeholder theory strictly speaking is more than a single theory. In its original form, and in its more moderate formulations, it reflects a view of decision making consistent with the religious world-view. Before human beings promote their own preferences, human beings need a framework to critique and alter those preferences. The austere theory of the firm, to the extent that it relies on the rational view of decision making, is at odds with the vast majority of Jewish sources.

At last count, at least twenty-nine states have adopted statutes, consistent with the stakeholder theory, that extend the range of permissible concern by boards of directors to a host of non-shareowner constituencies, including employees, creditors, suppliers, customers, and local communities (Orts 1992). At the same time, many major U.S. corporations are adopting goals similar to the goals described in the Johnson & Johnson credo (Pava and Krausz 1995). This evolution in corporate law and management thought suggests an increasing acceptance of the stakeholder view. It deserves at least two cheers from a Jewish perspective.

References

Akerlof, George A., "Loyalty Filters," *American Economic Review* 73, no. 1 (1983), 54–63.
Bowie, Norman E., "New Directions in Corporate Social Responsibility,"

first printed in 1991(a), reprinted in Hoffman, W. Michael, and Frederick, Robert E., *Business Ethics* (New York: McGraw-Hill, Inc., 1995), 597–607.

Bowie, Norman E., "Challenging the Egoistic Paradigm," *Business Ethics Quarterly* 1, no. 1 (1991[b]), 1–21.

Caux Roundtable, *Principles for Business* (Minneapolis, Minn.: Caux Roundtable, 1994).

Donaldson, Thomas and Preston, Lee E., "The Stakeholder Theory of the Corporation: Concepts, Evidence, and Implications," *Academy of Management Review* 20, no. 1 (1995), 65–91.

Evan, William M., and Freeman, R. Edward, "A Stakeholder Theory of the Modern Corporation: Kantian Capitalism," first printed 1988, reprinted in Hoffman, W. Michael, and Frederick, Robert E., *Business Ethics* (New York: McGraw-Hill, Inc., 1995), 145–154.

Freeman, R. Edward, "The Politics of Stakeholder Theory: Some Future Direction," *Business Ethics Quarterly* 4, no. 4 (1994): 409–421.

Friedman, Milton, Capitalism and Freedom (Chicago: The University of Chicago Press, 1962).

Friedman, Milton, "A Friedman Doctrine – The Social Responsibility of Business Is to Increase Its Profits," *The New York Times Magazine* (September 13, 1970), pp. 32–33, and 123–125.

Friedman, Milton, and Friedman, Rose, *Free to Choose* (New York: Avon Books, 1980).

Goodpaster, Kenneth E., "Business Ethics and Stakeholder Analysis," *Business Ethics Quarterly* 1, no. 1 (1991), 53–74.

Goodpaster, Kenneth E., "In Defense of a Paradox," *Business Ethics Quarterly* 4, no. 4 (1994): 423–429.

Jensen, Michael C., and Meckling, William H., "The Nature of Man," *Journal of Applied Corporate Finance* 7, no. 2 (1994), 4–19.

Levine, Aaron, "Aspects of Ideology of Capitalism and Judaism," 1994, Paper presented at the 1994 Orthodox Forum, New York.

March, James, with the assistance of Chip Heath, *A Primer on Decision Making: How Decisions Happen* (New York, The Free Press, 1994).

Mekilta de-Rabbi Ishmael, Vol. 2 (Philadelphia: Jewish Publication Society of America, 1961).

Orts, E.W., "Beyond Shareholders: Interpreting Corporate Constituency Statutes," *The George Washington Law Review* 61, no. 1 (1992), 14–135.

Pava, Moses L. and Krausz, Joshua, *Corporate Responsibilities and Financial Performance: The Paradox of Social Cost* (Westport: Quorum Books, 1995).

Singer, Andrew, "Can A Company Be Too Ethical?" first printed 1993, reprinted in Hoffman, W. Michael, and Frederick, Robert E., *Business Ethics* (New York: McGraw-Hill, Inc., 1995), 590–597.

Stone, Christopher, "Where the Law Ends: The Social Control of Corporate Behavior," first printed in 1975, reprinted in Hoffman, W. Michael, and Frederick, Robert E., *Business Ethics* (New York: McGraw-Hill, Inc., 1995), 141–145.

Walton, Clarence C., *Corporate Social Responsibilities* (Belmont, Cal., Wadsworth Publishing Co., 1967).

Wicks, Andrew C., Gilbert, Daniel R., and Freeman, R. Edward, "A Feminist Reinterpretation of The Stakeholder Concept," *Business Ethics Quarterly* 4, no. 4 (1994), 475–498.

Normative Values and Expressions:
Commitment or Manipulation?

Ji-Hwan Song[*] and Hun-Joon Park

Abstract

This chapter critically reviews the existing framework developed for grasping ethical conduct in a business context. Pointing out the limits of ethical decision-making process and integrative social contracts theory, we go on to contemplate a point missing even in the stakeholder management theory. To enrich the theory's merit of comprehensive considerations of multiple constituencies, we stress that the theory needs to be elaborated by an understanding of the strategic conduct of stakeholders deployed in the arena of business transactions. The argument is focused on the ways in which the strategic conduct of both management and employees is socially constituted in the context of new managerial discourses. To specify the strategic conduct of stakeholders, a distinction between "shared values" and "shared expressions" is significantly articulated as an analytic construct. Importantly, we suggest that different stakeholders, through the circulation of selected expressions, socially manipulate corporate morality. The conduct of shared expressions is construed as penetrating the mechanisms whereby both management and employees make use of the components of corporate culture in an ethical ethos of "sharing." We present empirical evidence of the narrowed use of expressions found both in an insurance company in Britain and company in Korea. The empirical evidence illustrates a current state of how the corporately espoused ethical standards are, in reality, appropriated.

The normative stance to business ethics is basically predicated on the assumption that members of a company ought to share the corporate values that are acceptable under the rationale of ethical principles. The corporate culture approach to business ethics (Sinclair 1993) endorses this collective norm of sharing "corporate morality" in the name of "ethos" which is adopted by corporate management and urged to be shared by employees. The main spirit of The Caux Roundtable is also founded on a normative requirement that businesses and stakeholders should devote themselves to practicing the principles for business, which are specified in The Caux Roundtable (see previous chapters of this book).

However, this idealistic pursuit of *normativity*, supported by a commonly accepted value of integrity, is most apt to silence the other side of "sharing" which is doomed to be divisive and manipulative. First, in recognition of these contrasting aspects of normativity, an existing body of framework for ethical conduct in business is critically reviewed in this chapter, and an analytic concept for explicating the collective conduct of sharing is presented with a focus on the distinction between "shared values" and "shared expressions," in order to supplement a critique of one-sided recognition of normativity. Based upon this understanding of the mechanisms of sharing, this chapter discusses that a corporate manipulation of morality is facilitated through the course of "shared expressions." We elaborate these conceptual understandings by reference to two case illustrations from business where "new managerial practices" have come into play.

Normative Approaches to Business Ethics

The business ethicists' efforts to understand the dynamics of ethical conduct of both individuals and corporations have been crystallized into a variety of conceptual frameworks. These frameworks basically represent the processes in which ethical issues are socially constituted, revolving around interactions between the corporations' espoused moral norms and the members' attitude to the corporate morality in the context of general social norms. According to different focuses of diverse approaches to business ethics, these frameworks can be classified into three areas of ethical concerns: (1) ethical decision-making process, (2) social contract theory, and (3) stakeholder theory.

The framework focused on ethical decision-making process is typified by general causal models. For instance, Trevino's (1986) person-situation interactionist model attempts to explain how individual moral subjects behave in situations that influence their ethical choices. By the same token, many other frameworks address the determinants of ethical behavior – significant others, opportunity, individual factors, and the social and cultural environment (Ferrell and Gresham 1985); cultural environment, industry environment, organizational environment, and personal experiences (Hunt and Vitell 1986). However, these general causal models fall short of genuine generality because, as Brady and

Hatch (1992) argue, such models solve no problems and raise only general issues. Moreover, Brady and Hatch (1992, 314) pinpoint that contrary to the intent of their authors, these models serve the purpose of reviving interest in the empirical research tradition rather than providing any new theoretical insights.

Given that any new theoretical insights are to be grounded on descriptive ethics and not prescriptive ethics, Donaldson and Dunfee's (1994) integrative social contracts theory (ISCT) seems more suggestive of a realistic description of ethical conduct in the business arena. This is because their theory is premised on the moral subjects' bounded moral rationality. In recognition of this boundedness, the theory highlights a normative and hypothetical contract among economic participants who are members of specific communities including firms, departments within firms, informal subgroups within departments, national economic organizations, professional associations, industries, and so on. ISCT is trying to incorporate as many aspects of ethical conduct in business as possible into a contractarian network of moral subjects as economic participants by contriving such notions as a macrosocial contract, moral free space, consent and exit, authentic norms, legitimacy and hypernorms, and priority rules (pp. 259–271). Although the theory allows a more detailed normative assessment of particular ethical problems in economic life (p. 279), it merely applies an integrative normative frame to ethical issues that may occur in the "contractarian" network of economic participants. By not delving into how the moral subjects acquit themselves in situations which demand them to deploy morality for their self-interests, it is devoid of a deep investigation of the economic actors' subjective experiences (Taka 1996).

The integrative social contract theory is intertwined with multiple interest groups giving rise to a need for connecting between multiple moral subjects' ethical conduct and stakeholder management theory (Freeman 1984). Donaldson and Preston (1995) suggest that stakeholder management theory explicitly or implicitly contains descriptive/empirical, instrumental, and normative types of theory. Descriptive/empirical formulations of the theory are intended to describe and/or explain how firms or their managers actually behave. Instrumental theory purports to describe what will happen if managers or firms behave in certain ways. Although the stakeholder management theory, held as a normative stance, posits that managers should be accountable to such stakeholders as shareholders, creditors, employees, suppliers, and publics, it is certain that the theory should be elaborated by the underpinnings of both theoretical development and empirical testing. The normative legitimacy of stakeholder theory is echoed in the requirement that it is debated not on the basis of ownership or of a contract or an agency relation, but in terms of public policy (Boatright 1994). Moreover, Freeman (1994) specifies three principles to serve as constitutive elements of attempts to reform the law of corporations – the stakeholder enabling principle, the principle of director responsibility, and the principle of stakeholder recourse. In contrast to this normative buttress of the theory, a voice for critical advancement is also noteworthy. Langtry's (1994) tinged stockholder theories contend that stakeholder theorists preoccupation with the emphasis on multiple constituents' welfare can lose sight of the centrality of a corporation's fiduciary duty to stockholders. The tinged stockholder theory argue that managers' duty to pursue their stockholders' interests subject to various legal and moral side constraints should be central to preserving the other stakeholders' benefits. Rivoli (1995) furthers the argument on stakeholder theory by pinpointing an assumption of stakeholder theory that stakeholders conduct themselves in a self-interested manner. Illustrating a trend of changes in U.S. shareholders' resolutions toward social issues other than their wealth-maximizing self-interests, Rivoli argues for a communitarian ethic that surpasses the assumption of self-interests in stakeholder theory.

A finding that stockholders may sustain their own way of conduct inconsistent with the self-interest of maximizing their wealth highlights a nature of the strategic conduct deployed by each different stakeholder. Basically, the stakeholders' strategic conduct is assumed to oscillate between legal constraints and moral obligations. The stockholders in the Rivoli's case seem to align their strategic conduct with moral obligations beyond the bottom line of legal constraints. Their moral conduct takes on a strategic nature because they may believe in more benefits to reap in the long run in return for their resolution for social issues. However, a significant question is raised about the nature of managers' strategic conduct deployed in managing a variety of stakeholders. Despite the legally stipulated requirements for protecting stakeholders' interests, let alone moral obligations emphasized in stakeholder management theory, top managers in particular are likely to manipulate stakeholders' interests by circumventing a discretionary scope of corporate control by stakeholders (Huse and Eide 1996). Worse is the case that middle managers are entrapped in role conflict and ambiguity in their relations to stakeholders, as positioning the middle managers in the managerial labor process (Teulings 1986) is most apt to leave the managers accountable to no-one in particular (Brittan 1996). This is so because the managers' status as a composite of "part of labor" and "part of capital" (Carter 1985) can easily lead them to avert accountabilities on the excuse of not belonging to a particular faction of "capital" or "labor" (Song 1996).

This weakness in the stakeholder management theory raises the issue of agent-principal relationship because, as we have discussed above, the shape of agent-principal relationship is dynamically contingent upon different situations in which both corporate management and their stakeholders are bound to contend against each other. Quinn and Jones (1995), rebuking the inherent defects of instrumental ethics, put an emphasis on the four principles of moral obligations for the principal-agent model itself to hold. They are "avoiding harm to others," "respecting the autonomy of others," "avoiding lying," and "honoring agreements" (p. 34). Quinn and Jones contend that managers as agents should observe the four moral principles in practicing the business policy, prior to their obligation of increasing the shareholders' wealth. Although these four moral principles are assumed to fill the gap between the managers' intrinsic moral obligations and their extrinsic obligation to stakeholders, it is still questionable whether such normativity can be secured purely within the multi-faceted principal-agent relationship. As Abrahamson and Park (1994) argue, top managers may try to maintain their interests over other stakeholders by not being strict in observing the required normativity of "avoiding lying," for example, by intentionally concealing negative organizational outcomes in a self-serving way. The mechanism revolving around the concealment strategy is reported to be complicated in connection with different interests of such stakeholders as boards of directors, large institutional investors, and accountants when, as stakeholders, they influence the concealment mechanism in a systematic way.

The basic stance common to the above three normative approaches to the discourse of business ethics can be recapitulated as the following. Normativity predicates that social order can be achieved by means of setting up moral norms as a bridge to the attainment of such a social order, which is assumed to help maintain an integration of organizational values and individual members' values. However, as moral norms are put into a manageable state by a situational logic, their application to organizations can never be credited with absolute, universal validity. Rather, they tend to be absorbed into such relative reference systems as firms' productivity, efficiency, and profitability. As a consequence, organizational norms are bound to fall short of eliciting the organizational members' whole-hearted commitment. The basic problem of "normativity" lies in a gap between the ideality of releasing organizational values and the reality of their conflict with the members' values (Liedtka 1988). It is, thus, crucial to recognize that ideality often tends to neglect unintentionally, or marginalize intentionally, what is really going on with regard to the moral subjects' ethical conduct in the business arena. As Trevino (1986) works:

> Normative ethical theory is not designed for the purpose of explaining or predicting behavior. Rather, normative ethical theory represents an ideal that may not reflect accurately the processes engaged in by people in actual situation (p. 604).

If there is a missing point in accurately reflecting the processes engaged in by people in actual situations, this chapter is to provide a description of what has been disregarded in the discourse of business ethics in which a normative approach is predominant (Mitnick 1995; Kjonstad and Willmott 1995; Nicholson 1994; Jones 1995). Nonetheless, the intent of this chapter is, however, not to negate the significance of the normative stance but to complement it by descriptively diagnosing the processes in which moral norms are corporately appropriated in the context of new managerial practices (Storcy 1995; Kerfoot and Knights 1995). The analytic position developed in this chapter is grounded on skepticism towards the adoption of "shared values" as a tenet of corporate culturism (Peters and Waterman 1982; Schein 1986), which leads to an epistemological position that only "expressions" of the values are expediently shared by organizational participants for corporate objectives.

The Other Side of Normativity: Engineered Moral Norms

Problematizing the Notion of "Shared Values"

When normativity is engineered as corporate values to be shared by members, this process begets some ethical contestations. This is because the mechanisms of "sharing," espoused by corporate culturism in particular, is geared to engineering values in the form of moral norms in intentional and often compelling ways. As Willmott (1993) notes, a range of values to be engineered is limitless as long as they are contributory to all-encompassing corporate performances (efficiency, effectiveness, profitability, and quality). This limitlessness of values has to be efficiently controlled, and hence the idea of "corporate core values" comes into play. Principally initiated by top management, these values come to be cornerstones for maintaining "strong" corporate culture.

However, behind the issue of whether or not values should be shared lies a further matter. The question that this chapter critically reflects upon is the assumption that values can be shared in the scheme of corporate culture. The descriptive question of whether values *can* be shared has been obscured by the debate over the normative question of whether they *should* be shared. Basically, the normative prescription that values should be shared may circumscribe the boundary of moral application within individual companies (Dahler-Larsen 1994). Insofar as moral norms are calculated to be a good asset for managerial prescriptions, they become ready to be harnessed in a corporately circumscribed way. It follows that employees are bound to constitute their subjectivity by efforts to identify with those corporate moral norms that are legitimated as corporate core values. However, a question still remains whether employees' efforts to identify with corporate core values are genuine or instrumental. If employees consent to the corporate imposition of core values and norms only to maintain their membership and avoid excommunication, an explanation should be given to the employees' strategic conduct of "sharing" as compared with an acquiescent act of sharing. As Willmott (1993) argues, instead of the production of committed, enthusiastic, and self-disciplining subjects, the possible effect of a corporate imposition of core values and norms may be the reinforcement of instrumentality amongst employees who comply with corporate demands without internalizing the core values and norms.

When strategic conduct is lacking in a deep identification with core values and norms, their compliance may be understood as selective and calculative. In this case, employee behavior is (minimally) congruent with "realizing" the corporate values and norms, but only insofar as it may be calculated that material and/or symbolic advantage can be gained from managing the appearance of consent (Willmott 1993). The corporately legitimated tenet of "shared values" in the name of corporate ethos is a discursive practice that may be socially exploited both in an intended managerial prerogative and a calculative employee consent (Sturdy et al. 1992). This claim is echoed by the notion that "sharing" has two essentially opposing constructs in one word: unite and divide. The Oxford English Dictionary (1989) shows the following explanation of the word "share": (1) to participate in (an action, activity, opinion, feeling, or condition); to perform, enjoy, or suffer in common with others; to possess (a quality) which other persons or things also have; (2) to cut into parts, divided, cloven. Given that ethicality is significantly concerned with the harms brought to others in ways that are outside their own control (Hosmer 1994), the "unity" ethos of corporate culture may bring about unethical practices if it hinders the individual members' job rights. Employees' individual rights predicated on their competing views of corporate morality are marginalized and structurally divided from the corporate core values and norms.

Strategic Conduct of Sharing "Expressions"

It is, therefore, conceivable that employees in the company, when they are induced to share the values and norms initiated by corporate management, employ their own strategic conduct to cope with them. The ways of strategic conduct may vary according to the degree of employees' perceived compulsion accompanied by the imposition of corporate core values and norms. It is crucial that the generally expected mode of reaction will be to share only "expressions" rather than "values" enacted upon them by the corporate management. This contrasting act is more of a general social act. Cohen (1985, 15) explicates this tension in terms of the contrast between shared "meanings" and shared "symbols":

> Such categories as justice, goodness, patriotism, duty, love, peace, are almost impossible to spell out with precision. The attempt to do so invariably generates argument, sometimes worse. But their range of meanings can be glossed over in a commonly accepted symbol – precisely because it allows its adherents to attach their own meanings to it. *They share the symbol, but do not necessarily share its meanings.* Community is just such a boundary-expressing symbol. As a symbol, it is held in common by its members; but its meaning varies with its members' unique orientation to it. In the face of this variability of meaning, the consciousness of community has to be kept alive through manipulation of its symbols (emphasis added).

In the business firm in particular, the circulation of such "expressions" in the form of a uniform and lip service not only gives an appearance of observing a corporate code of ethics, it is also deployed as a means by which employees maintain membership and secure their self-preservation in the company. The distancing of one's self from corporate core values and norms may be mediated by the strategic conduct of sharing expressions as a preferred means of preserving and asserting self-identity. Notably, even corporate management can also deploy the strategic conduct of sharing expressions. For instance, the corporate management is often not committed to securing their employees' job rights – protectable by autonomy in organizational practices – such as discretion in decision making, etc. Rather, the corporate management's main concern is more likely to engineer autonomy so that the employees' lack of capacity to handle their autonomy is complemented and steered by the determinate power of the corporate management. To the extent that corporate management is not authentically committed to the ethical value of autonomy, all they share with their employees is the normative expression of autonomy, which the corporate management is eager to justify them in endorsing. Indeed, the dynamics of deploying normative expressions should be central to explicating the agents' strategic conduct as Abrahamson and Park (1994, 1330) suggest:

> Agency theorists have said little about how agents use *language and other symbols* to further their own interests (emphasis added).

The employees' identity work, to maintain their self-identity and self-interests from being identified with the corporate values and norms, is a basic behavior pattern of sharing "expressions," to the extent that they are at least not committed to the imperatives of "core values and norms." This is related with the employees' own ways of defining reality. Among the ways to interpret reality is the circulation of "phrases" in people's accounts to each other. Given that "accounts" are an important means by which to represent employees' competing value-standpoints, a consideration of some particular modes of verbal accounts is of significance. It may take on a form of idiomatic phrases by which the employees' collective attitudes towards the "corporate values and norms" is aphoristically conveyed. Just as employees are seduced to minimize the anxiety-laden experience of having to cope with an excess of autonomy by complying with a few core values (Willmott 1993), a few core phrases may be selectively coined and circulated by employees. Of significance is that these phrases convey the employees' ambivalence. The content of the phrases may carry an ethos of shared core values, but simultaneously can imply a pejorative nuance in a marked way. More importantly, it may contain elements of the employees' innermost aspirations, which are banned under the potentially totalitarian regime of corporate core values. Therefore, the phrases are bound to convey mixed messages. This is, in a sense, inevitable since the regime of corporate culture as the context for the constitution of phrases itself is a sourceful arena of contradictory practices.

The willingness and ability to circulate "chosen phrases" is to confirm the employees' belief that they have autonomy to define the reality according to their competence. Contrary to this self-affirmative aspect of constituting the chosen phrases, the "divisive" nature of sharing can be accomplished through a very intricate work of iteration and circulation of phrases through production and reproduction of languages. That is, words are selected for validating corporate core values and norms. As a result, some expressions are allowed to be shared or circulated while others are not. For instance, the managers in Watson's (1994) ethnographic study were not allowed to share the word "job." Employees, in the new scheme of things, were in "skill grades" instead of "jobs" and could be required to carry out any task appropriate to their skill level. Hence, nobody "owned" a job. To use the term "job" was to be slapped down by the injunction to "wash your mouth out" (p.115). This practice of seclusion leads the managers to be passively complying with the corporate values and norms in the situated practices by crossing off corporate. Consequently, employees' strategic conduct of sharing "expressions" can be formed around the pretense of "as if" as a behavior pattern. Because employees cannot survive in the company while completely resisting the corporate values and norms, they may pretend to share the values and norms as if they are actively committed to them. The negative effect of this mode of conduct is self-deceptive. An excess of instrumental compliance is likely to make employees lose the competence to criticize or resist the prevailing system of cultural logic and accordingly acquiesce to it. As a result, they are habituated into taking the reality defined by corporate core values and norms for granted as if it could be legitimated in every respect. This fetishism is likely to paralyze the employees' competence of ethical judgment (Bauman 1993).

In summary, a question of how the employees' efforts for identity work are secured and obscured in the process whereby corporate values and norms are engineered is central to a reflection of normative prescriptions of corporate culturism. It should be stressed that if the range of expressions open to "sharing" are directed and narrowed by both corporate management and employees, then this is a condition of possibility for the social manipulation of morality. Here, it is of crucial importance to spell out the distinction between "corporate values" and "shared expressions" with regard to their ethical import. The yardstick is the extent to which moral subjects commit to their conduct of sharing in terms of being accountable to consequences of sharing as well as being responsible for unintended consequences of sharing. However, the yardstick is itself vulnerable to the employees' subjective opportunism (Jones 1995) because they can accommodate an ethically relativistic attitude for unintended consequences on the excuse of not sharing corporate core values and norms. The engineered norms by corporate culturism thus reproduces the conditions of "demoralization" and "degradation" for which it is presented as a remedy (Willmott 1993). This subversion of "moralization" into "demoralization" as an outcome of engineering norms is meant to reveal some crucial discrepancies between the front and the backstage of strong corporate culture companies.

Effects of Shared Expressions: Manipulation of Moral Norms

Given that any aspect of instrumental rationality in the social act (Weber 1968) is morally *problematized* as manipulative (Sorell and Hendry 1994), the managerially expedient formula that "good ethics is good business" should be reflected (Quinn and Jones 1995) in the light of its susceptibility to a social manipulation of morality (Bauman 1991). The notion of "moral manipulation" indicates that morality is intentionally "engineered" and "exploited" by certain interest groups or individuals for their supposedly amoral interests. Because meaning is by nature alienable, movable, and manipulable (McCracken 1986), moral values and norms as meanings can instrumentally function for such utilities as corporate performance, impression management, etc. Morality is not respected for its own sake, but it is appropriated in a corporate way.

The social actor's interest in manipulating morality can also be expressed in the form of "impression management." Studies of impression management contribute to a broad understanding of people's moral conduct by assuming that people may strive to attain the benefits of being recognized as fair, but without actually behaving fairly. Such self-promotions of fairness lacking in substance may be referred to as "hollow justice." Indeed, fairness is a socially constructed reality, which is a desired label that people seek to attach to their behaviors (Greenberg 1990, 139). The pervasiveness of people's pursuit for "looking fair" induces them to partake of a collective complicity by employing impression management tactics like justifications, apologies, entitling, and reputation-building in order to appear to share "fairness" as a moral expression (pp. 127–138). Consequently, the effect of this collective complicity is to produce a hypocritical culture inducing moral cynicism amongst the members.

The other typical mode of manipulating morality is to resort to "moral norms" as the obligatory force. As Kunda's (1992) study of Tech corporate culture illustrates, the elements of "strong" corporate culture agenda are aimed at a normative control by elevating them as moral norms within the company. To the extent that the ethos of corporate culture is generated within the company and preserved in distinction from the influence of a general society (Dahler-Larsen 1994), the obligatory force of the ethos of shared values can be an impetus for manipulating moral norms. Insofar as the ethos is considered by members to be a unique set of norms for governing their conduct and soul (Rose 1989), a replacement of general social norms with corporate values and norms becomes effective for managing the members. However, the corporate values and norms are destined to serve the preservation of the identity of any particular company, which sustains its binding force through socialization and punitive sanctions. Therefore, the realm of members' democratic individuality (Gilbert 1990) would be relatively narrowed and inflicted by the predatory power of corporate values and norms. In spite of these infliction, the sovereignty of corporate culture over its members is legitimated on the premise that the sovereignty of corporate culture is more powerful than that of society in general because corporate culture is enforced by its differentiation from the society (Dahler-Larsen 1994).

However, legitimizing the sovereignty of corporate culture as the corporate norm may produce self-contradictory traps. When individuals are content with relying upon the sovereignty of corporate culture as a reliable greater power, the moral hazard is that they are indulging in that habitual practice of attributing the outcome of personal wrongdoings not to themselves but to the sovereignty of corporate culture. Indeed, a normative control by recourse to corporate culture is most likely to result in the members' collective egoistic attitude to the unintended consequences. Here, Kelley's attribution theory (1967) is more than illuminating. According to Kelley, "consensus" as an attributional cue indicates whether all the persons engaged in behavioral responses to a certain situation respond in the same manner or not. When the degree of consensus is high, they tend to attribute the unintended consequences to external factors rather than internal factors. This indicates that a construction of "consensus" by means of corporate culture (Willmott 1993) may lead members to partake in a complicity to exploit an ethic of consensus in the name of the corporate culture in order to secure a "safe haven," where they are exempted from responsibility for any possible unintended consequences.

Insofar as the members' complicity to appropriate moral expressions needs to be systematically checked by corporate management, a surveillance mechanism becomes more tightened beyond the apparent dominance of the visual dimension addressed by others (e.g., Lyon 1994). Surveillance over the use of words repeated in the members' day-to-day practices is to reinforce a corporate management's imposition of corporate core values upon its members through which the ways of how members share the corporate values and norms are monitored. In effect, management is partly done by surveillance over the members' accounts. The surveillance mechanism works as a more intelligent monitoring to check when and where moral expressions pertinent to the core corporate values of "quality" and "profit" are displayed. Managing is partly accomplished by surveillance over "expressions" or the use of expressions through which morality is conveyed in an ethos of sharing. Although employees may address moral issues in their company, they are bound to be cautious. They may share expressions of moral talk but limit them in ways that do not threaten organizational harmony and/or efficiency, and their own reputation for power and effectiveness (Bird et al. 1989). Indeed, morality is socially manipulated by a mechanism to produce social conformity and obedience to a prevailing system of inequalities and existing power relations. This is most salient in the business firms where morality is systematically susceptible to the corporate appropriation through the medium of circulating selected expressions. The conceptual arguments advanced so far can be succinctly diagrammed as follows:

Figure 1: Normative Values and Expressions: Commitment or Manipulation?

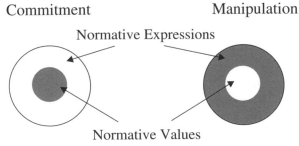

The 'jam' doughnut with its content core of integrity   The 'ring' doughnut with its hole empty of values

The diagram is guided by a metaphor of a "doughnut." The illustration on the left (commitment) is compared to a "jam" doughnut, which indicates a state of moral integrity where normative values become sufficiently realized. In contrast, the illustration on the right (manipulation) is compared to a "ring" doughnut, which indicates a state of empty values where only expressions of the normative values are expediently shared. Illustrations are now presented to clarify the theoretical concepts discussed so far and elaborate them in an empirical setting.

Case Illustrations

Edinso: A British Insurance Company

An empirical study was carried out by focusing on ethnographic interviews (Spradley 1977) with a cluster of middle managers in a British insurance company. The interviews were conducted in a "conversational" manner with an emphasis on "open" questions related to their everyday routines in the company. The interview accounts present some illustrations as to how a corporately espoused ethos of shared values and norms remains empty and, instead, only expressions of the values and norms are shared both by corporate management and employed middle managers.

As a typical insurance company, Edinso (a pseudonym) is keen to implement such popular business strategies as "corporate culturism" and "quality agenda (or, TQM)." What is going on in Edinso can be identified as an attempt to engineer a shift from a "family" metaphor to a "corporate" metaphor. However, because the corporate engineering of the family metaphor as a collective norm would likely bring about the effect of manipulated consensus (Archer 1988), the myth of cultural integration, attempted by Edinso's corporate management with recourse to new managerial practices, needs to be reflected in light of ethical contestations. As mediating concepts by which to assess "ethicality" embedded in the social act revolving around the myth of cultural integration, Archer's analytic concepts (p. 4) seem to be helpful for a deep understanding of the cultural dynamics in and around Edinso. These are logical consistency and causal consensus. Logical consistency is the degree of internal compatibility between the components of culture. Causal consensus is the degree of social uniformity produced by the imposition of culture by one set of people on another through the whole gamut of familiar techniques – manipulation, mystification, legitimization, naturalization, persuasion, and argument.

A salient example in questioning the degree of logical consistency was found to be the incompatibility between the collective ethos of sharing and the individuated imposition of . Both of these were affected by what Storey (1995) has called the new managerial discourses. A representative instance of this incompatibility was the allegedly strong "family atmosphere" in Edinso. As it was revealed in the managers' interview accounts, expressions of family imagery were applied sparingly. They were paternalistically appropriated mainly for relationships between corporate management and employees rather than for relationships among the employees. This paternalistic style of management (Kerfoot and Knights 1993) led only the preferences of "somebody upstairs" to be shared. Other competing voices were excluded. The employed managers' strategic conduct in relationship to their boss was bound inevitably to share the expressions which were "chosen phrases," delivering an implied consent to the boss' preference of values and norms. It follows that the moral expressions of family imagery were only hierarchically valid between the paternalistic leader and the loyal followers, leaving lateral relationships among the employees far from genuine family-like relations. The absence of intimacy between the different departments in Edinso was evidenced in the interviewed managers' accounts, showing their indifference to what was going on in other departments. As Mr. Marketing Manager alludes to this problem:

> Because the Service department is a mile and a half away, I don't feel I've got an accurate feel of how morale is or what the main issues are. And it is very much a view that is filtered by Mr. Service Director that I get, which might not always be the same view I get by being face to face with a lot of the finance people on a regular basis.

Indeed, family imagery as a moral expression is fractured by the expediency of its users, and the fragment of a family imagery is exacerbated when it is limitedly deployed for consolidating group cohesiveness within individual departments that lay claim to supremacy of their own expertise in the formation of corporate strategy (Knights and Morgan 1991). This expedient use of family imagery as a fragmented moral expression brings about segmentalism as its main effect (Kanter 1983). It is notable that segmentalism is fuelled by the individuated imposition of accountabilities which is simultaneously effected by new managerial practice as TQM (Munro 1995). Recognition that such an individuated imposition of accountabilities is incompatible with the collective ethos of sharing as a tenet of corporate culturism leads to the conclusion that the fragmented use of moral expressions gives rise to a serious doubt over the degree of "logical consistency" within Edinso.

Figure 2: Family Values and Expressions in Edinso

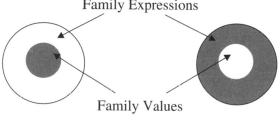

Inter-Departmental Horizontal Relationship

Intra-Departmental Hierarchical Relationship

Family Expressions

Family Values

Another example of weakening the degree of "logical consistency" was the implementation of "quality agenda" in Edinso. It was by means of the very "quality agenda" that Edinso tried to change what one of their managers referred to as "a whole sort of culture quite significantly towards serving the customer and getting things done right the first time." However, the legitimacy of changing "a whole sort of culture" is confined to Edinso's declared core values such as "serving the customer" and "getting things right the first time." Moreover, the incorporation of quality into Edinso's corporate culture does not entail its intended consequences. Such terms implying collective ethos of quality as "openness" and "team briefing" are no more than expressions lacking in substance. These expressions carry their own consequences, intended or not. In Edinso, an official espousal of sharing good ideas through an open door communication brought about the effect that openness was confined to those ideas, which must be contributory to corporate core values and norms to the exclusion of any other competing views. A corporate morality of openness was fractured when it was delivered with an insinuation that the superiors' time was money, and consequently amplified the distance between superiors and subordinates. It was also found that the Team Briefing System in Edinso, while carrying an ethic of sharing collective information, was perceived by the members only as a structure-added expression of organizational communication which amounted to less than a lauded decentralization of decision-making.

Rather than open up issues and disseminate much of the important information, which the members anticipated to share, it was perceived as reinforcing top down direction setting as mandatory.

These "decentralizing" practices are most likely to provoke the members' skeptical attitude to Edinso's espoused core values like "family" and "quality," and to result in their estrangement from those values. That is, the degree of "causal consensus" on the part of the members of Edinso is to be low in proportion to the low degree of logical consistency in such direct components of Edinso's corporate culture as internal strategies of "family imagery" and "TQM."

In contrast to "family imagery" and "quality agenda" as internal strategies to control Edinso's labor power, both Edinso's relations with IFAs (Independent Financial Advisors) and Edinso's "ethical unit trust" as an investment product were the mediators to convey Edinso's internal manifestations of corporate culture to other stakeholders externally. Edinso's staunch support for IFAs was identified to be used as an objective indicator by which to impose more accountabilities upon employees, exploiting the surplus from labor. We suggest that the members might be skeptical about the compatibility between the enactment of non-fiscal personnel policy like that of "family atmosphere" and the implementation of performance-based pay on the basis of IFAs' objective indicators of the members' individual performance. In short, the ethical expression of "independence" was peripherally directed at the objective indicator of individual performance rather than centrally directed at the IFAs' comprehensive assessment of Edinso as a recommendable company for customers in terms of Edinso's internal ethical integrity.

Edinso as an institutional shareholder was required to show up with the most impeccable image possible to the policyholders of ethical unit trust. The criteria of ethical unit trust were intended to upgrade the ethical standards of the invested companies as high as possible. Any company which manufactures armaments or nuclear weapons, etc. is not currently considered suitable for ethical investment. However, both Edinso and their policyholders were found to be passive in their involvement with the ethical unit trust. Their main interest was not so much in upgrading the ethical standards of the invested companies as in making money by means of using it as a marketing strategy for Edinso and as a tax-advantageous insurance commodity for policyholders.

Perversely, the members of Edinso were estranged from any potential effort to scrutinize the congruity between the ethical standard of Edinso's internal corporate culture and the ethical unit trust, which is supposedly credited with the moral superiority of Edinso's corporate culture. Indeed, the conduct of all agents surrounding the ethical unit trust was peripherally directed at marketing strategy or tax advantage and not centrally directed at genuine, proactive concerns with the ethical standards of invested companies.

These "decentralizing" practices would most likely lead the members of Edinso to be skeptic about and consequently less committed to, the corporately espoused values and norms. That is, the degree of "causal consensus" is to be low insofar as the members perceive that such channels of Edinso's business transactions as "IFAs" and "ethical unit trust" do not centrally focus on their authentic normativity.

Kaymo: A Korean Motor Company

The corporate culture of a Korean motor company, Kaymo, also carries the same example as in Edinso discussed above. The most outstanding example of the Korean corporate core values and norms is the collective commitment to a realization of harmony (which is called "*hwa*" in Korean) (Lee 1993). However, the corporate core value of harmony is confined to organizational behavior within the individual firm's inward relations and is not extended to outward relations with other subcontracting firms. The big firm's senses of relative superiority with regard to firm size and the level of technology make them exceedingly stingy in stretching their officially espoused value of harmony to their relations with small businesses in Korea. An interview excerpt with a middle manager in a small subcontracting firm which produces automobile parts (Yoon and Kim 1995, 20) is more than suggestive:

> They do not share information and technology with us at all. Instead they are only threatening a cut of transactions with us if we do not follow them as we are told.

A division of "them and us" is derived from differences in firm size and the level of technology between big and small firms. Most disappointingly, Kaymo's proclaimed ethos of harmony does no good for overcoming these distances arising out of the relative sense of superiority. Rather, such corporate ethos remains only a moral expression which is appropriated for shaping employees' self-image to be narrow in the corporate image, not to be broad as a member of a national economy. As Kunda (1992, 225) argues, shaping citizens by such a restricted expression of corporate morality may, in the long run, undermine the foundations of collective action. He raises a question of what will happen to the theatre of reality and its elaborate props when, or if, times change and assumptions no longer hold. His worry is even predictive of the effects brought about by a demise of the Japanese strong corporate culture where for a long time both management and workers enjoyed a kind of mutual agreement under which job security was exchanged for subordination (Takayama 1996).

Figure 3: Harmony as a Core Value and Expression in Kaymo

Intra-Firm Relationship   Inter-Firm Relationship

Harmony Expressions

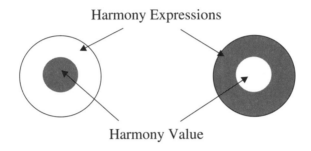

Harmony Value

We have so far illustrated some cases which evidence the effects of "shared expressions" in the context of new managerial practices. Although the number of cases necessary to underpin the notion of "shared expressions" is not great, the existence of corroborative accounts across East and West corporate cultures helps to buttress the validity of our argument. Based upon the further elaboration of theoretical arguments and its application to empirical evidence, the conceptual distinction between "shared values" and "shared expressions" could enhance the degree of its universalizability (Benhabib 1990).

Conclusion

This chapter identified that the normative prescription of "shared values" as a fundamental assumption in the Principles for Business in The Caux Roundtable is problematic in view of a descriptive position that only "expressions" of the values can be shared. We discussed that the members' strategic conduct of sharing expressions is constituted by the imperatives of new managerial practices. We warned that the moral prescriptions by diverse modes of managerialism are peripherally directed at the "other" rather than centrally internalized into the moral subjects' subjectivity. Managers with a status of employed stakeholder also partake in a complicity to exploit morality through the medium of shared expressions in both active and often negative manners such that they become entrapped in a vicious circle of moral cynicism and dependence. Indeed, their ambivalent subjectivity is constituted around the tension between a genuine commitment to normative values and the manipulative use of moral expressions.

The current status of the discourse of business ethics needs to be supplemented by an understanding of the other side of normativity, one which is doomed to be "divisive" and "manipulative" in the context of new managerial practices. A serious reflection should be cast upon whether gains from instrumental ethics for business are greater than losses from a vicious circle of moral cynicism and dependence. In order to prevent normativity from losing its authenticity through the narrowed sharing of moral expressions in the context of new managerial practices, the competing views of corporate morality should be nourished as part of an authentic organizational culture. The discretionary capacity of freely raising the competing views of the existing moral norms is indispensable to developing a full theory of normative referencing towards more desired states of normative guidance (Mitnick 1995). This chapter highlighted a notion that more desired states of normative guidance can be hampered by the stakeholders' strategic conduct of sharing expressions.

Therefore, the aim of a full theory of normative referencing should be to realize normative values through a mutual harmony between logical consistency of cultural elements and its resulting causal consensus at a level as high as possible. As the level becomes high, normativity, which is otherwise apt to be expediently relativized by the shared expressions of norms, could recover its authenticity and acquire the moral subjects' commitment.

Endnote

* Ji-Hwan Song died of leukemia in 1997. This chapter is a testimony to his dedication and his enthusiasm for his emerging career.

References

Abrahamson, E., and Park, C. S., "Concealment of Negative Organizational Outcomes: An Agency Theory Perspective," *Academy of Management Journal* 37, no. 5 (1994), 1302–1334.

Archer, M., *Culture and Agency: The Place of Culture in Social Theory* (Cambridge, UK: Cambridge University Press, 1988).

Bauman, Z., *Postmodern Ethics* (London: Blackwell, 1993).

Benhabib, S., *The Communicative Ethics Controversies* (Boston: The MIT Press, 1990).

Bird, F., Westley, F., and Waters, J. A., "The Uses of Moral Talk: Why Do Managers Talk Ethics?" *Journal of Business Ethics* 8 (1989), 75–89.

Boatright, J. R.. "What's So Special About Shareholders?" *Business Ethics Quarterly* 4 (1994), 393–408.

Brady, F. N., and Hatch, M. J. "General Causal Models in Business Ethics: An Essay on Colliding Research Traditions," *Journal of Business Ethics* 11 (1992), 307–315.

Brittan, S., "The Snares of Stakeholding," *Financial Times* (Feb. 1, 1996).

Carter, R., *Capitalism, Class Conflict and the New Middle Classes* (London: Routledge, 1985).

Cohen, A., *Symbolic Construction of Community* (London: Routledge, 1985).

Dahler-Larsen, P., "Corporate Culture and Morality: Durkheim-Inspired Reflections on the Limits of Corporate Culture," *Journal of Management Studies* 31, no. 1 (1994), 1–18.

Donaldson, T. and Dunfee, T. W., 'Toward A Unified Conception of Business Ethics: Integrative Social Contract Theory," *Academy of Management Review,* 19, no. 2 (1994), 252–284.

Donaldson, T. and Preston, L. E., "The Stakeholder Theory of the Corporation: Concepts, Evidence, and Implications," *Academy of Management Review* 20, no. 1 (1995), 65–91.

Ferrell, O. C. and Gresham, L. G., "A Contingency Framework for Understanding Ethical Decision Making in Marketing," *Journal of Marketing* 49 (1985), 87–96.

Freeman, R. E., *Strategic Management: A Stakeholder Approach* (Boston: Pitman, 1984).

Freeman, R. E., "The Politics of Stakeholder Theory: Some Future Directions," *Business Ethics Quarterly* 4 (1994), 409–422.

Gilbert, A., *Democratic Individuality* (Cambridge: Cambridge University Press, 1990).

Greenberg, J., "Looking Fair vs. Being Fair: Managing Impressions of Organizational Justice," in *Research in Organizational Behavior*, eds., B. M. Staw and L. L. Cummings (Greenwich, Conn.: JAI Press, 1990), 12, 111–157.

Hosmer, L. T. "Strategic Planning as If Ethics Mattered," *Strategic Management Journal* 15 (1994), 17–34.

Hunt, S. D. and Vitell, S., "A General Theory of Marketing Ethics," *Journal of Macromarketing* (Spring 1986), 5–16.

Huse, M. and Eide, D., "Stakeholder Management and the Avoidance of Corporate Control," *Business and Society* 35 (1996), 211–243.

Jones, T. M., "Instrumental Stakeholder Theory: A Synthesis of Ethics and Economics," *Academy of Management Review* 20, no. 2 (1995), 404–437.

Kanter, R. M., *The Change Masters* (London: Allen and Urwin, 1983).

Kelley, H. H., "Attribution Theory in Social Psychology," in *Nebraska Symposium on Motivation,* ed. D. Levine, vol. 15 (Lincoln: University of Nebraska Press, 1967).

Kerfoot, D. and Knights, D., "Masculinity, Management and Manipulation: From Paternalism to Corporate Strategy in Financial Services in Britain," *Journal of Management Studies* 30, no. 4 (1993), 659–677.

Kerfoot, D. and Knights, D., "Empowering the 'Quality Worker'?: The Seduction and Contradiction of the Total Quality Phenomenon," in *Making Quality Critical*, eds., H. Willmott and A. Wilkinson (London: Routledge, 1995).

Kjonstad, B. and Willmott, H., "Business Ethics: Restrictive or Empowering?" *Journal of Business Ethics* 14 (1995), 445–464.

Knights, D. and Morgan, G., "Corporate Strategy, Organizations, and Subjectivity: A Critique," *Organization Studies* 12, no. 2 (1991), 251–273.

Kunda, G., *Engineering Culture* (Philadelphia: Temple University Press, 1992).

Langtry, B., "Shareholders and the Moral Responsibilities of Business," *Business Ethics Quarterly* 4 (1994), 431–444.

Lee, H. C., *The Corporate Culture of Korean Companies* (Seoul: Bakyoungsa, 1993).

Liedtka, J. M., "Value Congruence: The Interplay of Individual and Organizational Value Systems," *Journal of Business Ethics* 8 (1989), 805–815.

Lyon, D., *The Electronic Eye: The Rise of the Surveillance Society* (Cambridge: Polity, 1994).

McCracken, G., "Culture and Consumption: A Theoretical Account of the Structure and Movement of the Cultural Meaning of Consumer Goods," *Journal of Consumer Research* 13 (1986), 71–84.

Mitnick, B. M., "Systematics and CSR," *Business and Society* 34, no. 1 (1995), 5–33.

Munro, R., "Governing the New Province of Quality: Autonomy, Accounting and the Dissemination of Accountability," in *Making Quality Critical*, eds., H. Willmott and A. Wilkinson (London: Routledge, 1995).

Nicholson, N., "Ethics in Organizations: A Framework for Theory and Research," *Journal of Business Ethics* 13 (1994), 581–596.

Peters, T. J. and Waterman, R. H., *In Search of Excellence* (New York: Harper & Row, 1982).

Quinn, D. P. and Jones, T. M., "An Agent Morality View of Business Policy," *Academy of Management Review* 20, no. 1 (1995), 22–42.

Rivoli, P., "Ethical Aspects of Investor Behavior," *Journal of Business Ethics* 14 (1995), 265–277.

Rose, N., *Governing the Soul* (London: Routledge, 1990).

Schein, E. H., *Organizational Culture and Leadership* (San Francisco: Jossey-Bass, 1986).

Sinclair, A., "Approaches to Organizational Culture and Ethics," *Journal of Business Ethics* 12, no. 1 (1993), 63–73.

Song, J. H., "Business Ethics and the Corporate Manipulation of Expressions" (unpublished Ph.D. thesis, Edinburgh University, 1996).

Sorell, T. and Hendry, J., *Business Ethics* (Oxford: Butterworth-Heinemann, 1995).

Spradley, J. P., *The Ethnographic Interview* (New York: Harcourt Brace Jovanovich, 1979).

Storey, J., *Human Resource Management – A Critical Text* (London: Routledge, 1995).

Sturdy, A., Knights, D., and Willmott, H., *Skill and Consent: Contemporary Studies in the Labor Process* (London: Routledge, 1992).

Taka, I., "Revising Integrative Social Contract Theory: Toward Solving Awareness Issue in Japanese Management," Paper presented at the First World Congress of Business, Economics, and Ethics. Japan, July 25–28, 1996.

Takayama, H., "The New Corporate Culture," *Newsweek* (March 25, 1996), 40–42.

Teulings, W. M., "Managerial Labor Processes in Organized Capitalism: The Power of Corporate Management and the Powerlessness of the Manager," in *Managing the Labor Process*, eds., David Knights and Hugh Willmott (Cambridge: Gower, 1986).

Trevino, Z. K., "Ethical Decision Making in Organizations: A Person-Situation Interactionist Model," *Academy of Management Review* 11 (1986), 601–617.

Watson, T., *In Search of Management* (London: Routledge, 1994).

Weber, M., *Economy and Society* (New York: Bedminster Press, 1968).

Willmott, H. (1993) "Strength Is Ignorance; Slavery Is Freedom: Managing Culture in Modern Organizations," *Journal of Management Studies* 30, no. 4 (1993), 515–552.

Yoon, S. J. and Kim, S. P., "A Study on the Institutionalization of Technological Innovation through Inter-Organizational Cooperation," *Yonsei Business Review* 32, (1995), 5–42.

Company Communication:
From the Ethics of Communication to the Communication of Ethics

Jacques Polet

Abstract

Parallel to the evolution of the world of enterprise and business, there has been a growing awareness of the importance of the ethical reference. It becomes particularly visible in the development of projects, charters, and enterprise contracts, which are giving a greater place to moral data and tend to become real tools of entrepreneurial communication, both external and internal. The concern for the values underlying good communication seems sometimes to become blurred behind the proclaimed concern for good communication of the values of the enterprise, taking the place of the product *itself: there is there a strategic reversal that leads one to wonder about the possibility of an instrumentalist recovery of the ethical approach. Critical reflection is necessary here if one intends precisely to preserve the axiological credibility of the enterprise and its communication.*

The Basis of the Ethical Reference System

It is a well known fact that for some years ethical preoccupations have come to play an important role in debates about the environment, biomedical sciences, the media, and corporate behavior. One could almost go as far as to maintain that no subject or issue is discussed and dealt with without a reference to ethics.

It is not our purpose here to speculate about the causes, various as they are, of this phenomenon. One may, indeed, cite the fears experienced in the face of the ecological hazards which threaten our planet, as well as the serious questions raised by advances in science and technology with their sometimes problematical applications in the human sphere. But there is also the revelation, widely depicted, of various manipulations which have affected the collection and processing of journalistic information. Finally, who can forget the avatars of easy money ("silly money") earned in the 1980s by "yuppies" and other "golden boys," or else by means of stock exchange dealings bordering on the crime of insider trading, not to mention the sensational raids by the heroes of the takeover bids overexposed in the media.

Although these excesses are not all new (let us not be candid, as if we came from a "Golden Age"), it does nonetheless seem fair to say that these different phenomena, and their conjunctions, have undoubtedly crystallized in our time in the collective conscience as a need to brace ourselves against an attack on *values*. The idea prevails that one can no longer do whatever one likes, that there comes a time when one must try to control the onrush of technologies and single interest groups. What matters is to rediscover *meaning*.

It is possible to suppose that there is a common denominator to these somewhat scattered, sectorial axiological concerns (the disrespectful relation to nature, medical experiments which are overbold, the information show, the economy of "business," etc.). Some have formulated the hypothesis that the increase in ethical concerns and discourse could be correlated with the gradual weakening and withering of ideologies and grand political designs. The new collective basis of the democracies would in some way be made up of the *ethical reference system*.

And it is true that, for some years now, one has seen a multiplicity of charters, codes, and draft codes materialize which are evidence of the desire to give a moral dimension to economic and social life (see Polet 1991).

Projects, Charters, and Company Contracts

As we know, this movement started in the United States, the cradle of business ethics, and it achieved an exceptionally significant breadth: most of the largest firms have now internal codes formulating rules of behavior.

In Europe, the phenomenon appeared later, and in less institutionalized, or, more precisely, less constricting forms. There are fewer *ethical codes* in the strict sense of the term; that is to say formalized series of principles (duties and rights), endowed with a certain coercive force, with failures in observance punishable (warning, blame, exclusion, etc.) by bodies within the profession set up for this purpose. The code of ethics is in this sense a para-legal system.

On the other hand, *company projects* have multiplied: they do not come directly within the sphere of ethics, however. Their aim is first of all to spell out the identity and the main objectives of a given company. For example: defining oneself as a financial institution which aims to respond more particularly to the expectations of one or other section of the public, or wanting to be one of the five largest banks in the country. The project proposes a vision; it is meant to express a shared collective will and contains a genuine *strategic* dimension (Lemaître 1990).

The company project is often rounded off with a charter, the *company charter*. This is not surprising, given the function of the concept chosen, which is endowed with a certain symbolic connotation. The charter is more in the axiological sphere, in fact: it lists what it gives as the *permanent values* constituting the substructure of its actions. For example: quality of service, which is based on a detailed understanding of the requirements of customers and colleagues; recognition of and respect for the value of the employees of the company as a whole; but also improvement of know-how and emulation through the power of "example" and again: profitability, which must express itself, in action, in a systematic search for an "added value" for the company;[1] and equally, often cited as such, a respect for professional ethics. The most recurring principles are without any doubt clarity, transparency, honesty, truth, or objectivity (negative and unpleasant information have to be communicated as well as the positive ones), credibility, coherence, loyalty, and respect of human being.

One can also see that the "project," supplemented by the "charter," may end with a *company contract*, a genuine *moral contract* which proposes a series of reciprocal undertakings: "The company *asks* you . . ." / "The company *offers* you . . ." For example: the company asks you to give total loyalty to the firm/the company offers you respect for private life.

While speaking both of "professional ethics" and of "profitability," the company charter (which is the instance of this structure of concepts, which no doubt is closest to our purpose because it is the place par excellence for "values") is a good reflection of the *mixture* which clearly defines the very essence of the company ethic. In other words, and to adopt a Kantian vocabulary, the axiological reference of the company proceeds not from a *categorical imperative* but rather from a *hypothetical imperative*.

In the first case, respect for what is "good" is imposed by *pure duty* (I do good because it is my duty to do so, full stop). In the second instance, on the other hand, which concerns that of company charters, conforming with what is good cannot be separated from an *external perspective* of pure duty: *the life of firms or of business.*

The sociologist and economist Max Weber would, in the first case, have used the term *conviction ethics*, based on *strict adherence* to a system of values, and, in the second, *ethics of responsibility*, taking into account the search for *any consequences* of acts subtended by the same values.

In less philosophical terms, then one would say: let us prevent from any "angelic" (non-realistic) behavior. For throughout and beyond the actual precepts, the preoccupation to fit into the finality of the *corporation* is emphasized by most of the people in charge of company communication. They point out that acts of communication suppose an adhesion to the principles of the company management but, having to be non-manipulating means, they aim to "let know" and to "listening in." In the same spirit, communication must serve the company (its shareholders, staff, and customers) without prejudicing third parties nor hurting respectable feelings. Basically, it should reflect the company project, expressing its goals, its strategy, and the corporate culture of which communication will deepen and diffuse the originality.

Tension and Dialectic of Values

It is clear in fact that the relations between ethics and companies are difficult to grasp outside a *tension of polarity*, which often defines the *dialectic,* and the difficulty, of company communication.

Let us take the example of *transparency*. One can certainly see it as an ethical precept par excellence and the very principle of communication (of "good" communication). But one can also grasp straight away that it is not possible in company communication to make it an absolute principle "in itself," in the manner of a categorical imperative. No company is alone in the world; it must take account of competitors and ensure that it is competitive, and profitable, to safeguard its margins. All of this cannot be done by telling everyone everything all the time, as Lionel Brault, manager of an agency which specializes in company communication, points out. One must, he says, communicate *signs* in line with the key values of the company, but not communicate *the company in its totality,* adding: "If the company is absolutely transparent, one can see through it, and it disappears . . . ; complete transparency is impossible" (Brault 1992, 100).

In other words, the precept of "transparency" cannot march alone; it has to go hand in hand with the principle of *confidentiality*. Company communication cannot avoid being part of this dialectical debate.

The same polarization can be analyzed in the field of *information for shareholders*. On the one hand, one finds the need invoked for shareholders to exercise to the full their rights of ownership, through genuine participation, in full knowledge of the facts, in the direction and control of management, through annual general meetings and the board of directors. Victor Scherrer, chairman of Pilstral, has become the shareholders' spokesman with his work *Dans la jungle des affaires* [In the business jungle] (Scherrer 1991). An interview given when his book came out shows him not mincing his words: annual general meetings and "boards of directors are rubbish. Everything is discussed at them, except, of course, strategies, restructuring, mergers, acquisitions. The real discussions take place before the official meeting and more than once I have been annoyed at having had to take part in such a farce" (*Trends-Tendances*, Weekly, Bruxelles, 27 June 1994). Where the real focus of power lies, they point to the need to direct strategy, to channel the flow of proposals all-round, and to prepare decisions, but also to the pressures of urgency, especially at a time of crisis, etc.

From Substantial to Instrumental Ethics

It is obvious: an ethics of company communication does not present itself in terms of a choice between Good and Evil (a question of Morality). In real life, there is a balance between "various more or less contradictory imperatives," as Gilles Lipovetsky emphasized in *Le crépuscule du devoir* [The Dawn of Duty] (Lipovetsky 1992, 248).

The ethics of company communication does not proceed therefore from a *substantialist* approach: the aim of an ideal, unconditional *end in itself*. Rather, it lies in an *instrumentalist* approach to the facts: finding the *fairest means for effective action*.

But what is particularly striking today is the increasingly common type of approach assumed by company ethics and the documents (charters and moral contracts) which are its material expression. It appears in fact that these texts establishing the company's values are gradually becoming genuine *tools of internal and external communication*.

First of all in internal communication

One can see that these guides to ethics are circulated increasingly among the staff, particularly when one just joins the company, as *vectors of employee adherence and participation*. Some employers do not hesitate in this respect to include the ethical aspect explicitly in the profile of the posts to be filled. For example, a large financial institution, outlining the stock profile of the young people it recruits, requires "a high level of intelligence, flexibility so as to be able to adjust to a changing environment, multiple skills, a commercial outlook, commitment to the job and a keen ethical sense" (See *La Libre Entreprise*, a weekly supplement to *La Libre Belgique*, Daily, Bruxelles, 18 September 1993). One even has the feeling in this list that the terms with the strongest connotations are precisely those referring to the ethics "item," if one dare say so, which is thus at the heart of the company's discourse as soon as the working relationship is likely to be confirmed.

Then in external communication

The concern with ethics, in fact, increasingly overflows into the sphere of external communication. Companies no longer hesitate to display their values externally and make them the subject of a communication with high visibility:

☐ to a *large public* (its customers):
For example, a financial institution not long ago drew up a charter which it entitled nothing less than a "Declaration of Rights," addressed to its customers in the form of a notebook containing a series of numbered principles which the addressee can expect to see followed;

☐ to the *general public* (via the media):
In various newspapers and magazines, a powerful group in the chemical industry published a poster that encapsulated unambiguously the "spirit" of the company. In the poster, the company said that it identified the notion of progress with that of "man, whether customer, partner or employee of the firm" – progress which, moreover, knows "no frontiers" over the "five continents" adding that "progress sees itself responsible," and providing as proof that, according to it, "concern for the environment is primordial" and letting it be known that "15 percent of its investment is directed to the safety of human beings and the protection of their quality of life." [2]

Here clearly is a type of communication for all publics plainly positioned in the sphere of values. Again, any incoherence or any contradiction between the *official* communication of a company and what is *experienced* by the staff or *perceived* by external publics must be avoided. One therefore has to watch for any discrepancy between *identity* and *image*! A company which falls into this trap through a communication which lacks credibility will sooner or later fall victim of it.

From this, it is clear that what we intend is no longer to discuss the ethics of communication, but rather the *communication of ethics*, a genuine about-face.

Towards the Communication of Ethics

This communication which is centered on values is particularly important in the sphere of *crisis communications*. There was the famous case of the American pharmaceutical company "Johnson & Johnson" recalled by Gilles Lipovetsky (1992, 269–270).

"In 1982, seven people died in the United States, after taking Tylenol capsules to which some unknown person had added cyanide. Even before Johnson & Johnson had obtained all the information on the cause of the tragedy and even before legal liability had been evaluated, it assumed moral liability for it: it recalled immediately from the market the 31 million bottles of Tylenol, with a market value of one hundred million dollars, it set up a help line to answer questions from the public, it opened up its meetings to the media, it offered a reward of 100,000 dollars to anyone able to supply information leading to the arrest of the culprit. There is no doubt as to the ethical orientation of the operation. It was nonetheless a triumph of communication which managed to dramatize the firm's responsible action. Johnson & Johnson's strategy combined the moral imperative with the ostentatious spectacle of the sacrifice of material goods, duty with the challenge thrust at strictly economic logic. The whole source of the operation was its radical nature, in the exhibition of its moral rectitude."

Here we see an exemplary manifestation of *strategic ethics*, which is presented as a *mixture of ethical absolute* and communication spectacle. Its strength "is that it transforms a catastrophe into a media event, a crisis into sympathy capital": the proof is that "eleven weeks after the start of the crisis, the Johnson & Johnson brand had recovered 80% of its initial market share and, in 1984, all its share."

At the root of this decision, we can find the statement of corporate responsibility set up by Johnson & Johnson under the denomination of "Credo," a document with ethical orientation, of which the first version goes back to 1947. It consists of a brief text, a set of values more than a rule book code, which appears as a common denominator grounding the action of the company. Comments one of the managers, "What we are doing here is not specifically *mentioned* in the Credo, but it is definitely *generated* by the Credo" (Nash 1988, 100). This common reservoir of decency enables the company to maintain a unity of spirit throughout the strong decentralization which characterizes this multinational.

But what the big Tylenol crisis pointed out is the great importance of the personal ethical commitment of the top management. For in these periods of extreme tension, in case of an issue particularly controversial and "with the best way" not obvious to everyone, Johnson & Johnson's chairman Jim Burke had no hesitation in assuming direct responsibility and control over deciding what the true "spirit of the Credo" is (80). As Laura L. Nash reports, "Jim Burke has often stated that the guidance of the Credo played the most important role in management's decision making during the crisis" (97).

Now again, we must emphasize the fact that the Credo doesn't consist in a list of tenets hovering in "the heaven of principles." It occurs in a strongly instrumentalized process in which the appropriate decisions are taken from both a business and a moral point of view, the Credo itself being not all about charity but remaining "tied to basic economic and ethical considerations at the same time" (101). At the occasion of the "Credo Challenge Meetings," where managers of different J&J's companies were gathered, one of them confessed, "The general consensus was that, through the values were 'somewhat idealistic', they were not far off from reality" (85). A member of the executive committee went so far as to state "Part of management's responsibility is to convince the doubters inside the company that, in fact, following the Credo is the best way to manage our business" (104).

One cannot fail to see that "Perrier" company had the same attitude as Johnson & Johnson much more recently in a situation of crisis when it withdrew from the world market millions of bottles of mineral water characterized by what was claimed to be an excessive proportion of benzene, and not at the price of prudent discretion, but accompanying it, quite the opposite, by a great communication operation implying the "responsible" nature of this costly decision.

The same point can be demonstrated *negatively*, when companies have neglected or underestimated the importance of values in their approach to the market.

Here the Johnson & Johnson case can be significantly compared to that of "Nestle" concerning the infant formula controversy. Between 1977 and 1984, Nestle was boycotted in the United States because of the multinational's marketing policy which tended to encourage mothers in developing countries to replace breast-feeding by bottle-feeding with powdered milk. As the water was polluted and the mothers knew nothing of sterilization procedures, the use of milk substitutes led to an increase in child mortality of several millions a year. More than 1,200 organizations, in the US and abroad, joined in the boycott.

In a comprehensive study, S. Prakash Sethi has reported and analyzed over the whole period this dramatic affair of irresponsible marketing (Sethi 1994; see also Akhter 1994). Instead of facing and assuming the horrible reality, Nestle sued the members of the Third World Action Group (TWAG) involved with the German translation and publication in Switzerland of the originally English pamphlet "The baby killer" (by Mike Muller and War on Want, a London-based activist group dealing with problems in developing countries) printed just earlier in 1974. Being judged guilty of libel, the TWAG happened to experience what often occurs on the occasion of a trial: the challenge of the group gained high attention of media and public opinion. Spreading from Europe to the U.S.A., the controversy led to the setting up of the "Infant Formula Action Coalition" (INFACT) which proclaimed on July 4, 1977 a consumer boycott of all Nestle products in the U.S.A. Various groups, many of which were private voluntary organizations (PVO's), joined in the controversy, persuading the World Health Organization to formulation an international code of marketing of infant formula. Years of negotiations between Nestle and the International Boycott Committee succeed in an agreement with a joint announcement in Washington D.C. on October 4, 1984. Here, the multinational had paid a heavy and long tribute to its mismanaging of a big crisis.

One can infer with Lipovetsky, who also calls to mind the Nestle case, that "the image of commercial cynicism and the placing of the ethical parameter in parentheses have become errors of communication which can cost companies very dear" (Lipovetsky 1992, 271). The ethical perspective is now a dimension of communication, reflecting less a categorical duty than a public relations imperative "in accordance with the well-understood interest of the firms." In other words, a strategic investment.

While the managing director of the firm declared in 1982 that "Nestle will need a generation to restore its image" (Lipovetsky 1992, 271), it has to be admitted that the handicap did not prevent the firm from giving rise, barely some ten years later, to conjunctural analyses attributing it many fine opportunities. In a weekly letter from investment advisors, there was the following promising opinion: "Nestle is continuing to expand; the group is reinforcing its positions in countries with immense potential for growth in Eastern Europe and in Asia. Excellent prospects," and it concludes that the share is an "interesting investment" (*Budget Hebdo,* Association des Consommateurs Test-Achats, Weekly, Bruxelles, no. 632, 20 September 1993). It might be said that Nestle has changed significantly from that moment on. Yet, one has to be cautious in evaluating the impact of an ethical deficit on the image of a company.

The Ultimate Avatars: Ethics as Performance and Ethical Investments

The public claim of a concern with ethics may go a further step, however. This is the case when one observes initiatives tending to recognize firms for action taken on the Human Resources level and recompense them, by awarding them "Prizes" or other "Trophies" for ethics. This is ethics engaged, no longer simply in the sphere of *communication*, but in that of *competition*.

Without calling into question the certainly laudable intention of the initiators, and prizes for excellence in other matters may do some good, one may legitimately ask oneself whether this type of operation which associates ethics with the "cult of performance" is not here reaching the *critical threshold* of its instrumental use.

However, the ostentatious communication of ethical preoccupation seems to have difficulty in progressing hand-in-hand with the new concept of *corporate citizenship* that has been increasingly accepted by the entrepreneurial approach. Going beyond the natural and legitimate objective of profitability, this concept means, in the context of economic crisis, to care about taking social and humanitarian initiatives. For instance:

- to support institutions and activities in favor of handicapped people;
- to help organizations committed to include various kinds of marginalized people into professional work; and
- to cooperate with preventive programs against drug abuse in schools;

In fact, such initiatives are underway and one cannot avoid noticing their traces in certain forms of commercial or institutional communication.

At the end of this contribution, there is, of course, no room to launch a debate about this controversial issue that requires a serious treatment for itself. Just one question might be raised: Is it not likely that social and humanitarian aid with corporate sponsorship appears as an excuse or unpleasant alibi at a point in time when companies lay off people?

Having said this, it must be emphasized that this type of demonstrative communication, still fairly modest and qualified as "ethical," is hardly compatible, precisely from a moral point of view, with spectacular communication. To put it bluntly, it could become indecent (if, for instance, a company promotes its good reputation by helping homeless people). For, as a spokesperson of a big Belgium group stated, "the gift is nobler if it is discreet,"[3] particularly in the context of those industries that are at the core of social conflicts.

Nevertheless, it appears important to differentiate and distinguish:

- the *external* communication where philanthropism seems to be somewhat indecent; and
- the *internal* communication within the company: generally speaking, the employees appear to be satisfied by, and even proud of, belonging to a company of generous solidarity. Moreover, such a policy can help to overcome hierarchical tensions and promote cohesion and social "pacification" within the firm (Walter 1996, 110).

It goes without saying how complex these issues are and, once again, how questionable it is to limit oneself to the conception of an *absolute* ethics.

No "angelic" attitude certainly. And let us repeat because, as Lipovetsky says, "Better, after all, 'self-interested' action capable of improving man's fate than incompetent good will" (Lipovetsky 1992, 20).

Nonetheless, one must, *all things considered*, inoculate oneself against any ethics which is nothing more than incantatory exhortation, moralizing injunction, or exhibitionist competition.

Fundamentally, ethics is not *said* nor is it *done*. It is *experienced*.

Endnotes

1. Note the ambivalence of the concept of "value" which may be understood in various senses of the term.

2. Advertisement inserted in *Talent*, a weekly supplement which appeared in *La Libre Entreprise* of 16 January 1993 in particular.

3. It concerns Tractebel Company. Cited by *Eco-Soir*, a weekly supplement to *Le Soir*, Daily Bruxelles, 16 February 1996.

References

Akhter, S. H., Book review of S. P. Sethi, *Multinational Corporations and the Impact of Public Advocacy on Corporate Strategy*, in *Journal of International Business Studies* (Third Quarter 1994), 658–666.

Brault, L., *La Com: La communication d'entreprise au-delà du modèle publicitaire* (Paris: Dunod, 1992).

Lemaître, N., "Culture, stratégie et image de l'entreprise" [Culture, strategy, and image of the firm], in *Guide des médias*. Public relations and company communication. Supplément 3 (Bruxelles: Kluwer, 1990).

Lipovetsky, G., *Le crépuscule du devoir: L'éthique indolore des nouveaux temps démocratiques* (Paris: Gallimard, 1992).

Nash, L. L., "Johnson & Johnson's Credo," in *Corporate Ethics: A Prime Business Asset*, February 1988 (New York: The Business Roundtable, 1988).

Polet, J., "L'éthique des relations publiques. Actualisation d'un questionnement" [Ethics of public relations. Updating a survey]. In *Les relations publiques: De la théorie à la pratique*. Proceedings of the First European Seminar of research workers and practitioners in public relations, held at the Collège d'Europe in Bruges, published by Centre Européen des Relations Publiques, 1991, 171–177.

Scherrer, V., *Dans la jungle des affaires* (Paris: Le Seuil, 1991).

Sethi, S. P., *Multinational Corporations and the Impact of Public Advocacy on Corporate Strategy: Nestle and the Infant Formula Controversy* (Dordrecht/Boston/London: Kluwer, 1994).

Walter, J. 1996. "L'entreprise saisie par le social et l'humanitaire: Contribution à l'étude de la reconnaissance d'un monde professionnel," in *Recherches en communication*, no. 6, Département de communication de l'Université catholique de Louvain, Louvain-la-Neuve, 1996.

Part III
Ethical Challenges for Business Leaders Around the World

Business Ethics in Islamic Context:
Perspectives of a Muslim Business Leader

Tanri Abeng

Abstract

The role of the business leader is key to developing the culture of an enterprise. To exemplify its importance in the national and global context, the Muslim author from Indonesia points with admiration to Konosuke Matsushita, founder of Matsushita Electric Corporation, who already in the 1930s set up the seven ethical principles for healthy business growth, which also are commended by the Islamic imperative. Due to the current dynamic business environment, Muslims find themselves confronted with serious dilemmas and need guidance from a clearly developed Islamic business ethics. For this purpose, the author offers, first, the essentials of such an ethics: the utmost importance of all sort of productive work and the distribution of wealth in society; the vocation of trade; the fundamental principles of freedom and justice for business conduct; the prescription of certain manners such as leniency, service-motive, and consciousness of Allah; and mutual consultation. He, then, presents his personal view on leadership in business. It involves three basic ingredients: an inspiring vision of high and achievable standards; a value system based on the principles of freedom and justice and promoting fairness, business integrity, and efficiency; and courage to face tough decisions while putting one's complete trust in Allah.

I am privileged to be given the honor to speak on the subject that I know so little, and that is Business Ethics in Islamic Context: From the Perspective of a Muslim Business Leader.

I would like to first quote Gordon Pearson, who argued that "There has always been a natural tension between behavior which is broadly accepted as being ethical and the imperatives of a successful business." (Pearson 1995, 1) Indeed, driven by the dynamic of business environment, this tension is increasing as competitive pressures rule the globalized business world today. Additionally, there seems to be a common perception, though still inconclusive, that society in general, and business along with it, is becoming less ethical.

Ethics, I believe, is a product of social environment. Ethical conduct of a business enterprise cannot therefore be totally isolated from the conduct of government, political institutions, as well as professional organizations. Prime tasks and core competencies, to be sure, are different for every organization, but to function effectively and efficiently, every organization needs an ethical framework, not just laws and regulations. Noordin Sopiee and Rozali Mohamed Ali (1995) put it right, when they said that "Laws and regulations do play an important part in curbing excesses, but can never entirely replace ethical-driven responsibility, transparency, and accountability, exercised through discipline and self-regulation." And, titled "A New Top-Down Moral Reform," a financial institution of United Mexican States articulated in *Leaders* magazine (September 1987) that:

> The act on accountability of Public Servants is, in fact, a code of ethics that demands of public employees the kind of behavior that adheres to the highest legal principles of morality. This code sets forth the concepts of impartiality, economy, efficiency, loyalty and honesty as principles to be lived by, by every public employee. It also specifies procedures for investigating and defining administrative accountability.

People in business, in fact, are as ethical as any other group in society, but their professional predicament is complex and evolving, from the time a business is first set up through its mature development as a large scale organization. Capitalism, as the main driver of modern business today, in itself is based on a foundation which many regard as a dubious morality. Profit maximization, practiced by many entrepreneurially driven business leaders, tends to lead to unfair distribution of resources and pushes at the ethical boundaries.

Nevertheless, despite what many feel about business, in terms of its conduct and behavior, modern society and the global world cannot deny the role of business in leading a better life for humankind. Business institutions with effective management are needed to generate wealth and create employment for the society at large. In fact, the entrepreneurial nature of business leaders which drives creativity for successful enterprises may not necessarily be in conflict with what is accepted as being ethical. The role of the business leader indeed is key to the development of the culture of an enterprise.

It can be said, therefore, that business ethics, reflected in the behavior of business organizations, more often than not is the transformation of the moral value of its leader. Konosuke Matsushita, founder of Matsushita Electric Corporation, on May 5th, 1932 declared his business philosophy to be shared by his employees and formed part of the company's culture. He said:

> The mission of a manufacturer is to overcome poverty, to relieve society as a whole from the misery of poverty and bring it wealth. Business and production are not meant simply to enrich the shops or the factories of the enterprise concerned, but all of society. And society needs the dynamism and vitality of business and industry to generate its wealth. Only under such conditions will businesses and factories truly prosper (Matsushita 1984, 24).

The following year, in July 1933, this philosophy was translated into operational activities by setting forth code of attitude consisting of five principles, namely:

1. Spirit of service through industry
2. Spirit of fairness
3. Spirit of harmony and cooperation
4. Spirit of striving for progress
5. Spirit of courtesy and humility.

In 1937, he added two more principles:

6. Spirit of accord with natural laws
7. Spirit of gratitude.

Interestingly enough that not only none of these principles is against the Islamic teaching, but they are all commended by the Islamic imperative, as I will try to elaborate later on.

In the case of Matsushita, these seven principles remain today, as they have been since that time, the basic foundation of Matsushita Electric employees' code of conduct. It is worth noting that nowhere in the seven principles, a word about profit let alone profit maximization, was mentioned. They did not, and I believe still do not, overvalue management and undervalue everything else. The important thing is that the company and its social surroundings (strategic environment) must grow healthy.

If "that is easier said than done," to borrow the words of Shintaro Ishihara (1995), then we absolutely need new ways of thinking (and of course new paradigms according to Ishihara) about how companies and their consumers relate to each other. And the relationship must be a positive-sum game. That will make a company respected. And yet, Matsushita Electric has matured into one of the most world respected enterprises, in terms of its size and the quality of its business.

Of course, any business enterprise has the right to making profit. In fact, it should always aim at generating positive cash flow through profitable business activities. The moral value attached to the business process, though, dictates the ethical standards acceptable to society at large. In the *Not for Bread Alone,* Matsushita had said that:

> The rationale of business is, of course, to make available good-quality, reasonably-priced goods to fulfill the needs of the consumers. We must, therefore, be constantly on the lookout for new ways of making better products, as well as devising more effective sales methods and offering better service. At the same time, we should always try to make a fair profit (Matsushita 1984, 81–82).

The Islamic Perspectives

Business has always played a vital role in the economic and social life of all people throughout the ages. This is equally true, if not more so, of our contemporary world. As part and parcel of the contemporary world, Muslims cannot be an exception to this rule. Their religion (Islam) not only permits them, but also encourages them to do business. The prophet of Islam was himself a full-time businessman for a considerable period of time. However, contemporary Muslims find themselves confronted with serious dilemmas. Despite their active participation, they are not sure whether some of their business practices are valid or not. It is not the business *per se* that has confused them, but rather the brand new forms, institutions, methods, and techniques of modern business.

Whether the problem is real or mere illusion, resulting perhaps from lack of knowledge, needs to be thoroughly investigated. The current dynamic business environment warrants the need for a clearly formulated theory of Islamic business ethics. Ideally, such a "theory" should have the capability of serving as a touchstone for ascertaining the validity of any business practices.

As a Muslim, I am convinced that rules and guidelines for all aspects of life, including business phenomena, are found in the *Quran*. I must confess, however, that my knowledge of Islamic sciences and the interpretation of the *Quranic* verses is less than marginal. I was fortunate to have met Dr. Alwi Shihab, professor in Islamic science and senior fellow at Harvard University, Center for the Study of World Religion.

There is no doubt, according to Dr. Shihab, about the fact that the legality of business is duly acknowledged by the Quran. The Quran has not stopped just at the pronouncement of its legality, but alluded to quite a number of explicit and implicit imperatives and prohibitions regarding business transactions. It also pointed out through unequivocal statements the importance of distribution of wealth in society. There as well as other relevant injunctions, would have to be taken into consideration in order to construct a "theory" of business ethics based on an appropriate synthesis of all such injunctions.

Islam attaches utmost importance to all sort of productive work. Not only has the Quran elevated *al-'Amal* (productive work) to the level of a religious duty but it mentioned such a work consistently, in more than 50 verses, in conjunction with *imaan* (faith). The relationship between faith and work is similar to that of root and tree – one cannot exist without the other. The Quran, for instance, enjoins upon Muslims to resume their work after the congregational worship. Furthermore, it is a person's duty to work harder and smarter (as *khalifah* or vicegerent on earth) in order to build this world and to utilize its natural resources in the best possible manner. Therefore, the Quran is very much against laziness and waste of time by either remaining idle or by engaging oneself in an unproductive activity.

Moreover, the Quran encourages humans to acquire skills and technology by calling it *fadhl* (grace) of God, and highly praises those who strive in order to earn for living. The ethics of Islam clearly counsels against begging and being a parasite living on the labors of others. The importance of business activity can also be seen from the Quranic extensive usage of business terminology. The Quran is not only replete with a variety of exhortations to the vocation of trade, but it encourages traders to undertake long trips and conduct business with the inhabitants of foreign lands. In fact, globalization of business and trade has already been envisaged over thousand years ago.

Besides its general appreciation for the vocation of business, the Quran often speaks about honesty and justice in trade. (See Quran 6:152; 17:35; 55:9). The Quran also presents Allah as the prototype of good conduct. Muslims, therefore, are supposed to emulate Him throughout their lives, including, of course, their conduct in business. The attributes of Allah and the principles ordained by Him, as propounded by the Quran, cannot but influence both the thought and the behavior of the Muslim, molding them into a desired ethical shape. The knowledge of Allah's attribute and principles forms a vital prelude to the unique concept of business which the Quran has expounded.

Among others, the Quran calls for an equitable and fair distribution of wealth in the society. Besides its moral exhortations to *al-infaq* (voluntary charitable acts) and its condemnation of concentration and hoarding, the Quran has established, through its legal enactment, several institutions for the distribution of wealth, such as *zakat* (alms giving) and the law of inheritance. While the Quran seeks to eradicate absolute poverty *(faqr)* absolutely and ensures social security for every member of the society, the distributive system of the Quran eliminates the exploitative element from the realm of business. Thus it helps not only in maintaining the business activity on just and ethical lines but, also, in its growth and enhancement.

The approved business conduct in Islam is founded on two fundamental principles, namely freedom and justice. The Quran's emphasis on justice in general and maintenance of straight balance in particular is evident from its forceful and oft-repeated injunctions. The fundamental mission of all the prophets, according to the Quran, was to keep the balance straight and to uphold justice. "The Quran commands Muslims to be fair even when dealing with those opposed to them," according to Hisham Altalib (1992). And this is exactly stated, for example, in the Quran (4: 135), commanding that "O you who believe! Stand out firmly for justice, as witnesses to Allah, even as against yourselves, or your parents or your kin, and whether it be against rich or poor, for Allah can protect both" (See also the Quran 4: 58 and 5: 8).

Freedom in matters of business transactions envisages the right of owning property, the legality of trade, and the presence of mutual consent. Mutual consent, however, can exist only when there is volition, honesty, and truthfulness over-against coercion, fraud, and lying. Nevertheless, constructive criticism should not be avoided and "the leader should strive," according to Altalib (a Ph.D. holder in Electrical Engineering at Purdue University in Indiana), "to create an atmosphere of free thinking, healthy exchange of ideas, criticism, and mutual advice so that the followers feel very comfortable in discussing matters on interest to the group."

On the other hand, justice in matters of business transactions includes:

1. *Fulfillment of promises* (pacts and contracts, or verbal and written).
2. *Exactness in weights and measures* (specifications) in all business related items including work, wages and payment, and labor movement.
3. *Truthfulness, sincerity, and honesty.* While lying and cheating are condemned, the quality of truthfulness, sincerity, and honesty is not only commended but commanded by the Quran (Quran 55:7–9 and 83:1–6).
4. *Efficiency,* i.e. jobs should be carried out without any lapse or omission, with best planning and to be the best in efficiency and competency.
5. *Selection of merit.* The Quranic standard of eligibility is the required merit and competency for the job (Quran 28:26).
6. *Investigation and verification.* They are essential because they constitute a prelude for the right and ethical conduct. The Quran commands to probe and verify any given statement or piece of information before making a decision or taking any action accordingly (Quran 17:36, and 49:6).

The Quran, as well as the tradition of the Prophet Muhammad, have prescribed certain manners and recommended certain others for the proper ethical conduct in business. Broadly speaking, such manners can be summarized under three headings:

1. *Leniency.* It constitutes the foundation and core of good manners. This quality of acts includes politeness, forgiveness, removal of hardship, and compensation.
2. *Service-motive.* In all business activities, Muslim should intend, according to the Quran, to provide a needed service to his/her own community and the humanity at large.
3. *Consciousness of Allah.* A Muslim is required to be mindful of Al-

lah even when engrossed in business engagements. Business activity, therefore, must be compatible with the morality and the higher values prescribed by the Quran.

In summary, the moral laws of the Quran, including its business ethics, are not left totally to an individual's personal choice or discretion. The Quran has made it clear that the leaders (even the Prophet himself) should consult their companions. The Quran defines this as mutual consultation or *shura* (see the Quran 42:38 and 3:159).

Therefore, any business activity bereft of ethical content or when pursued an end in itself is condemned by the Quran (Quran 9:38; 30:7; 4:47; 42:20). Likewise, all business practices involve explicit or implicit harm and injustice to the contracting parties or to the public at large are disapproved by Islam. Muslims are exhorted to seek the felicity of the day of the hereafter *(al-Akhiarh)* through making a proper use of the bounties provided by Allah here on earth. Although the Quran has declared business as lawful, yet it is equally explicit in reminding the Muslims that their business engagements should not become a hindrance in the way of compliance with God's imperatives (Quran 24:37).

Leadership in Business

The Prophet Muhammad told us that: "Every one of you is a shepherd and every one is responsible for what he is shepherd of" (as quoted by Altalib).

As a Muslim business leader, I try to manage on the premise that business exists and grows. So it must generate cash flow by making profits. One may ask how are the profits being made, and in the process whether or not the business should be ethical? There is an anonymous quote in Andrew Stark (1993): "To be ethical as a business because it may increase your profits is to do so for entirely the wrong reason. The ethical business must be ethical because it wants to be ethical." I tend to agree with this quotation. Business, after all, is people. The moral value of the individuals in business organizations, and in particular the leadership which plays the crucial role in shaping corporate culture in turn, dictates the behavior of the organization. (Again, I admire the code of Matsushita.)

As a Muslim, and I happen to be leading one of successful business organizations in Indonesia, I am grateful to have been able to learn and apply the three basic ingredients a leader must possess: vision, value, and courage.

Vision

"Without vision people shall perish," so the wisdom says. This is entirely true and can be accurately applied in business. There is nothing absolute in business. Everything is relative. Therefore, competitive position is the only relevant way to measure success, and, for that matter, survival, in business.

Visionary leadership in business will always aim for growth. Indeed, in business, it has been accepted that the only sign of life is growth. It is the vision that inspires the entire members of the organization to strive for achievement of challenging business objectives. What is important, of course, is that such vision must be translatable as well as achievable within the captive capability of the organization.

Stretching vision beyond reach of the available resources may push the conduct of the organization at the ethical boundaries.

Value

A leader must have a value system based on moral culture. This is where, I believe, the core influence of ethical conduct of any leader rests. The long term survival and growth of the business, in line with the approved business conduct in Islam, is founded on the principles of "freedom" and "justice." Freedom, which envisages, among others, the right of owning property, should be viewed in the context of organizational (business) long term objective to prosper and grow. In fact, the life of a business enterprise is manifested in its ability to accumulate assets or property. Assets, however, should not be limited to physical property such as building, equipment, monetary instruments, etc. but also and in some instances more importantly, capability, technological know-how, and image, which all together can be more valuable than all the physical assets combined.

The question is how does a business enterprise build up its assets base? This is where the second principle, justice, comes into the center stage. Based on the premise that a successful business, in the long run, does not depend on the monolith structure seeking to maximize profits from each transaction (but a series of partnerships so arranged as to benefit all parties in the spirit of win-win situation), the moral value attached to the business conduct should, among others, be including but not limited to:

First, *fairness.* Everyone is entitled to receive what he deserves. (In the old days, this referred also to fair weight and measurement, etc.) Fair also relates to the treatment of people or employees. It is to this aspect that internal company's policies and procedures are so important so that everyone is treated equally. Exceptions should be avoided as much as possible, otherwise it becomes the rule applicable to a non-level playing field (as a source of unfair practices).

Fair and transparent corporate policies, both internal and external, are the basic foundation for a successful management of any business organization. (My personal experiences in developing and/or turning around business enterprises, which have met certain degree of success, I believe, are indispensable to a principle that fairness must have its highest status in the order of multiple priorities.) In practice, it implies that management priority in developing a healthy organization is devoted toward development of a management system, policy and procedures, as well as human resource development. These are all aimed at building up the right infrastructure and the fair playing field for people of different cultural backgrounds and perhaps even different personal interests. Fairness unites people, fertilizing a healthy foundation for the strong teamwork necessary for successful business organization.

Second, *commitment to business integrity.* Business lives off the series of commercial transactions as well as the dynamic relationships among people within the business organization. These transactions as well as relationships are founded on the basis of pre-agreed terms and conditions, rules, etc., that must be fulfilled by all concerned. Business integrity does not reflect only the meeting of promises as well as the exactness of the weight and measurement, but also *sincerity* in fulfilling commitments.

There is no certainty in business, except uncertainty itself. Deviation from contracts, agreements, etc., is bound to take place. However, if sincerity has been built into the culture of the organization, corrective actions can be initiated to remedy the pain of unmet expectations. At the end, it is the honesty, integrity, and sincerity, as commanded by the Quran, that shape up the desirable *"image"* of the organization, an asset that is so difficult to nurture and yet so easily to lose.

Third, *value addition through efficiency.* The business community is a member of the larger society. Therefore, its existence should benefit society at large, not limited to entrepreneurs and their employees. Rent seeking business practices certainly do not add value to the society. In fact, such practices, which are common in developing countries, are counterproductive to both economic and social justice.

To create value through efficiency necessitates the application of an effective management system backed up by innovative as well as competent individuals who cause the functioning of the organization. Efficiency requires that management (the entire members of the management staff) not only do the right things but doing things right. In practical application, the organization must develop human resource "capability" through continuous learning. This is the only way business enterprise can keep up with the required core competence badly needed in today's highly competitive world.

Competence entails not only the possession of technical skills but also the right and positive attitude toward the achievement of the organizational goals. The bottom line of "globalization", which characterizes today's business environment, is competition. To manage competition, business leaders must be able to possess relative efficiency which, to a great extent, is a function of human resource competence. Therefore, the greatest challenge faced by business leaders today is the development, in the right direction, of human resources to alleviate the negative impact of competitive environment. At the end, this will bring wealth and prosperity to humankind, which in the Islamic teaching is a noble proposition.

Courage

Finally on the aspect of courage. More and more business leaders are faced with tough decisions. Management science alone, in its multiple disciplines, cannot cope up with the risk of making incorrect decisions. Judgment, therefore, plays an increasingly important role in today's dynamic business environment. As a Muslim, however, I believe in Allah's final reward or punishment. But I have to do the right things, apply my accumulated knowledge and skill at hands, with honesty and sincerity, with the conviction that final result is up to Him, and the One and the Only Almighty: Allah.

And for that, I agree with Dr. Histham Altalib that the five habits the Muslim leaders (including of course Muslim business leaders) should cultivate are:

1. *Know* where your *time* goes. Control it, rather than letting it control you, by making every second work.
2. *Focus* on concrete *result*. Concentrate on results rather than just the work itself. Look up from your work and look outward towards goals.
3. *Build* on *strengths,* not weaknesses. This includes not only your

own, but those of other brothers/sisters. Acknowledge and accept your strengths and weaknesses, and be able to accept the best in others without feeling that your position is threatened.

4. *Concentrate* on a few major *areas* where consistent hard work will produce outstanding results. Do this by setting and sticking to priorities.

5. *Put* your complete *trust in Allah and aim high* instead of limiting your goals to only the safe and easy things. As long as you are working for Him, be afraid of nothing.

References

Altalib, H., *Training Guide for Islamic Workers.* 1992.

Ishihara, S., *The Voice of Asia: Two Leaders Discuss the Coming Century* (Tokyo: Kodansha International, 1995).

Matsushita, K., *Not for Bread Alone: A Business Ethos, A Management Ethic* (Kyoto: PHP Institute, Inc., 1984).

Pearson, G., *Integrity in Organizations: An Alternative Business Ethic* (London: McGraw-Hill, 1995).

Sopiee, N., Mohamed Ali, R. 1995. *Business, Ethics and Politics.*

Stark, A., "What's the Matter with Business Ethics?" *Harvard Business Review* (May–June, 1993): 38–48.

Cultivating Moral (

Jack M

PART III: ETH

250

If the previous t

"quandary" e

680–682),

cal thin

"cha

j

Abst

Recent developments in business e
seeking ethical solutions to various
moral qualities of the agent in ter.... ..y ...rue   ethics. Prominent
among the traditional Western moral virtues is that of courage, and this
has important implications for the conduct of business by individuals
when they are required to face and manage risks of various kinds. In ad-
dition, the idea of moral courage can be usefully adapted to apply also
to business corporations, with valuable conclusions on ways in which
firms can create a climate of corporate moral courage, both with regard
to present challenges and also in facing the future.

The study of business ethics tends to concentrate on ethical issues which can arise in a business situation, such as behavior to customers, the treatment of employees, environmental sensitivity, or international bribery. In other words, it can devote its attention to various ethical challenges and choices which arise in the conduct of business. This attention to analyzing and resolving typical ethical situations forms a long tradition in the history of ethics. It is in fact the presupposition underlying the development of the various major ethical theories of utilitarianism, deontology or duty ethics, natural law and human rights ethics, all of which are aimed at analyzing situations and identifying the solutions to ethical dilemmas and choices.

Agent-Centred Ethics

In the history of Western ethics, however, there has also been another tradition, which has been lost to view since about the time of the Enlightenment and the Age of Reason, and which is in process of being recovered today. It is the tradition which directs our attention not to moral actions and what moral decision is called for in various situations, but instead focuses on the moral agent, the person who is faced with moral choices, and on the personal qualities which he or she possesses or can acquire which will enable them to make the correct choice and act on it.

...ype of ethical thinking is becoming known today as ...hics, or, as I prefer, "issue ethics" (Mahoney 1992, ...en increasing attention is now being given again to the ethi-...ing and reflection which goes by the name of "virtue" ethics, or ...acter" ethics (see Pence 1993, 249–258). It directs our attention not ...st to questions about what is the ethical thing to *do*, or how we are to *act* ethically, but what does it mean to *be* an ethical sort of person. In other words, we have now moved from considering what states of affairs we ought to bring about to looking at various personal qualities, or virtues, which people may possess and which can influence them as they consider which states of affairs to bring about and which to avoid.

Moral Virtues

If we are to talk about virtues as they apply to business people, and later, by extension, to business companies, then it will help to be clear about what we mean by them. From one point of view, a virtue appears to be a permanent disposition of a person to act in a particular way when faced with various situations, almost, in a significant phrase of Aristotle, as if it were "second nature" to act in such a way (see Aristotle, *Ethics*, VII, x, 4). This is why some writers refer to virtues as habits (Pincoffs 1992, II: 1283–1294). Good habits, that is; bad habits are what we commonly mean by vices. It can also be suggested that a virtue is a sort of moral skill, an ability to deal with various situations with a certain measure of facility, or at least without too much difficulty. And talking of virtues as skills also brings out the fact that a virtue is not just a matter of knowledge. I may well know in theory how to cook an omelette, or drive a car, because I have read an article or a book on the subject, but that does not necessarily mean that I actually can make an omelette or drive a car. Actually to be able to do it requires not just knowledge, but also familiarity and practice in acquiring the personal ability to do it (Aristotle, *Ethics*, II, iv, 3).

One final general point about virtues is that it would be a mistake to concentrate on seeing them just as inner resources which enable us to function or behave in certain ways. They are also personal qualities or attributes, aspects of the individual who is not just *able* to act justly or generously, but who actually *is* a just or generous person. For many people, following Aristotle, the possession or the pursuit of virtues as such personal qualities or endowments sums up what it means to live a good life, or actually to be a morally good person, which they would view as the ultimate in human flourishing, and indeed as what essentially constitutes human happiness (Aristotle, *Ethics*, X, 8; see MacIntyre 139–141).

Moral Courage

The whole approach to ethical behaviour in terms of personal qualities and dispositions which equip one to bring about appropriate ethical states of affairs goes back to Plato, and to his famous quartet of what came to be called the "cardinal" virtues on which all the rest hinge: the four basic moral qualities of practical wisdom, justice, moderation, and courage (Plato, *Republic*, Bk IV), which were later taken up by the Judaeo-Christian Book of Wisdom (*Wisdom* 8:7), and thus acquired immense religious as well as philosophical authority in the history of western ethical thought.

One significant example of how this virtue approach to ethics can be applied to business is by looking at the last of these great qualities, courage, since, quite apart from its practical applications in business, it seems particularly to focus attention on the character of the moral agent, and not just on what he or she does. In the literature addressed to business ethics, the idea of moral courage seems to have been first popularised by O'Toole, although he confined himself to describing it as the leadership quality of taking a public stand on controverted social and other issues (O'Toole 1985, 354, 370–371). Later reference to it by De George explained its importance in acting ethically in difficult situations (De George 1993a, 110–112), and this author applied the topic to situations involving bribery and extortion in a paper delivered at a Hong Kong conference on business ethics (Mahoney 1995, 241–242).

Courage in general involves the capacity to cope with difficulties and dangers, and not to be discouraged by them or be unduly fearful of them. As a personal disposition to handle difficulties and risks, courage may on occasion take on dramatic or even heroic significance in highly critical situations. Yet, in general, the ability to cope with dangers and difficulties seems a desirable quality for everyone to be able to call upon regularly in more mundane matters as they go about their daily lives or ordinary occupations, including the occupation of business.

The particular role of courage in the face of difficulties and dangers is commonly seen as the capacity to cope with the fear which such situations can arouse in us. In his study, *The Anatomy of Courage,* Winston Churchill's physician, Lord Moran, was reflecting on his medical experience during the two World Wars when he defined fear as "the response of the instinct of self-preservation to danger," and identified courage as the "will-power" to handle that instinctive reaction (Moran 1945, 46–47). He was writing about the supreme physical danger of losing one's life in battle, but what he calls the instinct of self-preservation covers many other unpleasant contingencies apart from losing one's life or sustaining serious physical injury, such as the loss of one's job and one's livelihood, the loss of one's prestige or authority, or the loss of one's reputation. An earlier writer on the subject of courage and fear, Thomas Aquinas, expressed the view that "fear is born of love." In other words, fear is the apprehension of losing something that we love or value (Thomas Aquinas, *Summa Theologiae*, II-II, q. 123, a. 4 ad 2; q.125, a. 2). If so, then the greatest fear we have at any time will be to lose what we love or value most at that time, and courage will be the capacity to combat that fear.

As such, it may not, of course, necessarily be *moral* courage. A fraudulent accountant may well possess the courage to overcome the fear of being caught out, or a cat burglar may need to acquire the courage to overcome a fear of heights. What seems to make the difference between such courage which is merely psychological or physical, on the one hand, and moral courage on the other, is when the action which will result in unpleasant consequences is itself a moral action, such as being honest, or keeping a promise, or resisting various pressures to do something one knows or believes to be unethical. Then being able actually to do the right thing and resist or manage the fear of unpleasant consequences can rightly be termed the exercise of moral courage.

Bravery in Business

What have these general reflections on courage and fear to do with business behaviour and business decisions? Quite a lot, I suggest. No one ever claimed that it is always easy to be ethical in one's business dealings, either at an individual or a corporate level. The pressures to act unethically can be considerable, in large matters as well as small, particularly in an occupation which is so result-orientated, not just for a business as a whole but also for the individuals who work for it and in it. Further, the difficulties and risks which are of the very nature of modern business, and the unpleasant results which could follow from failure, can place considerable strains on what Moran called one's instinct for self-preservation, strains which can call for considerable reserves of moral courage when those pressures, and one's fear of them, are driving one towards acting unethically. In this context, it was relevant to read the forthright verdict of *The Economist* some years ago on the explanations which were being offered for the conduct of some members of the British government in the Churchill Matrix mess involving the illegal export of arms, that "nine-tenths of the explanation boils down to cowardice" (*Economist*, 14 November 1992). If it was cowardice, that is, the absence of moral courage, then what were they afraid of losing, and what were they seeking to protect?

Moral courage, then, appears to be the capacity to do what one judges is ethically called for in spite of one's instinctive reaction to the perceived dangers and difficulties in which such an action will result. Cicero usefully identified three elements of courage which again can have ready application to the exercise of moral courage in business. He envisaged such courage as composed of confidence, patience, and perseverance in the handling of one's fears: *confidence* in the sense of one's belief or trust in the ability to succeed in doing the right thing, or a well-founded hope of succeeding; *patience* as the willingness to endure difficulties and setbacks in the pursuit of one's goal; and *perseverance* in the sense of steadily adhering to the ethical course of action and bringing it to completion (Cicero, *De Inventione Oratoria,* II, 54). He also made the important point that courage involves confronting such dangers and difficulties, and identifying them realistically for what they are. In thus defining courage as the "considered" confronting of dangers and accepting of difficulties, Cicero recognised that such an approach needs to be reasoned in its assessment of the dangers and difficulties looming up or looming ahead. Part of the virtue of courage must lie, then, in accurately identifying the real enemy and not allowing oneself to be overwhelmed by vague or irrational imaginings and fears. Perhaps it was this sort of dread fear Napoleon had in mind when he said he had rarely encountered "two o'clock in the morning" courage, or unprepared courage, *courage à l'improviste*!

Calculated Risks

This measured confronting of dangers, of course, is something which business knows all about, in its ways of managing risk and its familiarity with risk-benefit analysis, which is central to competition and the market economy. It is a set of skills which business could usefully teach the rest of society, in bringing the cool light and calculations of reason to so many other human and social risky situations. It is interesting to note that one of the factors which helped post-mediaeval Europe to throw off the Christian Church's blanket condemnation of usury, or the charging of any interest (not just excessive interest) on loans for their "use," was the recognition that the risk of loss of the capital (*periculum sortis*) is a central factor in all business dealings and a contingency for which one should be entitled to charge compensation (see Mahoney 1991). Such consideration of calculated risks is an inherent part of realistic courage.

There is also another aspect of courage where realistic calculation can be important, and not just in assessing how to handle fear. Aristotle was, and remains today, one of the most influential thinkers in the whole area of virtue ethics, and he is best known for his argument that virtue, any virtue, lies in finding the mean between two extremes (Aristotle, *Ethics*, II, 7; III, 7). Perhaps he was over-optimistic in claiming this in the case of every virtue but at least in our present case of courage, what his approach serves to bring out is that one's courage can be defective in two ways: one by having too little courage, as when we can be overwhelmed by our fears; and the other by having too much of it, as when courage really becomes recklessness and we pay no regard, or not sufficient regard, to dangers and difficulties. We do not call people courageous when they take stupid risks with their cars; we call them reckless drivers. In general, we condemn people as rash if they do not stop to think, or do not give enough forethought to the possible results of their actions. Paradoxical as it may sound, there may be a closer connection than at first appears between courage and caution, or equally paradoxically, proper moral courage may lie in taking due thought and care in all one's actions. It is, then, not only lack of wisdom, but also lack of genuine courage to rush in foolishly and unfearingly where even angels fear to tread!

Whose Risk?

When this thought is applied to risk management as a fertile field for moral courage in business, then it raises certain ethical questions which must apply to any risk-benefit analysis. The standard components of such analysis appear to cover the stakes, the odds, and the compensations; that is, the amount of potential loss foreseen, the degree of likelihood of such loss being sustained, and the acceptability of such stakes and odds when they are assessed alongside the benefits hoped for or anticipated. Apart from the inherent difficulties involved in quantifying such considerations for the purposes of comparison, and ultimately financial comparison, there arise highly pertinent ethical questions about who incurs the risk or the potential loss, who reaps the foreseen benefits, and who is properly to decide on whether the risks for such benefits are acceptable. So, for example, questions need to be asked about safety standards at work or in products ranging from nuclear power to children*s toys, and about what risks are on balance acceptable in such instances, and acceptable for whom. We cannot lightly take risks with other people*s lives or well-being, however uncaring or heroic we may choose to be about our own.

The Ford Pinto case has become regarded as one classic example of risks for car drivers being deliberately accepted by the manufacturer, based on the calculation that the estimated risk of litigation in the wake of accidents to drivers would prove less costly to the company than the certain costs of delaying and redesigning the product (see De George 1993b, 130–137; 111). We may call that a business decision, but it was also a decision which was widely perceived and condemned as ethical callousness. Even more morally reckless was the decision of some government and health officials in France in 1985 who deliberately and knowingly issued HIV-contaminated blood products to hemophiliacs, and by their actions of criminal negligence did not just accept the risk to themselves of being brought to justice, as did happen, but also accepted the deadly risks to the recipients, of whom by 1993 more than a thousand had contracted the disease and more than 300 had died (see *The Times,* 4 June 1993). And for what?

Courageous Companies

In applying modern virtue theory to business ethics, one may also explore whether we can apply such virtues not just to the individual people who are involved in business but to business firms themselves. It may appear strange to enquire whether we can speak of a company being morally brave or courageous, and yet it is possible to make some useful sense of the idea in several respects. For instance, one aspect of courage which has not yet been mentioned is the capacity to respond to emergencies or sudden crises, and to cope with the sudden rush of feelings and fears which these can engender. For individuals, the very acquiring of the habit of courage means one is already predisposed to handle such sudden instinctive and unforeseen reactions with some measure of practice, skill, and preparedness. And, by analogy, one can say the same of a company which already possesses procedures for handling crises and emergencies, so that corporate responses are not just a series of panic measures or instinctive cover-ups or other frightened *ad hoc* attempts at evasion or damage limitation.

At the European Business Ethics Network conference held in Paris in 1992, I was introduced to an organisation, and indeed to a subject of research, of which I had previously been unaware, *l'Institut européen de Cindyniques*. It was only when I recalled that the Greek word for danger is *kindynos* that I appreciated that the purpose of this European Institute was to study danger and the various ways of handling it. One of the maxims of such *cindynology*, or study of danger, is that "catastrophes are not accidents"; and this conclusion is based on the findings of various post-disaster enquiries which indicate that technological catastrophes result less from chance than from various cultural, organisational, and managerial deficits or failings (see Kervern 1993, 140–142). If that is so, then I suggest that one of the best ways for companies to acquire the calculated corporate "courage" to be able to avoid disasters is by regular managerial and organisation audits, and by setting up contingency procedures which will move smoothly, that is, "virtuously," into action as occasion requires.

Another built-in capacitator for corporate moral courage can be the mutual support of like-minded directors in a company. If one of the features of whistle-blowing is the feeling of isolation on the part of the potential whistle-blower, as is generally recognised (see Vinten 1994, 10–11), then another generator of courage in a business firm is the company of like-minded people. There is not only safety, there is also courage in numbers. One of the reasons why the then Director General of the Confederation of British Industry, John Banham, advocated an increase in the number of non-executive, or independent, directors in unitary company boards in Britain was precisely to provide them with the collective confidence to take difficult and possibly unwelcome stands on various issues of company policy or behaviour (Banham 1992, 23–24; see *Report of the Committee on the Financial Aspects of Corporate Governance*, 4.10–4.17).

A third way in which a firm can develop what I have called corporate moral courage is by creating and applying a code of conduct for all its members. For this can do much to promote a climate of moral courage in a business company. If courage, as we have seen Cicero analyse it, is composed of confidence, patience, and perseverance in the face of dangers and difficulties, then to the extent that a company can devise structures to promote these qualities in its corporate decisions, and to facilitate them in its personnel, it is creating a climate of courage for its dealings and all its members. Confidence, for example, as I have said, is belief and trust in one*s abilities to cope successfully with dangers, and here is where codes of conduct can have a part to play by creating such moral confidence in all the members of a firm. This codes can do not only by publicly expecting individuals to act ethically in discharging their duties in the face of pressures, they can also equip people with a resource to overcome the fears which such pressures can create, in providing them with corporate support and approval when they do act with moral courage.

Courageous Vision

Finally, such a climate of compliance as a matter of course with approved corporate procedures can not only facilitate ethical behaviour resulting from accordance with such procedures. It may also hopefully, and literally, "en-courage" individuals as the occasion requires to exercise moral independence and to have the courage to act in ways which on occasion may not be foreseen by established procedures, or which may even seem to be at variance with those ways of acting which have been decided on for the general run of situations. Broadening this consideration can lead us to consider what some writers have come to identify as the power of moral imagination (Mahoney 1994, 40–41), or moral creativeness (Barnard 1992, 170–173), in the conduct of business, where ethics is seen as not simply literal obedience to the letter of a code, but fidelity to its spirit, and adherence to the purpose of the company to satisfy a whole variety of human needs and aspirations.

Perhaps the ultimate expression of moral courage is the courage to be visionary towards the future in spite of inevitable uncertainties and the fears which they understandably raise. Such a visionary and courageous approach can apply to every honourable enterprise in human living, and not least to the activity of business in society. This in turn raises fundamental issues about attitudes to change and adapting to new circumstances on the part of a company. The courage of a chief executive or a board to leave the security of the past and face the uncertainties of a conjectural future is, in the traditional philosophical distinction, courage which is necessary, but not sufficient. It has to be communicated and shared throughout the whole enterprise, on pain of delay, obstruction, and possible failure. Structures have to be created and called upon which will make provision for those two other Ciceronian elements of patience and perseverance, thus making not only the goal of change but also the way towards achieving it a matter of considerable sustained corporate courage.

Managing with Integrity

Ultimately, what virtue theory brings out more than any other ethical theory applied to business activities is that there is really no substitute for the integrity, including the trustworthiness, loyalty, and moral courage of the individual person working within the company and for its best interests. There can be an element of quiet moral leadership about the behaviour of such an individual for which no amount of exhortation or codification can substitute, yet individuals live in societies, and interact with their societies. Accordingly, while it can be hoped that virtuous individuals in a business company can have a steady, and perhaps unsung, influence on their colleagues and on the company as a whole, it is also to be hoped that companies themselves will not just leave their own proper ethical concerns to the virtuous individuals whom they may be fortunate to possess from time to time. This is something which should not be left to chance, nor delegated. Companies themselves must set about the pursuit of virtue, or the increase of virtue, in order to attract, encourage, and profit from the sort of personnel whom I have been describing, and in order each to *be*, and be seen to be, an organisation which is habitually and characteristically concerned about the ethical quality of its corporate life and behaviour. If companies and the individuals within them are not able to work together to identify the ethical principles for which they stand, and to exemplify them by acting with the courage of their convictions, then at the very least they may well find themselves ending up with convictions of a somewhat different kind!

References

Banham, J. M. M., interviewed, "Top Salaries in UK Privatised Companies," *Business Ethics: A European Review* 1, no. 1 (January 1992): 23–24.

Barnard, C. I., "The Nature of Executive Responsibility," in *Mission and Business Philosophy*, eds., A. Campbell and K. Tawadey (London: Butterworth Heinemann, 1992), 170–173.

De George, Richard T. (1993a), *Competing with Integrity in International Business* (Oxford: Oxford University Press,1993).

De George, R. T. (1993b), "Ethical Responsibilities of Engineers in Large Organizations: The Pinto Case," *Business and Professional Ethics Journal* 1 (Fall 1981), in *Ethical Theory and Business*, eds., T. L.

Beauchamp and N. E. Bowie, 4th ed. (Englewood Cliffs, N.J.: Prentice Hall, 1993).

Kervern, G.-Y., "Studying Risks: The Science of Cindynics," *Business Ethics. A European Review* 2, no. 3 (July 1993): 140–142.

MacIntyre, A., *After Virtue: A Study in Moral Theory* (Notre Dame, Ind.: University of Notre Dame Press, 1981).

Mahoney, J., "Ethical Aspects of Banking" in *The Banks and Society: The Gilbart Lectures 1990* (London: Chartered Institute of Bankers, 1991).

Mahoney, J., "The Challenge of Moral Distinctions," *Theological Studies* 53, no. 4 (December, 1992): 680–682.

Mahoney, J., "How to Be Ethical: Ethics Resource Management," in *Business Ethics: A European Approach*, ed. Brian Harvey (New York: Prentice Hall., 1994).

Mahoney, J., "Ethical Attitudes to Bribery and Extortion," in *Whose Business Values? Some Asian and Cross-Cultural Perspectives*, eds., S. Stewart and G. Donleavy (Hong Kong: Hong Kong University Press, 1995).

Moran, Lord, *The Anatomy of Courage* (London: Constable, 1945).

O'Toole, J., *Vanguard Management. Redesigning the Corporate Future* (New York: Doubleday, 1985).

Pence, G., "Virtue Theory," *A Companion to Ethics*, ed., P. Singer (Oxford: Blackwell,1993), 249–258.

Pincoffs, F. L., "Virtues," in *Encyclopedia of Ethics*, eds., L. C. Becker and C. B. Becker (Chicago and London: St James Press,1992), II:1283–1284.

Report of the Committee on the Financial Aspects of Corporate Governance (The Cadbury Report) (London: Gee, 1 December 1992).

Vinten, G., ed., *Whistleblowing – Subversion or Corporate Citizenship?* (London: Paul Chapman, 1994).

Information and the Ethics of Business Leaders

Joanne B. Ciulla

Abstract

This chapter is about how information affects the moral relationship between leaders and followers. Knowledge redistributes power and responsibility. Trust is based on the knowledge we have of other people and it is essential for cooperation. Hence, this is why the ethics of leaders matter more now than ever before.

The personal ethics of business leaders on and off the job matter more today than they did in the past because of people's access to information technologies and the mass media. In the information age, the world is a fishbowl, and business and political leaders are the fish. The spread of televisions, phones, faxes, and computers hooked up to the Internet inevitably change society. Information inside and outside the workplace has a dramatic impact on the moral relationship between employers and employees. Knowledge redistributes power and responsibility. While the particular challenges of leadership in the information age are new, some of the moral lessons about a leader's relationship to followers and the personal integrity of leaders are universal lessons found in ancient sources. In this chapter, I will talk about how information affects the relationship between leaders and followers. I conclude that trust is the greatest challenge for business leaders in the information age.

The Press

The mass media have made life more personal. News reports about business and political leaders make us feel as if we know them better, and because we know them better, we take more interest in their personal ethics. People all over the world benefit when the watchful eye of the press unmasks the atrocities of war, the misdeeds of companies, and personal improprieties of leaders. Cameras and satellite links make it possible to capture and transmit information from the most remote outposts of the world. New and miniaturized transmission technologies make it difficult for countries to censor information. Nowadays, anyone with a modem and a computer can find almost anything he or she wants through the Internet.

People enjoy reading stories about powerful people who are dishonest and behave in personally inappropriate ways. This is a favorite topic of TV soap operas and news stories. In democratic societies, the media supply so much information about celebrities and leaders that heroes and moral role models are almost impossible. Few people lead lives so morally perfect that they can stand up to the scrutiny of the press. Even revered national figures like George Washington have lost some of their shine in recent probing biographies. Information about leaders' lives demystifies them and they become more like everyone else. In the U.S., constant revelations of the moral flaws of public figures have gotten so bad that it seems as if the only people who can be leaders are those who have never engaged in sex, politics, or business. Failure to scrutinize the morality of leaders is dangerous, but if we scrutinize them too much, fewer people will want to lead and the ones who do may not be the best ones for the job.

Public access to information and in particular access to information about leaders has changed the very nature of leadership in business and politics. In democratic societies, politics focuses more on the personal ethics of leaders than on their effectiveness or views on the issues. The dark side of this is that in many countries, ethics has become a key form of political assassination. As Elia Chepaitis points out in the chapter "Ethics Across Information Cultures," information technologies may also offer "new and frequently antisocial means of unprecedented self-aggrandizement and mobility in societies where information sources are scarce" (Chepaitis 1999). For those without access to original sources of information or those lacking the ability to separate good information from bad information, it is difficult to tell the good leaders from the bad. As a result of this, people in some countries no longer trust any of their leaders.

In the past, the public was not privy to the personal lives and private dealings of their leaders. Trust without knowledge is a blind faith that the powerless have in institutions or holders of offices or positions of power. It rests on the hope that people in high places will be trustworthy. In authoritarian workplaces and countries, the issue of trusting followers is not a great concern because strong systems of social and physical control ensure that people behave in the prescribed way. People have always gossiped about those in positions of authority, but today a curious press elevates gossip to fact or the appearance of fact. Knowledge about the personal morality of a leader counts more today because it is and can be known. Once knowledge about the other comes into a leader-follower relationship, trust becomes a central issue. The more you know about a person, the more you can tell if he or she is trustworthy. Knowledge about the actions and personal lives of leaders affects people's emotional response to them. It also limits the influence that leaders have over followers.

Cultures vary in terms of what is morally repugnant personal behavior in leaders. For example, in some cultures, customers and employees might be reluctant to give their total commitment to a company whose CEO beats his wife, regardless of the executive's competence on the job. We primarily assess business leaders on their ability to make profits and get things done. However, when their private behavior becomes public knowledge, it becomes a factor, even though it seems irrelevant to the business. It is not always fair of the press to pry into the personal lives of leaders, but they do, and in doing so they have made personal integrity, not past record or effectiveness, the central issue of public debate about leaders. Nonetheless, without public disclosure of the behavior of business leaders (who are often hidden behind disclosures about the actions of corporations), business ethics is difficult and so is democracy. Both require informed participants, whether those participants are employees, consumers, or citizens.

Information, Power, and Followers

Access to information, goods, and services in a global economy redistributes power between ordinary people and those who hold official positions of power. The spread of information fragments power, and good and evil become particularized. The introduction of information and communication technologies has a democratizing affect on a culture regardless of the culture's political philosophy. This does not mean that access to information alone creates democratic institutions and workplaces. It means that widespread access to information will change the relationship of people to institutions and businesses. This change can be for better or for worse. For example, James Coleman believes that economic development not only depends on knowledge and skills, it depends on social capital, or the ability of people to associate with each other and work together for a common purpose (Coleman 1995). Francis Fukuyama takes this idea one step further and argues that a nation's well-being and ability to compete is conditioned by the level of trust in a society. He says that there are high and low trust societies, and that high trust societies are socially and economically better off than low trust societies.

There is an intimate relationship between knowledge gained form information technologies and the media about people, institutions, and organizations, and our ability to trust them. The level of trust in a society or organization determines the level of social cooperation. Information contributes to more or less trust and more or less cooperation, to democracy or anarchy. In his book *Jihad vs. McWorld,* Benjamin Barber contends that the global commercial values conveyed by mass media will lead to a conflict between global commerce which he calls "McWorld" and parochial ethnicity, which he calls "Jihad." In his scenario, nether Jihad nor McWorld carry democratic values. The conflict is between the bloodless economics of profits and the bloody politics of identity (Barber 1996, 7–8).

Individual citizens and employees are now able to do greater harm and greater good than ever before. Not long ago, only the leaders of powerful nations held the tools of destruction. Today almost any group or individual can gain access to the formulas and materials for building powerful bombs. Consider the scale of destruction caused by the bombing of the government office building in Oklahoma City and the horror and fear caused by the Aum Shinrikyo sect in Japan when its members released poison gas in a subway. Businesses have been destroyed or humiliated by the acts of individuals such as Nicholas Leeson at Barings Bank and Toshide Iguchi at Daiwa. Employees have caused trouble for companies in the past and terrorists are not new. What is different is that they can do harm on a far greater scale than ever before. In a sense, life is more personal today because we are more dependent than ever on the ethical integrity of our colleagues and total strangers for our safety and physical well-being. In this environment, the ethics of everyone, leaders, followers, employees, and employers, are *really* important.

Computers that give employees access to information change the relationship between employees, customers and other stakeholders, and the business. Information is power. Employees know more about the company and employers have to trust employees to maintain confidentiality and not abuse information. Consumers know more about the company through the news media. Unhappy employees can go to the newspaper with unflattering information. Corrupt and angry employees can pass on sensitive information to a competitor. In this respect, access to information on the job equalizes the power of employers and employees. Trust becomes a fundamental component of that relationship because information gives employees more power, which in turn gives them more responsibility. Management yields more power and control to employees when it gives them access to information.

Sheep, Cloth, and Cats

The problems of people living and working together are problems that recur at different times and in different forms. Plato thought a lot about leadership. In the *Republic*, he portrays leaders as philosopher kings who are wise and benevolent. They rule over a stratified society where everyone has a place based on his or her abilities. People still believe in the ideal of the powerful wise leader who is better and smarter than ordinary people. While there is much to commend the philosopher king, it is hard to imagine him being very effective in the ancient or modern world. It takes more than knowledge of universal forms to lead. Plato's depiction of the philosopher king errs in setting an ideal of leadership that fails to take into account the nature of followers (Kelly 1991).

Plato's views on leadership evolved during three disastrous trips to Sicily. The tyrant Dionysius I invited him to Sicily the first time. The luxurious lifestyle of Dionysius' court disgusted Plato. He returned to Athens, convinced that existing forms of government were corrupt and unstable. Plato then wrote the *Republic* in which he argued that the perfect state could only come about by rationally exploiting the highest qualities in people. Such a state would be led by a philosopher king.

About twenty-four years after his first visit, Dionysius' brother-in-law Dion invited Plato back to Sicily. By this time, Dionysius I was dead. Dion had read the *Republic* and wanted Plato to test his theory of leadership education on Dionysius' very promising son Dionysius II. This was an offer that Plato couldn't refuse, although he had serious reservations about accepting it. The trip was a disaster. Dionysius II exiled Plato's friend Dion because of court intrigues. Plato left Sicily in a hurry, despite young Dionysius' pleas for him to stay. Upon returning to Athens, Plato wrote:

> The older I grew, the more I realized how difficult it is to manage a city's affairs rightly. For I saw that it was impossible to do anything without friends and loyal followers... The corruption of written laws and our customs was proceeding at such amazing speed that whereas when I noted these changes and saw how unstable everything was, I became in the end quite dizzy (Plato 1971, 1575).

Plato's despair is similar to the despair that some people feel today. The world is changing too fast and it is full of corruption. It is difficult to control what is going on and hard to cooperate without people that you can trust. Perhaps in his own way, Plato realized the importance of social capital.

Dionysius II lured Plato back to Sicily a third time because he promised to make amends with Dion and allow him back into the country. Instead, Dionysius sold all of Dion's property and put Plato under house arrest. When he finally returned home from Sicily, he had completely changed his view of leadership. Plato no longer believed that people could be perfected. Having observed leaders up close he concluded that leaders shared the same human weaknesses as their followers.

In the *Republic*, Plato entertained a pastoral image of the leader as a shepherd to his flock. After his experiences in Sicily, he wrote the *Statesman*. In the *Statesman*, Plato realized that a leader is not at all like a shepherd. Shepherds are obviously quite different from their flock, whereas human leaders are not much different from their followers. Furthermore, people are not sheep. Some people are meek and cooperative, and some are contentious and stubborn (Plato 1992, 275b–c). Hence, Plato revised his view of leaders and followers. He said leaders have to be like weavers. Their task is to weave together into a society different kinds of people, such as the meek and self-controlled and the brave and impetuous.

If we follow the progression of Plato's thought on leadership, he goes from the belief that it is possible for some people to be wise and benevolent philosopher kings, to a more modest assertion that leadership is getting people who sometimes don't like each other, don't like the leader, and don't want to work together, to work towards a common goal. This is clearly the challenge of business and political leadership today. The more people know about their work and their leaders, the less they are like sheep and the more leaders are like them. James O'Toole says that leadership is more like being a shepherd to a flock of cats than a flock of sheep (O'Toole 1995, 6). The only way to herd a flock of cats is to get them to make up their minds to follow. People trust and respect leaders based on the information they have about them. Near the end of the *Statesman*, Plato contends that leaders aren't always morally good, and that is why we need the rule of law. The reason we need laws to regulate business is that we cannot always depend on business leaders to do what is morally and socially right. Good business regulations can substitute for leadership, but to work they require good information. They help businesses and industries survive immoral leaders and followers. In the absence of regulations, attentive media and consumer watchdogs play a central role in protecting people from unethical leadership.

Abuse of Power

We all know that knowledge is a form of power and that power can corrupt people. An inherent part of the ethics of leadership is the way in which a person gets power and the way that he or she wields power. Leaders from all walks of life have to understand the moral hazards of power for themselves and their subordinates. The most common way we predict if someone will be an ethical leader is by looking at his or her past. We do this when we hire people and when we decide whom to vote for in an election. This is a very complicated process because we have to first pick out what facts about a person are relevant and then project those behaviors into future behavior. Unfortunately, the press and the public frequently choose what is most important about a person on the basis of what is most interesting to the public. This is often determined by a kind of telepathy between mass media and the public. In politics, sex and money are more interesting than legislation, even if they aren't always what is most relevant. Businesses traditionally pick people for leadership roles who have produced the most or done the best job and reward them by giving them power over other employees. Managers often receive power as a reward, not because they are good at leading people.

Philosophers have long debated how you judge the morality of a person. John Stuart Mill said that the end of a person's act tells you about the morality of the act. The intentions and the means of doing the act tell you about the morality of the person (see Mill 1957). This sensible view of morality is problematic when it comes to leadership. Public discussion concerning the ethics of leaders is sometimes unable to sort out the morality of the means and ends of the leader's actions. In many businesses, managers are tempted to promote the person who has made the most money for the company without looking into the means that a person used to be successful.

The moral foible that people fear most in a leader is personal immorality that involves abuse of power. Dean Ludwig and Clinton Longenecker call this the Bathsheba Syndrome (Ludwig and Longenecker 1993). In the biblical story of David and Bathsheba, King David comes home from the battle front and relaxes. While walking around his palace, he happens to see Bathsheba bathing. He sends his servants to bring Bathsheba to him. King David seduces her, and she gets pregnant. King David tries to cover up his actions by calling Bathsheba's husband

Uriah home from the front and getting him drunk so that he will sleep with his wife. Bathsheba's husband refuses to sleep with his wife because he feels it would be unfair to enjoy himself while his men are still on the front. David then arranges to have Uriah killed in battle. In the end, God makes David suffer for these actions and the *Bible* teaches us all a lesson about the abuse of power in leadership.

The Bathsheba story demonstrates our worst fears about the private morality of leaders in business and in politics. First, we fear that successful leaders will lose strategic focus because of their vanity, lust, and greed. David should have been thinking about the war, not watching Bathsheba bathe. Second, power leads to privileged access. Leaders have more opportunities, hence more temptations to indulge themselves. David can have Bathsheba brought to him by his servants, no questions asked, because he's the king. Third, powerful leaders have control over resources, which sometimes gives them an inflated belief in their ability to control outcomes. David gets involved in escalating cover-ups of his actions.

The interesting thing about the Bathsheba Syndrome is that it is hard to predict because people get it *after* they have become successful. It is a reaction to the temptations of power. Someone may have been perfectly ethical in his or her past professional life and then change. The Bathsheba Syndrome often occurs when businesses or political leaders have been in power for a while and lose sight of the interests of the citizens or their company. Leader's loose sight because they no longer get good or relevant information, and/or they stop asking critical questions about the information they get. Ironically, people in positions of power usually assume that because they have power, they have the best and most complete information, when they often have the worst information because it has been filtered and sanitized by subordinates.

Unethical followers are what make unethical leaders possible. That is why it is so important to pay attention to the ethics of employees as well as business leaders. Ethical behavior is difficult for employees because they have less power than their employer. Business ethics is full of stories about the lone whistle-blowing employee, and not many of them have happy endings for the employee. Jack Mahoney discusses the importance of moral courage in business in his chapter, "Cultivating Moral Courage in Business" (Mahoney 1999). He defines courage as "the capacity to cope with difficulties and dangers" and cites Thomas Aquinas, who said, "fear is born of love." People fear because they don't want to lose something of value. For employees, that "something" is their livelihood. Ethical employees need something more than courage; they need perspective on the meaning of work and its place in their lives. In "Career Counseling and Moral Responsibility in Developing Countries," J.C. Lamprecht and G.J. Rossouw's outline a program of counseling for the "lost generation" of young black men in South Africa (Lamprecht and Rossouw 1999). They emphasize the importance of teaching young people how to find personal satisfaction in their careers and preparing them to play a morally responsible role in the labor market. This sort of training and reflection should be a central part of business ethics. It not only develops ethical employees, but it keeps leaders honest and develops future leaders. You need to learn how to follow before you can learn how to lead.

Leaders as Teachers

Leaders have always abused power, but that fact shouldn't stop us from trying to prevent its abuse. Telling these stories to future leaders is one form of moral education. That's what the writers of the *Bible* had in mind. Some of the stories are told globally via news broadcasts such as CNN. A bright side of the information age is that it is getting harder for leaders to cover-up their unethical dealings and control the outcomes of their actions for long. Heads of state and corporate leaders need to think twice lest they be embarrassed in front of the whole world.

In a volatile business environment, businesses have to change rapidly and employees have to keep learning. Employees have to be flexible and leaders have to help them to be able to quickly adapt to new technologies and market conditions (Heifitz 1994). Fewer businesses will be run like monoliths with strong leaders in total control at the top. For example, Johnson and Johnson has become a decentralized company of 160 businesses, operating in 50 countries and employing 81,000 workers. Each operates in its own way; however, the glue that holds the company together is the strong commitment of its leaders to the ethical code of conduct (*The Economist* 1995, 71–72). Corporate control does not stem from a small group of people, but from a set of moral commitments that people respect as guides to their behavior.

Plato teaches us the importance of trust in the leader-follower relationship. The Bathsheba story emphasizes the importance of personal morality and the dangers of abusing power. In the complex and fast changing business environment of the information age, leaders will be more like teachers (Winslow 1994; Sims and Lorenzi 1992). Their job is not only to help employees learn, but to make them want to learn and take responsibility for their work. The Zen philosopher Wuzu sums up the relationship between the personal morality of a leader and the way that followers respond to moral leadership. In a letter to Fojian, Wuzu writes:

> As a leader it is essential to be generous with the community while being frugal with oneself...when the community is impressed, things get done even when no orders are given . The wise and the stupid each naturally convey their minds, small and great each exert their effort. This is more than ten thousand times better than those who cannot help following them, oppressed by compulsion (Cleary 1989, 18).

If people today want business leaders who have complete control, they are bound to be disappointed. This is one reason why there is wide dissatisfaction with leaders in many countries. Our disillusionment with leaders is not just a problem with leaders, but a problem with followers. Leaders aren't able to control as much as they used to, which means that followers have to control and take responsibility for more. A complex world requires a new kind of leader and follower, yet many people desire all-powerful and wise leaders who will show them the way.

As I have pointed out, technology, the mass media, and the free market redistribute power and responsibility, regardless of a culture's values and political ideology. Hence, in the twenty-first century, the quality of business leaders will be measured by the quality of their employees. We determine the quality of employees by their ability to work together to solve problems, adapt to change, take on leadership roles, and assume responsibility for achieving the goals of the group, organization, or community. Good followers will also require ethical accountability from their leaders.

People, not technology, are the greatest challenge for business leaders in the twenty-first century. The more people know, the greater their demand for moral integrity in their leaders. The more employees know, the greater their responsibility for their work. Inside organizations, employers and employees will both have to act with integrity in order to establish trust. The more employers and employees know about each other, the higher the standards of ethics will be. Without trust between employers and employees, businesses will not be able to compete. Businesses have to be strong on the inside to compete in a turbulent business environment. Zen thinker Fushan Yuan sums this idea up in a Letter to Master Jingyin Tai. He writes:

Nothing is more essential to leadership and teachership than carefully discerning what to take and what to leave aside. The consummation of taking or leaving is determined within; the beginnings of safety and danger are determined without (Cleary 1989, 7).

References

Barber, Benjamin R., *Jihad vs. McWorld* (New York: Ballantine Books, 1996).

Chepaitis, Elia V., "Ethics Across Information Cultures," in this volume.

Cleary, Thomas, trans., *Zen Lessons: The Art of Leadership* (Boston: Shambahala Publications, Inc,. 1989).

Coleman, James S., "Social Capital in the Creation of Human Capital," *American Journal of Sociology* 94 (1988): 95–120. Also see Robert Putnam, "Bowling Alone," *Journal of Democracy* 6 (1995): 65–78.

The Economist, "Dusting the Opposition," (April 1995).

Heiftz, Ronald, *Leadership/Without Easy Answers* (Cambridge, Mass: Belknap/Harvard University Press, 1994). Heifitz argues that a leader's job uses the values to help employees do adapt to environmental changes.

Kelly, Robert, *The Power of Followership* (New York: Doubleday Currency, 1991). This is one of the best works on the nature of followership.

Lamprecht, J. C., and Rossouw, J. G., "Career Counciling and Moral Responsibility in Developing Countries," in this volume.

Ludwig, Dean, and Longenecker, Clinton, "The Bathsheba Syndrome: The Ethical Failure of Successful Leaders," *Journal of Business Ethics* 12 (1993), 265–273.

Mahoney, Jack, "Cultivating Moral Courage in Business," in this volume.

Mill, John Stuart, *Utilitarianism* (Indianapolis: Bobbs-Merrill, 1957).

O'Toole, James, *Leading Change* (San Francisco: Jossey-Bass Inc., 1995).

Plato, Letters VII, 325c–326, transl. by L. A Post, from *Plato: Collected Dialogues*, ed. Edith Hamilton and Huntington Cairnes (Princeton: Princeton University Press, 1971).

Plato, *Statesman,* transl. by J. B. Skemp (Indianapolis: Hackett Publishing Co., (1992).

Sims, Henry P., Jr., and Lorenzi, Peter, *The New Leadership Paradigm: Social Learning and Cognition in Organizations* (Newberry Park, Cal.: Sage Publications, 1992).

Winslow, Charles D., *Future Work: Putting Knowledge to Work in the Knowledge Economy* (New York: Free Press, 1994).

Entrepreneurs, Multinationals, and Business Ethics

Richard T. De George

Abstract

Business ethics has been primarily concerned with large corporations and has paid little attention to small business. This neglect has become clearer as the literature on international business ethics has developed. This chapter argues that it is often not appropriate to hold local entrepreneurs to the same standards as multinationals, because they are in different situations even though in the same country. I argue this by looking at four different issues involving entrepreneurs: apartheid in South Africa, child labor, bribery, and neighborhood stores. As International business ethics develops, it will be necessary not only to clarify principles and resolve general issues of ethical relativism, but it will also be necessary to consider the ethics of local entrepreneurs.

As business ethics has developed, it has considered five levels of activity: the level of the individual, the level of the firm, the level of the industry, the national level, and the international level. Correspondingly, there are individual ethics,[1] corporate ethics codes,[2] industry-wide codes,[3] national laws and groups and studies,[4] and a growing number of codes proposed for transnational or multinational corporations.[5] In this division, the local entrepreneur has been largely ignored.

The neglect of the small entrepreneur has become clearer as the literature on international business ethics has developed. Multinational corporations (MNCs) have been in the forefront of internationalizing business. The large corporations have come in for attack by critics, often justifiably, and the large corporations have been struggling with the correct way to act as they cross borders, cultures, and traditions, and as they interact with local suppliers and customers in very many different settings. Not only is it proper for MNCs to develop and adhere to a code of ethics in their world-wide operations, but also, if other firms, contractors, suppliers, partners, and customers are to know what the MNCs

stand for, the MNCs must have some clear policy wherever they operate.[6]

Yet, just as the American business ethics literature has tended to ignore the small entrepreneur in the United States, and the national business ethics literatures in other countries have tended to do likewise, so
the difficulties and conflicts that arise from the interaction of large multinationals and small entrepreneurial enterprises in various parts of the
world have largely been ignored as well. The result has been a literature
that tends to argue against ethical relativism and that treats ethical relativism as a mistake to be overcome, without paying much attention to
the conditions that often lead to the differences. International codes,
such as the transnational code that the UN Commission on Transnational Corporations has been developing, or the Caux Principles for Business, and most others, specify norms that all multinationals should follow wherever they operate. This is appropriate, but some of the interesting questions of business ethics are not on that level but on the level of
the local entrepreneur.

What I shall briefly investigate is whether it is appropriate to hold
local entrepreneurs to the same standards as multinationals. I shall claim
that often it is not. Whether it is depends on whether the background institutions of a society are such as to create a level playing field for all
business, large and small, and whether the structures are basically just. It
is when the local structures are not just that cultural relativism is a serious issue and that ethical relativism is a problem.

I shall consider four different kinds of issues involving entrepreneurs: apartheid in South Africa, child labor, bribery, and neighborhood
stores.

Apartheid in South Africa

In the case of South Africa, where apartheid was written into law, many
countries judged the South Africa social and economic systems to be
immoral, boycotted the country, and applied various sanctions until its
structures were changed. It was appropriate for American multinationals not to invest in South Africa, or if the companies remained there at
least to follow the Sullivan Principles[7] and not obey the apartheid laws.
But among business ethicists there was not much thought about the local
entrepreneurs.[8] The local white entrepreneurs in South Africa did not
have the luxury of ignoring the apartheid laws and of following the
Sullivan principles. If they had broken the law, presumably they would

have suffered the legal penalties. Does it follow that since obeying the apartheid laws meant engaging in unjust discrimination, every white entrepreneur in South Africa, every white local businessperson acted immorally and ethically should have closed up shop?

That conclusion seems both logically necessary and yet somehow too strong. It seems too strong because it means that since white business people could not be ethical entrepreneurs, all ethical white people were precluded from being entrepreneurs and had to earn their living by working for unethical entrepreneurs or unethical large corporations. Even then they might be faulted, since as white workers they profited from the existence of apartheid, even though they did not make the laws or have responsibility for the rules of the company for which they worked. The only other alternatives seemed to have been either to leave the country or to start a business in which one worked for oneself but did not employ others. If whites could neither be entrepreneurs nor be workers without being unethical, in many cases they were necessarily unethical, since they had no other alternatives by which to make a living. But any doctrine that says people are necessarily unethical is too strong because one can only be held responsible for doing what it is possible for them to do.

So two questions deserve close examination. The first is whether it would actually be possible to be an ethical entrepreneur in South Africa under the apartheid laws. Could an entrepreneur quietly ignore the apartheid laws and not be prosecuted by the government? Was there a way to obey the apartheid laws and still treat one's black workers decently? Could local entrepreneurs with a conscience possibly be justified as carrying on their business in an unjust social structure and claim that doing so is the lesser of two evils, the greater evil consisting of leaving all business activity to those who do not care about being unethical or who believe that apartheid is not unethical? Could workers be held not ethically responsible for profiting from apartheid if they had no part in supporting it? Although I am inclined to think that local entrepreneurs and white workers who did the best they could – whatever that turns out to be in concrete terms – cannot be morally faulted, and that less could be expected of them than of foreign multinationals or large South African enterprises, I have not argued the answers to any of these questions. I raise them to indicate the kind of questions that were not raised, and so not answered in the business ethics literature which focused almost exclusively on multinationals.

Child Labor

Can a similar sort of analysis be made with respect to companies that operate in countries that allow child labor?[9] American multinationals, it is widely and I believe correctly held, should not use as suppliers firms in India or Bangladesh or Pakistan that use child labor, where that is defined as using children under the age of fourteen. There is good reason for holding this. Firms that use child labor tend to stunt the children's growth, and they preclude their developing the rudimentary skills learned in grade school so they can get decent jobs as adults and so they can lead fulfilling lives. Thus hiring children full-time instead of letting them go to school does harm to those children. It usually violates their human right to education, a right recognized by the UN Declaration of Human Rights.[10] In some cases, child labor is very close to slavery.

It is appropriate to claim that American multinationals and multinationals from other developed countries, should not use such suppliers. If the MNCs do use them, they indirectly support child labor and contribute to its continuance. They would do so to keep their costs minimal and either to benefit their customers at home with low prices for finished goods or their shareholders with larger profits from using cheaper suppliers, who in turn use cheaper labor. Both justifications are insufficient to justify the harm they do. The multinationals have other suppliers they can use, even if the cost may be somewhat higher. Their customers have no right to lower prices if derived from the exploitation of children, and their shareholders have no right to larger profits if similarly derived. So far the argument is sound.

However, there is remarkably little literature on or study of the position and role of the small entrepreneur in India or Bangladesh or Pakistan. If we take child labor as an instance, on whom do we blame the practice and what is the proper ethical attitude to adopt concerning individual entrepreneurs? Unlike the case with apartheid and South Africa, child labor is not required by law, and in some of the countries in question it is prohibited by laws that are often flouted with impunity. The countries are very poor and developing. From an ethical point of view, we can say the society is morally deficient, since it has and tolerates child labor. Yet in a poor country, where the use of child labor is widespread and customary, the income provided by children may be just enough more for a family to survive. From the outside, and even from the inside, people may call the social structures unjust, and from an ethical position they are unjust. Outsiders cannot ethically profit from that injustice. But what are those to do who are caught within the structures?

Must we say that unless an entrepreneur is able to start and operate a business without using child labor, even though all his competitors do, he is unethical if he operates it? If his business can be run by himself, then he may exploit himself all he wishes, in the sense that he can work sixteen hours a day, seven days a week. If the business is run by a husband and wife, providing they both agree, then again they may exploit themselves all they wish. They may also have their children help them, providing the children also have an opportunity for the education they will need to operate as full members of their society when they grow up. If the small entrepreneurs do well enough to need further help, they may hire others, presumably at the going wage. Suppose that going wage is not really a living wage, although that is what their competitors pay. Must they only expand and hire people when they can pay enough above the going wage to pay a just wage? The answer seems to be yes. But this places enormous burdens on the ethical local entrepreneur and will make it enormously difficult for him successfully to compete in a system that is unjust and skewed against him. Are local entrepreneurs really required to live up to ideal rules when the social structures are basically unjust? If they are basically unjust, must we say that all those who engage in them are unjust and that it would be better for them if they did not become entrepreneurs but lived as best they could by being exploited by others as the system requires?

Of course it would be better to change the system and to make it fair and just. But if ought implies can, then the small entrepreneurs, just as the individual workers, may plead that they cannot change the system. The conclusion that it is better for them to suffer injustice rather than to try to improve their lot, if this means engaging in the system, is a harsh doctrine indeed.

Perhaps this is why discussions of ethical relativism and international corporations remain on the higher level of the multinational. The multinational clearly has the choice of not operating in certain countries and of not using suppliers who use child labor. The multinational is large and powerful and rich enough that it cannot justify using suppliers who use child labor. Moreover, it can take the lead in setting the example, in paying somewhat higher prices to suppliers who do not use child labor, thus making it possible for them to compete. Yet whether it is the obligation of the multinationals to change the unjust structures of countries by paying higher wages is certainly open to question. Why go to a country where there is child labor and pay the same prices that one might pay in a country in which there is no child labor? Multinationals have no obligation to search the world for places where they can improve the social structures or help raise wages or the standard of living.

So we are brought back to the local entrepreneur. Should all the ethical local entrepreneurs forego developing beyond a family-run enterprise, rather than pay less than a living wage or rather than employ any child labor, even when the mothers of their workers ask for such employment for their children, will not send their children to school anyway, and would leave them on the streets? If that is required, then all entrepreneurial activity will be left to those who are unethical, who are content to continue the practices that support them, and who continue to defend the social structures from which they benefit.

If a multinational comes in and pays higher than the customary wage to a supplier, with the understanding that the supplier will not use child labor and will pay his employees a living wage, what happens to the small local entrepreneur who does not have a multinational as a customer and must compete without the benefit of such a contract? If such an entrepreneur pays the same wages as his competitor, who is in fact subsidized by the multinational, he will be forced to close up shop. May he temporarily follow local custom, develop his product to the point where he might attract a multinational as a customer and so eventually be able to operate as ethically as he would like? To adequately answer this question it is necessary to determine what is and what is not actually possible for local entrepreneurs. Do some operate without using child labor? Can one compete without doing so? Why are young girls not sent to school and what are the real alternatives for them if they do not go to school? Until the local background conditions are changed, what is the role of the local entrepreneur? Given the conditions that exist, what do local entrepreneurs and local workers wish from multinationals? These are questions that require empirical study. The proper role of the multinational cannot fully be discussed without this information.

Bribery

In countries in which bribery is endemic, it is possible for multinationals either to refuse to operate there or to refuse to pay bribes.[11] They have both the power and the resources to make those choices, and the literature in business ethics is almost unanimous that they should do so. And surely the literature is correct. But what of the local entrepreneur? May the local entrepreneur pay the bribes that he claims, probably correctly, that he must in order to do business? He does not have the luxury of not operating there, since that country is where he lives. Either he operates there or he does not operate. Nor does he have the power to force those who demand bribes to pass his goods or give him his permit or allow him to operate without paying the bribe. By paying he reinforces the corrupt system. But his choices seem to be either to do so, or not to operate and to leave all entrepreneurial activity to those who do not mind being corrupt. In this situation, I suggest that paying the bribe is the lesser of two evils, providing the entrepreneur will try to change the system to the extent that he can (and of course he has an economic incentive to do so). Although the practice is corrupt, the entrepreneur in this case suffers injustice but does not impose it on others. The entrepreneur is the victim here. In hiring child labor, the entrepreneur is not the victim but the perpetrator, even though it is the system in which he operates that makes his activity arguably necessary.

As in the other two cases, the interaction of multinationals and of local entrepreneurs is not without relevance, and can help throw light on both the ethics of the actions of multinationals and possibly on cultural, if not ethical, relativism.

Neighborhood Stores

The fourth case concerns small businesses that go to make up neighborhoods. They serve a social function in many cities in many countries, but being small they do not get the benefits of scale that large corporations do. In the United States, the large corporations have more and more driven out the small retailers. The story of WalMart is well known, as is the story of supermarkets driving out the local grocery store, meat market, and fruit and vegetable stand. In places like Paris and Tokyo, the neighborhood still survives. Yet there is tension between protecting the small store and keeping the large discount and other large retailers from competing as they would wish. In Japan, the laws until recently protected the small shop owner and tended to make it difficult for large discount stores, such as Toy-R-Us, to penetrate the Japanese market.[12] What seemed unfair to the large corporations seemed perfectly fair from the point of view of the local stores. A negative result for the Japanese people was higher prices for their goods, but on the positive side they preserved their neighborhoods, which tend to help promote safety and community. The ethical conflict has been little investigated and detailed, but there are clearly ethical issues involved. How can small businesses protect themselves against their large competitors? Does ethics simply say that if they cannot compete on the terms set by the large corporations, they must give way? Are laws and other social structures that defend this view ethically defensible? Who speaks for the small business and the small entrepreneur? The tension and conflict are not easily described and the ethical issues are not entirely clear. They form part of the concrete research that international business ethics in its next stage demands.

Conclusion

The conclusion I draw is that the literature on business ethics is correct in claiming that ethical relativism is a mistaken position and that multinationals should not engage in corrupt practices even when they are practiced in a host country. The multinational should not engage in apartheid, it should not engage in slavery or child labor, it should not pay bribes to government officials. But saying that and agreeing that these practices are ethically wrong is compatible with asking whether the same rules apply in the same way to the local entrepreneur. Here the answer is not as clear as it is in the case of the multinational. The reason is that the local entrepreneur and the multinational are really in two different situations, even though they operate in the same country. The multinational does not have to operate there. The local entrepreneur must operate there or not operate at all. The multinational has resources from its other operations upon which to draw. The local entrepreneur has no such resources. The multinational has the power and wealth to stand up to local corruption and does not have to accede to it. The local entrepreneur does not. The multinational often brings jobs, taxes, and other benefits to the country that makes it attractive to the host country. The local entrepreneur has much less in that respect to offer. Because their real situations are different, what can and should be expected of them may well be different.

The conclusion that all local entrepreneurs in a society that has unjust social structures act immorally is a judgment that the local society probably would not make. This is what some of those who defend ethical relativism take as their central point. But even if those who suffer from the exploitation of the system say it is unjust, would they prefer that there be no employment and that no one of them take any initiative to move from the ranks of the exploited to that of the entrepreneur? These are difficult questions to answer, and business ethics would profit from close empirical studies of local entrepreneurs, of their own perceptions of the ethics of their actions, and of the perceptions of the ordinary people in the society in question. Where child labor continues, is it because it is preferable to the existing alternatives, such that if engaging in it is necessary for an entrepreneur to succeed it is the lesser of two evils, or is the system such that it is run by the rich and laws prohibiting it are blocked and, if passed, not enforced, because of the influence of those who profit from it?

Although it is clearly unethical for multinationals to use child labor or suppliers who use child labor, what is not as clear is whether people in such societies prefer multinationals to help set standards or whether they consider that interference. What is the impact of multinationals in such situations and what is the effect on local entrepreneurs? How does the presence or lack of presence of multinationals affect the situation of local entrepreneurs? These are questions to which it is important to find answers, and they are questions that ethical theory cannot answer.

Developments in international business ethics have somewhat paradoxically shown a gap in the study and development of business ethics on the national level in the consideration of small businesses and individual entrepreneurial activity. As international business ethics develops, it will be necessary not only to clarify principles and resolve general issues of ethical relativism, but it will also be necessary to consider the ethics of local entrepreneurs.

Endnotes

1. The individual is often the focus, but there is special emphasis on the individual in the "virtue ethics" approach. As one example, see Jack Mahoney, "Cultivating Moral Courage in Business" in this volume.

2. Most of the Fortune 500 companies in the United States have corporate codes and some companies in Europe have adopted codes. In addition, the focus of much of the writing in business ethics has been concerned with the corporation and its activities.

3. Among others, see the WHO International Code of Marketing Breast-milk Substitutes, and the Chemical Manufacturers Association "Responsible Care" Guiding Principles.

4. In the United States two laws have played an especially important part in the development of business ethics: the Foreign Corrupt Practices Act (1977), and the Corporate Federal Sentencing Guidelines (1991). The business ethics literature as it developed in the United States typically focused on U. S. business and U. S. practices. As business ethics has flourished in other countries, the literature in those countries has tended slowly to the problems and conditions in those countries. See the Country Reports published in *The Journal of Business Ethics* (October 1997), and articles such as those by J. C. Lamprecht and G. J. Rossouw ("Career Counseling and Moral Responsibility in Developing Coun-

tries") and Eduardo Schmidt, SJ ("Ethical Formation That Makes Sense for Business Men and Women in Latin America") in this volume.

5. Among these are the proposed U.N. Code of Transnational Corporations, the Caux Roundtable Principles for Business, the OEDC Guidelines for Multinational Enterprises and Social Policy.

6. Two books devoted to international business ethics both focus on multinationals: Thomas Donaldson, *The Ethics of International Business* (New York: Oxford University Press, 1989), and Richard T. De George, *Competing With Integrity in International Business* (New York: Oxford University Press, 1993).

7. The Sullivan Principles, developed in 1977 by Leon Sullivan, a Baptist minister on the Board of Directors of General Motors, prohibited signatories from following the apartheid laws and required non-segregation and equal treatment of employees regardless of race. He proposed it as an experiment to break down apartheid from within. In 1987 he declared the experiment a failure, and called for American companies to leave South Africa. By that time 280 American companies had signed the Principles.

8. This is true as well of the few South Africans writing on business ethics, who were also concerned with abolishing apartheid.

9. On child labor, See "Danger: Children at Work," *Futurist* 1 (January-February 1993): 42–43; Martha Nichols, "Third World Families at Work: Child Labor or Child Care?" *Harvard Business Review* 71, number 1 (January-February 1993): 12–23; and "Slavery," *Newsweek* (May 4, 1992): 30–39.

10. Article 26.

11. For a history of bribery, see John T. Noonan, Jr., *Bribes* (New York: Macmillan, 1984). Even in countries in which bribery is endemic it is usually against the law. In no country is bribery publicly justified as ethical. If it were, it would not be a means of getting special privilege and so would not be bribery but simply a cost of doing business.

12. For a discussion of some of the issues between the U.S. and Japan, see Richard T. De George, *Competing with Integrity in International Business* (New York: Oxford University Press, 1993), 159–175.

Ethical Formation That Makes Sense for Business Men and Women in Latin America

Eduardo Schmidt

Abstract

In an attempt to make business ethics more relevant to Latin Americans, a new pedagogical method has been developed. It is called "interactive teaching." James W. Fowler's theory of human development has played a key role in this process. The principle insight upon which this methodology is based is that in order to be effective as professors of business ethics, we must understand how our students make sense out of life. Another key insight is that, contrary to what we may think, the ethical concepts which Latin American students assimilate and take with them are not generally organized by means of abstract ethical paradigms. Given their way of making sense out of life, characters to whom they can relate are a more effective vehicle. These characters, presented in specially designed cases, can serve as powerful symbols which help make possi ble the transition from theory to practice in their professional lives.

Introduction

Some twenty five years ago, it became evident in Latin America that the moral formation being offered to business men and women was rapidly becoming irrelevant. Our students of business ethics learned what they needed to know in order to pass their examinations. However, they considered our courses to be very idealistic and impractical given the complex social, economic, and cultural context in which they would have to apply what they had learned. Attempts to use a case study method were often perceived as sterile casuistry. Due to their perceived irrelevance, courses in business ethics were reduced to their minimum expression or eliminated from many university curriculums. It was obvious that something had to be done if business ethics was to remain alive and well in Latin America.

The purpose of this chapter is to share the results of a search for a better way to teach business ethics which began at the "Universidad del Pacífico" in Lima, Peru, in 1972. Over the years, a new pedagogical method has been developed, complete with a textbook for students, a book for professors which also serves as an additional text book for graduate students, class notes for professors, and access via the Internet to a bank of more than one hundred and thirty Latin American business ethics cases.[1] Many of these cases include variations which take into account different social and economic variables such as hyper-inflation, local legislation, and changing cultural customs. This new pedagogical method is known as "interactive teaching." University professors have been trained to use it effectively in Peru, Uruguay, Bolivia, Venezuela, and Spain. An experimental course, designed and coordinated via the Internet, has been presented at the Universidad Católica Boliviana. On line e-mail support is provided to professors who use the text books in their courses.

A Starting Point: What We Know about Our Students

What do we know about our Latin American business ethics students that should be taken into account when considering their moral formation? In the following pages, we will examine what little empirical data is available. We will also take into account the experience of professors who teach business ethics in Latin America.

Pessimism toward the Ethical Climate in the Business World

To begin with, the vast majority of business men and women, as well as students of business ethics, tend to be pessimistic when assessing the ethical climate of the business world in their respective countries. The data presented in Table 1 are very illustrative. However, it should be noted that the data shown for countries other than Peru are merely preliminary indicators which will have to be confirmed by further study.

Table 1: The Opinion of University Students Concerning the Ethical Atmosphere of Business in Their Respective Countries

"In our country businessmen tend to pass over ethical principles when making their decisions. What interests them is doing business."

	PERU N = 675 1990–1996	URUGUAY N = 110 1992	VENEZUELA N = 158 1994	SPAIN N = 172 1994
In agreement	35%	13%	36%	29%
More in agreement than disagreement	53%	58%	43%	62%
Indifferent	2%	10%	3%	4%
More in disagreement than in agreement	8%	15%	12%	5%
In disagreement	2%	4%	6%	0%

Admitting this limitation, a certain pessimism would seem to be prevalent in all of the countries for which data is available. Between 71% and 88% of those who responded were at least more in agreement than in disagreement with a statement that can be translated as, "In our country businessmen tend to pass over ethical principles when making their decisions. What interests them is doing business."

This pessimism makes it difficult for our students to accept ethical values and principles as realistic and operative elements within the decision making process. The phrase "business ethics" tends to be seen as a contradiction in terms. This problem becomes acute when, due to a lack of economic and social stability, the main objective in business becomes the maximization of short term profits. Unfortunately, ethics tends not to be compatible with this objective.

Reference Points for Determining That Which Is Ethical

What points of reference do Latin American business men and women most frequently use for determining "that which is ethical"? Table 2 offers some interesting insights. In the case of Uruguay, it should be noted that we only have data for "professionals" (Prof.). In the case of Spain, the only data available are for "university students" (Univ.).

Table 2: What Business Students and Business Men and Women in Various Countries Understand by "That Which Is Ethical" in the Business World

RESPONSES	PERU 1990–1996		VENEZUELA 1994		URU-GUAY 1992	SPAIN 1994
	Univ. N=675	Prof. N=809	Univ. N=158	Prof. N=96	Prof. N=110	Univ. N=172
1. That which is in my own interest	0%	0%	0%	0%	1%	1%
2. That which is in agreement with the saying: "Do unto others as you would have them do unto you"	17%	17%	5%	18%	26%	25%
3. That which does good to the greatest number of people possible	24%	14%	19%	20%	17%	16%
4. That which is accepted as normal in society	8%	13%	13%	16%	21%	4%
5. That which is legal	3%	12%	25%	19%	5%	1%
6. That which is in agreement with my religious convictions	8%	4%	3%	1%	5%	5%
7. That which is in agreement with my feelings of justice	41%	40%	35%	27%	25%	49%

Note: Some of the columns do not add up to 100% due to rounding off the percentages. The abbreviation "Univ." means "university students," the abbreviation "Prof." means "professional business men and women."

Each of the possible responses indicates something about our students which may be of importance when trying to design more effective pedagogical methods. With the possible exception of the first response, something can be said in favor of all of them. However, each response also has certain limitations which, for the most part, are evident. These also must be taken into account. In this chapter, we will not analyze in detail each of these seven responses. Rather, we will discuss the most important conclusion to be derived from the data presented.

Option 7, "That which is in agreement with my feelings of justice," elicits the greatest response. Between one fourth and one half of those who answered the questionnaire preferred this option. Even in groups of university professors, we find that as many as half of those who respond choose this point of reference. What does this tell us? It indicates that for a considerable number of professionals, ethical conduct is determined by referring to deeply rooted feelings, which may or may not be expressed as clearly articulated moral principles. When cases are discussed in class, it becomes evident that what is really operative is a pre-reflexive sense of morality. If someone asks why a certain practice is not ethical, the typical response is "I couldn't sleep at night if I did such a thing." Positive ethical obligations are perceived in much the same way – "I just feel that it is the right thing to do." Professionals in the fields of business and economics seldom use traditional philosophical concepts to articulate ethical principles. Such paradigms are not perceived as useful for making sense out of business ethics. They can be learned, but with few exceptions, those who learn them will not apply them when making business decisions.

When examined in the light of ethical principles considered to be objective, this deeply rooted ethical feeling manifests three categories of values: values which are correctly perceived (perhaps 80 percent); values which are exaggerated; and values which are not perceived. The most notable case of an exaggerated value is "loyalty to friends." Friendships are so sacred that one must do almost anything for a friend. In countries where civil society is all but disintegrated, this tendency is even stronger. When the structures of society no longer offer a forum for obtaining justice, the only thing that a person can depend upon is a "friend," and a friend in need is a friend indeed.

The most notable example of a value which is not perceived has to do with the obligation to respect professional secrets. A "professional secret" in most Latin American business contexts is something so sacred that one should only reveal it to his ten best friends who, in turn, not only "may" but "should" reveal it to their ten best friends, and so on. According to this way of thinking, that is what friends are for in the business world!

Why Business Men and Women Make Decisions That Are "Ethical" or "Not Ethical"

Why do Latin American business men and women respect, or fail to respect, the demands of business ethics when making their decisions? The data presented in Table 3 provide us with an answer – it is "a person's code of personal conduct." When we examine the columns labeled "ethical," we discover that for university students this factor has a value of 1.32, which clearly indicates its relative importance. As can be seen, this same tendency exists among professionals for whom this factor has a value of 1.52. For both groups, there is a considerable difference between the relative importance of one's "code of personal conduct" and the factor which is in second place – "the behavior of one's superiors in the company." If business men and women are ethical, apparently it is because of their own virtues.

When we examine the columns labeled "not ethical," we find that "a person's code of personal conduct" is also important when explaining why business men and women are not ethical; however, it is relatively less important than it is when trying to explain why they are ethical. As can be seen, this factor and "the behavior of one's superiors in the company" are almost equally important when trying to understand why people are not ethical. Bad example is much more contagious than is good example. Furthermore, the data contained in the columns marked "not ethical" show a much greater degree of dispersion. This indicates a certain tendency to look for scapegoats instead of questioning a "code of personal conduct" when trying to explain why people are not ethical.

What do the respondents understand by a "code of personal conduct"? Surprisingly, they do not refer to a written code, nor are most of them capable of articulating moral principles which might be included in such a "code." Rather, they refer to "their feelings of justice."

Table 3: The Relative Importance of Five Factors Which Influence the Ethical Conduct of Business Men and Women According to the Opinion of Peruvian Business Students and Professionals: 1990–1996

Responses	University students Total = 675		Professionals Total = 809	
	Ethical	Not Ethical	Ethical	Not Ethical
1. A person's code of personal conduct	1.32	2.50	1.52	2.49
2. Formal company policy.	3.74	3.92	3.07	3.38
3. The climate or ethical atmosphere of the industry	3.47	2.84	3.53	3.01

Responses	University students Total = 675		Professionals Total = 809	
	Ethical	Not Ethical	Ethical	Not Ethical
4. The behavior of one's superiors in the company	2.96	2.50	3.01	2.60
5. The behavior of those who are of the same category in the company	3.52	3.24	3.87	3.53

Note: The numbers indicated are weighted averages of the responses given for each factor (1, 2, 3, 4 or 5), assigning a value of 1 to the most important factor and a value of 5 to the least important factor.

A General Profile of Latin American Business Ethics Students

Based on the data presented in these pages, we have developed a general profile of Latin American business ethics students which has served as our starting point when developing "interactive teaching." With few exceptions, it is valid for university students as well as for business men and women in general. According to this profile, we find that most of our students are guided by a deeply rooted moral sense. They manifest a pre-reflexive morality in which many genuine ethical values are present. However, they have not developed the ability to express these values as articulated moral principles or norms of conduct. This makes them vulnerable when others demand that they explain their positions. Business ethics becomes a taboo. No one desires to talk about it, precisely because they do not know how to explain rationally what they feel, and feelings don't count in the "school of hard knocks."

James W. Fowler's Theory of Human Development: A Tool for Understanding How Business Men and Women Make Sense Out of Life

According to James W. Fowler's theory of Human Development, before deciding how to present ethical contents to our students, we must first understand how they make sense out of life.[2] "What" makes sense for our students is one thing; "how" they process different contents in order to make sense out of life is quite another. Unless we are able to present our ethical contents in such a way that our students find them useful for making sense out of life, our courses will not be perceived as relevant.

James W. Fowler is a structuralist in the tradition of Piaget and Kohlberg. According to his theory, in order to understand how people make sense out of life, we should examine what he calls the seven aspects by means of which this process may be observed. These aspects are: form of logic; social perspective taking; form of moral judgment; bounds of social awareness; locus of authority; form of world coherence; and symbolic function. Explaining what is meant by each of these aspects is beyond the scope of this chapter. For our purposes, it is sufficient to note that we will be effective in teaching business ethics to the degree in which we are able to take into account as many of them as possible.

As an example of what can be done, let us examine how paying attention to "symbolic function" can help us design more effective business ethics cases. Persons who are guided by a pre-reflexive morality relate more easily to "people" as symbols than to "abstract principles." This being the case, we can portray characters in our cases who will serve as symbols of ethical or unethical conduct. Such a case can be presented in class by means of a socio-drama. The discussion of the case can center around the attitudes taken by the characters and the attitudes of the students themselves toward these characters. We can encourage the participants to form moral principles in *their own words* as a way of justifying their opinions.

Given the general profile of our students, this type of case discussion will be far more effective than analyzing a case in terms of abstract ethical principles. In more than twenty five years of teaching in Latin America, not a single alumni has come back to thank me for having taught them a given moral principle. When they return, they say things such as, "Do you remember Rosie the little white liar in that case we studied? Well, thanks to all we learned about her, and about ourselves, I have been able to defend my ethical values in any number of situations." As this expression shows, in general the ethical contents which our students assimilate as useful for making sense out of life are not organized around abstract ethical paradigms. They tend to be organized around the characters presented in our cases. This is a key concept for understanding how to be more effective when teaching business ethics in Latin America. I suspect that it may also be important in other areas of the world.

The "Objectives" to Be Achieved in Business Ethics Courses

We propose to achieve the following objectives in business ethics courses given at the undergraduate level:

- By the end of the course, the participants will be able to do the following with reference to their future professions:
- Identify the values reflected in their own feelings of justice;
- Formulate moral principles in their own words which reflect these values;
- Evaluate their moral values and principles in the light of objective values and principles; and
- Integrate objective moral principles into the decision making process.

When teaching courses at the graduate level, we add an additional objective:

- In the light of James W. Fowler's theory of human development, develop a strategic plan for improving the ethical climate in the business in which you are employed.

The first four objectives are not achieved in sequence. Rather, the students perfect the skills necessary to achieve all four of them as the course advances.

"Interactive Teaching": The Means by Which to Achieve These Objectives

In "interactive teaching," we make use of three elements. The first is a textbook which serves as the primary source for the content of the course. Students should read the assigned chapters before coming to class. We try to keep other assigned readings to a minimum. We consider it far more important for our students to use their available time for discussions and for resolving cases in writing, since these activities are more conducive to the objectives we wish to achieve.

The second element in "interactive teaching" is the discussion in class of a case which has been prepared to highlight the topic under discussion. Four or five students participate in each discussion group. During a plenary session which follows, each group presents their responses to a set of uestions about the actions and attitudes taken by the characters presented in the case. The key element in both the group discussions and the plenary sessions is explaining *why* they think that their answers are correct. It should be noted that these so-called "pedagogical cases" have no one, concrete solution. We have deliberately left room for the students to "read between the lines" in order to take into account local conditions in the country where they may live. The students soon learn that *how* they arrive at their conclusions is far more important than the conclusions themselves. In the process, they learn how to formulate moral principles in their own words in order to be able to justify their position. At the end of the plenary session, the professor underlines important points and, if necessary, completes the theoretical framework related to the topic under discussion.

The third element is what we call "cases for measuring acquired skills." These cases should be resolved in writing by each student. A four-step methodology should be followed:

1. The identification of the moral issues which are involved in the case.
2. The identification of basic objective values which should be respected when analyzing and resolving the case.
3. The formulation of objective moral principles which should be respected when analyzing and solving the case.
4. Analysis and solution of the case in the light of the objective moral principles developed in the previous step.

As students resolve successive cases using this approach, they gradually achieve the objectives proposed at the beginning of the course. This individual work compliments the discussions which take place in class.

Interactive Teaching: Does it Really Work?

As in any pedagogical methodology, the "bottom line" has to do with results. Does interactive teaching really work? To be quite honest, due to a lack of financial and human resources, we have yet to scientifically prove the effectiveness of our methodology. However, we have observed certain indirect indicators of success.

To begin with, almost all of the professors who use "interactive teaching" are highly rated by their students. In the graduate school, the undergraduate division, and the extension service of the "Universidad del Pacífico," professors of business ethics who use this methodology are consistently among those who are most highly rated. We reason that when this happens, we can safely assume that the course has been perceived as useful for making sense out of life.

Another indicator has to do with the amount of informal discussion of business ethics cases which takes place outside of the classroom. Our students frequently continue discussing in the cafeteria the cases that have been presented in class.

The academic performance of our students is another positive indicator. They work hard and their grades show it. At the undergraduate level, they are required to do a final project which involves interviewing a high level manager, an office employee, a blue collar worker, and a street vender. They must prove that they are capable of discussing business ethics in a meaningful way with people at all levels. The quality of their work shows that they do have this ability. In the graduate school, more than one student has had his or her strategical plan for improving business ethics accepted by their respective employers as a realistic way of bettering the ethical climate in the company.

While it is true that we lack concrete scientific evidence which would prove undeniably that our students do indeed apply what they learn, these indirect indicators lead us to believe that we are doing a better job then before. As more and more professors make use of "interactive teaching," we are receiving valuable input in the light of which will make improvements in the future.

Endnotes

1. The title of the textbook is: Schmidt, Eduardo, *Ética y negocios para América Latina* (Lima: Universidad del Pacífico, 1995), 610 pp. The title of the second book is: Schmidt, Eduardo, *Moralización a fondo: Un aporte a la luz de la teoría del desarrollo humano de James W. Fowler* (Lima: Universidad del Pacífico, 2ª edición 1995), 335 pp. Class notes for professors are available on diskette. A bank of business ethics cases, written in Spanish, may be accessed via the following website: http://www.up.edu.pe/up/docentes/eschmidt Further information can be obtained via E-mail from Dr. Eduardo Schmidt, SJ: eschmidt@up.edu.pe.

2. The basic book for understanding Fowler's theory is: Fowler, James W., *Stages of Faith: The Psychology of Human Development and the Quest for Meaning* (San Francisco: Harper & Row, 1981), 332 pp.

Career Counseling and Moral Responsibility in Developing Countries

J. C. Lamprecht and G. J. Rossouw

Abstract

In this chapter the emphasis is on a specific sector of those who are often characterized as a "lost generation," namely the militarized youth in black townships in South Africa. The present challenge is to reorientate the militarized young people with a view of integrating them into the new South African society. First, a brief outline of the formation of these groups is given. This is followed by a problem analysis which indicates that their lack of knowledge of the network of relations presumed by the market economy prejudices their entry into and adjustment to the market economy. In conclusion, specific reference is made to the role that the career counselor can play in rectifying this problem.

Introduction

Businesses do not exist in isolation but are embedded in a complex network of relationships and contexts (Rossouw 1994, 7). As far as contexts are concerned, business exists first and foremost within a nature (or ecological) context and is dependent on this ecological basis for survival. Besides that, it also exists within a social (or societal) context. Within this social context, business stands in relation to both the state and the civil society and is dependent on both for survival. Furthermore, and in a more specific sense, the business enterprise stands in direct relation to suppliers and clients. These relationships are indispensable for the business. In an even narrower sense, businesses stand in relation to their shareholders and in the narrowest sense, employers and employees stand, of necessity, in an intimate relation to each other. Businesses depend on this network of social relationships to survive and flourish (Esterhuyse 1991, 27–29). This implies that businesses with moral responsibility must act in relation to each of the parties named above. There are, therefore, moral playing rules underlying the market economy that must be respected by the players in that economy (cf. Jones 1982, 211).

This network of relationships is, however, different, more so in South Africa where the overwhelming majority of citizens of the country were excluded as a result of both formal and informal forms of discrimination from the top echelons of the economy. In this way, a generation of young people grew up without any identification figures to introduce them to the complex network of relationships and the moral responsibility that go hand in hand with the maintenance of this network.

In this chapter, the emphasis falls on a specific sector of those who are often characterized as a "lost generation," namely the militarized youth in black townships in South Africa. The authors of this article were approached by the Minister for Safety and Security and the Minister of Education of the Gauteng Province to research the problems surrounding militarized young people in townships and to devise a business strategy that could meaningfully reassimilate these young people into society. Hence, the specific focus is on this sector of the community.

First, a brief outline of the formation of these groups will be given. Thereafter a problem analysis will be made, which will indicate that their lack of knowledge of the network of relations presumed by the market economy prejudices their entry into and adjustment to the market economy. In conclusion, specific reference will be made to the role that the career counselor can play in rectifying this problem.

Background to Militarized Youth

To understand the problem surrounding the militarized black youth in South Africa, it is necessary to refer briefly to some political developments since the accession to power of the National Party in 1948.

Since the National Party assumed power in 1948, a policy of separate development, later known as "apartheid," was implemented. For the first time, unwritten "apartheid" ideology and practices were increasingly enforced by a series of laws. The Mixed Marriages Act (1953) prohibited marriages between whites and people of other colors. The Group Areas Act (1950) was the instrument whereby the National Party government consolidated physical separation between races. The Separate Amenities Act (1953) regulated public amenities on the basis of racial separation. Signs reading "Whites only" or "Non-whites only" became visible everywhere. This situation demanded that black people carry identity documents (pass books) at all times. Serious discrimination against black people in the workplace was practiced. Numerous jobs were reserved for whites (Esterhuyse 1991, 52). Among other things, black people were prohibited from training as artisans or to do skilled labor in a city or town.

Black people revolted against the discriminatory measures of the white government. From 1960, the resistance of the African National Congress (ANC) acquired a strong revolutionary emphasis. The first serious conflict between police and black people took place in the Sharpeville township when sixty nine black people were shot dead. Skirmishes between police and black agitators occurred regularly. In 1976, school unrest began and spread to virtually every black area in South Africa. Conditions in black areas deteriorated progressively. Clashes between the police and black youths became virtually a daily occurrence.

In black areas, the residents began to organize themselves into street committees. Young people were divided into paramilitary units with commanders in charge. Under the wings of the ANC, the Self-Defense Units (SDU) were formed and the Inkatha Freedom Party (IFP) organized the Self-Protecting Units (SPU). In the process, thousands of young people sacrificed their school careers to join these paramilitary units. In the meantime, the SDU and SPU members began to fight one another. Infrastructures in black areas were paralyzed. No-go zones were the order of the day. Black citizens depended on the protection of the SDUs and SPUs.

These conditions in black areas only began to normalize with the election of Nelson Mandela as first President of a non-racial democracy in South Africa.

Problem Analysis

In this section, the problem surrounding militarized young people is analyzed by means of two theoretical constructs. The *first* is *Brueggemann's (1977) sociological model of change* in which people may find themselves in one of the following three phases or in a process of transition between phases:

Orientation:

In this phase, people find themselves in a social framework in which they have clarity on their social roles and in which they experience meaning in their existence.

Disorientation:

This refers to the erosion of the framework that gave role clarity and meaning to the person's existence (Brueggemann 1993, 18v). This phase can be initiated either by a loss of confidence in the existing framework or when a person moves into a new social framework in which neither role nor meaning is clear.

Reorientation:

This phase arises as the person once again finds meaning in a new social framework and once again experiences role clarity and meaning. (Orsmond 1989, 9v, 104v).

The second theoretical construct is a three-phase model of moral development according to which people find themselves in one of the following three phases of moral development or in a process of transition between these phases (Rossouw 1994, 8–10).

Survival morality:

This phase is, strictly speaking, a pre-moral phase since the essential element of ethical action, namely the consideration of the interests of others, is absent (Velasquez 1992, 153). In a struggle for personal or business survival in the work environment, the person or business is prepared to fight for survival at all costs, regardless of the potential consequences to others. It becomes a case of "bread first, morals later."

Reactive morality:

In this phase, people and businesses realize that success in the work environment depends on their acceptance by the environment within which they operate. They try, therefore, to satisfy the demands made upon them by society in order to gain acceptance.

Pro-active morality:

In this phase, people and businesses themselves take the moral initiative. They act on their own initiative to contribute in the form of their own personal or their business activities, to the improvement of the environment in which they operate (Rossouw 1994, 8–10).

On the basis of these two theoretical frameworks, the situation of militarized youth can be analyzed as follow:

Orientation phase:

SDU and SPU members experienced a meaningful existence in their respective townships during the "struggle years." These young black people created a living-space for themselves in which they were at home and where they could live life to the full. They knew the rules of the game and therefore felt safe. They had, in their specific community context, a clear role description. Through their task to protect the community, they gave meaning to their own lives. The community, in spite of the fact that they feared them, recognized the SPU and SDU members as the protectors of their safety. The youth gained worth in a community sense. In the spirit of *ubuntu* (we care unconditionally for one another and help one another), they remained alive and were provided with their basic necessities in life.

Disorientation phase:

The personal situation of the SDU and SPU members change immediately, however, when they have to hold their own outside the boundaries of the township. Within the boundaries of the community, they know the rules of the game; outside the boundaries of their communities, they find it difficult to operate with confidence. They are now expected to play a new game that makes them feel unsure and unsafe. It is especially problematic for them to move from a township culture to a business culture. The rules of the game inherent to business-undertakings are strange and unfamiliar. The new demands in terms of moral responsibility differ from their township world. Insight into the nature of the business game is limited, as are the responsibilities implied by a network of relationships in the business world.

On entering a job, such youngsters observe a survival morality. Such employees fight only for their own existence. Their dominant driving force is a fear of financial ruin. In this process, they place their own interests first and are prepared to do almost anything to avoid losing their income. They can consequently experience their existence as meaningless because they cannot find meaning in what they do on a daily basis. Their existence is aimed at survival because they experience no long-term security. Sabotage, indifference, irresponsibility, low motivation, and low productivity are visible consequences of the predisposition merely to serve their own interests. In this phase, moral responsibility is often absent.

Reorientation phase:

Reactive morality comes to the force only when the youth begin to experience security in terms of their future; only then does the readiness for moral responsibility, and the insight that there is more to the game than their own survival, develop. "Other" now becomes a factor that influences their moral behavior. The realization now begins to penetrate that in business they stand indissoluble in relation to others requiring of them to respect certain rules in order to be accepted. This implies an insight into a network of relationships and a readiness to consider others, in other words, a moral responsibility towards other people (Cederblom and Dougherty 1990, 279).

Pro-active morality can follow on reactive morality as the highest form of moral development. Instead of only reacting to demands, people start displaying initiative. This can only happen when employees begin to experience themselves as an integral part of the specific enterprise system within which they find themselves (Olyn and Barry 1996, 21–23). Such employees identify with the enterprise and have a desire to contribute to the creation of a stronger and healthier society, as a result of their involvement with the business. In this commitment, people find a reason for their existence. Survival and acceptance are in harmony with moral commitment.

Reactive and pro-active morality are, however, only possible when certain preconditions are met. Some of these pre-requisites will be discussed. The reorientation through which militarized young people must go makes demands on a number of role players. Specific focus will be placed on the role that the career counselor can play in this reorientation process.

The Challenge to Integrate Militarized Youth Back in Society

The challenge that presently exists in South Africa is to guide the militarized young people to a reorientation within the new South African society. This means that the youth must be demilitarized and become economically active.

Before considering how this can be done, two matters should be addressed: The moral responsibility of militarized youth towards society; and moral responsibilities in a market economy.

Moral responsibility towards society

It must be accepted that the militarized youth are not prepared for the workplace. They were brought up in a township with a completely different value system. Their values were shaped in an environment where they had to fight to survive, where little value is placed on human lives, and criminal activities are the order of the day. They lack a clear idea of the moral responsibility towards the broader community. If this basic realization of responsibility towards society is lacking, there is no reason for the existence of any form of ethics – and neither for business ethics. The situation in which these militarized youth found themselves has eroded precisely this fundamental realization of responsibility towards society. To act morally in business, one should be aware of the network of responsibilities associated with holding down a job.

This dilemma of the militarized youth stands in strong contrast to the majority of youths from unaffected backgrounds. An assumption can rightly be made that the latter have an idea of their moral responsibility to society, also in so far as it concerns their future work via their socialization in their communities and families.

Moral responsibilities in a market economy

The introduction indicated that employers and employees find themselves in a complex network of relationships and contexts. It was then argued that respect for each of these relationships is a necessary condition for survival and success in the market economy. The reorientation of the militarized youth is impeded since they have little insight into this network of relationships and the moral responsibility that these relationships presuppose. There are a number of reasons for this state of affairs:

- The militarized youngsters were excluded from the mainstream of society and taken up into a subculture of military and criminal activities where they received little exposure to the market economy.
- Many were also excluded from normal family life, since groups of militarized youngsters began living together on the borders of the No-go Zones in houses that had been deserted by the rest of the community since it had become too dangerous to stay there. In this way, they lost contact with their parents who were economically active. They thereby forfeited socialization in the market economy.
- The militarized youth is also a severely politicized group, as is evident from the strong bonds between the groups and political parties. The freedom ideology to which they were exposed in the struggle against apartheid was permeated by communist conceptions of the economy. These ideas are very simplistic and repre-

sent the market economy as an antagonistic system of mutual exploitation between capitalists and proletarians. The capitalist system as such is represented as immoral. Capitalism and morality are seen as exclusive concepts (Cederblom Dougherty 1990, 157–158; White 1993, 12–13).

All these factors have contributed to the fact that militarized young people have an imperfect insight into the nature and workings of the market economy. Consequently, they also find it difficult to understand why they have a moral responsibility within the workplace to, inter alia, the following parties: Employers; shareholders; suppliers; clients; state; civil community; and natural environment.

The question now arises of how this problem should be addressed. Who will be responsible to guide the militarized youth to this new value system and teach them the rules of the market economy, as well as introducing them to the unwritten moral responsibilities associated with it.

An option that should be considered seriously is to involve a career counselor, as a registered psychologist, in the process of assisting the traumatized youth back into society.

Career Counseling and Reorientation of Militarized Youth

Before discussing a model of counseling, three approaches towards counseling will be discussed briefly. A fourth approach will be added as a link between psychology and business ethics.

The point of departure of the *first approach* is the human resource requirements of the community and, in a broader context, of the country. This approach emphasizes the optimal utilization of the available human resources. According to this approach, career counseling can be seen as an instrument for channeling people to careers where the greatest need exists. The focus is on the needs of a certain community or country rather than on the individual as such.

The point of departure of the *second approach* is the personal needs of the individual in terms of career satisfaction. The emphasis of this approach is placed on the personal possibilities of individuals and how these can be utilized maximally in their choice of careers. In practice, this includes determining their specific aptitudes, interests, personality characteristics, and career values through psychometric testing, and then relating these to certain careers before a final career choice is made (Lindhart 1985, 11–13). For this reason, it can be stated that this approach focuses on the individual and not on the broader community as such.

When these two approaches are examined more closely, it would seem that the first approach is applied mainly in developing countries. The danger implied in this approach is that the personal potential of people are denied and they are utilized only to do a job. The second, more luxurious approach is indeed the ideal sought after, but is not feasible in developing countries where work opportunities and money are scarce.

The *third approach* is a compromise between these two approaches (Diagram 1). On the one hand, it focuses on the unique personal possibilities of the individual, while on the other hand the specific needs of a country are brought into the calculation. The youth must get a better un-

Diagram 1: Traditional Career Counseling

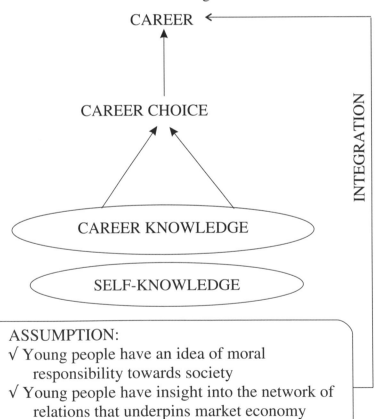

derstanding of themselves, namely self-knowledge. They must match this self-knowledge with corresponding careers and choose the best possible career, keeping in mind the human resources requirements of the country. This approach can be seen as a traditional approach to career counseling (Peterson and Nisenholz 1991, 299–303).

This point of departure is, however, still incomplete when career counseling is given to youth from deprived communities in the case of this chapter, to the militarized youth). Two important components are

Diagram 2: Counseling: Traumatized Youth from Deprived Communities

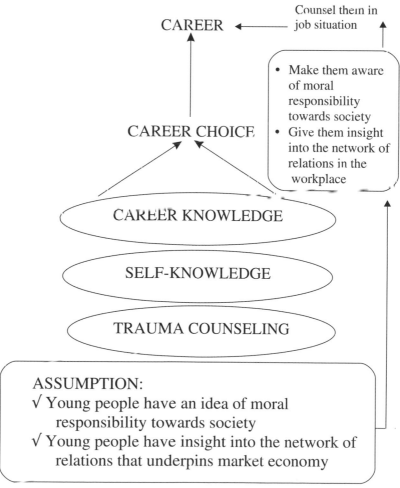

missing, namely trauma counseling and counseling-in-insight into the moral rules of the game of the market economy. When these assumptions cannot be made, career counselors should follow the *fourth approach* (Diagram 2).

First, before militarized youngsters can receive guidance in future possibilities, events in their pasts must be addressed psychologically. They must, in other words, receive help in working through the traumas of the past before they dare to explore the future. It implies that they must move through a process of healing and develop a cognitive grasp of emotional issues that occurred in their lives (Gillis 1992, 160–161). Should their personal traumas not be addressed, they will remain trapped in their own problems. Not only will they not be able to make peace with themselves, but they will with difficulty reach out to others and take others' needs into account when they have co-operate in an undertaking that presupposes a network of relationships. Trauma counseling will prevent unresolved problems from the past that can negatively influence their relationships with themselves and with others from emerging in the future.

Second, they must receive career counseling. They must discover their unique personal possibilities, career options should be matched, and the most appropriate career chosen.

Third, the career counselor must introduce these youth to the basic nature of the market economy as well as the unwritten rules and moral responsibility associated with it. The career counselor must, in other words, awaken them to their moral responsibility towards society and give them insight into the network of responsibilities in the workplace. The career counselor should assist them before they enter the workplace, but also guide them through the first phase while they adapt in their new job.

This assumes a reconsideration of the nature of career counseling. In addition to the traditional function of reconciling career choice and self-knowledge, the aforesaid two matters need also to receive attention. The demands this will place on the career counselor will quite possibly exceed the competence that career counselors receive from their traditional training. This new role will, in most cases, entail retraining career counselors or, alternatively, demand that an interdisciplinary approach to career counseling be followed.

Career counselors will have to cut across the traditional boundaries of career guidance to introduce the militarized youngsters to the basic nature of the modern economy as well as to the unwritten rules and moral responsibilities associated with it.

This approach to career counseling is in its essence a long-term approach. To implement it cost- and time-effectively, it is important that the counselors initially concern themselves intensively on an individual basis with the young people, gradually less intensively and in groups, until these youngsters eventually accept full responsibility for their own behavior.

Conclusion

The reorientation of the militarized youth as a career guidance programme presently being investigated is to begin a central career-counseling centre (CCC) that can serve all the militarized young people in the Gauteng province. Counseling will have to be generated to satisfy the needs of militarized young people.

A solution that is at present being investigated is to begin a CCC that can serve all the militarized young people in the Gauteng province, irrespective of the school or training centre to which they may be attached. This will also serve the group already in the process of training for a job.

The proposed CCC will not only provide help in guiding members of the militarized youth in making career choices, but the other two matters discussed above will also enjoy attention. With the help of specially selected and retrained career counselors, or through interdisciplinary co-operation between career counselors, clinical psychologists, and economists, militarized young people can be prepared to enter the labor market with moral sensitivity.

References

Brueggemann, W., *The Land: Place as Gift, Promise, and Challenge in Biblical Faith* (Philadelphia: Fortress Press, 1997).

Brueggemann, W. *Praying the Psalms* (Winona, Minn.: Saint Mary's Press, Christian Brothers Publications, 1993).

Cederblom, J., and Dougherty, C. J., *Ethics at Work* (Belmont, Cal.: Wadsworth Publishing Company, 1990).

Donaldson, T., and Werhane P. H., *Ethical Issues in Business: A Philosophical Approach* (Englewood Cliffs, N.J.: Prentice Hall, 1988).

Esterhuyse, W., *Sake-etiek in die praktyk* (Pretoria: J. L. van Schaik, 1991).

Gillis, H., *Counseling Young People.* (Saxonwold: Lynne Publication, 1992).

Green, N., and Lascaris, R., *Third World Destiny* (Cape Town: Human and Rousseau, 1988).

Jones, D. G., *Business, Religion and Ethics* (Cambridge, Mass.: Oelgeschlager, Gunn and Hain, 1982).

Lindhard, N., *Career Choice* (Cape Town: College Tutorial Press.1985).

Olyn, J., and Barry, V., *Applying Ethics* (Belmont, Cal.: Wadsworth Publishing Company, 1996).

Orsmond, E. C., *Teologie and Politieke bevryding : 'n Kritiese evaluasie van D. Sölle se poging tot rehabilitasie van die Westerse-protestantse tradisie en waardesisteem vanuit 'n hermeunitiek van ervaring.* (M.A. thesis, University of Stellenbosch, 1989).

Peterson, J. V., and Nisenholz, B., *Orientation to Counseling* (Boston: Allyn and Bacon, 1991).

Rossouw, D., *Business Ethics: A Southern African Perspective* (Johannesburg: Southern Book Publishers (Pty) Ltd., 1994).

Rossouw, G. J., "Rational Interaction for Moral Sensitivity: A Postmodern Approach to Moral Decision Making in Business," *Journal of Business Ethics* 13 (1994), 11–20.

Velasquez, M. G., *Business Ethics: Concepts and Cases* (Englewood Cliffs, N.J.: Prentice Hall, 1992).

White, T. I., *Business Ethics: A Philosophical Reader* (New York: Macmillan Publishing Company, 1993).

Part IV
Emerging Business Ethics in East Asia and Japan

Ethics in Developing Economies of Asia

Akira Takahashi

Abstract

This chapter aims to deepen our comprehension of the economic ethics of different peoples in Asia, as well as realizing a degree of cultural relativism, in order to enhance amicable economic associations. It counterbalances the conventionally strong West-oriented views which regard exotic features of non-Western economies as backward and illogical elements that disturb smooth and orthodox development and, hence, should be eradicated. The author, first, recalls a number of facts which depict the eruptive economic transformation in Asia. He, then, criticizes the imposition of Western-style development and exploitation without excluding Japan's colonialism in Taiwan and Korea, and pleads for multiple forms of development and modernity. Economic transactions should be analysed in relation to sociocultural aspects, and, therefore, communities and ethics groups play a substantive role between the public and private sectors, the market, and individuals. For instance, small farmers in Southeast Asia, struggling with the weakness of tenant farmers and pressures of the market mechanism, developed ingenious and participatory forms of survival, increasingly supported by non-governmental organizations. Case studies from Thailand, Malaysia, and the Philippines give a vivid picture of these activities. Because the developing economies are composed of market and non-market sectors, reasonable attention should be given to the ethics beyond market principles, with particular emphasis on community as foundation.

Introduction

Economic activities are regulated by a variety of factors related to the environments in which they occur, and the values and culture of society affect crucially the conducts of transaction. It is natural, therefore, that economic ethics are imbedded deeply in the soil of the locality where such endeavors are carried out. Of course, economic ethics have considerable levels of universality which are brought forth by the basic nature of human beings, and commonality is also necessary to promote mutual interaction between areas as well as peoples. But more important and urgent at this moment for us is to deepen our substantive understanding of the ethic dimensions of different peoples. In that sense, looking under an interdisciplinary and internalized approach, realization and comprehension of economic norms, as well as realizing a degree of cultural relativism, are necessary to enhance amicable economic association. In other words, methods of the area studies are fairly applicable in the field of studies on economic and business ethics.

We have to admit, however, economics in general tended to look at only the development courses of non-Western nations, perhaps due to strong West-oriented views. Until recent years, exotic features of non-Western economies were simply regarded as backward and illogical elements which disturb smooth and orthodox development, and eradication of such characteristics was said to be indispensable for economic progress – assimilation to the modern West was prescribed as an inevitable step toward economic growth. But the current situation in the Third World, especially the enormous transformation of the Eastern Asian economy as it maintains its distinct cultural tradition, urges us to reconsider a more conventional approach.

In this paper some of those instances are explored based on the personal findings of the writer in the region to understand cultural diversity and its relevant tradition for international business (see Takahashi 1970, 1977, and 1990). Points of emphases are: (1) economic ethics of Asia should be understood in substantive functions; (2) in rural Southeast Asia, interaction of individual and community is deployed along subsistence ethics, which ensure the common man's rights to survive; and (3) that the community is crucial for formulating the ethics of the society.

Eruptive Transformation in Asia

It is well known that the economic growth of Eastern Asia has been remarkably rapid in the last few decades, over two times of that of the OECD countries. Furthermore, real growth rate of GDP of Asia shows a steady rise as it was 5.6% in the 1960s, 6.9% in the 1980s, and 7.4% in 1990-93, while the other parts of the world rather stagnated. It is natural that this corner of the globe attracts international attention and is often called "the growth center." South Asian countries are also following the locus of Eastern Asia. India in the 1990s showed substantial changes in its economy and the *Economist* (London) used the phrase "tiger set out of cave." In 1993, the share of Asia, including Japan, in world GDP was 26.2%, which exceeded that of the United States. Per capita GNP of Singapore and Hongkong are above US$23,000, which is higher than many of the OECD countries.

Eastern Asia now strengthens its self-confidence, and claims its presence and identity in the world. Hitherto for long, even after their independence, they kept a low profile to the West, but the growth greatly changed trends of the times. The absence of the Malaysian Premier from the APEC summit meeting in Seattle in 1993, the judgement of a Singaporean court to an American youth in 1994, tension between Southeast Asia and the West relating to the formation of the EAEC, and the comprehension of democracy in China and Burma, all of these instances reflect the economic resilience of the region and the setting of a new kind of international relations. The tendency of cultural indigenization is widely observed in Asian countries, and traditional values and languages are positively appreciated in society and education, which have been neglected under colonial heritage. Sometimes limitation of the use of Western words in billboards and advertising is also implemented in various parts of Asia.

Japan's economy experienced structural transformation as production bases of manufacturing moved to other countries, particularly to Eastern Asia, in the later half of the 1980s, because of labor shortage, the higher value of the Yen, mounting trade frictions with importing countries, and deregulation of foreign investment policies in recipient nations. Such shifts started in the field of labor intensive types of manufacturing but then high technology followed, like the case of automobile and electronic industries.

The trend brought forth the deindustrialization of Japan and a considerable portion of manufacturing plants closed down, and the relocation of industrial facilities to other Asian countries took place. This, in a sense, accelerated development of an international division of labor and helped to form the new industrial structure of Japan, especially in the mid-1990s, when the Yen's value was further raised and exports of Japanese-made parts were made infeasible.

Recently a new feature of economic activity is observed in Eastern Asia. Until the 1970s, many of these countries were basically exporting primary commodities, but this share of manufactured goods in export gradually increased, sometimes quite extensively. Also, geographically, Asia depended on the developed countries like the U.S., Japan, and the European Community for the export of product and the supply of investment and parts, but from the mid-1980s mutual depending of trade and investment within Eastern Asia grew. We may say that the formation of a structure of regional circulation is going on. This means that the developing countries in Eastern Asia now rely on each other for export of their products and for investment. Asian countries are emerging out from under the control of the West.

Now the Eastern Asian economy strengthens its inter-dependency, and substantial regional cooperation is in progress. Economic transactions across borders are growing. Operating for nearly three decades, the Association of Southeast Asian Nations (ASEAN) is a solid organization that plays a significant role in political, economic, and cultural dimensions, and with membership increasing, all ten Southeast Asian countries are closely cooperating within the network of the ASEAN.

Interregional economic zones are being formed in various locations from the Japan Sea to the Indian Ocean. In the case of the "Growth Triangle," steady collaboration among Singapore, Malaysia, and Indonesia is active, to combine the resources of three nations for development. In the Batam Island of Indonesia, industrial estates were constructed based on an agreement three countries signed in 1990, and many industrial plants generated employment for over 10,000 workers, mainly from Indonesia. Frequent ferry services of forty minutes provide easy access from Singapore. It represents a bright future of interregional cooperation in Southeast Asia.

Thus the recent development of Asian economies enhanced economic interaction as well as international exchanges in the region and in the world, and while the market mechanism integrates and unifies these economies beyond cultural banners at some extent, we also realize that the economies of the areas still rigidly maintain individualistic features related to the roots and the uniqueness of its peoples.

Western Bias on Asian Economies

Due to its genesis in modern Europe, economics tended to interpret development processes of the non-Western world analogous to Western experiences. Conventional economists used to assume that the natures of economies of respective areas of the world were virtually universal and, thus, they disregarded the cultural relevance of economic relations. For them, consequently, modernization was usually conceived as assimilation and subsuming of varied non-Western economies with the Western models through the penetration of market principles of the economy.

But contemporary situations of the world such as the emergence of the Third World powers and enlarged economic discrepancy among nations along with issues related to environment and energy have forced economics to concern itself more seriously with the substantive reality of economies beyond market relations. This resulted in an increase of economic works with profound insights and appropriate emphasis on interrelations between economic and sociocultural factors, to comprehend basic characteristics of Asian and African societies.

The Western world accomplished the Industrial Revolution in advance of the rest of the world, and integrated other regions into a world market system, so that the development of the world economy centered around Europe. Economics, therefore, was also constructed and progressed in a framework based on the civil society of modern Europe. Naturally, principles of economics were postulated on the experiences of the Western societies, while little attention was paid to the rest of the world, which was colonized or set to be colonized.

Western economists sometimes observed uniqueness in economic activities of the non-Western world and contrasted them to that of the West, such as transaction and other economic relations, which were contradictory to the doctrines of the market economy. Theories such as the reversal curve of the labor supply or the concept of absenteeism were used as weapons by the colonists for keeping wage levels lower in the countries where the livelihoods of workers usually consisted of two categories of market and subsistence sectors.

But for them such relations were considered to be irrational and premodern. They took it for granted that the penetration of the market mechanism into the backward, illiterate, and uncivilized regions would eventually result in complete integration and assimilation of such awkward economies with an orthodox market economy based on Western principles. The very process is termed modernization, and transformation achieved by the process is called development.

The contemporary situation of the world, however, revealed that the economy was hardly able to solve problems confronting it nationally and globally, unless it reorganized itself through internalizing elements and approaches which have been ignored for a long time. For example, we have environmental problems that surpass mere market relations. Japan's economic success in recent years is to be explored not only in economic relations but in cultural environment of the economy. The increasing economic disparity between industrialized and developing countries is the most serious problem facing the world today. Modern economics is vulnerable in facing all sorts of unprecedented cultural challenges now, such as Islam economics.

Then what can economics learn from the Third World? Now economics must step out of the century-long deterministic model and take
into account the non-market aspects of the economy both in the Western
and non-Western world. In this regards, economics has to learn from the
Third World and create a new paradigm of comparative economics
based on substantive understanding of the non-Western societies as
well. For instance, development economics, based on profound concerns of local specificity, should elaborate itself in order to more appropriately meet local specificities.

The first point is regarding the disparity between industrialized and
developing countries, and its enlarging trends. Economics used to explain the situation in the analogy of forerunner and slow starter on a race
track, like the Marxian stage theory based on nineteenth century
ethnographic knowledge and Rostow's West-centered linear model for
interpretation of growth.

The fact that premodern Europe owed so much to the non-West is
totally forgotten here. It is undeniable that Western development and
prosperity was built only on the exploitation of the non-West in various
direct forms like the enclosure of land and natural resources and transfer
of colonial revenue to homeland, as well as indirect measures such as
exchanges of unequivalents. In some cases, the West destroyed local
communities by extremely violent measures through such activities like
slavery. Glory of modern England versus poverty in India, the prosperity of the Netherlands versus miserable conditions in Java after introduction of the culture system, are just two sides of the same coin.

We cannot see the reality of Pax Britannica without recalling the
flow of the home charge sent from India to London directly, as Indian
economic historians pointed out long before the group of the Depen-
dencia Theory formulated the dichotomy of center and periphery.

Even now, industrialized countries still exploit the Third World in
rather latent measures. One such case is African low-wage menial workers in Europe whose reproduction is totally born by village communities
and families in rural Africa, as Meillassoux (1975) demonstrated using
his concept of domestic community.

Such a situation is found not only in Europe, but also in Japan. Although Japan is proud of its economic success in modern history, count-
ing considerably high level of market economy or educational achievement at the start of modernization in the mid-nineteenth century, it
rarely mentions the role of colonies like Taiwan and Korea in the initial
stages of its economic development. In recent years, Japan is also very

proud of being one of the leading donor countries in regard to economic cooperation.

For a long time, economics took it for granted that the experiences of the modern West is the standard and orthodoxy. Development used to be conceived as a way to trace the locus of the Western nations, while deviation from the track was condemned as stagnation or irrationality. Non-Western characteristics found by British in the economy of colonial India were simply branded as retrogression and irrationality, then it became the "white-man's" obligation to let the ignorant Indians give up such premodernity and to civilize them according to Western standards. Thus the colonial rule was legitimatized under the name of "modernization."

Capitalistic society, however, is not eternal and universal in the history of mankind, but if we look back in history we easily realize that its significance is limited to the specific periods of specific regions with specific cultures. Regions of the world interact each other, but at the same time each region has it own value and its own dynamism of development. Economics has to understand the internal logic of the region based on the perception of the multiplicity of the world. Here, the alternative development should be sought by Third World countries, and then the word modernity becomes plural: modernities.

Western experiences are certainly one of the models for developing nations but peoples of various regions have to look for their own paths appropriate to their history and culture. The concept of development in India, for example, must be in accordance with harmony of Hinduism, sacred cows, and the caste system. What is needed for us is to shake off the fetters of the modernization approach and our tendencies to object the modern West.

Culture and People in Economics

Hitherto, households, enterprises, and governments have been generally conceived as basic units of economic activities within the framework of economic theories, for economists used to assume that the economy of the world is universal, thereby disregarding cultural relevancies. But to comprehend economies of the Third World, and in the industrialized society too, sociocultural characteristics of the economy should be given appropriate emphasis since, as historians claim, each ethnic group (as well as respective regions) has innate value systems and a particular path of development. In other words, it must be necessary to look at the economy as a facade of culture.

Economists seem to comprehend that the constantly forwarding Juggernaut of the market economy crushes down all the pre-capitalistic remnants and that ultimately the world is dominated by an effective market and a rational economic man. This brought forth the fictitious concept of "the formation of the world economy, " instead of "the formation of the world market economy," disregarding non-market and non-economic elements in the economy.

That is reasonable enough if we remain at the level of the national economy, since the market is the core of a capitalistic society. But to understand problems of the contemporary world, we have to go beyond that level because the substantive aspects of economies of peoples cannot be grasped only from the viewpoint of national economy. Here a concept of people or ethnicity, in the sense of people with culture, has to be appreciated.

The so-called Japanese way of management or Japanese type labor relations, for example, are certainly a matter of ethnicity in Japan. Particularly in the case of developing countries, which share two-thirds of total world population, it must be improper to make diminutive the substantive economy of the people to the market economy of the people. In this regard, reexamination of the economy in relation with non-market economic factors as well as a re-evaluation of market economy in the light of non-market relations should be crucial. In other words, we should not analyze economic relations apart from region, but we must observe economy in relation to sociocultural aspects and try to understand the people innately. In this regard, emphasis should be given to community as substance between the public and private sectors, the market and individual.

Moral Aspects of Economic Practices

In Southeast Asia, small farmers have been facing varied categories of social and economic problems. The following points seem to be important: (1) Impacts of land relations on small farmers of weak position such as tenant farmers; (2) Communal ethic measures as countervailing force against pressure of the market mechanism; (3) Participatory endeavors of local farmers in protecting their livelihood; and (4) Role of non-governmental organizations (NGOs) in rural development.

We also must pay proper attention to the area diversification of rural issues in Southeast Asia because of the striking differences in ecological and historical backgrounds of countries and localities in the area, though we have to be careful not to be trapped in the particularities of a region.

Let's start with general conditions of Southeast Asia as prerequisites to understand current issues of rural transformation in the region. Trends of changes in Southeast Asia can be summarized as follows. The region is in the process of rapid economic transformation. Foreign direct investment and industrialization are taking place. Income level is rising in urban areas. Rural to urban exodus and international migration are growing, especially in the Philippines and Thailand. Improvement of infrastructure such as roads and communication accelerates the mobilization of population. The disparity between rural and urban levels of living is enlarging. Deterioration of the environment for agricultural production such as deforestation is increasing. Food shortages are being solved partly by enhanced productivity through technological innovation, though it is limited by the stratum of cultivators and the infrastructure of the particular area. Inequality of land holding and disappearing public land for pioneers often cause agrarian unrest. Increases in population bring forth general land hunger. The tradition of peasant resistance against the landed class still exists. Principles of market economy penetrates to the traditional patterns of society and economy, but still community is the basis of rural functions. The world of moral economy is still positive where maximum welfare of community members is often given priority over individual benefit.

The writer has been observing a small rice-growing village in the central Luzon plains in the Philippines repeatedly from the mid-1960s. Due to high population pressure and the traditional land ownership patterns of large estates, share-tenancy was the most popular form of cultivation of the paddy until the agrarian reform programs were implemented under the Marcos regime in the 1970s.

The rent was often as high as a half of all the net produce on a contractual basis, but in reality all the net produce (gross output minus labor and other cost) was taken away by the landlords at the time of harvest because of amazingly high interest rates of debt (often two hundred percent per annum) to the landlords. Even immediately after the harvest season, cultivators never had a single crop harvested from their tenant farm for consumption of families. The interest rate is not felt as much by the borrowers because it is not repaid in practice. Rather for the landless workers, or share tenant, the increase of credits due to the high interest rate strengthens the bond and dependency as well as the linkage between landlord and the landless.

An interesting fact was that tenant farmers hired labor gangs for the major steps of farm works, though they themselves suffered from low productivity of paddy and underemployment because of the small size of the farmable land. It seemed to be too irrational, but detailed observation of farmers' behavior patterns demonstrated that it was the way they made their livelihood secured.

Around thirty percent of output of the farm was rendered to the workers as wage for transplanting and harvesting. Naturally it reduced the amount of tenants' share (nominally half of net produce), but net produce and the tenant's share did not have serious meaning for the cultivators as, anyway, cultivators did not receive any portion of output of their farm land under the circumstance. In return on subsequent days, the tenant farmers and their family members were hired by neighboring farmers on equal terms. The landlords, who arbitrarily took away all the net produce of the land, did not request repayment of credits from the grains the tenants obtained as wage on and off the farm.

In this sense, dependence on hired workers of nearby communities was the substantive choice of farmers to maintain their livelihood because, under the land relations, they could not realize compensation for their farming work on their tenant farm land. Payment of wages to hired workers could be understood as securing compensation for his own work as neighbors, too, followed the local practice of dependence on hired workers.

The paddy taken by landlords went to the market and farmers had to purchase rice at local market for consumption, so that paddy paid to hired workers as wage in kind was a way to secure a part of output of the village land in the community. In Central Luzon villages, the landlord are expected not to watch too closely the dispose of the harvest of the farm land.

In this case, the landlords compromised with the farmers by ignoring the farmers' gains from their off-the-farm employment. The latitude might be partly derived from the history of peasantry uprising in the locality, and landlords needed a certain social safety valve to prevent a rise of discontent. From the farmers' viewpoint, the practice was needed and approved by the community. If one did not follow the practice, social sanction followed.

Often economists, historians, and political scientists claim that landlord-tenant relations in the Philippines are much more severe in comparison to other parts of Asia. But when we observe closely the various aspects of the relationship, we are impressed by the presence of considerable latitude such as rent reduction, occasional credit, gifts, and other patriarchal postures of the landlord other than economic transaction of farming on tenant land. Such an oblige is an indispensable part of attributions of elites, particularly in a typical two-class structured society like the Philippines.

Communal Ethics versus Market Mechanism

Another example of communal ethics is the practice the writer called the "shadow circulation" of the grain in the village community. At the time of harvesting, family members of the community who have no direct concern in farming of the land come to the field to glean the paddy of what is left by the reapers. Quite often gleaners are relatives of hired reapers, so that the poor job of the hired workers means richer returns for the gleaners.

Villagers also take grains by winnowing remained stalks at the threshing site after the landlord's threshing machine completes work. In the rainy season, when the threshing machine is not used, village women sit beside the hired-hand threshworkers and beat the bundles of paddy with sticks, which have been threshed by hired workers, to collect remaining grains. Often both parties of hired threshers and grain-collecting women belong to a family or are close kin. The poorer the job of hired workers, the more the grain collected by women. Furthermore, each hired reaper takes back a sheaf of paddy home as a bonus at the end of day's work, often claiming that the grain is to be given to the chicken.

It is observed that the total amount of grain carried away by villagers in this practice counts as much as twenty to twenty-five percent of what is considered formal output. Again the cultivator as well as the landlord accepts the practice as a social custom of the community. If this is done by the tenant- cultivator on his farm land, it is a criminal conduct because it violates tenancy contract but as far as it is committed by the villagers, it is socially admitted as tradition of the community. The family members of the cultivator collect grains by gleaning the neighbors' fields the following days.

Significant is that this portion of grain is critically important for the lives of the poor farmers and the landless. Yet the portion is formally ignored by the national government and the landlord, and they overlook it, pretending as if the portion is minor and negligible. Of course, many people realize the economic importance of this practice, but this portion of the local economy is supposed to be invisible in social account.

Thus, together with a dependence on hired labor, communal practices, which seem to be obsolete and irrational in outlook, are working as a means of income-sharing among the villagers under landlordism, and are substantial measures in protecting their lives. We see resilient social security functions in community relations of the area.

Of course gleaning is a popular practice, having been written about by Leviticus in *The Bible* and it is still observed as an important sort of aims in Islamic nations as well as in nineteenth-century France as Millet painted, but in the Philippines it is quite a substantial part of the livelihood of the landless families even today. The same function is observed in villagers participation in harvesting of paddy on *bawon* practice in Java.

In the 1970s, technological innovation prevailed and agrarian reform measures took place (to a certain extent). Newly born owner-farmers and fixed-rent tenants are becoming more farm management oriented and cost conscious. We observe changes in the relationship between individual farmers and the community, but the general setting of rural regions remains unchanged due to the lukewarm implementation of agrarian reform and even after the 1986 political turmoil, small farmers have to rely on community relations for betterment of their living.

In Southeast Asia, we have to give special attention to the community sentiment of the people. The role and value of a sense for community property that is neither public goods nor private property are significant to understand the behavior of the populace. And the sense of communal property is the basis of participation.

Small farmers in Southeast Asia know how to use their community organizations to confront external forces such as government, foreign aid programs, and market powers, basing on their confidence of participation. Here several cases are presented from Thailand, Malaysia, and the Philippines.

A Forest in Northern Thailand

Hundreds of small farmers have been utilizing a communal irrigation system constructed by their forefathers some sixty years ago. Recently, they faced the menace of losing their watershed by sale of the portion of national forest to an urban entrepreneur. With the help of the local NGO and "development oriented monks" of the Theravada Buddhism, farmers built a shrine shelter for praying and other religious facilities in the forest.

Thus converting the area into a sanctuary of Buddhism, occasionally they held religious ceremonies in the forest. Now cutting trees in the forest means abusing the Buddha. This group action was possible because most of the farmers shared a sense of participation as they thought the irrigation system belonged to them.

The local NGO is trained and supported by a group of social scientists of Chianginai University. In Southeast Asia today, we see vital activities of NGOs in helping peoples and organizations in rural regions, and the linkage between the faculty of universities and NGOs are being promoted in many countries like Thailand, the Philippines, and Indonesia.

Irrigation Project in Northwestern Philippines

Ilocos Norte is a province noted for the presence of numerous small, communal irrigation systems constructed some sixty to eighty years ago. In 1980, with Japan's ODA, the National Irrigation Administration planned extensive renovation of irrigation facilities covering twenty thousand hectares, but the local farmers refused to be included in the modern scheme. A striking fact was that half of the farmers of one thousand hectares of the pilot area, where irrigation facilities such as diversion dam, canals, and ditches, and service roads were to be granted without payment for construction, opposed and dropped out of the project.

Though obsolete in outlook, the traditional systems, *zanjeras*, were maintained quite well by the community with minimal costs. To become a part of national irrigation systems meant higher cost for beneficiaries (yearly 250 kg of unhusked rice per hectare), and farmers sensed that increment of productivity was smaller than what the government estimated. Compensation for the expropriated land was to be paid only to the land owners; farmers were left at the mercy of landlords. Moreover, the landlords, who allowed cultivation of the land, were able to use the water for communal irrigation, now started to redeem the land, claiming that the water will be provided by the state, thus the background of farmers' reaction.

Finally, the government compromised with local farmers and a participatory approach was undertaken. Original organizations of communal irrigation systems were preserved, and the water of national facilities were distributed to the farmers at a reasonable cost.

From the viewpoints of the government and the landlords, important is the rise of production as a whole but as to cultivators, their concerns are the amount of grains which ultimately remains in their hands.

Double Standards of Tenancy in West Malaysia

In a kampong (village) of Perlis, a northern state of Peninsular Malaysia, a variety of tenancy relations is observed in the paddy field. Most typical contracts are (1) share tenancy called *pawah* and (2) fixed rent called *sewa*. The striking fact is that the burden of rent is so different between pawah and sewa. In case of pawah, usually half of the output of the tenant field is paid to the owner as rent, while under sewa a contract proportion of the fixed rent is equivalent to some fifteen percent of normal output. Therefore, the amount of rent is nearly *three times* higher for pawah than sewa. This gap of the rent in a small village puzzled economists, who tended to interpret economic transaction mainly from the production aspects (Ouchi, Takahashi, et al. 1977).

Combining the social factors of the community with tenancy relations, it was revealed that pawah was often practiced between father and son. In bilateral kinship, different from societies of unilateral kinship principles, the position and dignity of the aged member of the family are not necessarily well insured and legacy is not inherited by children before death of fathers. Instead, a farmer usually lend out farm land to his sons. In this case, land rent is not a mere compensation for the use of personal property, but it implies familial support of the senior member by the younger generation. Also renting the land is not an economic transaction but a transitional form of securing the family property corresponding to the life cycle from a generation to the next one.

Role of NGOs for Development

As briefly touched above, the activities of NGOs are growing in Southeast Asia, especially during the 1980s. Collaborating with foundations and NGOs of the developed world, they have been organizing meaningful networks in rural areas of Southeast Asia for income raising, building village level credit systems, environmental preservation, and so on. A recent feature of NGO activities is network of links with universities which have technology and manpower.

One remarkable example is the network of NGOs, people's organizations (POs), and governmental organizations (GOs) in the Philippines to accelerate implementation of agrarian reform policies which was enacted in 1987 but delayed by the passive posture of the government, due to strong resistance by the landed class. Endeavors of local agency of agrarian reform have been stagnant due to hostility and resistance of the former land owners.

With help and guidance from university faculties and Western foundations, NGOs, POs, and GOs formed a close network, TriPARRD, the "Tripartite Partnership for Agrarian Reform and Rural Development" in

1991, and started collaboration in solving obstacles of agrarian reform in six provinces. University groups are taking on the additional role of research and documentation.

This sort of trial seems to be suggestive in formulating new action plans for solving social insecurity in the Third World countries.

Ethics Beyond Market Relations

Facing the new world disorder in the post-cold war era, looking at the rise of the non-Western world in recent years, especially the emergence of the East and Southeast Asian countries as growth centers of the contemporary world, it is exigent for us to reexamine the nature of economic development in the context of competitiveness of the non-Western nations. Economics has been seeking universality of economic principles and was much too nomothetic, but economy is substantively carried out by human individuals who are after all entities of cultural being.

Development economics tended to interpret development processes from viewpoints of Western modernism. Sacred cows in India, for example, were looked at as an irrational tradition, not from the ecological reasoning of necessity to increase the number of cattle in the region. The caste system used to be seen only from its discrimination aspects and has been blamed as being a hindrance to progress, but redistributive functions of the caste system were totally ignored. Theravada Buddhism was said to have been wasting resources, but aspects of alms as part of the social system and the roles of "development monks" were seldom given attention. Social systems exist because they have uses for the people. Otherwise people are smart enough to transform the tradition by themselves.

What is important for us is to look for alternative paths of development indigenous to localities. Development economics has to learn and to understand more precisely the insights of the country and its people. As indigenization of the learning in social sciences and humanities are prevailing in the Third World as mentioned above, studies of development and economic ethics ought to indigenize the approach.

Here in this chapter, presenting description of economic substances of Asian actors, the writer intended to emphasize that in the contemporary world, when the globalization of economy proceeded rapidly and when universalization of business ethics was needed for building harmonious interaction among components, it was urgently requested to have explicit understanding of the differences of the economic ethics by region and by people instead of following Western standards. We have to refrain from judging local ethics with an exclusive outside view. Relative stance is indispensable. Value and moral should be conceived in plurality.

Dialogue of the U.S. and Japan on the Structural Impediment Initiative (SII) in early 1990s was a useful trial as far as it sought a mutual approach to eradicate trade barriers. But there was a tendency that one party stressed its specific pattern of economic practices as fairness and condemned that of the other. More important is the realization that economy is, by its nature, highly individual by region and by people, since it is transacted by man and man is product of culture.

Any economy has its own specific characteristics, and it can be universal only in exceedingly abstract level. Relativism is requested to be basis of that sort of negotiation.

Japanese business in other parts of the world sometimes face friction with local ethics of workers and management. This seems to be intensified by the fact that interaction is based not on direct dyadic relations but through interpretation of Western language and concepts. It is crucial to have a direct understanding of the local logic of economy and its ethics without depending too much on a Western medium.

Ethics are formulated in relation of the human actor and the society. What is most imperative for us is indigenization of ethic understanding. We have to be patient enough to take sound steps to comprehend the morals and values of areas. The economies in the Third World are composed of market and non-market sectors. We have to give reasonable attention to ethics beyond market principles, with particular emphasis on community as foundation.

References

Meillasoux, C., *Femmes, Graniers et Capitaux* (Paris, 1975).

Ouchi, T., Takahashi, A., et al., *Farmer and Village in West Malaysia* (Tokyo, 1977).

Scott, J. C., *The Moral Economy of the Peasant* (New Haven, 1976).

Takahashi, A., *Land and Peasants in Central Luzon* (Honolulu, 1970).

Takahashi, A., "Rural Labor and Agrarian Changes in the Philippines," in *Hired Labor in Rural Asia,* ed. S. Hiroshima (Tokyo, 1977).

Takahashi, A., "Agrarian Reform and Rural Industrialization," in *International Issues in Agrarian Reform,* ed. Ministry of Agrarian Reform (Quezon City, 1990).

Business Ethical Perceptions of Business People in East China:
An Empirical Study

Xinwen Wu

Abstract

This chapter deals with the ethical perceptions of business people and the current state of business ethics in East China. After surveying eight hundred business people in fifty-nine enterprises and interviewing forty-two chief executive officers, chairs, and senior managers among them, the following conclusions can be drawn: First of all, business ethics has become a new and popular topic in East China. Second, quite a lot of business people are pessimistic about the ethical standards of their superiors and co-workers, and about the ethical climate of their enterprises. Third, more and more business leaders begin to realize the importance of business ethics. Finally, in East China, the establishment of the market economy and the improvement of business ethics will depend on each other. In short, business people in East China have various ethical perceptions, and the current state of business ethics in East China is also complex and changeable.

Introduction

Business nowadays plays an ever more important role in the People's Republic of China. With the fast growing economy, a multitude of ethical problems arise such as kickbacks, bribery, fraud, environmental pollution, unethical sales practice, violating employee rights, false or misleading advertising, and so forth. Thus public concern for business ethics is quite widespread.

In the fall of 1995, an empirical study was conducted in several cities of East China: Shanghai, Qingtao, Jinan, Changzhou, Hangzhou, and Tianjin. Its purpose was to collect data on business people's ethical perceptions of the social transition, and to comment on the current and expected future state of business ethics in East China. The study was jointly sponsored by the Philosophy Department and the Centre for Applied Ethics at Fudan University, Shanghai. The research group included four faculty, of whose the author was one, and twenty-six undergraduate students of the two institutions. This study used a combination of a survey and personal interviews.

Methodology

The Sample

We made a *convenience sampling* from enterprises in various industries: manufacturing, wholesale and retail trade, finance, construction, advertising, consulting, and other services. In order to ensure the representative character of the sample, we also sampled different types of enterprises, including state-owned enterprises, collective enterprises, private enterprises, and foreign-invested enterprises. Out of this convenience sample, seventy enterprises were chosen for the survey, but eleven enterprises refused the survey by reason of "being too busy" or "not being permitted by the superior." Finally, we sampled eight hundred business people in the remaining fifty-nine enterprises. From eight hundred questionnaires that were sent out, we received seven hundred usable responses.

The response rate was 87.5%. A demographic summary of the respondents is as follows:

Gender	61% males, 39% females
Age	24% under the age of 30
	29% between the ages of 30 and 40
	31% between the ages of 40 and 50
	16% were over the age of 50
Education	34% received advanced education
	66% did not go beyond high school
Job title	6% senior business leaders
	15% middle-level managers, directors, and chiefs (whom we also regarded as business leaders)
Enterprise type affiliation	42% worked in state-owned enterprises
	17% worked in collective enterprises
	14% worked in private enterprises
	26% worked in foreign-invested enterprises
	1% did not indicate the type of their enterprises

Industry affiliation	45% worked in manufacturing industry
	24% worked in wholesale and retail trade industry
	13% worked in finance industry
	18% worked in advertising, consulting, construction, and other industries

The Questionnaire

The questionnaire contained six sections:

Section I: Background information. In this section, there were six issues with several choices. The respondent was asked to indicate his/her gender, age, education, job title, and type and industry of his/her enterprise.

Section II: Degree of satisfaction. Here the respondent was asked to indicate his/her degree of satisfaction with the following categories: work itself, payment, welfare, training, promotion, superiors' and co-workers' ethical standards, and the enterprise's ethical climate and culture. The degrees of satisfaction were divided into five ranks from "strongly satisfied" to "strongly dissatisfied."

Section III: Degree of approval. This section offered eight enterprise activities related to business ethics. The respondent was asked to indicate his/her degree of approval from the following five ranks: strongly approve, approve, neutral, disapprove, and strongly disapprove.

Section IV: Views on business ethical issues. This section presented twelve business ethical issues concerning the enterprise's image, the enterprise's social responsibility, advertising, sexual harassment, relationship between management and workers, enterprise and consumers, and so on. Each issue had four or more possible answers. The respondent was asked to choose one or more as his/her view on the issue.

Section V: Reactions to business ethical cases. This section described ten situations that had happened in Chinese business. The respondent was asked to indicate his/her reaction on each situation from various choices.

Section VI: Opinion on the survey. Here the respondent was asked to answer the following open-ended question: "What is your opinion of this survey?"

In order to establish the truth of the collected data, the survey questionnaire was distributed to every respondent by our survey participants and was anonymously completed by the respondent.

The Interviews

Among the respondents, 6% were chief executive officers, chairs and senior managers of enterprises. We gave them personal interviews of thirty minutes each in order to remedy the defects of the survey. In each personal interview, we asked the interviewee three questions:

1. Does your enterprise have a formal and written code of ethics or similar standards and norms of proper behavior? If not, is your enterprise planning to develop them?
2. Did you often take ethical aspects into consideration in your process of decision-making?
3. Do you think that developing a market economy is good (or bad) to improve Chinese business ethics? And why?

The Statistics

Owing to the lack of computer and the defects in the questionnaire design, we had to do our statistics by hand. We spent nearly one year to complete most of the statistics in the questionnaire survey and the interviews. This backward method of statistics added to our difficulties in analyzing and studying the collected data. It should be mentioned, moreover, that we could not accomplish all kinds of statistics because the recovered questionnaires had become completely ragged after they were used too many times.

Findings

Degree of Satisfaction

The business people's degree of satisfaction with the enterprise, especially with the ethical standards of superiors and co-workers and with the ethical climate of the enterprise, is an important basis for commenting on the state of business ethics. Table 1 presents the results of our survey regarding the respondents' degree of satisfaction.

Table 1: The Respondents' Degree of Satisfaction

	strongly satisfied	satisfied	neutral	dissatisfied	Strongly dissatisfied
Work itself	13%	28%	22%	30%	7%
Payment	8%	25%	29%	24%	14%

	strongly satisfied	satisfied	neutral	dissatis-fied	Strongly dissatis-fied
Welfare	9%	17%	32%	34%	10%
Training	11%	19%	44%	18%	12%
Promotion	4%	10%	48%	23%	15%
Superiors' ethical standards	7%	12%	34%	31%	16%
Co-workers' ethical standards	14%	20%	39%	19%	8%
Ethical climate and culture	6%	13%	42%	30%	9%

From Table 1 we can see that, at the aggregate level, 47% of the respondents were dissatisfied or strongly dissatisfied with the ethical standards of their superiors; 27% were dissatisfied or strongly dissatisfied with the ethical standards of their co-workers; and 39% were dissatisfied or strongly dissatisfied with the ethical climate of their enterprises. It is worth noting that most of these people were also dissatisfied or strongly dissatisfied with their payment, promotion, welfare, and training. These findings imply that many respondents were pessimistic about the ethical aspects of their enterprises, and their degrees of satisfaction with these aspects have something to do with their degrees of satisfaction with their self-interests in enterprises.

It is worth noting, however, that nearly 33% of the respondents who were satisfied or strongly satisfied with work itself were dissatisfied or strongly dissatisfied with the ethical climate and culture of their enterprises. Twenty-nine percent of those who were satisfied or strongly satisfied with payment were dissatisfied or strongly dissatisfied with the ethical standards of their superiors. These two percentages suggest that there is no necessary relationship between the respondents' degree of satisfaction with work itself and payment and their degree of satisfaction with the ethical aspects in the enterprises. This result is out of our anticipation.

In addition, at the aggregate level, those respondents who were business leaders had much higher degrees of satisfaction with the eight categories than the respondents who were ordinary workers or employees.

The different degrees of satisfaction between business leaders and ordinary business people indicate their different judgments of the current situation in their enterprises. Moreover, those respondents who had received advanced education and those who were over the age of forty were more dissatisfied with the above categories than the others. This means they had higher expectations of their enterprises than the other respondents.

Degree of Approval

Business people's degree of approval of different business activities usually reflects their values and ethical perceptions in some sense. The results of our survey on the respondents' degree of approval are presented in Table 2.

Table 2: The Respondents' Degree of Approval

	strongly approve	approve	neutral	dis-approve	Strongly disapprove
Doing business completely ignored ethical considerations	1%	4%	3%	66%	26%
Applying business ethics instead of business law as the main means for coping with business conflicts	31%	45%	8%	11%	5%
Institutionalizing ethical codes or norms for business activities	34%	53%	4%	8%	1%
Popularizing Japanese style management in Chinese business	7%	24%	15%	37%	17%
Appointing university professor of ethics as business consultant	4%	28%	21%	35%	12%
Raising staff's salary so as to strengthen enterprise's solidarity	8%	33%	24%	29%	6%

	strongly approve	approve	neutral	dis-approve	Strongly disap-prove
Using reward and punishment as the major instruments of business manage-ment	4%	36%	17%	35%	8%
Increasing business profits at the cost of business ethics when they contradict each other	10%	18%	33%	23%	16%

Table 2 shows that 92% of the respondents expressed their disapproval or strong disapproval of those business activities which completely ignored ethical considerations. Eighty-seven percent, of whom nearly 20% were business leaders, approved or strongly approved to institutionalize ethical codes or norms for business activities; 76% approved or strongly approved to apply business ethics instead of business law as the main instrument for dealing with the conflicts of interests inside and outside the enterprise. It followed from this result that a substantial number of respondents began to realize the significance of business ethics. Nevertheless, the disagreement of the business people surveyed was obvious when a conflict existed between business profit and business ethics. Specifically, 28% of the respondents approved or strongly approved to increase profits at the cost of business ethics, 33% were neutral, and 39% disapproved or strongly disapproved it. This result suggests that many respondents did not have a clear and right conception of business ethics. Under such a situation, unfortunately, most of the respondents still rejected or neglected the guide of ethicist. Such an attitude is a great challenge to Chinese ethicist in academia when they want to communicate and cooperate with business practitioners in East China.

The second focus of our survey on the respondents' degree of approval is to find out their attitudes towards various management styles and instruments, and to further analyze their ethical perceptions. As Table 2 shows, most of the respondents disapproved or strongly disapproved of popularizing Japanese style management in Chinese business. The reason seems to be attributed mainly to Chinese people's nationalism. According to our statistics, however, 62% of the senior and middle-level business leaders surveyed approved or strongly approved of Japanese style management. This result may imply that the efficiency of

Japanese style management had so a strong appeal to these business leaders that they could surpass their nationalist standpoint when they were managing enterprises.

In recent years, money stimulation, reward, and punishment were popular instruments of management in quite a lot of Chinese enterprises. Therefore, we surveyed the respondents' degree of approval of these instruments in order to grasp their attitudes. With regard to raising salary as the instrument of strengthening enterprise's solidarity, 35% of the respondents, of whom 29% were senior and middle-level business leaders and 44% received advanced education and 57% worked in state-owned enterprises, expressed their disapproval or strongly disapproval. In those respondents who approved or strongly approved of money stimulation, 73% did not go beyond high school and 48% were females. Those respondents who kept neutral, 34% were business leaders and 49% were over the age of forty. These results indicate that most of those respondents who were business leaders and who had received advanced education could not approve of pure money stimulation, while most of the respondents who were females and did not receive advanced education were prone to accept it. This finding seems to be inconsistent with the finding on the degree of satisfaction above that several respondents who had received advanced education were more dissatisfied or strongly dissatisfied with payment and welfare than the others; thus, we can infer from this fact that those business people who were dissatisfied with their salaries and welfare did not necessarily approve of using money stimulation in business management.

With regard to using reward and punishment as the major instruments of business management, 43% of the respondents, of whom 32% were business leaders, indicated their disapproval or strong disapproval. This result shows that more and more business people in East China began to express their aversion to the rigid way of business management, which implies that it is possible to establish ethical management in Chinese enterprises.

Views on Business Ethical Issues

Generally speaking, business people's views on business ethical issues are central to their ethical perceptions. By asking the respondents twelve close-ended business ethical questions, we basically grasped their views on some important business ethical issues. The main findings are as follows:

As for *the values of the respondents*, 46% chose seeking for self-development and self-fulfillment as their main purpose of working for the enterprise; 21% seeking for making more money; 18% for lively working rhythm and good working atmosphere; 10% for good ethical relationship, climate, and culture; and 5% for the others. From this result we can see that most of the respondents did not regard their jobs in enterprises merely as a means of life any longer.

As for the *image of enterprise*, we asked the respondents to choose no more than three given answers which could represent the image of enterprise. The result is presented in Table 3.

Table 3: The Respondents' Views on the Image of Enterprise

The image of enterprise is represented by	Chosen in percentage	Ranking
(a)Values, spirit, and culture of enterprise	19%	4
(b) Total business strength of enterprise	28%	3
(c) Advertisement and propaganda of enterprise	6%	7
(d) The superiors' impression on enterprise	5%	8
(e) Products or services of enterprise	43%	1
(f) Contribution of enterprise to society	16%	5
(g) Mental style and features of enterprise staff	30%	2
(h) Artificial environment of enterprise	13%	6

The result shows that business people in East China had various views on the image of enterprise and many respondents devoted more attention to the ethical aspects and the total business strength of enterprise while they despised the role of advertisement, propaganda, and superiors' impression in shaping the image of enterprise. It should be emphasized that nearly 70% of business leaders surveyed all chose (a), (e), and (g) as the representation of the image of enterprise. This result implies that business leader in East China had improved their ethical consciousness.

As for the *primary responsibility of the enterprise*, 31% of the respondents held that the enterprise is primarily responsible to consumers, 26% to employees, 18% to stockholders, 14% to the government, and 11% to the society and the environment. According to our statistics, 53% of the respondents who worked in manufacturing industry held that the enterprise is primarily responsible to consumers, while only 16% of the respondents who worked in wholesale and retail trade industry thought so. In those who chose the government as the answer, 67% worked in state-owned and collective enterprises and 32% were business leaders in these two type of enterprises.

As for *the nature of advertising*, 27% thought that advertising "as a kind of marketing strategy" always contains false factors; 31% thought that advertising "as a means of business competition" always contains misleading factors in spite of its possible truth; 33% thought that advertising as an introduction of the products and services of enterprises does not always contain false or misleading factors, and that true advertising should be distinguished from false or misleading advertising; only 9% thought that advertising "as a bridge between enterprises and consumers" is trustworthy. From this result, we can find out that there is serious confusion in most of the respondents' views on advertising.

As for the preference for *the type of advertising*, we asked the respondent to specify no more than three types of advertising which he/she likes from the given answers. Table 4 presents the main results.

Table 4: The Respondents' Preference for the Type of Advertising

Type of advertising	Percentage	Ranking
(a) Being simple, brief and understandable	21%	3
(b) Employing well-known persons	3%	6
(c) Employing people with sex appeal	2%	7
(d) Employing experts or institutions of sciences	15%	4
(e) Employing lovely children	5%	5
(f) Embodying distinctive originality	24%	2
(g) Offering the true and overall information about products or services	37%	1
(h) Others	1%	8

From Table 4, we can see that the respondents more like the type of advertising of (g), (f), and (a) than the others. This result is under our expectation. It is unexpected, however, that such a few respondents chose (b), (c), and (e) which are popular types of advertising in today's mainland China. It should be added, moreover, that nearly 10% of the respondents did not specify any answer of this question. The reason may be that they did not like advertising itself.

As for *the relationship between management and workers*, 36%, of whom 31% were business leaders, thought of it as one between managing and being managed, leading and being led, 23% as one among equal comrades, 18% as one among brothers and sisters, 14% as one among friends, and 9% as one among opponents and competitors. In those who chose the equal comrades relationship, only 15% were under the age of 40 and in those who chose the relationship among brothers, sisters or friends, 25% were business leaders. This result suggests that business leaders surveyed had formed two main circles in their views on the relationship between management and workers. Moreover, from the fact that 32% of the respondents chose the relationship among brothers, sisters, or friends as one between management and workers, we can understand the ethical characteristics in Chinese business.

As for *the relationship between enterprise and consumers*, 34% thought that the relationship is pure self-interest of the enterprise; 41%, of whom 32% were business leaders, thought of the relationship as mutually beneficial one on the basis of selling and buying; and 22% regarded it as equal, free, and friendly, one which is beyond pure interest. But 3% of the respondents thought of it as the relationship between deceiving (enterprise) and being deceived (consumers). This result reflects more or less the current situation of the relationship between enterprises and consumers in the process towards market economy.

As for *the relationship between government and enterprise*, 46% hoped that government should reduce its control of enterprise; 25% expected government should abolish its control of enterprise; 23% thought that government should keep its macrocontrol of enterprise although it should not intervene in specific affairs of the latter; only 6% thought that enterprise should be under the comprehensive control by government. We can see from this result that 71% of the respondents, nearly 20% being business leaders, thought that enterprise should get rid of the control by government. This finding indicates the yearning of most of the respondents for changing the traditional relationship between government and enterprise under the plan economy system.

As for *the popular practice of offering and accepting kickbacks* in present Chinese business, 17% regarded it as ethical and legal, 22% as ethical but illegal, 27% as legal but unethical, 31% as unethical and illegal, and 3% regarded it as having nothing to do with ethics and law. It should be noted that in those respondents who regarded kickbacks as unethical and illegal, only 16% were business leaders. In those who regarded kickbacks as ethical and legal, 48% worked in private enterprises and 29% in foreign-invested enterprises.

As for *the way of emerging business management*, 24% thought that management should emerge by the election in all staff members in the enterprise, 45% by the election in the representative assembly of enterprise, 17% by the appointment from the board of directors, 6% by the appointment from the government, and 8% by the other ways. This result shows that most of the respondents did not approve of emerging business leaders by the appointment of government, which was the usual method under the traditional plan economy system. Meanwhile, only 17%, 43% being business leaders, held that management should be appointed by the board of directors. This fact implies that most of the respondents, especially those who were not business leaders, still refused to accept the internationally popular way of emerging business management.

As for *the critical elements of a successful enterprise*, the respondents were asked to choose no more than four elements from the ten given possible answers. The major results are presented in Table 5.

Table 5: The Respondents' Views on the Critical Elements of a Successful Enterprise

Elements	Percentage	Ranking
(a) Strong economic investment	15%	6
(b) Leaders with abundant business experience and great working ability	45%	1
(c) Definite and feasible business idea and development strategy	42%	2
(d) Harmonious interpersonal relationship	16%	5
(e) Perfect credit of products or services	19%	4
(f) Staff members with high quality	33%	3
(g) Good relationship with the community	4%	8

Elements	Percentage	Ranking
(h) Concern and support by the government	11%	7
(i) Unique business characteristics	3%	9
(j) Others	2%	10

Table 5 indicates the respondents' main views to the question what are the critical elements of a successful enterprise. It is obvious that many respondents paid more attention to the spiritual and human elements than to the others. In those who chose (c), nearly 45% were business leaders.

This result means that many business leaders realized how important business ideas and development strategies for enterprises are. In those who chose (b) and (f), 26% and nearly 50%, respectively, were business leaders. This fact shows that business leaders emphasized more the role of staff members than that of leaders in the development of enterprise. In those who chose (h), nearly 82% were business leaders. We can infer from this percentage that many business leaders did not ignore the role of government in business success. This finding forms a sharp contrast to the result on the relationship between government and enterprise (above) that 14% of business leaders surveyed thought that enterprise should get rid of the control by government.

With the exception of the above twelve questions, the respondent was also asked to answer a question about sexual harassment. The question was a manager expressed sexual desire to a subordinate with the bait of promotion and higher salary. Do you think the subordinate should: (a) accept it; (b) reject it tactfully; (c) charge the manager; or (d) resign from the company. Out of all respondents, no one chose (a), nearly 49% chose (b), 23% chose (c), and 26% chose (d). In those who chose (c) and (d), 69% and 82%, respectively were female respondents. It followed from this percentage that female business people had a stronger reaction to sexual harassment than male ones. In addition, it was interesting that 2% of the respondents who were all business leaders did not answer the question.

Reactions to Business Ethical Cases

After surveying business people's views on twelve business ethical issues, we presented the respondents with ten business ethical cases concerning product quality, employee rights, unemployment, environmental pollution, and so on, in order to better understand their ethical perceptions. Here we will explain these cases one by one and present the respondents' reactions to them.

Case 1: Destroying overdue food.
A food company decided to destroy one hundred tons of candy in stock which had exceeded its expiration date. How should this decision be evaluated? Sixty-one percent thought that it was ethical and deserved commendation; 32%, of whom 36% were business leaders, kept neutral; and 7% held that it was completely wrong and should be criticized. This result was obviously inconsistent with the finding on the degrees of approval (above) that 92% of the respondents disapproved or strongly disapproved of doing business while completely ignoring ethical considerations. We can infer from the inconsistency that it is easy to approve of business ethics in words while it is difficult to put it into practice under specific business situations.

Case 2: Dealing with a harmful product.
A TV set with bad quality exploded and did a great harm to the consumer. Who should take the responsibility to compensate for the loss? With regard to this question, 26% regarded it as the responsibility of the manufacturing factory, 9% as one of the selling enterprise, and 65% as the common responsibility of both sides. It is worth noting that in those who merely emphasized the responsibility of manufacturing factory, 71% worked in wholesale and retail trade industry, while in those who merely emphasized that of selling enterprise, 86% worked in manufacturing industry. This fact implies that some business people surveyed were prone to shirk their own responsibilities when their products or services did harm to the consumers.

Case 3: Violating employee rights.
A foreign-invested toymaking factory made a body search on the female workers when they went off work in order to prevent the toys from being stolen by them. With regard to this case, 1% thought that the factory was right to do so; 6% thought it was feasible because it was legal in spite of being unethical; 27% held that the factory ought to stop doing so because it was unethical although being legal; 66% maintained that the factory was wrong to do so in law as well as in ethics. In those who regarded the action as right or feasible, four were business leaders in private or foreign-invested enterprises. This result suggests that few business leaders surveyed lacked respect for employee rights.

Case 4: Dismissing an employee.
A state-owned airline company dismissed a staff member because she violated the formal codes of ethics in the company. With regard to this case, 13% thought that the company was right to dismiss her; 18% thought that it was right but unethical; 54% thought that the reason to dismiss her was insufficient; and 15% maintained that the company did not have any reason to dismiss her because the codes of ethics were legally invalid. In those who chose the answer that the company was right, 30% were business leaders. From this finding, we can infer from the respondents' different views on the question what role the codes of ethics should play in enterprises.

Case 5: Dispute about intellectual property right.
An new machine equipment was invented by a engineer when he worked in a machine-making factory. Two years later he resigned his position from the factory and was reemployed by a corporation. When he contributed his invention to the corporation, however, he was charged by the factory that he violated the property right of the factory. With regard to the case, 21% thought that the engineer was the owner of the invention and he had right to arrange it; 18%, of whom 46% were business leaders, held that the invention was owned by the factory and the factory was right to charge the engineer; 52% maintained that the invention was the common property of the engineer and the factory, and neither side could arrange it without the agreement by the other; and 9% thought that they could not judge who had the intellectual property right because the current business law in China was ambivalent on this issue.

Case 6: Business contribution to education, culture and charity.
In 1994, a large foundation was founded by a well-known steel corporation in order to support education, culture, and charity in China. With regard to this case, 43% thought of it as a pure advertising strategy and a potential investment; 36%, 35% being business leaders, considered it as the social responsibility to which the corporation ought to take; 15% regarded it as a unwilling choice which was forced by the government; and 6% took it as a wrong decision at the expense of the interests of employees and stock holds. This result implies that most of the respondents did not yet understand the social responsibility of business which is different from its economic responsibility. Nevertheless, many business leaders surveyed had a explicit conception of business' social responsibility.

Case 7: Helping unemployed employees.

In recent years many workers who were usually over the age of 40 and had low cultural and educational quality lost their jobs in enterprises. Who should take the responsibility to help these unemployed people be reemployed? With regard to this question, 23% of the respondents considered it as government's responsibility because the unemployment problem was the problem of government, 20% regarded it as one of the related enterprise, 19% took it as the unemployed people's responsibility, and 39% considered it as the common responsibilities of the three parties. In those who emphasized the responsibility of government, nearly 80% were over the age of 40 and 73% did not go beyond high school; in those who held the responsibility of the unemployed people themselves, 65% were business leaders.

Case 8: Dealing with a bankrupting state-owned enterprise.

A state-owned enterprise was on the brink of bankruptcy in the period of economic transition. We asked the respondents what proper step the government should adopt under such a situation. Fourteen percent thought that the government should provide favorable policy and a interest-low loan so as to help the enterprise pass the difficult period; 53%, of whom 58% worked in state-owned enterprises, held that the government should change the leaders in the enterprise and raise its efficiency in management; 7% maintained that the government should let it alone and let it bankrupt naturally; and 26% chose the step that the government should encourage the other enterprises to annex it. From this result, we can see that several respondents did not approve of the usual step that government offered the bankrupting enterprise policy and financial support. It is worth noting that in those who chose the annexing step 45% were business leaders, most of whose worked in state-owned or collective enterprises.

Case 9: Importing foreign rubbish.

A chemical plant imported a great quantity of foreign, everyday rubbish as its raw materials of production, a situation that did not violate the current law in China. It made a lot of money as well as serious pollution. With regard to this case, 5% thought that the plant as an independent legal person that had right to do anything legal, including importing and processing foreign rubbish, although it caused pollution; 16% thought that the plant should decrease the pollution as far as possible although it had right to import and process rubbish; 23% maintained that the plant should abandon the right to import and process rubbish unless it could avoid the pollution; 56% held that the plant ought not to have the right to import and process foreign rubbish. We discovered that, in those who maintained the absolute right of the plant, 72% worked in private or for-eign-invested enterprises, and in those who maintained the limited right of the plant, 43% were business leaders. This result indicates that most of the business leaders surveyed maintained the plant's right to import and process foreign rubbish.

Case 10: Closing a pollution-made enterprise.
A large state-owned paper mill made serious water pollution. There is no better way to avoid the pollution than closing the mill, so the local government decided to close it, although this step would make thou-sands of people unemployed. With regard to this case, 7% of the respon-dents thought that the local government was illegal and unethical to close the mill, 24% regarded it as legal but unethical, 32% regarded it as ethical but illegal, and 47% thought of it as legal and unethical. From this result, we can see that the respondents were divided into different groups about what is legal and what is ethical in dealing with the rela-tionship between employment and environmental protection.

From the survey, we found that most of the respondents realized the difference between business ethics and business law, while they could not yet correctly understand the relationship between them. We also found from their reactions to several cases that more than 30% of them emphasized the role of business law in business activities. This finding seems to be inconsistent with the result on the degrees of approval (above) that 76% approved or strongly approved to apply business eth-ics instead of business law as the main instrument for dealing with busi-ness conflicts. Moreover, those business people surveyed often had different reactions to the same business ethical cases. We found that the different job title, affiliation, education, and age of the respondents often produced an impact on their reactions to these cases. These disagree-ments reflect the complex nature of the problem of right, duty, and re-sponsibility in business activities.

Ethical Beliefs of Business Leaders

In addition to the survey on business leaders who were 6% of the total seven hundred respondents, we also personally interviewed them on three questions. Here are the significant results:

Codes of ethics and similar statements:
Among forty-two business leaders, sixteen confirmed that their enterprises had formal and written codes of ethics or similar standards or
norms of proper behavior; twenty-six admitted that their enterprises did
not have them; eleven of them were planning to develop such a code. All
sixteen business leaders whose enterprises had such a code or standard
showed and explained us their codes and standards. They believed that
formulating a business ethics code and standards could improve the
good operation of the enterprise. Most of them, however, thought that
their enterprises did not need setting up a special ethics organization or
an executive ethics officer to supervise the implementation of the business ethics code or standard. This finding seems to be inconsistent with
the result on the degrees of approval (above) that 17% of the business
leaders surveyed approved or strongly approved the institutionalization
of ethical codes or norms for business activities.

Considering ethical aspects:
As for decision-making, thirty-five business leaders often, and three occasionally, took ethical aspects into consideration in their processes of
decision-making, but four, of whose three were private business leaders
and one was a collective's business leader, thought that business decision-making had nothing to do with ethics.

Role of the market economy for improving business ethics:
With regard to the importance of market economy in improving Chinese
business ethics, thirty-six business leaders thought that developing a
market economy was good to improve Chinese business ethics because
the market economy system was helpful in fostering the independence
and autonomy of the enterprise and the individual in it, and to make their
rights and duties clear. But six, who were all leaders in state-owned and
collective enterprises, thought developing a market economy system
was harmful to improve Chinese business ethics. The first reason was
that market economy was self-interested oriented while ethics always
presupposed somewhat altruism, and the second one was that developing market economy would destroy Chinese ethical tradition and socialist morals. In their opinions, socialist business ethics with Chinese
characteristics could not coexist with market economy. This result suggests that some senior business leaders in East China had not understood
the ethical dimension of market economy.

Opinions on the Survey

Concerning the last open-ended question, 11% of the respondents said nothing about the survey, 74% considered it good, meaningful, or necessary, and most of them expected that we could report our survey findings to related enterprises and government departments as the reference of their decision-making. But 15% regarded it as meaningless or a waste of time (two were senior managers in state-owned enterprises and one was chief executive officer in a private business group).

Conclusions

A number of conclusions can be drawn from this empirical study. First of all, business ethics has become a new and popular topic in East China. Most business people are sensitive to business ethical issues, and they have various ethical perceptions. Second, the findings indicate that quite a lot of business people are dissatisfied with both the ethical standards of their superiors and co-workers and the ethical climate of their enterprises. Third, more and more business leaders begin to believe that high business ethical standards are advantageous both to the enterprise and to the individuals in it, while some business leaders have not properly understood the relationship between business ethics and business law as well as the right, duty, and responsibility in business activities. Fourth, because of the social transition, the ethical perceptions of some business practitioners in East China are self-contradictory and the great disagreement with ethical perceptions exists when they face the same business activities. This fact implies that the current state of business ethics in East China is complex and flexible, and it will remain so in the not too distant future. Finally, because most business people have approved the development of a market economy and realized the impossibility of market economy without business ethics, the establishment of the market economy and the improvement of business ethics will strongly depend on each other in East China.

Of course, there are certain limitations to this study. For example, the sample of enterprises was a convenience sampling; the number of the issues asked in the questionnaire was too large; the statistics were artificial; and in the questionnaire we could not eliminate possible effects of the bias of the respondents toward social desirability. Particularly, we did not survey the degree of influence of traditional Confucian ethics on the respondents' business ethical perceptions. We also did not use the experience and findings of similar studies in foreign countries for reference. Moreover, the regions of the People's Republic of China have different levels of economic development. Because East China as the most developed economic region in China is very particular, the survey can not represent the ethical perceptions of Chinese business people in the whole country.

It should be emphasized, however, that such a large scale empirical study of business ethics was the first one in the People's Republic of China which presents a viable starting point for developing a Chinese business ethics as an academic discipline. On the basis of this empirical study, we will further strengthen the cooperation between academia and enterprises in order to improve Chinese business ethics in theory as well as in practice.

Ethical Contexts of Korean Chaebols:
An Exploratory Study on Ethical Subjectivity of Managers

Jegoo Lee and Hun-Joon Park

Abstract

This chapter explores the ethical subjectivity to which members of various business organizations in Korea adhere. This study is carried out by using the "Q-methodology," which enables the revelation of the systems of ethics that members of each organization possess. It specifically concentrates on the common values shared among members of each of the three Korean conglomerates, or Chaebols, and compares the traits of each organization's ethical characteristics. It provides possible insights into the Korean business ethics from organizational as well as institutional perspectives. Implications for business ethics practice and research are discussed.

Introduction

It has only been widely recognized that individuals in business organizations hold diverse ethical criteria. Consequently, organizations tend to possess their own ethical values. Interpreting and reasoning the real contexts for each society as well as organizations must be settled without delay. Although numerous researches have been carried out for constructing the ethical decision making model, there exist limitations and problems with the previous researches. First, most of the existing ethical decision-making models focus largely upon a few factors (for examples, Akaah and Lund 1994; Dukerich et al. 1990; Glenn 1994; Grover and Chun 1994; Hansen 1992; Harris 1990; Jones 1990; Mitchell et al. 1992; and Posner and Schmidt 1993). Second, these studies still remain at a conceptual level (for recent examples, Johnson and Greening 1994; Thomas and Simerly 1993; Weber 1994; and Zahra et al. 1993). Furthermore, most pioneering works on the subject adopt insights from the individual cognitive process on psychological basis which confine themselves within a narrow perspective (Jones 1991; Reed et al., 1990; Weber, 1993). Third, fundamentally, the reason why the business organizations should be moral has not been sufficiently presented thus far (Frederick 1987; and Swanson 1995). Finally, the majority of existing researches has been dominated with Western perspectives, not with the viewpoints of non-Western society or local contexts.

This chapter explores the ethical subjectivity which members of various organizations adhere to. The study will be carried out by using the "Q-methodology," which enables the revelation of the system of ethics that members in each organization possess. It will, specifically, concentrate on the ethical values of the three Korean conglomerates, or Chaebols, and compare the traits of each organization's ethical contexts. While the ethical contexts of Korean Chaebols will be examined, the moral standards of Korean managers will be shown in comparison with those of South East Asian managers and foreign expatriates. Finally, some normative organizational logic of Korean business ethics will be discussed. Discussing the implication for business ethics research and practice concludes it.

Methods

The Q-methodology (Brown 1980; McKeown and Thomas 1988; and Stephenson 1983, 1985) was used to inspect and observe the ethical subjectivity of the members of Korean Chaebols. Q-methodology is a method for inquiring all forms of moral recognition and self-references of individuals. It focuses on disclosing each individual's subjective standards for a given event. Q-methodology is not the equivalent to the Q-sort technique (Bougon 1983), the latter being a method for arranging opinions. It distinguishes itself from the conventional statistical approach by being abductive rather than being inductive or deductive. On abductive, or retrospective, logic, any kind of hypothesis found in real phenomena is worth of intellectual consideration (Peirce 1940). Abductive reasoning could be interpreted as one sort of the inference to the best explanation (Harman 1970). Using Q-methodology, the researcher should collect as many statements as possible within a society and let P-samples sort Q-items (refined statements) according to their own subjective standards. Individual subconscious criteria can be revealed through the expression of their own subjective standards. Therefore, Q-methodology is well suited to an exploratory, direction-deficient theme and/or to a qualitative inquiry.

Gathering Q-Statements

At first, we collected statements from interviews with managers and executives in Korean business organizations as well as foreign expatriate managers in Korea. In order to gather as many opinions as possible, situation-specific scenarios were given (Beauchamp 1983; David 1954; and Maclagan and Snell 1992). Among the five scenarios dealing with ethical dilemmas, the most effective in screening the diverse perspectives of an individual was "whether or not you should expose a previous employer's core technology to your new organization." As a result, over 200 statements were compiled from responses to this situation.

Building Q-Items (refined statements)

For the final questionnaire, two kinds of techniques were applied: structured Q-items and unstructured Q-items. *Structured Q-items* were designed based on the gathered statements that showed the following four predominant response categories: 1) issue-perceived attitude (perceiving ethical dilemma or justifying self-interest); 2) ethical perspectives on the basis of ethical theories (egoistic, utilitarian, and deontological); 3) final decision to participate (active or passive); and 4) reaction level to a situation (individual or organizational level). For the final structured Q-items, we combined the above four categories and built 24-structured Q-items. Six statements were generated from the field, while applying or compounding the established theories mostly formed structured ones. Those six *unstructured Q-items* are: 1) structural barrier in organization, 2) the importance of individual praxis, 3) the logic of caring, 4) the fair competition in a market, 5) rules of the game, and 6) the profit maximization.

Q-Sorting and P-samples

Instead of adopting unforced or hands-off Q-sorting, a forced or instructed Q-sorting method was chosen. *Forced Q-sorting* controls the respondents' ranking of Q-items according to the imposed pattern of item distribution, whereas unforced Q-sorting allows respondents to decide for themselves on the distribution of Q-items. Respondents should interpret all Q-items based on their own operant logic as opposed to considering each Q-item separately in their responses. Samples used in the Q-sorting were named *P-samples* for the purpose of differentiating them from Q-samples as a source of Q-items. Unlike conventional statistical approaches, reliable outcomes can be extracted with relatively small samples (Brown 1980; and Stephenson 1985). In this study, 120 Q-sorting were obtained from 120 Q-samples. Among them, 81 Q-sorting warranted Q-factor analysis. 67 Q-sorting were made by managers from the three Korean conglomerates, or Chaebols, i.e., 24 managers from Chaebol A, 26 from Chaebol B, and 17 from Chaebol C, respectively. In order to secure representativeness, P-samples are from electronics, semi-conductor, general trading, and consulting companies. Also, 10 Q-sorting was obtained from South East Asian managers and 4 from foreign expatriate managers in Korea.

Q-Factor Analysis

First, all 81 Q-sorting made by Korean managers as well as foreign managers were analyzed as a whole. In this analysis, we can explore the question of how distinct and peculiar Korean business ethics are compared to those of foreign ones. Then we need to answer such questions as "What are the ethical contexts of Korean Chaebols?" and "How different are the ethical subjectivities from each Korean Chaebols?" In order to discover answers to these questions, 67 Q-sorting made by Korean managers from the three Chaebols were analyzed independently. Since Q-methodology is used to reason and abduct the relative contexts in P-samples' ethical subjectivity, two analyses are not following the same logic, rather independently. *Censort 2.0* was utilized to filter out Q-factors.

Results

Korean and Foreign Business Ethics

Table 1 shows how distinct and peculiar Korean business ethics are as compared to Southeast Asian and other foreign business ethics.

Table 1: Korean and Foreign Business Ethics

Group (S/T)	Factor 1	Factor 2	Factor 3	Factor 4
Korean (20/67)	5	12	2	1
Foreign (8/14)	6	–	1	1

S: subtotal / T: total number of P-samples belong to 4 factors

(1) Q-Factor 1. In this Q-factor 1, the majority of Southeast Asians and foreign P-samples are clustered together. Table 2 illustrates how managers in this factor postulate the perspectives based on individual criteria and teleological criticism. From the items of these P-samples showing the highest disparity, they seem to have negative feelings about the indifferent attitudes toward unethical actions, but they also appear to be passive.

Table 2: Foreign Business Ethics (Q-Factor 1)

Rank	Brief Statement	Rank of Factor 2
1	Individual capability and autonomy (1.6081)	16 (-.0245)
2	Organizational deontology, legitimacy (1.5700)	4 (1.0981)
3	Criticism based on the results (1.1237)	15 (.0661)
4	Caring (1.1100)	1 (2.3887)
5	Individual deontology (1.0645)	17 (-.0843)
29	No problem to act immorally (-1.3190)	24 (-.7965)
30	Reveal only if it is better for my position (-1.3483)	26 (-1.0447)

Number in parentheses: Z-score

(2) Q-Factor 2. In Table 3, the items with which the majority of Korean P-samples agreed are shown, yet none of the foreign P-samples accompanied are enumerated. This factor can be called the Korean business ethics factor. Korean P-samples recognized and granted the importance of individual action and the structural hindrance at the same time. Furthermore, the most unique item of the Korean factor is "for the good of the society." This item stems from the utilitarian and the public interest perspective.

Table 3: Korean Business Ethics (Q-Factor 2)

Rank	Brief Statement	Rank of Factor 1
1	Caring (2.3887)	4 (1.1100)
2	Importance of individual praxis (1.6190)	15 (-.0341)
3	Structural barrier (1.3313)	16 (-.1247)
4	Organizational deontology, legitimacy (1.0981)	2 (1.5700)
5	For the good for whole society (1.0368)	14 (-.0140)
29	Fear of being fired and harm to family (-1.7063)	24 (-1.0329)
30	Everyone is doing so (-1.7727)	19 (-.5184)

Number in parentheses: Z-score

Ethical Contexts of Korean Chaebols

Korean P-samples from three Chaebols were examined and compared with foreign P-samples. This first analysis, however, has limitations to the extent that Korean managers were analyzed as a whole and were put alongside those of foreign managers. In the ensuing analysis of 67 Q-sorting by Korean managers, 4 Q-factors were acquired. As shown in Table 4, each P-sample from each different organization keeps its particular belongings respectively. Individual managers of Chaebol B appear in every Q-factors, but most of those in the Q-factor K1, and those of Chaebol B are partially homogeneous. Members of Chaebol A are seen in Q-factor K2 and K3, but none in Q-factor K1 and K4. Moreover, it can be said that P-samples of Chaebol A are very much homogeneous.

Table 4: Ethical Characteristics of Korean Chaebols

Group (S/T)	Factor K1	Factor K2	Factor K3	Factor K4
A (12/24)	–	3	9	–
B (11/26)	8	1	1	1
C (7/17)	2	–	2	3

S: subtotal / T: total number of P-samples belong to 4 factors

Members of Chaebol C, however, cannot make any unique scattering and are idiosyncratic in that they show no uniform ethical characteristics. Thus Q-factor K1 and Q-factor K3 were chosen to be examined in detail since most P-samples from Chaebol B and Chaebol A belonged to their unique factors.

(1) Q-Factor K1 (Chaebol B). P-samples that belong to Q-factor K1 use individual-oriented and principle-centered criteria to examine the problem. They highly regarded inner voice and fair situation, but disagreed with the profit maximization logic of market and a shrewd attitude as seen in Table 5. In this factor, the majority of P-samples is from Chaebol B. For the sake of convenience, Q-factor K1 is titled "the factor of Chaebol B."

Table 5: Ethical Characteristics of Korean Chaebol B (Q-Factor K1)

Rank	Brief Statement	Rank of other factors		
		Factor K2	Factor K3	Factor K4
1	Individual deontology (1.5856)	2 (1.7784)	22 (-.3839)	13 (.0295)
2	Rules of the game (1.3037)	23 (-.6089)	4 (1.3523)	11 (.6046)

Rank	Brief Statement	Rank of other factors		
		Factor K2	Factor K3	Factor K4
3	Caring (1.2511)	4 (1.2023)	1 (2.0723)	12 (.3449)
4	Fair competition (1.2204)	6 (-.8341)	5 (1.1847)	2 (1.4810)
5	The importance of individual praxis (1.1937)	13 (.0918)	2 (1.4633)	17 (-.2607)
29	Profit maximization (-1.7703)	3 (-.0328)	27 (-.3229)	18 (-.4156)
30	Keeping principles is naive (-1.7780)	16 (1.2024)	19 (-1.2453)	20 (-.3788)

Number in parentheses: Z-score

(2) Q-Factor K3 (Chaebol A). Q-factor K3 is extremely biased to Chaebol A, although some P-samples from Chaebol B and Chaebol C belong to it. Thus, this factor is named "the factor of Chaebol A." As shown in Table 6, P-samples in Q-factor K3 consider the organizational situation as well as the individual attitude. Especially, organizational conscience is rated as an important canon, whereas the individual conscience is treated as the most important item in Q-factor K1's, or "the factor of Chaebol B" case.

Table 6: Ethical Characteristics of Korean Chaebol A (Q-Factor K3)

Rank	Brief Statement	Rank of other factors		
		Factor K1	Factor K2	Factor K4
1	Caring (2.0723)	3 (1.2511)	4 (1.2023)	12 (.3449)
2	The importance of individual praxis (1.4633)	5 (1.1937)	13 (.0918)	17 (-.2607)
3	Organizational deontology (1.3809)	8 (.9989)	30 (-1.8855)	9 (.6567)
4	The rules of the game (1.3523)	2 (1.3037)	23 (-.6089)	11 (.6046)
5	Fair competition (1.1847)	4 (1.2204)	6 (.8341)	2 (1.4810)
29	Fear of being fired and harm to family (-1.5811)	28 (-1.6023)	29 (-1.7609)	24 (-.7930)
30	Everyone is doing so (-1.9457)	22 (-.6434)	26 (-1.1848)	19 (-.4088)

Number in parentheses: Z-score

In this analysis that inquired into Korean organizations, we were able to draw up a few clues. First, members of Chaebol A are very much homogeneous and are convergent to the Q-factor K3. They interpret ethically problematic situations through a window of organizational conscience. In addition to that, members in Chaebol A pay attention to individual praxis and yet admit structural problems. For Chaebol B, members tend to think of basic principles and moral consciousness as individual criteria. They are not so much homogeneous as Chaebol A. As explained previously, members of Chaebol A are very homogeneous and individualistic, but they might be bewildered and perplexed when and if confronted with organization-centered values. Members in Chaebol A possibly could commit ethical harm when they are urged to conform to their organizational mandates. Although members of Chaebol are not as homogeneous as members of Chaebol A, they are more likely to hold basic principles and moral consciousness as criteria than the latter.

In Table 7, the ranks of Korean Chaebol companies in terms of general company images and ethical images as perceived by the public are presented. From these viewpoints, it is recognized that unbalanced images between two images exist. In detail, semiconductor and electronics companies generally hold higher ranks and reputation for ethical images. While this is not true for general company images, in terms of ethical images, the individual companies of Chaebol A do not hold consistent images. The situations are different for Chaebol B companies in that they maintained higher ranks for ethical images than for general company images.

Table 7. Images of 3 Korean Chaebols

Rank	Total Company Images	Ethical Images
1	A (semi-conductor)	A (semi-conductor)
2		B (electronic goods)
3	A (electronic goods)	B (semi-conductor)
4	C (automobiles)	
5	C (construction)	
6	B (electronic goods)	
8	C (heavy industry)	A (electronic goods)
9		C (electronic goods)

Adapted from "Images of Korean companies," *The Weekly Economist* (1/16/96, No.321)

Discussion

Logic of Korean Business Ethics

Two Q-items, "caring" and "fair competition," were found throughout all 4 Q-factors compared to foreign business peoples' standpoints during the second analysis. In addition, other Q-items belonging to both Q-factor K1 and Q-factor K3 are "the rules of the game" and "the importance of individual praxis." In light of these common facts and compared to foreign business peoples' standpoints, we could suggest some provisions tentatively: 1) Korean samples tend to be individual-oriented, so they are likely to perceive the importance of individual praxis and to establish and preserve the positive institutional logic for the good of the whole society; 2) but simultaneously they are embarrassed with the structural hardship and the importance of such situational bounds as the rules of the game and the need for assurance of fair competition. Korean business people not only regard individual willingness but also structural pressure as the important factors in ethically problematic situations. They also want to keep and wish to be kept well in favorable circumstances for business organizations. Further, the particular item that we need to take into consideration for Korean business ethics is "I should disclose the secret (of a former company) on the condition that it is for the good of the whole public and is not to be fatal to anyone." They seemed to hold utilitarian and somewhat egalitarian perspectives. In short, they are likely to establish and preserve the normative institutional logic of their own.

Ethical Contexts Inside Korean Business Organizations

In interpreting the Q-factors in organizational and societal contexts, it was revealed that members of Korean business organizations maintain diverse facets of ethical subjectivity and their own organizational logic as well as institutional ones. In this analysis that inquired into Korean organizations, we were able to reason that members of Chaebol A are very much homogeneous and are convergent to the Q-factor K3, meanwhile, for Chaebol B, members tend to think of basic principles and moral consciousness as individual criteria. Business people from Chaebol A tend to hold such logic or values for satisfying the needs and desire of the society. At the same time, they possess alternative ones in favor of their organizational benefit, irrespective of social desirability. In Chaebol B, managers are more likely to blow whistles when they encounter moral conflict circumstances, for they can sustain individual standpoints.

From outside, Chaebol A is projected as perfect and fine teamwork, but Chaebol B seems like a mixed bunch or rabble. The interpretation is reversed, however, when ethical values are considered, the latter is evaluated in finer image than the former. This proposition is backed up by the public perception, as shown in Table 7. As a result, the organizational contexts of Chaebol A is titled *"homogeneous opportunists,"* and for Chaebol B, *"principle-centered individualists."* Homogeneous people may commit ethical problems (Daboub, et al. 1995) or show a "groupthink" phenomenon (Janis 1972). Therefore, homogeneity among members in Chaebol A might be pressured for conformity (Festinger 1954; Schacter 1951; and Tajfel 1982) and for convergence on a single solution (Steiner 1982). Thus, members in Chaebol A might be bewildered and perplexed; moreover, they possibly could commit ethical harm, when and if they are urged to conform to their organizational-oriented values. In the Q-methodology research process, they interpret ethically problematic situations on the basis of organizational conscience.

Implications and Suggestions

As explained above, most members of Korean organizations represent their own emotional and self-referent criteria toward moral dilemmas rather than legal or theoretical standards. It is reasoned that Korean organizational members tend to prefer their own moral criteria to existing norms. Moreover, they appear to preserve double standards and organizational logic for their own companies and institutional logic for the society. Korean business people have created a unique value (Janelli 1993), which is dualistic and syncretistic (Kim 1992). Koreans were also sensitive to whether organizational interest and individual concern can be compatible. In addition, they tend to regard the cause of accidents, which often give rise to the public criticism, as institutional and structural evils instead of by cunning actors. Hence, what is the organizational member's ethics-in-use and practical logic should be studied and inquired in addition to proposing normative theories.

Generally, in any organization members share values, beliefs, and assumptions for the advantage of a particular social world, regardless of social desires. Institutions are beneficial to the society directly, while organizations pay attention to their benefits (Donaldson 1989; Selznick 1992; Sethi 1979). There might be a collective conscience which is more than a collective sum of individual organizations (Halme 1995). Institutions could sort out organizations which adapt only to technical requirements from those which adapt to social values beyond technical requirements (Selznick 1992). The former is termed organizational logic, whereas the latter institutional logic. In this dynamic context, individuals themselves are participants in shaping all kinds of logic, whether they are organizational or institutional. The ethical contexts are a mediator between an inside organization and outside world (Halme 1995). The actions (ethical or unethical decision making) also have an effect on both the internal and external environment.

Figure 1: A Suggested Inquiry Perspective onto Ethical Contexts

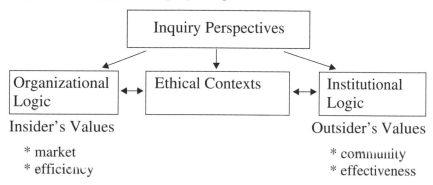

In this context, the directions for future research would be suggested in Figure 1. As explained above, both organizational values and societal morals affect ethical contexts. Members of organizations, therefore, hold the double values. Business people are generally often afraid of the failure of efficient outcomes for the sake of moral values (Etzioni 1988; Friedman 1962, 1970; Sen 1987), i.e., the bounds of incompatible perspectives of efficiency and morality (Cavanagh et al. 1981; Frederick 1987; Swanson 1995; and Wood 1991). For the prescriptions and praxis, there could be no more important notion than individuals be participants in shaping the logic of organizations as well as institutions (Jackall 1988), not only being subjected to that logic. A few pathfinders concerned it and named ideational culture (Schein 1992), belief system (Donaldson and Lorsh 1983), interpretative scheme (Bartunek 1984), organizational paradigm (Etzioni 1988; Johnson 1987, 1992; and Pfeffer 1981) and institutional logic (Jackall 1988). Hence, as the suggested direction, for inquiring into the genuine ethics of business people, important questions are as to what are ethics-in-use or practical contexts of business organizations.

We analyzed managers's ethical subjectivity who belong to Korean conglomerates, Chaebols, that consist of significant part of Korean economy. Managers sometimes make decisions for satisfying not only interests as a member of family and society but also those of their company. There is no "one ethical logic" among business managers but they adopt various ethical criteria due to the changing contexts. Ethical subjectivity implies such a kaleidoscope of ethical standpoints. Therefore, inquiring ethical subjectivity should be a learning process for acknowledging and bridging the gaps between espoused ethics and ethics-in-use.

References

Akaah, I. P., and Lund, D., "The Influence of Personal and Organizational Values on Marketing Professionals' Ethical Behavior," *Journal of Business Ethics* 13 (1994), 417–430.

Bartunek, J., "Changing Interpretative Schemes and Organizational Restructuring: The Example of a Religious Order," *Administrative Science Quarterly* 29 (1984), 355–372.

Beauchamp, T. L., *Case Studies: In Business, Society, and Ethics* (Englewood Cliffs, N J : Prentice-Hall, 1983).

Bougon, M. G., "Uncovering Cognitive Maps: The Self-Q Technique" in *Beyond Method: Strategies for Social Research*, ed., G. Morgan (Beverly Hills, Cal.: Sage, 1983).

Brown, S. R., *Political Subjectivity: Applications of Q-Methodology in Political Science* (New Haven and London: Yale University Press, 1980).

Cavanagh, G., Moberg, D., and Velasquez, M., "The Ethics of Organizational Politics," *Academy of Management Review* 6 (1981), 363–368.

Daboub, A. J., Rasheed, A. M. A., Priem, R. L., and Gray, D. A., "Top Management Team Characteristics and Corporate Illegal Activity," *Academy of Management Review* 20, no. 2 (1995),138–170.

David, D. K., "Foreword" in *The Case Method at the Harvard Business School*, ed. M. P. McNair (New York: McGraw-Hill, 1954).

Donaldson, G., and Lorsh, J., *Decision Making at the Top* (New York: Basic Books, 1983).

Donaldson, T., *The Ethics of International Business* (New York: Oxford University Press, 1989).

Dubinsky A. J., and Loken, B., "Analyzing Ethical Decision Making in Marketing," *Journal of Business Research* 19, no. 2 (1989), 83–107.

Dukerich, J. M., Nichols, M., Lippitt, E., Dawn, R., and Vollrath, D. A., "Moral Reasoning in Groups," *Human Relations* 43 (1990), 473–493.

Etzioni, A., *The Moral Dimension: Toward a New Economics* (New York: The Free Press, 1988).

Festinger, L., "A Theory of Social Comparison Process," *Human Relations*, 7 (1954), 117–140.

Frederick, W. C., "Theories of Corporate Social Performance," in *Business and Society: Dimensions of Conflict and Cooperation*, eds., S. P. Sethi and C. M. Falbe (New York: Oxford University Press, 1987).

Friedman, M., *Capitalism and Freedom* (Chicago: University of Chicago Press, 1962).

Friedman, M., "The Social Responsibility of Business Is to Increase Its Profit," *New York Times Magazine* (September 13, 1970), 33, 122–126.

Glenn, J. R., Jr., and Van Loo, M. F., "Business Students' and Practitioners' Ethical Decisions over Time," *Journal of Business Ethics* 12 (1994), 835–847.

Grover, S. L., and Chun, H., "The Influence of Role Conflict and Self-Interest on Lying in Organizations," *Journal of Business Ethics* 13 (1994), 295–303.

Halme, M., "Environmental Issues in a Product Development Processes: Paradigm Shift in a Finnish Packaging Company," *Business Ethics Quarterly* 5 (1995), 713–733.

Hansen, R. S., "A Multidimensional Scale for Measuring Business Ethics: A Purification and Refinement," *Journal of Business Ethics* 11 (1992), 523–534.

Harman, G., *Introduction, Acceptance, and Rational Belief*, ed., M. Swain (Dordrecht: Reidel, 1970).

Harris, J. R., "Ethical Values of Individuals at Different Levels in the Organization Hierarchy of a Single Firm," *Journal of Business Ethics* 9 (1990), 741–750.

Jackall, R., *Moral Mazes: The World of Corporate Managers* (New York: Oxford University Press, 1988).

Janelli, R. L., *Making Capitalism: The Social and Cultural Construction of a South Korean Conglomerate* (Stanford, Cal.: Stanford University Press, 1993).

Janis, I. L., *Victims of Groupthink: A Psychological Study of Foreign Policy Decisions and Fiascoes* (Boston: Houghton Mifflin, 1972).

Johnson, R. A., and Greening, D. W., "Relations between Corporate Social Performance, Financial Performance, and Firm Governance," *Academy of Management Best Paper Proceedings* (1994), 314–318.

Johnson, G., *Strategic Change and a Management Process* (Oxford: Basil Blackwell, 1987).

Johnson, G., "Managing Strategic Change – Strategy, Culture, and Action," *Long Range Planning* 1 (1992), 28–36.

Jones, W. A., Jr., "Student Views of Ethical Issues: A Situational Analysis," *Journal of Business Ethics* 9 (1990), 201–205.

Jones, T. M., "Ethical Decision Making by Individuals in Organizations: An Issue-Contingent Model," *Academy of Management Review* 16 (1991), 366–395.

Kim, C. S., *The Culture of Korean Industry: An Ethnography of Corporation* (Tucson: University of Arizona Press, 1992).

MacIagan, P., and Snell, R., "Some Implications for Management Development of Research into Manager's Moral Dilemmas," *British Journal of Management* 3 (1992), 157–168.

McKeown, B., and Thomas, D., *Q-Methodology* (Beverly Hills, Cal.: Sage, 1988).

Mitchell, W. J., Lewis, P. V., and Reinsch, N. L., Jr., "Bank Ethics: An Exploratory Study of Ethical Behavior and Perceptions in Small, Local Banks," *Journal of Business Ethics*, 11 (1992): 197–205.

Pfeffer, J., *Power in Organizations* (Marshfield, Mass.: Pitman Pub., 1981).

Peirce, C. S., *Philosophical Writings,* ed., J. Buchler (New York: Dover Pub., 1940).

Posner, B. Z., and Schmidt, W. H., "Value Congruence and Difference Between the Interplay of Personal and Organizational Value Systems," *Journal of Business Ethics* 12 (1993), 349–357.

Reed, L., Getz, K., Collins, D., Oberman, W., and Toy, R. 1990. "Theoretical Models and Empirical Results: A Review and Synthesis of JAI Volumes 1–10," in *Corporation and Society Research: Studies in Theory and Measurement*, ed. L. E. Preston (Greenwich, Conn.: JAI Press, 1990), 27–62.

Schacter, S., "Deviation, Rejection, and Communication," *Journal of Abnormal and Social Psychology*, 46 (1951), 190–207.

Schein, E., *Organizational Culture and Leadership* (San Francisco, Cal.: Jossey-Bass, 1992).

Selznick, P., *The Moral Commonwealth* (Berkeley: University of California Press, 1992).

Sen, A., *On Ethics and Economics* (Oxford: Blackwell, 1987).

Sethi, P. S., "A Conceptual Framework for Environmental Analysis of Social Issues and Evaluation of Business Response Patterns," *Academy of Management Review* 4 (1979), 63–74.

Steiner, J. D., "Heuristic Models of Groupthink," in *Group Decision Making*, eds., H. Brandstatter, J. H. Davis, and G. Stocker-Kreichgauer (London: Academic Press 1982), 503–524.

Stephenson, W., "Communication Review and Commentaries" in *Communication Year Book*, (1983), vol. 13.

Stephenson, W., 1985. A Lecture on the 50th Anniversary of Q-Methodology. University of Missouri.

Swanson, D. L., "Addressing a Theoretical Problem by Reorienting the Corporate Social Performance Model," *Academy of Management Review* 20, no. 1 (1995), 43–64.

Tajfel, H., "Social Psychology of Intergroup Relations," in M. R. Rosenzweig and L. W. Porter, eds. *Annual Review of Psychology*, 33 (1982): 1–39.

Thomas, A. S., and Simerly, R. L., "Strategic Leadership and Corporate Social Performance: An Empirical Examination," *Academy of Management Best Paper Proceedings* (1993), 331–335.

Weber, J., "Institutionalizing Ethics into Business Organizations," *Business Ethics Quarterly* 3 (1993), 419–436.

Weber, J., "Influences upon Managerial Moral Decision Making: Nature of the Harm and Magnitude of Consequences," *Academy of Management Best Paper Proceedings* (1994), 329–333.

The Weekly Economist, No.321. 1/16/96. Seoul.

Wood, D. J., "Corporate Social Performance Revisited," *Academy of Management Review* 16 (1991), 691–718.

Zahra S. A., Oviatt, B. M., and Minyard, K., "Effects of Corporate Ownership and Board Structure on Corporate Social Responsibility and Financial Performance," *Academy of Management Best Paper Proceedings* (1993), 336–340.

Trust and Filipino Family Business

Alejo José G. Sison

Abstract

This chapter pursues a three-fold objective: First, to trace the evolution of the concept of "human resources" from "labor" to "social capital"; second, to seek in Francis Fukuyama's transcultural analysis of trust and its relationship with business a suitable framework for understanding the particular Filipino environment; and third, to establish the trust parameters of select Filipino family businesses.

On "Human Resources": From "Labor" to "Social Capital"

Over the decades, we have been witnessing some very significant developments in the field of human resources. This evolution has occurred from the more abstract and universal conceptions of human resources to the more concrete and particular ones. Aside from capturing better the distinctively human – that is, personal and unsubstitutable – contribution to business and the economy, it has likewise had repercussions on the valuation and retribution of the same.

Traditional microeconomic models simply considered human resources as one more among several production factors, like land and capital. For many, "manpower" referred to abundant, low-skilled and poorly-remunerated labor: Pakistani kilim weavers, Zairean diamond miners, Chinese prisoners who make toys, Filipina domestic workers, they represent that flimsy wage advantage that people from developing countries supposedly have. Manpower was analogous to "horsepower," the measure in Physics for energy or the capacity to do work. In this perspective, and the assumptions of maximizing behavior, stable preferences, and market equilibrium notwithstanding, Gary Becker's work on the notion of "human capital" signals a very welcome breakthrough (1975).

Like the professional managerial class, the notion of "human capital" reconciles two historically clashing factors: labor and ownership of capital. Only when human resources are conceived as capital does it begin to make sense to invest in their upkeep and improvement. "Human capital" brings with it an appreciation for the differential characteristics of sex, age, training and experience among people who, until then, were regarded almost uniformly as "commodities."

With Becker's pioneering research, human resource experts have later formulated the concept of "intellectual capital" (Stewart 1994), which includes intangibles such as expertise, knowledge, and information. Larry Prusak defines it as the "intellectual material that has been formalized, captured, and leveraged to produce a higher-value asset." Attempts have been made to quantify "intellectual capital," transforming it into an accounting item in financial statements. Implicit is the belief that a corporation's "intellectual capital," as its R & D efforts and services, occupies a prominent place in its assets portfolio. Besides, there is a growing awareness among accountants that the old system, with its entries of cost of material and labor, has become obsolete. This attitude is detected, for example, in the subsector of information technology and management. A consensus exists here on the higher value of patented software over hardware. Once the knowledge assets of a company have been identified, management could implement processes that describe, measure, and enhance them, to the benefit of the firm's financial performance. London Business School fellow Charles Handy estimates that in any given corporation, intellectual assets are worth three to four times their tangible book values. In more sophisticated versions, intellectual capital results from the interplay of human capital (the skills of the employees, as the source of innovation and growth, although these are not assets the company could own), structural capital (the firm's organizational capabilities, which shareholders may claim), and customer capital (a corporation's franchise or market).

As early as in the 1960s, Fritz Machlup (1962), had already coined the term "knowledge-industries," to designate the emerging protagonists in the creation of wealth and value in the economy. Peter Drucker (1978) later heralded the birth not only of "knowledge-based industries or economies," but also of an entire "knowledge-based society." The call made Robert Reich (1992) for more "symbolic analysts," the equivalent to Drucker's "knowledge workers," to relaunch the American economy is just another confirmation of this belief.

In the last five years, two milestones stand out. The first is the concept of "cultural capital," authored by Thomas Sowell (1994). By this term, he refers to that set of productive capacities or "skills" and cultural values (e.g., work habits and dispositions, propensity to save money, attitudes towards education, entrepreneurial spirit, etc.), inasmuch as these provide an explanation for the level and degree of development of specific countries, races, and civilizations. On account of their cultural capital, for example, overseas Chinese succeed in their business ventures, be it in the Philippines, Thailand, Los Angeles, or Vancouver.

Discussion over "cultural capital" has gone beyond pluri-ethnic American society and its obsession with political correctness. Offshoots of this issue are the debates regarding the role of Confucianism in the ascent of the East Asian economies, or the superiority of "Asian values" over the enlightened individualism of the West (see Mahbubani 1995; Lingle 1996; Sen 1999).

Oftentimes, "political correctness" is camouflage for "cultural relativism," the belief that development or progress is a function of the treatment that a social group receives from others, some sort of an all-pervading self-exculpating victim complex. Sowell avoids falling into this trap by recourse to common sense. In the same way that books are better than papyri as reading matter, arabic numbers are better than roman numerals for mathematical computations, and rifles and pistols more effective war weapons than bows and arrows, we may also say that cultures which invented the former are better than those which invented the latter in the specific areas considered.

The second reference point along the line of "human resources," is the notion of "social capital" by Francis Fukuyama (1995). "Social capital" may be defined as "the ability of people to work together for common purposes in groups and organizations," or "the ability to associate with each other," which in turn depends on "the degree to which a community shares norms and values and subordinates individual interests to those of larger groups." In the absence of trust and cross-cultural understanding, a borderless economy, as the one described by Ohmae (1990), would necessarily bring with it spiraling insurance, legal and litigational costs. Earlier, Ronald Coase (1960) had called our attention to these "transactional" or "social" costs. He expressed the paradox according to which the more opportunistic people become with their "bounded economic rationality," the less trustworthy they are. In lieu of trust, bureaucracy and corruption are bound to flourish. On the contrary, a corporate culture wherein one's word is one's bond, a business environment where every agent delivers on his promises, oblivious to the sanctions for doing otherwise, could almost have guaranteed success.

A Transcultural Analysis of Trust and Its Impact on Business

Trust involves committing something valuable belonging to oneself, such as material resources or information, to another (see Bond 1991). Revealing a personal identification number for the automatic teller machine or a computer password, hiring a caregiver for one's infant children or choosing a heart doctor, getting engaged and getting married, all these are "trust" actions. In such voluntary and deliberate self-giving, the protagonist loses effective control over how the other person makes use of the matter entrusted.

Trust deals primarily with information that is "vital," one which spells a difference in the life of an organization. This information is a source of power. (Here "social capital" connects with "intellectual capital.") Yet, this knowledge is not held by the trustee as his own property, of which he can freely dispose, but rather, it is held in deposit, as entrusted by the owners for a specific purpose. This knowledge is not intended to be used for the trustee's personal gain. If so, he would have fallen to the mercenary-like attitude by some rogue traders who profit on the basis of insider information (see Werhane 1994). Sometimes, these brokers defend themselves from theft by alleging that their earnings did not belong to anybody else in the first place. Their profit was simply based on a "privileged" information, the proprietorship of which is difficult to determine. Until laws for the protection of intellectual property have been enacted, these arguments do have a point. Yet, the real issue lies in their having abused the confidentiality of information, in not having been able to keep a secret. And it is by virtue of this breach in fiduciary responsibility that they would deservedly stand accused.

Fukuyama's thesis lies in isolating trust or "social capital" as the key factor for the success of business and the economy. The higher the trust level of an organization, the more successful one could expect it to become, however "success" may be defined. Secondly, Fukuyama understands trust as a cultural trait (thus allowing linkage with Sowell's "cultural capital"); that is, the trust level is homogenous in a socio-cultural group. Undeniably, "culture," "ethnicity," and "race" are contested terms in scientific language; all the more so, to suppose a homogenous culture for any group, given the state of communication technology and the permeability of life worlds. Yet, these contentions are not enough to invalidate the proposition that the trust level in a cultural group is homogeneous, at least to the same extent that culture itself is acknowledged to be homogenous in the group considered.

Seven different cultures are analyzed and compared by Fukuyama on the basis of their inherent social capital endowments: China (including Taiwan and Hong Kong), Italy, Korea, France, Germany, Japan, and the United States. The lowest trust levels are to be found in China and Italy, whereas Japan and the United States are rivals on the top end. Similarities have likewise been established not only between these pairs of countries, but also between Korea and France in their levels of social capital.

The most significant criteria in gauging the degree of trust present in a cultural group are its family structures, the strength of "associationism," and the extent of government or state intervention in business. Among these three, only "associationism" registers a direct proportion with a society's trust level, while family structures and state intervention seem to have an ambivalent effect. Nonetheless, a particular society's family structure is the strongest net conditioning factor of its stock of social capital, insofar as it determines the degree and type of "associationism" and, ultimately, the configuration of civil society.

The family represents the most effective universal institution for socializing individuals, irreplaceable by either broader community groups or government programs. It is the prime vehicle for the transmission of both intellectual and cultural capital. Furthermore, it constitutes the elementary unit of economic organization, not only from the side of consumption but from the side of production as well. A family enterprise can thrive in the absence of a stable structure of property rights because its cohesion is based on the moral, cultural, and emotional bonds of an original social group.

On the other hand, ever since Max Weber (1951), the idea that "familism" is detrimental to economic development has been put into circulation. According to the German sociologist, overly restrictive family bonds constrain the development of universal values and impersonal social ties necessary for modern business organizations. Family ties have to weaken before economic progress occurs, from the extended families of agricultural societies to the nuclear families of industrial societies, and further on to the single-parent families of post-industrial welfare societies. For this reason, the "familistic" societies of China, France, Italy and South Korea are considered to be low-trust: they all have difficulties in creating large organizations beyond the family, and, consequently, the state has had to intervene to promote durable, globally competitive firms. In this regard, a sharp contrast may be drawn with the high-trust societies of Japan and Germany which have found it easier to spawn large-scale firms not based on kinship ties (i.e., professionally managed).

The challenges to family business and to "familistic" societies are therefore "spatial," in graduating to scale, and "temporal," generational succession is hardly guaranteed with the Buddenbrooks phenomenon ("shirtsleeves to shirtsleeves in three generations") often taking place. Nonetheless, a familial set-up such as that of the Chinese may prove to be advantageous in sectors which are labor-intensive, fast-changing, highly-segmented, and atomistic: apparel, textiles, plastics, electronics, and furniture markets, for example.

That associationism is the only factor with a direct proportion relationship with the trust level of societies indicates that, in truth, is but another name for the build-up of social capital. For Fukuyama, it is synonymous with "spontaneous sociability," that capacity to form new associations and to cooperate within the terms of reference that these groups establish. In a sense, it is very similar to what Durkheim (1933) called "organic solidarity," founded more on shared values rather than on stipulations of a contract.

Associationism rests on cultural roots. By "culture," we understand, aside from whatever is not natural, the institutionalized (stable, shared, organizational) and "inherited" ethical values and habits of society. By "ethics," we mean a common perception, judgment, and language of good and evil. Associationism could only flourish in an atmosphere of regular, honest, and cooperative behavior, where persons have an experience of, are committed to, and reasonably expect from others loyal and dependable conduct. Associationism is encouraged, rather than by the proliferation of laws, but by the practice of social virtues. Such is the importance of associationism that even societies with relatively weak family ties would be able to develop, by virtue of their vigorous private non-profit organizations like clubs, schools, and churches, strong private economic institutions of scale.

Government intervention is manifested in the number of state-owned, -subsidized, -protected, or -sponsored enterprises, and in the centralization and concentration of information, power, and authority in a society's organizations. American society is traditionally anti-statist, although this does not mean hostility towards the community. The country that pioneered in anti-trust laws is the same one that first successfully produced corporate giants, internationally-known market leaders, and brand names.

Japanese and German experience regarding government intervention points towards the opposite direction. There exists a very high degree of collusion between public agencies and private businesses in Japan, to the extent that it is practically impossible to discern the public from the private. In place of vertically-integrated companies, the Japanese have developed *keiretsus* (the pre–World War II *zaibatsus*), flexible networks built usually round a bank. The Japanese market is protected, dominated by cartels, and oligopolistic. Similarly, the German economic structure is composed of the *Interessengemeinschaften* (communities of interest), which are bank-centered industrial cartels, and *Konzerne*, which are smaller, cross-shareholding arrangements. Germany, likewise, possesses a strong *Mittelstand* (medium-sized industries), vigorous trade associations, and *Verbände* or industry-wide unions, in addition to a pervasive welfarist tradition ever since Bismarck.

Trust Parameters of Select Filipino Family Businesses

The 1990s mark the long hard climb on which the Philippine economy and nation has had to embark to once more occupy its place in the global arena. Much of the effort and the credit rests upon Filipino family enterprises, specifically, on those headed by the new billionaires and "taipans": Aboitiz, Conjuanco, Concepcion, Gokongwei, Lim, Sy, Tan, Ty, Tan Yu, and Yuchengco. Their history, however, is still all too recent to be written. The Zóbel de Ayalas and Sorianos who represent continuing sagas of business leadership notwithstanding, there already existed since the beginning of the century a group known as "Manila's old rich" which has now quietly faded into the background: the Palanca, Elizalde, Ysmael, and Puyat families. This particular characteristic has made them a more suitable object of study regarding the idiosyncrasies of Filipino family business (see Debuque and Cabacungan 1995).

Among these families, the Palancas and the Puyats are of Chinese extraction, whereas the Elizaldes and the Ysmaels have Spanish roots. *Carlos Palanca*, whose forbearers come from Fookien, China, started building his business empire with *La Tondeña Incorporada*, founded 1902, which became the country's premier liquor maker and distributor. In 1924, he purchased the *Destilería Ayala*, manufacturers of *Ginebra San Miguel*, a drink popular among Filipinos since 1834. He was also a co-founder of the China Banking Corporation, one of the country's top banks. In 1950, he was succeeded by his son, Carlos Palanca, Jr., who was responsible for the family's diversification into mining, hotel, textile, sugar, food, pulp and paper, cement, and lumber industries. Carlos

Palanca, Jr. relinquished control of these concerns to his sons, Carlos III and Miguel Carlos, in the mid-1980s, a specially turbulent period marked by the Aquino assassination, the EDSA revolution and the Marcos ouster, and the coup-plagued government headed by Aquino's widow, Corazón (see Debuque and Cabacungan 1995).

Gonzalo Puyat laid the foundations for the "House of Puyat" in 1918, when he began manufacturing award-winning billiard tables. Soon after, he entered into the production of all sorts of furniture and construction materials, as well as the exploitation of timber concessions. One of his sons, Gil, became a senator, and this branch of the family later acquired the financial and insurance concerns (The Manila Bankers Corporation) through a "stock swap" in 1976. The remaining third-generation family members, José Puyat, Jr. and Edgardo Puyat Reyes, now manage the flagship company "Gonzalo Puyat & Sons" which is into steel, flour milling, construction, agri-business and real estate. The decline of the Puyats from the Thirtieth slot in the country's top corporations to outside of the Two Hundred List is traced to a family decision to divide its businesses twenty years ago (see Villadiego 1995).

The Elizaldes started business as traders in the early 1900s. From among their ranks have later on emerged patriots, diplomats, philanthropists, politicians, sportsmen, and artists. Manolo was the one principally responsible for the consolidation of the Elizalde Empire which, at its height during the 1950s and the 1970s, was involved in sugar, rope-making, insurance, steel manufacturing, floor wax, beverage, and radio and television. He was famous for his strongly paternalistic style of management. He had two male heirs, Manda and Fred. Manda was the older one and for this reason, despite the fact that his interests were more cultural and anthropological, having served as head of the government agency for minorities (PANAMIN), he ended up inheriting and later divesting himself of the family's better companies. Fred retained the Manila Broadcasting Company, which presently runs fifty radio stations nationwide (see Espina and Espino 1995).

Juan Ysmael was a Spanish national of Lebanese descent who, in the 1890s, together with his wife Magdalena, started a retail business and acquired large tracts of land. Soon afterwards, they put up Ysmael Steel, in an attempt to produce basic home, kitchen, and office fixtures. In 1951, the clan matriarch ventured into home appliance manufacturing, and theirs became the country's leading brands ("Ultra Cold" and "Admiral," from an American license). The second generation of Ysmaels was practically bypassed, with management being transmitted from

Magdalena herself to her grandchildren, Carlos Ysmael, Sr. and Felipe Ysmael, Jr. In the early 1970s and in the wake of the declaration of Martial Law, the Ysmael heirs decided to sell out their business concerns and migrate to Australia (see Narisma 1995).

In accordance with the parameters established by Fukuyama and after a careful examination of the histories of the aforementioned family corporations, one may identify Philippine society as a low-trust society, akin to a hybrid between Chinese and Italian or Latin models. For this reason, the troubles that beset Filipino family businesses with the change of generations are not at all unlike those of other low-trust societies (see Debuque 1995).

Like in Chinese society, there is a primacy of blood and fictive kinship (*pagkakamaganak*) in social relations, economic or political (see Timbermann 1991). The development of Filipino family businesses somehow mimics that of Chinese family businesses, both of which go through three distinct stages.

The first stage consists in the foundation of the business by an entrepreneur, usually a strong patriarch, who places his relatives in key management positions and lays down the rules for the running of the company, almost in an authoritarian manner. There is no formal division of labor nor a managerial hierarchy strictly speaking, which is decentralized and multidivisional. All the problems associated with a bureaucracy – unnecessary delays, weak decision centers, impersonal and irresponsible activity, etc. – are therefore absent, but so are the benefits that a bureaucracy is supposed to bring, in terms of specialization and a more participative style of management. Instead, there is a highly centralized hub, the founding entrepreneur, to which all branches report directly. Management style is personalistic and charismatic. Such have been the cases of Carlos Palanca, Gonzalo Puyat, Manuel Elizalde, and the couple formed by Juan and Magdalena Ysmael-Hemady.

The second stage commences with the demise of the founding patriarch. The principle of equal inheritance among the heirs is usually followed, regardless of whether the latter display any interest or a minimum of competence in discharging organizational functions. Certain exceptions are to be found in the case of the Ysmaels, where the second generation family members or the direct heirs were completely bypassed in favor of the grandchildren. In the case of the Elizaldes, the variant introduced was that of the older brother, Manda, inheriting the lion's share of the corporations, despite the fact that he had showed a stronger inclination towards culture and the arts, and clearly manifested a less developed business acumen than his younger sibling, Fred. Although the second generation family members have a social and economic headstart in comparison to the founding patriarch-entrepreneur, practically none of them have been more successful than their forebears. The experience of Carlos Palanca, Jr. would be the only debatable issue, inasmuch as he was responsible for their family concerns' diversification.

The third stage is marked by the inevitable break-up of the business empire when its ownership and control is passed on to the third generation family members, who present an even wider disparity in age, interest, and capacity than their parents. The grandchildren inevitably grow up in comfortable and affluent surroundings and tend to take their inherited wealth for granted. They are, therefore, less motivated and less self-sacrificing in their work than those who have preceded them. At this point, sometimes, the best solution lies in dividing the family businesses as amicably as possible, and each going on its own, independent way, as the Puyats had done.

After the principle of kinship, the second most powerful force in the shaping of Filipino societies, business organizations included, is that of *patronage*. Patronage, or the preferential treatment extended towards one's workers or the members of one's town, province, or linguistic group, eliciting in return a deep sense of indebtedness (*utang ng loob*), is, in the final analysis, also patterned after the paternal-filial relationship. Its influence is most keenly felt in the realms of government and politics, on which the fates of business organizations in the Philippines heavily depend. If current elected officials are favorable to a family because they have received financial support in their campaigns or they foresee to benefit economically from future ventures, then that family's businesses are bound to flourish under that administration. That family begins to form part of the elected officials' "cronies," and receive preferential treatment from government in business opportunities. It does not really matter that the financing for the government projects that favor a certain family's businesses comes from the citizens' tax money; insofar as that family is concerned, it will always be a "personal" favor from the elected officials, a favor that sometime and somehow will have to be repaid. (The exorbitant rise in the fortunes of certain families during the Marcos regime would warrant an independent study.) On the other hand, if the political climate is perceived to be adverse to a prominent business family, then its members may very well decide to close shop, liquidate its interests, and migrate elsewhere, as the Ysmaels had done soon after the declaration of Martial Law in 1972.

After the value of *utang ng loob* that integrates Filipino families vertically, comes the value of "*pakikisama*," normally translated as "smooth interpersonal relationships," which integrates Filipino families and their members horizontally. This means giving in to group or peer pressure, even at the expense of objective truth or justice (which adopt a very "plastic" or "manipulable" nature), for the sake of convenience of not having to "rock the boat" and in order to save face or acceptability within the group (*hiya*) (Talisayon 1990). Contrary to what would be expected, such a concern for "smooth interpersonal relationships" has not at all favored the cause of associationism in the Philippines, the indexes of which have remained very low.

Filipinos have continued to be a very insular people, quite incapable of looking beyond the immediate interests of their families and family-assimilated groups (barangays, town- or province-mates, etc.). Strongly influenced by a culture of endemic poverty, Filipinos tend to be quite short-term and self-centered in their mind-frames. The so-called "public sphere" (*res publica*) does not enter the field of the ordinary Filipino's considerations. For example, with regard to personal and domestic hygiene, Filipinos may be considered second to none, but these very individuals will never think twice nor hesitate to throw their garbage into the streets, outside the perimeter walls of their domiciles, reasoning out that such public space does not belong to anyone in particular, giving themselves *carte blanche* to do with it as they please. A similar form of reasoning is adduced in order to justify what as a matter of fact are petty thefts, acts of pilferage, or plain and simple wastefulness: the so-called "souvenirs" from restaurants, hotels, and other service establishments, that may range from free publications, stationeries, and complimentary toiletries to towels, ash trays, china, and cutlery.

Extremely significant in this regard is the listing of theft and cheating, in the first place, among the undesirable Filipino habits that are to be changed, according to a university-based public opinion survey (ADMU 1988). If ever the "public realm" were to merit any concern or care at all, it would necessary have to come from government exclusively, and never from private citizens (see Sison 1995; Roces and Roces 1985). Such is in the particularly Filipino form of statism. To help oneself to government or public property would hardly be labeled as theft; it is considered to be up for grabs, free for all, with the "strong" or "influential" (*malakas*) and the "smart" (*matinik*) as those who stand to benefit the most.

If ever one were able to overcome these notable drawbacks spring-ing from a lack of respect for public and private property and achieve en-trepreneurial success, he would still have to contend, nevertheless, with the notorious "crab mentality" (*talanka*), an endemic form of envy among Filipinos. The term for this cultural vice derives from the obser-vation that crabs in a basket do not even need to be tied in order to be pre-vented from leaving the receptacle: as soon as a crab ventures to leave, another one with its pincers would take care of pulling it down to the fold. After the end of centuries of colonial rule and the dismantlement of American bases in its territory, Filipino entrepreneurs find that they have no one else to blame but themselves for lagging behind in the race for economic development, especially when compared to their already prosperous East Asian neighbors.

In the aforementioned species of statism, together with the influence derived from the Catholic religion, is where the likeness of the Philip-pines with Latin countries such as Spain and Italy could best be seen. Left alone to take care of the public sphere, the state becomes as enor-mous as it is ineffective, and instead of the proverbial Confucian sub-mission towards the community, there is a robust sense of individualism (*kanya-kanya*) (see Senate Committee Study 1988), based on the Catho-lic teaching that each person is naturally endowed with reason, free will, and certain inalienable rights in consequence. As such, each individual is ultimately responsible for designing and carrying out his or her own actions. This is, perhaps, the most significant contribution of the Catho-lic religion – the defense of private property and initiative, tempered with an unrenounceable commitment to the common good – to a coun-try's economic culture, rather than a purported link between Catholic "other-wordliness" and a pervasive and complacent poverty as hypothe-sized and popularized by Weber.

As was stated earlier, associationism, among all the factors exam-ined by Fukuyama, is the only one that registers a parallel growth with respect to trust or social capital. But neither is associationism, or the high degree of membership in organizations of the most varied persua-sions, independent of a culture's family structure. It is, as a matter of fact, in the bosom of a family where one earns his first – and by far, his most important – experience of membership within a society. In the family, a person is respected and loved unconditionally, both for what he is in himself (his individuality) as well as for what he is with respect to the others (his relatedness). Rather than as a cost, each family member is valued as a resource and an asset. If ever human beings are to behave in an organization according to rules other than those of selfishness, they need a strong sense of belonging. This sense of belonging, the collective pride in family traditions and the co-responsibility for them, are matters which families and family businesses have always known to make use of to their full advantage. Families are communities of trust; and it is only through the well-spring of families that trust could be generated and transmitted to the other forms of associations, including business firms.

So far, we have argued, explained, and insisted on the economic value of trust or social capital. Before concluding, we would only like to establish and safeguard, together with Arrow (1974), that despite its economic value, trust is in itself of a non-economic nature: "Now trust has a very important pragmatic value, if nothing else. Trust is an important lubricant of a social system. It is extremely efficient; it saves a lot of trouble to have a fair degree of reliance on other people's word. Unfortunately this is not a commodity which can be bought very easily. If you have to buy it, you already have some doubts about what you've bought. Trust and similar values, loyalty or truth-telling, are examples of what the economist would call 'externalities.' They are goods, they are commodities; they have real, practical, economic value; they increase the efficiency of the system, they enable one to produce more goods or more of whatever value one holds in high esteem. But they are not commodities for which trade on the open market is technically possible or even meaningful."

References

Arrow, Kenneth, *The Limits of Organization* (New York: Norton Publishers 1974).

ADMU Ateneo de Manila University, *Public Opinion Survey: February 1988* (Quezon City: Ateneo de Manila University Press, 1988).

Becker, Gary S., *Human Capital*, 2d ed. (New York: Columbia University Press, 1975).

Bellah, Robert N., et. al., *Habits of the Heart* (Berkeley: University of California Press, 1985).

Bond, Michael Harris, *Beyond the Chinese Face: Insights from Psychology* (Hong Kong: Oxford University Press, 1991)

Coase, Ronald H., "The Problem of Social Cost." *Journal of Law and Economics* 3 (1960), 1–44.

Debuque, Margarita, "Manila's Old Rich. In the end, business needs good management, dynamism," *Philippine Daily Inquirer* (October 27, 1995).

Debuque, Margarita, and Cabacungan, Gil, Jr., "Manilas Old Rich: Fading into the background." *Philippine Daily Inquirer* (October 23, 1995).

Drucker, Peter A., ed. with a new introduction, *The Age of Discontinuity: Guidelines to Our Changing Society* (New York: Harper & Row, 1978).

Durkheim, Emile, *The Division of Labor* (New York: Macmillan, 1933).

Espina, Katherine, and Espino, Margie, "Manila's Old Rich: Elizalde Heirs Go Separate Ways," *Philippine Daily Inquirer* (October 24, 1995).

Fukuyama, Francis, *Trust: The Social Virtues & the Creation of Prosperity* (New York: The Free Press, 1995).

Handy, Charles 1995: "Trust and the Virtual Organization." *Harvard Business Review* (May–June 1995), 40–50.

Lingle, Christopher, *Singapore's Authoritarian Capitalism. Asian Values, Free-Market Illusions, and Political Dependency* (Virginia: The Locke Institution, 1996).

Machlup, Fritz, *Production and Distribution of Knowledge in the United States* (Princeton: Princeton University Press, 1962).

Mahbubani, Kishore, "The Pacific Impulse," *Survival* 37, number 1 (1995),105–120.

Narisma, Connie S., "Manila's Old Rich: Martial Rule Drove Ysmael Heirs Out of RP," *Philippine Daily Inquirer* (October 25, 1995)

Ohmae, Kenichi, *The Borderless World* (London: Collins, 1990).

Reich, Robert, *The Work of Nations: Towards 21st Century Capitalism* (New York: Knopf, 1992).

Roces, Alejandro, and Roces, Grace, *Culture Shock Philippines* (Singapore: Times Books International, 1985).

Sen, Amartya, "Economics, Business Principles, and Moral Sentiments," in this volume.

Senate Committee on Education, Arts and Culture, and on Social Justice, Welfare and Development, *Moral Recovery Program: Building a People, Building a Nation.* May 9, 1988.

Sison, Alejo José G., "The Public and the Private in Contemporary Philippine Society: A Study on Political Dynasties," *The Third International Jerusalem Conference on Ethics and the Public Service* (1995).

Sowell, Thomas, *Race and Culture: A World View* (New York: Basic Books, 1994).

Stewart, Thomas A., "Your Company's Most Valuable Asset: Intellectual Capital," *Fortune* (October 3, 1994).

Talisayon, Serafín D., *Filipino Values: Determinants of Philippine Future* (Makati: Economic Development Foundation, 1990).

Timbermann, David, *A Changeless Land: Continuity and Change in Philipine Politics* (Singapore: Institute of Southeast Asian Studies, 1995).

Villadiego, Rita, "Manila's Old Rich: Puyat Heir Split Ownership of Patriarch's Conglomerate," *Philippine Daily Inquirer* (October 26, 1995).

Weber, Max, *The Religions of China: Confucianism and Taoism* (New York: The Free Press, 1951).

Werhane, Patricia H., "Ethical Issues in Financial Markets: The American Experience," *Fundación BBV Encuentro sobre la Dimensión Etica de las Instituciones y Mercados Financieros* (Madrid, 1994).

Ethics and the Japanese Miracle:
Characteristics and Ethics of Japanese Business Practice

Mitsuhiro Umezu

Abstract

In this chapter, I will argue that there are ethical elements behind the post–World War business success in Japan. By pointing out this ethical aspect of the "Japanese Miracle," I would like to avoid a culturally interpretation of Japanese style management which emphasizes the incommensurable element in a culturally contextualized management style. Rather, I would like to examine a possibility and condition of the transplantability of Japanese style management which goes beyond Japanese cultural limits. I will point out the similarity between communitarianism and Japanese ethical values. I will also argue that some aspects of Japanese style capitalism are justifiable from a quasi-Rawlsian argument. The structure of the chapter is as follows. 1) a brief summary of a few differences between US and Japanese business practices; 2) an analysis of the ethical values behind Japanese style capitalism; 3) and an examination of the commensurable character with Western ethical traditions and the transplantability of Japanese style capitalism.

Introduction

In 1982, Chalmers Johnson published an epoch-making book entitled *MITI and the Japanese Miracle* (1982), in which Johnson claimed that there is no miracle about the Japanese post–World War II economic development. According to Johnson, the miraculous Japanese economic development should not be attributed to the cultural uniqueness of Japanese people, but instead to the excellent economic policy which was carefully planned and guided by the bureaucratic machine, MITI. I borrowed my chapter title from this book, but as my title suggests, my conclusion will be a different one. My conclusion is "don't forget ethical elements behind the post–World War Japanese economic success!"

Before I advance my arguments, there should be several clarifications in order to avoid misunderstanding. First, together with Johnson, I deny the culture theory of the Japanese miracle; that is to say, that the uniqueness of Japanese sociocultural characteristics, such as group-orientedness, the diligent national character of the Japanese people etc., is the cause of this defeated resource-less small island nation's development into a technological economic giant. This reductionistic explanation only describes a partial reality. Probably the most comprehensive and quite self-evident answer is that there are multiple reasons for Japanese businesses' success.

In addition, the phrase "uniqueness of Japanese culture" is carelessly used by both Japanese and foreign writers. It creates a sense of nationalistic pride within the Japanese, feelings of discrimination among foreigners, and, eventually, has developed into the revisionism among the foreign media (see Honma 1990). It is not productive to emphasize an incommensurable cultural trait as a key factor of economic success. After all, all cultures are unique in some sense. Rejecting the myth of "uniqueness of Japanese culture," I clearly deny the ethnocentric, nationalistic interpretation of the Japanese miracle.

Second, I also deny the purely political economic explanation of the Japanese miracle; that is to say, that Japanese economic development has been planned and guided by the well-calculated paternalistic industrial policy, which is prepared by the elite Japanese bureaucracy, MITI. It is true that there are effective industrial policies; however, it is not correct to claim that these are the only cause of the Japanese economic miracle. This is another reductionistic theory that dismisses the Japanese people's ethos behind this business success. Unless there is implicit agreement among the Japanese people, nobody will accept such a half-coercive administrative intervention. Here is my point – there should be certain ethical values that are implicitly agreed to and which motivate both Japanese management and workers to create such a dynamic synergism.

My intent is not to create another reductionistic explanation of the Japanese miracle. My message "do not forget the ethical element behind the Japanese miracle" means there are some forgotten elements, of which ethics would be one. It would be significant to identify the ethical roots of the Japanese miracle.

Finding the ethical roots of Japanese style business means finding the universalizability or transplantability of Japanese style management. Some claim that "Japanese style business practices" only work within Japan. This relativistic view is widely spread and includes a serious challenge to business ethics in a global/borderless business era. Because relativism (both cultural and normative) ultimately makes it impossible to find trans-cultural norms of human activities, including economic transactions, it eventually nullifies the efforts of business ethicists to establish new norms among nations.

Considering the fact that Japanese multinational corporations practice borderless business transactions every day and that many Japanese companies have already transplanted Japanese style management to other countries, it is not realistic to claim the impossibility of transplantability. But some might argue that Japanese corporations are touting their style of management by utilizing their economic power. Without extracting the ethical essentials of Japanese style business from Japanese cultural setting, there might be no excuse for proselytizing Japanese style management. However, if there are universalizable/transplantable ethical values or principles behind Japanese style business, they can apply to other cultures and societies. In other words, ethical roots of Japanese style business could be culturally contextualized in other countries and societies.

In order to accomplish these goals, I will take a cross-cultural approach to argue the ethical validity of Japanese-style management. First, I will briefly summarize a few differences between US and Japanese business practices. Second, I will attempt to analyze the ethical values behind Japanese style capitalism. Third, I will try to argue that these ethical values behind Japanese-style management can be justified on the basis of recent American ethical-sociologial perspectives, namely communitarianism and the Rawlsian theory of justice. This cross-cultural justification indicates the commensurable character with Western ethical traditions, and the core value of traditional Japanese ethics.

US and Japanese Business Practices: Macroscopic Differences

So far I have used the terms "Japanese style business," "Japanese style management," and "Japanese style capitalism" interchangeably. These three aspects are interlinked and make up an organic unity called "the

Japanese Miracle." Therefore, in fundamental reality, these three aspects are not clearly separable. However, for the sake of discussion, I will temporarily define "Japanese Capitalism" as a macroscopic socio-political agreement among the Japanese people, and "Japanese style management" as the microscopic particular corporate level agreement. When I use "Japanese style business," it indicates the totality of the Japanese business system, both at the macro- and micro-level.

Since the space of this chapter is limited, I will focus on Japanese style capitalism and try to find its macroscopic ethical roots. I will also use a comparative method to contrast Japanese style capitalism and American style capitalism. The reason I chose American capitalism as the comparative partner is that I am relatively familiar with these two capitalist societies. Also, it seems to me that these systems are two extreme types of capitalism; other forms of capitalism, such as European capitalism, NIES capitalism, ASEAN capitalism, etc., could be located somewhere in between US-Japan systems.

Table 1 is a summary of these two different types of capitalism (rearranged from Johnson 1982, 18, and Dore 1987, 29).The main characteristic of Japanese style capitalism is its plan rationality and goal-orientedness. The government or the bureaucracy with the specific national goal intervenes in markets in a paternalistic manner on the basis of plan rationality. Often corporate freedom in the market place is limited by this administrative guidance (which is not total coercion but half-coercive in its nature). In return, by accepting this paternalistic intervention, each corporation can enjoy a certain amount of organizational stability. Limiting market competition often creates a situation where the pricing mechanism and business transactions deviate from the theoretical market rational expectations, but people of Japan tend to accept long-term teleological rationality over short-term market rationality.

In contrast, the US people seem to accept more market rationality. Governments are expected to behave as a referee to make sure that free market competition efficiently functions according to market rules. Therefore, the government only intervenes in the market in a regulatory manner and not paternalistically. This position also coincides with the classical liberal position in which the government functions as a regulator of freedom maximization in the society, and as long as each player in the market plays within the minimum norms, such as the no-harm principle, the government should refrain from any intervention.

Table 1: Two different types of capitalism

Japanese Style	The US Style
Plan Rationality	Market Rationality
• Paternalistic	• Classical Liberalistic
• Goal-oriented Intervention	• Regulatory Intervention
• Purpose-governed State (telocratic)	• Rule-governed State (nomocratic)
• Stable Organization	• Mobile Organization
• Organizational Capitalism	• Mechanical Capitalism
• Well-averaged Society	• Diversified Society

As a result of these differences, the two societies show quite different characters and distributional shapes (see Figure 1). Japanese style capitalism has resulted in a well-averaged society where there is a relatively small difference from the top to the bottom layer of society in terms of income, information, and other resource distribution. Japanese society as a whole and Japanese organizations tend to prefer stability rather than change. Meanwhile, as the result of liberal market-oriented capitalism in US style capitalism, the society is more mobile and diversified, i.e., income distributions etc., indicate sizable differences from top to bottom.

Figure 1: Different distributional shapes of society

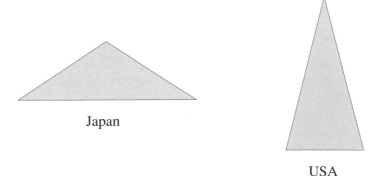

Japan

USA

The two triangles here are images of two societies; the tall triangle represents the shape of US society, the shorter one represents Japan. These illustrations could explain the difference in social characters and results. I could, for example, use these triangles to explain US vs. Japanese corporate salary structures. In the US, corporate executives' salaries are extremely high, while their Japanese counterparts earn relatively modest salaries. Another characteristic is the difference from the top to bottom. It has been calculated that US executives earn forty times more than bottom line blue collar workers. In Japan, this difference is approximately seven times (Hasegawa 1986). This distributional characteristics in the corporate setting can be observed in such areas as benefit distribution, information sharing, decisional power structure, etc.

Furthermore, it is probably true that this structural trait can also explain the situation of educational opportunities, medical care system, etc. In the US, the best educational opportunity and medical care are available primarily to the most advantageous layer in the society; at the same time, the worst and most miserable situation exists for the least well off members. In Japan, the top is not as high as the US but at the same time, the bottom is not as low. One could say that, before your birth, if you know your social stratification will be in the top 5%, choose the US as your country; if you know your social stratification will be in the bottom 5%, choose Japan.

It seems to me that this consequential difference indicates that people of two countries have agreed upon and accepted quite different types of social values or ethical norms. In the case of Japan, people appreciate teleological, organization-oriented norms which are backed up by stable, well-averaged human relationships. In the US, people tend to welcome more mechanical, market-oriented norms which are based on mobile, diversified, and free human relationships.

Ethics behind Japanese Style Capitalism

In order to function in this operational system, people of society must have a sociocultural foundation/climate of acceptance and mutual agreement. Otherwise, the system and operation lose their legitimacy, the legitimacy of normative persuasiveness which makes people willingly cooperate to support the system.

To explain Japanese style capitalism from an ethical perspective, I will use two aspects of Japanese ethics. One is the ontological aspect that describes the view of human beings. The second aspect is the normative one which implicitly prescribes the justice principle, very similar to John Rawls' second principle of justice. These two aspects are by no means an exhaustive list of Japanese morality. For the sake of discussion in this chapter and a limitation of space, I have chosen only these two aspects.

The View of Human Being

One of the fundamental difficulties of explaining Japanese ethics in a Western context is its ontological nature. Fundamental arguments of Japanese ethicists do not start with normative principles, rules, virtues, and even acts. They tend to start with the ontological analysis or description of human beings, society, nature, cosmic energy, etc. From a Western perspective, it is puzzling to find an ontological, cosmological description in an ethics book. Trained in the Western analytic philosophical tradition, I myself had a hard time figuring out the Japanese way of argumentation. It does not make any sense until one figures out the simple fact that ontology *is* ethics from a Japanese philosophical perspective (possibly from many Asian countries philosophical perspectives). What Japanese ethicists are trying to say is the essential structure of "the way things are" suggests "the way things should be." In other words, they try to argue the ontological ground of normative rules in a highly descriptive, hermeneutical discussion.

A very important and interesting question is whether ethics should be grounded on the ontological foundation, or ontological theory (= world view), which reflects a normative element in each society. These questions, however, are beyond the scope of this chapter. I rather would like to focus on identifying the ethical element in Japanese capitalism and examine its compatibility with other cultures.

One good example is Tetsuro Watsuji's ethical theory (1934). According to this leading Japanese ethicist, who taught ethics at Tokyo University in the first half of this century, ethics is an ontology of basic human existence.[1] That is to say, the aim of ethics is to find a fundamental logic and law of human beings as a relational being ("Ningen sonzai no konpon-kouzou," Watsuji 1934, 45).

In the Japanese language, a human being *Ningen* consists of two Chinese characters, i.e., *Nin* (human) and *Gen/Aida* (between). Since the Japanese language does not distinguish between singular and plural, the word *Ningen* could be either singular or plural. Watsuji thought of this *aidagara* ("betweenness") aspect as ontologically primordial to any human existence. For Watsuji, a human being without this "betweenness" is not a person in its full sense. In other words, a person becomes the person in a social network, and an independent person without a social network is, even if it is possible, a deviation or negation of its original form.

The concept of *Aidagara* ("betweenness") is a natural development of the idea from his previous writing, in which Watsuji emphasizes that spatiality is the fundamental category of human existence. However, the Japanese word *Aidagara* means more than just physical spatiality. Watsuji himself did not articulate this, but it seems to me that *Aidagara* indicates the psychological as well as the physical space between people. As a matter of fact, the primary usage of *Aidagara* in contemporary Japanese has a strong psychological connotation, which usually means whether two people are close or distant.

Aidagara also provides a context of roles and the reasons of acts between two people. There is some dialectical relationship between *Aidagara* and human action, namely that the relationship between two persons limits the appropriate action in context; at the same time, the mutuality of actions enhances and visualizes this *Aidagara.*

For example, the relationship of father and child can be explained by the psychological tie between two people, but at the same time, this psychological tie can be visualized and enhanced by the father's "father-like" action towards the child (for example, protection of child from danger) and child's own reaction to it. If a father does not behave like a father (for example, he commits child abuse), there is no father-child relationship; the same thing could be observed in the case when the child does not behave like a child. (Remember also the Hegel's example of Master and Slave.)

Watsuji argues that a human being's life can exist only in the "betweenness." All human beings are born into, grow up within, and die in various human relationships. Even after an individual's death, the human relationships created by this person continue to exist. Nobody can escape this social network of human relationship. Even if a person tries to rebel against the order of this network, though he might be granted independence for a while, he will be forced to return to the network of the social order again. Insofar as his mode of behavior is concerned, a person is prescribed *a priori* by his/her position within a socio-psychological network and hierarchy of *Aidagara*

The task of ethics, according to Watsuji, is to define the nature of this relationship which already exists in our social life as customs and mores. His ethics does not start with the analysis of an individual's moral consciousness or reasoning, as is done in traditional Western ethics. Rather, it starts with the two-person community, the smallest unit of human relationship.

This theory could be interpreted as Confucian ethics which was also a basic ideology of feudalistic society. However, Watsuji talks about much more fundamental characteristics of human existence, which are the underlying cause and foundation of any social organization. Watsuji's point is that the context of human existence is universal and necessary to all human beings in any culture and in any time.

Watsuji's theory reminds me of the communitarianism of Charles Taylor, Michael Sandel, etc. I cannot explain extensively here, but analogous to the communitarian arguments, this ontological grasp of human beings provides the ethical roots of Japanese group/ organization orientedness. According to this view, since no one can live by him/herself, no individual can perform well without somebody else's assistance. Cooperation is emphasized over competition, because *Ningen* are complemental beings which become complete only with other human beings. Paternalistic intervention should be appreciated within a relationship between two parties whose power, knowledge, experience etc. are uneven. Finally, since the community of human relationship is prior to the atomic individual, it is better for each individual to adjust him/herself (sometimes even limit one's freedom or rights) to the community at large.[2]

The view of Justice: Quasi-Rawlsian Justification of Japanese Style Capitalism

The ontological view of *Ningen* and *Aidagara* by Watsuji will provide an ethical background of Japanese style capitalism, especially its organization-orientedness, cooperation over competition and paternalistic character. However, another aspect of Japanese style capitalism cannot be explained well from only an ontological aspect. In order to explain the well-averageness of Japanese society, there should be some other ethical principle.

As was mentioned in the previous section, Japanese society as a whole has attained a well-averaged shape which contrasts with the well-diversified society of the United States. In a sense, Japan has accomplished a more equal society than the United States.

Minimum differences from the top to bottom remind me of John Rawls' *Theory of Justice*. In fact, it looks as though the people of Japan are familiar with Rawls' "difference principle" and have actualized the social structure which embodies this principle. Obviously, the majority of Japanese are ignorant of this complicated theory of justice, so I cannot argue that Japan is a Rawlsian nation. However, it is possible to argue that Japanese style capitalism is justifiable from the quasi-Rawlsian perspective, and to assume there are similar ethical norms in Japan.

From the Rawlsian perspective, Japanese society is preferable in term of distributive justice, because it realizes a society where the least well-off members enjoy more advantageous benefits. I already mentioned the examples of income distribution, information sharing and decisional power structure within a organization, educational resource distribution, the medical care system, etc. Together with the fact that Japan is a basically free society and equal opportunity principles are sustained, Japanese society would probably earn an "A" from Professor Rawls!

However, while the consequential result in Japanese society exhibits a satisfactory character from the Rawlsian perspective, we should not forget that the ethical principle behind this Japanese social character might be different. The possible principle behind Japanese society is in the old Japanese proverb "the nail sticking out must be hammered down." This proverb teaches that an individual should not deviate too far from the average of society. It also suggests that social adjustment is required, when certain members of the society achieve unproportionally advantageous positions. Because of this averaging function, Japanese society provides an environment which produces few multimillionaires and few extremely poor.

I would like to call this function the "Averaging principle," separating it from Rawls' "Difference principle." Although it still needs more theoretical sophistication, the "Averaging principle" is a normative principle which guides individual judgment and institutional framework. While the Rawlsian "Difference principle" focuses on the advantage of the least well-off members, the "Averaging principle" requires a lowering of the advantage of over-achievers, as well as lifting-up of the disadvantage of under-achievers.

This "Averaging principle" is often criticized as a conformist proverb which discourages the over-achievers' flourishing talents and limits the range of individual expression. I agree that the cultural application of this proverb might be problematic; however, from an economic perspective, it actualizes justice in a society.

In addition to this, a well-averaged society helps create high-level of self-satisfaction among the people. Media polls repeatedly indicate that almost all Japanese identify themselves as a middle class and show overall satisfaction with their lives. This high-level of self-satisfaction contributes to maintain a sense of fairness among the workers and promotes high morale in a corporate context. In a social context, high self-satisfaction also secures a sense of community, and helps to reduce the number of crimes and disputes.

Thus, although there are several negative aspects in the "Averaging principle," there are quite a few positive aspects in this principle, too. As I have argued before, the consequential result of this "Averaging principle" actualizes the minimum difference from top to bottom in the society. This end result coincides with the Rawlsian ideal of a just society.

Conclusion

As a conclusion, I will make a number of observations and point out future issues. I have been trying to contrast Japanese and U.S. style capitalism. On the one hand, there is the teleological, organization-oriented Japanese style capitalism which emphasizes the importance of the stable, long-term human relationship. On the other hand, there is the mechanical, market-oriented U.S. style capitalism which are rooted in the ideal of free and mobile human relationships. Again, this is not the only way to interpret both forms of capitalism and, furthermore, both forms of capitalism have strengths and weaknesses.

In order to find commensurable points of these two contrastive forms of capitalism, I have tried to identify some ethical foundations of Japanese style capitalism. I characterize Japanese style capitalism from two ethical aspects: the "onto-anthropological" structure of human beings and the "averaging principle" as a variation of the justice principle.

These two aspects have similar ethical counterparts in Western philosophical theory, namely, communtarianism and the Rawlsian theory of justice. Therefore, even if the surface structures of two forms of capitalism exhibit considerable differences, U.S. and Japanese capitalism share commensurable ethical roots at the underlying level.

By identifying this ethical commensurability, I can dismiss the revisionistic theory of U.S.-Japan relations; at the same time, I can deny the relativistic assumption of the imcomensurability among culturally-bound economies. In principle, therefore, Japanese style capitalism is transferable to any community which accepts similar aspects of Japanese ethical presuppositions. Anywhere in the world, if there is a group of people that share the same ethical values, there is the possibility that Japanese corporations could be transplanted there easily.

My method of arguing the commensurability is to justify the ethical value of Japanese style capitalism on the basis of Western ethical theories. This diagonal, crosswise method reinforces superficially incommensurable communities. Unless I use this ethical approach to the diversity of capitalism and businesses to interpret the current situation, it is impossible to find underlying commensurable values. I believe this is one of the advantages of business ethics to sort out problems in the context of international and pluralistic societies of the future.

In the future, it will be nonsensical to talk about nation-state oriented distinction of business, such as Japanese business and the U.S. business. There might be an American corporation which adopts Japanese style management, or a Japanese corporation which is more like a U.S. style corporation. In this sense, my formulation of comparison, U.S. Style vs. Japanese style capitalism, is already becoming out of date. However, the distinction and comparison of two ethical values, which is currently exemplified by U.S. and Japanese style businesses, will remain in the future world. It will be formulated in different terms such as "market-oriented business vs. community-oriented business" or "mechanical capitalism vs. teleological capitalism," and so on.

These two sets of principles and ideals originate from the mutually irreducible view of the world, i.e. fundamental view of the world as a market or as a community. Epistemologically, world-in-itself can be interpreted in both ways, and both ways of interpretations contain valid ethical points. Finding the balancing point of these two extremes might become the task of conscientious choice.

Probably, future corporations will have to choose their own corporate ethical position somewhere in the spectrum of two extremes. From the Japanese perspective, which emphasizes the averaging principle, one would like to see the world business situation where the balancing point of each corporation converges on the medium of the spectrum. From the U.S. perspective, which emphasizes diversity, one would like to envision the maximumly pluralistic situation.

In either way, the emergence of the Japanese economy and the friction with the U.S. economy in the later century would be a good lesson and a paradigm case for the ethical positioning of twenty-first century businesses. In this sense, we should not forget the importance of the ethical elements behind American style business, just as we should remember those behind Japanese style business.

Endnotes

1. The term "ontological" needs to be explained. This is the direct translation from Watsuji's terminology. Some suggest that the term "anthropological" would be adequate, since Watsuji is describing the view of human beings. However, Watsuji was heavily influenced by Martin Heidegger's writings at

the time of this publication, so that he specifically used the term "ontological." Probably the term "Onto-Anthropological" or "Dasein" would be more suitable in this context, but I have decided to respect Watsuji's original terminology and keep it as it is.

2. See also the more recent argument by Eshun Hamaguchi.

References

Dore, Ronald, *Taking Japan Seriously* (Stanford: Stanford University Press, 1987).

Hasegawa, Keitaro, *Japanese Style Management: An Insider's Analysis* (Tokyo: Kodansha International Ltd., 1986).

Honma, Nagayo, "Nihon Tasha-ron no Kiken [Danger of Revisionism]," *Gaiko Forum* 13 (1990).

Johnson, Chalmers, *MITI and the Japanese Miracle: The Growth of Industrial Policy, 1925–1975* (Stanford: Stanford University Press, 1982).

Watsuji, Tetsuro, *Ningen no Gaku toshite no Rinrigaku* [Ethics as a Study of Human Being] (Tokyo: Iwanami Shoten, 1934).

Confucian Values, Japanese Economic Development, and the Creation of a Modern Japanese Business Ethic[1]

Gregory K. Ornatowski

Abstract

This chapter analyzes the adaptation of selected Confucian values by pre– and post–World War II Japanese industrialists and government officials toward the formation of a modern Japanese ideology of capitalist economic development. The use of Confucian values is examined in terms of three different areas: education, the workplace, and the government bureaucracy. While Confucian values were consciously used by elites to further economic development, they also reflected in many cases these elites' own personal ethical values. Moreover, although it is difficult to measure how much such values impacted modern Japanese economic development, it is clear that they did have an effect, both positive and negative. The use of Confucian values has also been subtly transformed over time to meet the changing needs of Japan's developing economic and social environment. At the same time, there is a consistent emphasis on the values of respect for learning, social harmony, loyalty, and familism.

Introduction

An important issue in explaining the successful economic development of Japan over the past century is in evaluating the roles of cultural values, economic policy, and political policy in contributing to this economic development. Generally speaking, while explanations focusing on cultural or social values have often come from the work of anthropologists and sociologists (Bellah 1970; Dore 1970 and 1979; and Glazer 1976), economists and political scientists have tended to support the role of economic and political institutions and policies (Johnson 1982; Lockwood 1954; and Ohkawa and Rosovsky 1973). A third approach which partially overlaps both of the above are explanations stressing historical or situational elements.[2]

None of these approaches by themselves, however, offer a complete explanation of modern Japanese economic development. Rather, a more balanced view which combines all three seems to offer important insights and a deeper level of explanation of why Japan was so successful. In this sense, the issue of explaining Japanese economic development becomes less a question of which set of factors (cultural, institutional/policy or historical/ situational) is most conclusive than a question of *how* these factors worked together and what was the role of each. For example, when analyzing particular policy decisions made during Japan's modern economic development process, these decisions must be analyzed not only as the consequence of rational policy choices made in light of what had worked elsewhere (the West), but also as the consequence of cultural values influencing decision makers toward certain choices rather than others among a larger array of possible policies, and of policymakers consciously making use of cultural values to support the implementation of policies that were chosen. In this way, the course of pre - and post–World War II Japanese economic development and the manner in which Japan adopted capitalism was not only the consequence of good leaders choosing "rational" policies applicable to Japan's historical situation, but of cultural values impacting the choices and their successful implementation.

Thus while not rejecting the important roles of economic and political policies and historical circumstances, this chapter will focus upon the particular role of *cultural* factors in helping to explain modern Japanese economic development. At the same time, it will also examine how such cultural factors, specifically Confucian-derived values and institutions, contributed to the creation of a modern Japanese business ethic, first in the prewar period by such leading industrialists as Shibusawa Eiichi, and later in the postwar period by large companies' use of Confucian values in the workplace and in relationships with suppliers. In this way, the role of Confucian values was two-fold: to support modern economic development and to help create a modern Japanese business ethic. As such, this chapter will look at how certain Confucian-derived values were both *utilized* by Japanese industrialists and government bureaucrats toward accomplishing the two above mentioned goals, and, simultaneously, *reflective* of these elites' own personal values. At the same time, since showing a clear quantitative relationship between cultural factors and economic development is difficult in Japan as elsewhere, this chapter will *not* focus on showing to what extent Confucian values were the "cause" of modern Japanese industrial development, but rather in showing the manner of their *use* as ideological support for economic modernization policies and the creation of a certain business ethic.

It is also important to differentiate between the "elite" nature of traditional Confucianism and more "popularized" forms which appeared in Japan beginning in the early eighteenth century. "Popular" Confucianism represented a different type of Confucian values than "elite" Confucian values in that it harbored no antagonism toward merchant life and profit-making but in fact justified them while preaching honesty, filial piety, loyalty, and righteousness (Rozman 1991).

In terms of this chapter then, "Confucian values" will refer to: (1) a high public regard for education and the overwhelming importance of entrance exams for placing talent in society; (2) an emphasis on mutual obligations between superior and inferior within social organizations based upon actual or quasi-family ties, where the prime virtue of the superior is benevolence and of the inferior is loyalty; and (3) an overall stress on "social harmony" rather than individualism, i.e. the individual "fitting" himself into groups and groups doing the same vis-à-vis society. All of these can be summarized in the key values: "respect for learning," "loyalty," "filial piety," and "harmony." The chapter will examine these Confucian values as they were used in three areas of Japanese social life: *education, the workplace,* and *the government bureaucracy,* during the pre- and postwar periods.

The Prewar Period

Education

In the area of *education,* after an initial surge of enthusiasm for Western learning in the 1860s and 1870s, by the late 1880s, a backlash began to form against what was perceived as over-Westernization in the area of morals. This resulted in a re-emphasis on Confucian ethics in the schools, highlighted by the government issuance in 1890 of the Imperial Rescript on Education. This document became the centerpiece of moral education (*shushin kyoiku*) in schools and was memorized and recited by all Japanese school children until the end of World War II (Saniel 1965, 131). Many phrases in the Rescript were direct translations of well known Confucian ideas. For example, four of the five Confucian relationships were directly referred to, especially those regarding the loyalty of "subjects" to the Emperor and children's "filial piety" to parents. The virtues of "benevolence" and "harmony" were also extolled as was the need to "pursue learning" and "advance public good and promote common interests."[3] In this way, these values were used by the government to aid economic development by helping to create loyal, hardworking, and public-minded subjects who felt a moral obligation to carry out the government's policies of building a "rich country and strong military" (*fukoku kyohei*).

Confucian values also were useful in promoting economic development through the institutionalization of meritocratic entrance examinations to schools and universities, beginning in the Meiji period. Although far from the traditional Confucian exams in terms of content (the new exams stressed knowledge of mathematics and the sciences rather than the Confucian classics), they nevertheless paralleled the traditional Confucian exam system in terms of function. That is, they funneled the best talent on a meritocratic basis to key leadership positions in society, in particular to the government bureaucracies and larger companies.

The Workplace

In the *workplace*, the pattern of the use of Confucian values in the period and the early twentieth century followed a similar pattern to that in education. That is, initially Western industrial practices were adopted with enthusiasm, and both companies and workers in the new industrial sector showed limited loyalty and long term commitment to each other. However, by the 1890s, as some in the government began to call for a Western-type national labor law to set minimum standards for working hours and factory conditions, the response of many industrialists was to appeal to the "special" relationships they claimed existed in Japan between management and labor as one reason why such a labor law was unnecessary. Since these relationships were based upon "affection," they asserted, and were similar to that between "parent and children" or "master and retainer," Western-style labor laws were out of place (Marshall 1967, 58). Such a paternalistic management ideology reflected the first attempts of modern Japanese businessmen to verbalize a new business ethic for the era of economic modernization.

The development of a modern Japanese business ethic, and one more specifically referring to Confucian principles, was advocated by Shibusawa Eiichi, one of the most important industrialists of the entire Meiji and Taisho periods (1868–1926) (Hirschmeirer 1965). After giving up a high ranking post in the Ministry of Finance in the early 1870s,

Shibusawa was involved in the creation and management of no less than five hundred companies over the next forty years. During this time, he continually referred to the need for Japanese industrialists to establish a new business ethic which would combine the wisdom of Confucius with modern business skills, while avoiding the old style business ethics of Tokugawa merchants based upon dishonesty and selfish money grubbing. Shibusawa put these ideas into a number of books, the most well known being *Rongo to Soroban* (The Analects and the Abacus). He also presented his ideas in numerous speeches to businessmen groups and formed his own society of young businessmen to put these ideals into practice (Kinzley 1991, 15–16). One of Shibusawa's key arguments was that there was no contradiction between commercial activities and the Way of Confucius. To prove his point, he went back to the classics of Confucius and argued that they had not condemned commercial activities or profit-making as such but only if such activity was done in a selfish manner rather than for the good of the community. In this way, Shibusawa made a major contribution toward combining selected values of traditional Confucianism with the business practices of modern capitalism to form a modern Japanese business ethic centered on business' role in serving the common good (Shibusawa 1992; and Tai 1989, 70–72).

With the end of World War I, however, management ideologies based upon traditional paternalism and familism began to show strains as the labor movement in Japan became more radical. Industrial disputes doubled from 1915 to 1916 and by 1917 were three times the number of 1915. At the same time, companies struggled to secure a stable supply of skilled labor without worrying about the tendency of workers with higher skills to move when they could get a better offer. Given these conditions, some of the larger companies began to search for a new labor management practices which could tie down well trained workers and at the same time lower the number of labor disputes. This led a few of the larger companies to institute the practices of lifetime employment, seniority based wages and promotion, and company-sponsored social welfare systems as ways to accomplish these goals. The number of companies using such practices, however, was limited, and even among them, employees were usually not able to gain a guarantee of lifetime employment until they were around forty years old and have proven their worth to the company (Dore 1979).

At the same time, the Allied victory in World War I in 1918 drew attention to Western approaches to the labor problem, with the implication that legal curbs and police repression alone were no longer adequate as ways to deal with labor disputes. Yet many in both Japanese government and business hoped to avoid simply adopting a Western approach to the labor problem, i.e. the adoption of legal measures to define labor rights and dispute settlement. Instead they looked for a solution which would encompass traditional Japanese values. These currents combined to result in the formation of the *Kyochokai* (Harmony Society) in 1919.

The two main leaders of the *Kyochokai* were Shibusawa and Home Affairs Minister Tokonami Takejiro. Together they created what they called a doctrine of *kyochoshugi* (harmonism). Although never a very clear and coherent doctrine, the general outlines of this philosophy were the avoidance of confrontation between labor and management through encouraging a "spirit of cooperation and harmony." The solution to labor-management problems therefore was viewed as practicing the Confucian "kingly way" (*wang tao*) by having labor and management come to understand that their interests were "common to each other" (Smith 1973, 23–24; and Kinzley 1991, 51–65) Thus, the fundamental problem was moral and not economic, and the solution was harmony and reciprocity between labor and management, to be accomplished by each carrying out their respective roles in society. Moreover, this appeal to industrial harmony was not only elite-imposed but relied for its effectiveness based upon the fact that the values of social harmony, "benevolence from above," and "loyalty from below" were still very much a part of the value system of workers as well (Smith 1988, 236–70). In this way, Confucian values were used by both industrialists and the government in efforts to establish a new Japanese business ethic during the prewar period which would both support modern economic development but also reinforce traditional social values of hierarchy, loyalty, and group harmony.

The Government Bureaucracy

Another area of the influence of Confucian values upon prewar Japanese economic modernization lays in the *role* and *attitudes of the government bureaucracy* toward economic development. Part of this influence was reflected in the paternalistic assumption that government should take the leading role in industrialization. As a result, beginning from the Meiji period onward, the Japanese bureaucracy functioned as a *developmental* state, as opposed to the *regulatory* state that tended to exist in early (and current) Anglo-Saxon forms of capitalism. This role was also clearly Confucian in character in that from the 1890s, onward the prewar Japanese bureaucrat showed a strong concern for the "moral" aspects of Japan's industrialization. This was seen above in the highly Confucian Imperial Rescript on Education in 1890 and the government's role in the establishment of the *Kyochokai* in 1919. It can also be seen in the revised Japanese Family Code of 1898, which made the authority of the male household head dominant, and Confucian type ideas about the family legally enforceable (Rozman 1991, 180).

Strong government moral concerns with the effects of economic development increased in the 1920s and 1930s, as spreading labor radicalism led to greater government efforts to encourage the dissemination of Confucian values as a way to maintain social order. One way such efforts were carried out was through government support for a new private Confucian organization, the *Shibunkai*, created in 1918 through the merging of a number of previously existing smaller organizations. Prominent politicians and heads of government ministries frequently attended *Shibunkai*, events during which they praised Confucian values for their role in stabilizing society and developing spiritual discipline. As time passed, they also increasingly referred to the connection between Confucian values and the Japanese *kokutai* (national polity), a term which had taken on nationalist and absolutist tones as a sacred symbol for the country itself. In this way, Confucian values came to be presented as having an important role to play in defending Japan's "national polity" against the excessive materialism and radicalism flowing into Japanese society from the West (Smith 1973, 26–27, 136).

In summary then, in the prewar period, Confucian values were used by both industrialists and the government to promote modern economic development and create a new business ethic capable of justifying industrialization and promoting harmony as the basis of management-labor relationships. By encouraging an individual moral ethic of sacrifice toward national goals, a work ethic of diligence and obedience toward workplace superiors, and a government bureaucracy which viewed its role as paternalistically promoting industrialization in order to build a "rich country and strong military," Confucian values were extremely useful toward these ends. At the same time, however, the use of Confucian values limited the range of possible solutions to social and economic problems. This was because they encouraged maintaining traditional social morals and relationships as the solution to certain modern economic problems (such as labor-management disputes or poverty in the countryside) rather than efforts to find innovative economic solutions to these problems.

The Postwar Period

In the period after World War II, similar to early Meiji, Confucian values initially lost much of their prestige as a general reaction set in against all "traditional values." However, by the early 1950s, "post-Confucian" values and institutions began to appear in the areas of education, workplace ethics, and the government bureaucracy, even while they were seldom ever referred to directly as "Confucian."

Education

In *education,* for example, the role of Confucian values in determining social stratification has continued in the national use of meritocratic entrance exam systems for college, high school, and junior high school. In fact, the role of such exams has expanded compared to the prewar period due to the greater percentages of students going on to higher education and the application of the system down to even the elementary school and kindergarten levels in some cases. The explosion in higher education in terms of the numbers of private colleges and universities, the rapid growth of *juku* (cram schools), and the high scores of Japanese students on mathematics and other standardized tests when compared internationally, all point to the tremendous stress on educational achievement structured into an educational system built around entrance exams.

As with the prewar period, the economic effect of this system has been to support high standards of performance in the workplace (Vogel 1991, 97) and to teach students the values of discipline and sacrifice as much as any specific body of knowledge. The meritocratic nature of the system also means that there has been a widespread sense of the fairness of the system, in spite of its competitiveness. Such a feeling of fairness has an economic benefit in that it encourages people to participate rather than drop out or protest. Competition, on the other hand, prepares students for the competition they will encounter in a modern capitalist economy.

The Workplace

In the *workplace*, Confucian values also have continued to play an important role, but seldom under the label of "Confucian." Instead, companies have utilized the concepts of "harmony," "respect" (for hierarchy), and "loyalty" to the firm as a "family," while usually identifying these values as Japanese rather than Confucian, or more often as simply part of the traditions of the firm itself. Harmony in particular continues to be the most emphasized value of all and is widely incorporated into company mission statements, ceremonial events, and new recruit training. "Spiritual education" (*seishin kyoiku*) in the form of training programs to instill such company values also is widely practiced, with some estimates putting its use in roughly one third of all medium and large size companies (Rohlen 1974, 34–61, 194–211).

The values of loyalty, harmony, and respect for hierarchy are not only reflected in company statements and new employee training programs but also in the actual operating policies of companies. For example, the three main institutions of the so-called "Japanese employment system" in the postwar period have been lifetime employment, seniority-based wages and promotion, and company-based unions. The lifetime employment system reflects Confucian values to the extent that it can be viewed as a system in which employee "loyalty" to the firm is rewarded with company "benevolence" in the form of a "lifetime" guarantee of work.[4] Seniority-based wages and promotion, on the other hand, reflect the Confucian value of maintaining "social harmony" by utilizing hierarchy based upon age as a means of determining social rank (Imai and Komiya 1994, 23–25). Finally, lifetime employment, seniority-based wages and promotion, and company-based unions all emphasize viewing the company as a "family" and encourage relationships between employees and the company which are not viewed as contractual but as moral commitments.[5]

The systems of lifetime employment and seniority-based pay and promotion in the Japanese postwar economy also directly contradict Parsonian theories about social value change during modern economic development (Glazer 1976). For example, the continuing existence of lifetime employment is an example of the "diffuse" and "affective" relationships between Japanese employees and their companies, relationships in which companies are concerned with the employee's overall welfare and life outside the company and not just the value of their labor inside the company, and in which the employee often has a stronger "collective" rather than "self" orientation. Second, seniority-based wages and promotions reflect a system in which rewards (salary and promotion) depend less upon individual achievements than upon how long and loyally the individual has served the company (i.e., an ascriptive basis).[6] Third, new employee recruitment methods emphasize a strong concern for "diffuse" rather than "specific" values, i.e. the recruit's personal qualities, family background, and "character" as equally important or more important than levels of knowledge or specific abilities (Rozman

1992, 315–17). All of these factors thus point to the divergence of Japanese practices from Parsonian (and Weberian) theory and to their partial congruence with more traditional Confucian social ethics.

The influence of Confucian-type values also can be seen in relationships between large manufacturing companies and their suppliers. In such relationships, the larger company is referred to as the *oya gaisha* (parent company) and the suppliers are called *kogaisha* (child companies). Under each child company, there are also often ten or more *magogaisha* (grandchild companies) so that the entire manufacturing *keiretsu* structure is a large pyramid-type organization of "family" companies. Each "child" or "grandchild" company is tied to its parent company through heavy dependence upon the latter for a large part of its total business. This dependence is encouraged by the parent company and is used to control the child company in many areas, including prices, product quality, and profitability. In this way, the parent company uses the child company for the latter's lower labor costs and to diversify its own risk. At the same time, the relationship is reciprocal in that the parent company is required to show "benevolence" towards the child company in the form of providing a steady supply of business, help with raising productivity and cutting costs, financial assistance, and technology sharing.[7] In return, the child company is expected to show "loyalty" by striving for continuous improvement in lowering costs and prices, showing great flexibility in responding to various demands for special orders and on-time delivery, and not abandoning the parent company in hard times. Overall then, the system is a hierarchical one which relies upon long term reciprocal quasi-family relationships to achieve close cooperation and high levels of economic efficiency.[8]

The Government Bureaucracy

In the third area of the roles and attitudes of the *government bureaucracy*, although there is no longer government participation in Confucian organizations, many Confucian-derived attitudes remain within the economic bureaucracies. For example, strongly "paternalistic" economic policies continue in the form of heavy government protection of domestic industry from foreign competition and support with subsidies, government-organized cartels, and a generous flow of low cost capital from government-owned or controlled financial institutions. While such "paternalistic" attitudes have been attributed partly to rational economic decision-making (though this is debatable since these policies are not seen as "rational" in the U.S. for example), they also are a carryover from an underlying Confucian mind-set toward the bureaucratic role vis-à-vis the economy.

In their effects, these government economic policies also tend to favor producers over consumer and as such have recently come to be labeled "producer economics" by economists such as Lester Thurow to contrast them with the "consumer economics" underlying Anglo-Saxon economies (Thurow 1992). That such "producer economics" also reflect deep-seated Confucian attitudes toward the economy is reflected in a well-known passage from the Confucian classic, *The Great Learning*:

> There is a great course [*tao*] for the production of wealth. Let the producers be many and the consumers few. Let there be activity in the production and economy in the expenditure. Then wealth will be always sufficient (Legge 1971, 379).

Specific examples of such policies in the postwar period included government programs to encourage high household savings (and thus less consumption), to funnel those savings under government guidance into the capital markets where they were loaned to industry (while consumers often found it difficult to get bank loans), and to allow widespread use of cartels by producers (Prestowitz 1988, 122–150; Cutts 1992, 48–55).

Conclusions

What then are the main themes in the adaptation of Confucian values by Japanese elites in the pre- and postwar periods, both to promote economic development and help create a modern Japanese business ethic? These themes seem to be as follows:

(1) Confucian values and institutions were consciously *adapted* and *appropriated* by political and economic elite groups in order to support policies and practices which they believed would promote economic development while preserving certain traditional Japanese social values. Such a use of Confucian values benefited economic development by encouraging hard work, frugality, diligence, and loyalty on the part of (a) individual workers to companies or workgroups, (b) "child" companies to "parent" companies, and (c) all groups and individuals in society to national goals. At the same time, such utilization of Confucian-derived values sometimes was detrimental to economic innovation by tending to

define "loyalty" and "filial piety" (or "familism") as unquestioning obedience to the ideas of earlier generations or organizational superiors rather than more creative responses to current problems. It also tended to restrict the range of possible solutions to economic issues defining them as moral problems (e.g., prewar labor/ management disputes or poverty in the countryside) and therefore their solution as primarily a moral issue (i.e., a need for the right ideology) rather than as issues also amenable to political, legal and organization, and technical solutions as well.

(2) Clear *continuities* exist between the use of Confucian values by pre- and postwar businessmen and government bureaucrats. While Confucian values and institutions have in one sense become "post-Confucian" values in the postwar period due to efforts to their increasing adaptation to modern economic and political circumstances, at the same time, a certain *continuity* is striking in an unchanging emphasis upon the values of "respect for education," "harmony," "loyalty," and "familism," even as the language used to express these becomes more indirect and their focus in the postwar period has shifted much more to corporations rather than the nation.

(3) Confucian-type values have been used to support a continuing emphasis on *communitarian* rather than *individualistically*-based decision-making within economic organizations in Japan (Vogel 1987), and on relationships within these organizations which are "diffuse" rather than "specific," "affective" rather than "affectively neutral," and in many cases "particularistic" rather than "universalistic." While individualism and universalistic values *have* made major inroads, especially in the postwar period, Japanese business ethics, especially as represented by corporate policies and actual economic behavior, remain clearly more communitarian than those predominant in most major Western countries (Taka 1994; Lodge and Vogel 1987).

(4) There is a consistently close relationship between the use of Confucian values and the *state* in most of Japanese history. This is true even though the state was clearly not the only user of Confucian values in the modern period, since private businessmen and companies in both the pre- and postwar years used them as well as has been shown above. Yet state use of Confucian values does have a much longer history, dating back to the seventh century.[9] Moreover, the key principle that has driven this use from the very beginning has been political leaders' recognition

that Confucian values were extremely helpful in both justifying their own position in society but also in mobilizing popular support (obedience) to state-directed goals. In this sense, the major break in this history of the elite use of Confucian values in Japan occurred when companies rather than the government took over in the postwar period as the major users (and benefactors) of such use.

The Use of Confucian Values in Japan and International Business Ethics

At the same time, this Japanese use of Confucian values for economic development and the creation of a modern business ethic seems to have a broader meaning for the field of international business ethics as a whole. Part of this is that it shows how a non-Western non-individualistic ethical tradition can be successfully adapted over time to serve the needs of modern economic development *and* in the process help shape the nature of that economic development itself. One example of this is the way Shibusawa and other prewar industrialists were able to interpret traditional Confucian ethics to support the profit motive and modern capitalism, and in the process create a modern Japanese business ethic which continued to shape business values and organizational dynamics throughout the prewar period. Another example is the manner in which both pre- and postwar Japanese bureaucrats have used Confucian-derived values and institutions to support economic development and their own dominant role in this process. Both of these exhibit an ability to *create* a specifically Japanese synthesis of "morality" and "economics," and at the same time to be *influenced* by the thinking of that synthesis in the structuring of economic-related organizations.

Second, the significance of this particular synthesis between traditional communitarian ethics and modern economic development does not end with the case of Japan. Rather, the postwar Japanese form of this synthesis became the model, with certain differences, for a similar synthesis of Confucian values and modern economic development policies in other high growth East Asian countries such as Korea, Taiwan, and Singapore, where Confucian values have played a major role in creating cultural support for government-directed economic development and have been reflected in workplace values emphasizing harmony and familism (Winckler 1987, 173–205; Janelli 1993; Redding 1993; Rozman 1992; and Robinson 1991, 216–225). While Korea was perhaps the closest to the "Japan model" in terms of its overall use of Confucian ideology by the state and companies,[10] the parallel between all four countries was particularly close in two areas: (1) educational values, especially in the role of the entrance examination system and in the use of a Confucian ideology of sacrifice by the central government to rally the population around national economic goals; and (2) attitudes of the government bureaucracy toward promoting economic development and protecting domestic industry.[11] In this way, the use of modified Confucian values and institutions in pre- and postwar Japan has much greater importance for theories and practices regarding modern economic development that only being limited to the historical case of Japan or as a specific one time case of the successful synthesis of traditional social values and modern economic development policies. As the "miracle" of East Asian economic development is increasingly looked to by the World Bank[12] and developing countries around the world as a model for others to follow, the record of how these East Asian countries adapted traditional values and institutions to meet the cultural needs of modern capitalistic development takes on an important meaning for developing countries as a whole today.

Third, the postwar economic successes of such East Asian countries as Japan, Korea, and Taiwan have a wider significance for developmental economics theory and especially Western assumptions regarding the relationship between modern economic development and traditional values (see also 1999). That is, in their postwar economic success, Japan (and later Korea and Taiwan) did not follow the classic Western model to modern economic development. At the same time, they also retained many traditional cultural values which they were able to synthesize with the goals and processes of modern economic development in a way that produced growth rates far superior to both Western industrialized societies and most other developing countries, and levels of income equality which were higher as well. That such growth rates in particular were achieved with what could be called a more "communitarian" cultural ethic than that which prevails (or previously prevailed) in most Western countries proves the important point that modern capitalism does not require modern Western style individualism, but can function quite effectively under communitarian social ethics.[13] For developing countries, the implication of this is that they do not have to make an "all or nothing" choice between maintaining traditional values or opting for modern development. Rather, modern economic development can take place while retaining at least some (though not all) of traditional values, which in most developing countries are some form of communitarianism.

Fourth, as the strong individualism and decline of "community" in

Western economic ethics leads to calls for a more communitarian ethic, the record of Japan's ability to synthesize parts of its own traditional communitarian ethics with modern economic institutions and create a modern business ethic offers valuable lessons (both positive and negative) for Western supporters of the adoption of more communitarian business and economic ethics in the West. That is, Japan's record of the use of Confucian communitarian values, albeit representing only one possible type of communitarian values, shows both the potential dangers (stifling of individualism, creativity and innovation, and focusing too much on purely moral solutions to economic issues) and the potential advantages (less adversarial relations between managements and labor unions, greater job security and social stability, and a more egalitarian economic system with a smaller gap between rich and poor and high and low incomes within corporations; see also Umezu 1999) of adopting more communitarian business and economic ethics in the West as well.

Fifth, there is the issue of the *future* of communitarian values within Japanese capitalism itself, an issue raised by Wokutch and Shepard (1999). My own prediction in this regard is that Japanese business and economic ethics *will* become more individualistic, as represented both by actual economic behavior and corporate policies. A good example is recent changes in corporate human resource policies.[14] Yet it is hard to imagine that Japan will move all the way to the Anglo-Saxon pole of individuality in terms of corporate human resource policies, government economic policies, or the general behavior of individual workers. The reasons for this are various, not the least of them being national pride and the slowness with which cultural and social values as deep as these usually change. Another reason is that to do so would be for Japanese corporations and the government to give up an important source of Japan's own current competitiveness.[15] As such, it is more likely that corporations and the government will attempt to find some middle ground between retaining current communitarian practices and introducing new more individualistic ones, with the goal of retaining the best of past practices while trying to eliminate certain disadvantages they hold for Japan's current economic circumstances.[16]

Endnotes

1. Parts of this chapter are derived from an earlier paper I wrote. See Ornatowski 1996.

2. For a discussion on these different types of explanation, see Johnson 1982, 7–17, who however brings a strong bias toward the role of economic policy as being most important.

3. For an English translation of the Rescript, see Smith 1973, 269.

4. "Lifetime" here usually refers only until 55 or 60 years of age, after which the regular employee is helped to find another job, often in a smaller affiliated firm. Lifetime employment does not apply to all employees in the Japanese workplace, but only to regular (rather than temporary) employees at the larger companies, although small and medium size companies try to implement it as much as possible.

5. Lifetime employment for example is never guaranteed contractually.

6. Seniority-based wages and promotion, however, have lost some ground as the merit component of pay has increased in the past decade. See Japan Employment Information Center 1996, 27–32.

7. Of course, to many "child" companies such "benevolence" may simply seem like an indirect means of "control." Yet the same could be said about the actual practice of traditional Confucian relationships in Tokugawa Japan and premodern China.

8. Some analysts describe this system as "feudal" rather than Confucian. See Sakai 1990. Since Confucian values themselves were the product of a feudal age in Chinese history it may not be meaningful to distinguish that closely between "feudal" and Confucian values in the Japanese case. This argument is supported by the fact that so-called Japanese "feudal" warrior values and Confucian ideology were closely intermingled during the 250 years prior to the beginning of Japan's modernization. As a result, Japanese feudal values and Japanese Confucian values are difficult to distinguish.

9. For more on the role of Confucian values in the pre-modern periods, see Collcutt 1991, and Warren Smith 1993.

10. There are many similarities between the use of Confucian values by the postwar Korean government and prewar Japanese government, and between postwar Korean companies and prewar Japanese ones, particularly in terms of government use of moral education and an ideology of self-sacrifice for the nation's welfare and companies' use of the values of harmony, loyalty and familism. At the same time, the specific roles of government and the relative power of government over the economy has varied between the two countries (with the Korean government having more power), and a more authoritarian form of top-down management and more flexible interpretation of "lifetime employment" being predominate in Korean companies (see Choe, Lee and Roehl 1996, 64).

11. See Vogel 1991, Chapter 5. The parallel in the area of education between prewar Japan and postwar Korea in particular is very strong since President Park instituted a type of "morals education" and "rescript on education" that

clearly resembled prewar Japan. Since Park himself was educated in a prewar Japanese military academy this resemblance is not surprising. Singapore also began in 1982 a mandatory public schools morals education curriculum which while differing from prewar Japan's or postwar Korea's, nevertheless is imbued with Confucian values. See Pan 1989.

12. See the World Bank 1993. This study focuses on the role of government policy in contributing to the successful postwar economic development of East Asian countries.

13. At the same time it does *not* prove that such traditional communitarian ethics *caused* such economic development. Instead as I mentioned in the introduction of this paper, I view the best causal explanation of modern Japanese economic development as lying in an approach which combines the factors of economic/political policies, cultural values and historical/situational elements. Moreover, even among contemporary Western countries, there are differences between the values of German and French capitalism, which lean more toward the communitarian pole, and British and U.S. capitalism, which tend to be more individualistic. For more details, see Lodge and Vogel 1987.

14. This is already apparent in the trend toward a greater emphasis on the merit component of pay and promotion, as opposed to seniority, and the recent emphasis on fostering individual creativity and less "group think" within large companies (Taylor 1996; Mallaby 1994).

15. Although this issue deserves a long discussion in itself, suffice it to say here that my assumption is that the "communitarian" values which produced and sustained such practices as the *keiretsu*, lifetime employment for core employees, and close government-business cooperation will continue even while being adjusted to fit the need for structural changes in the current Japanese economy and companies' needs to improve profitability and white collar productivity. In this sense, the Japanese business system currently is in a process of adjustment and "incremental evolution" rather than Westernization.

16. A good example is current changes being instituted in large companies to the seniority-based wage system (so as to improve individual employee motivation and thus overall white-collar productivity) while at the same time maintaining lifetime employment for core employees and its beneficial effect of tying strongly together the long term interests of employees and company. See Ornatowski 1998.

References

Bellah, Robert, *Tokugawa Religion: The Values of Pre-Industrial Japan* (Boston: Beacon Press, 1970).

Choe, Soonkyoo, Lee, Jangho, and Roehl, Tom, "What Makes Management Style Similar and Distinct Across Borders? – An Examination of the Influence of Growth, International Experience and National Culture in

Korea and Japanese Firms," in *Association of Japanese Business Studies Best Paper Proceedings*, ed, Mitsuru Wakabayashi and Allan Bird. (San Luis Obispo: The Association of Japanese Business Studies, 1996).

Collcutt, Martin, "The Legacy of Confucianism in Japan," in *East Asian Region: Confucian Heritage and Its Modern Adaptation*, ed., Gilbert Rozman (Princeton: Princeton University Press, 1991).

Cutts, Robert L., "Capitalism in Japan: Cartels and Keiretsu." *Harvard Business Review* 70, no. 4 (1992), 48–55.

Dore, Ronald, *British Factory Japanese Factory* (London: George Allen and Unwin, 1970).

Dore, Ronald, "Industrial Relations in Japan and Elsewhere," in *Japan: A Comparative View*, ed., Albert Craig (Princeton: Princeton University Press, 1979).

Glazer, Nathan, "Social and Cultural Factors in Japanese Economic Growth," in *Asia's New Giant*, eds., Hugh Patrick and Henry Rosovsky (Washington D.C.: The Brookings Institution, 1976).

Hirschmeirer, Johannes, "Shibusawa Eiichi: Industrial Pioneer," in *The State and Economic Enterprise in Japan*, ed., William W. Lockwood (Princeton: Princeton University Press, 1965).

Imai, Kenichi, and Komiya, Ryutaro, "Characteristics of Japanese Firms," in *Business Enterprises in Japan: Views of Japanese Economists*, ed., Kenichi Imai and Ryutaro Komiya (Cambridge: MIT Press, 1994).

Janelli, Roger L., *Making Capitalism: The Social and Cultural Construction of a South Korean Conglomerate* (Stanford: Stanford University Press, 1993).

Japan Employment Information Center, *Issues and Methods in the Advancement of the Annual Salary System* (Nenposei no susumekata to kadai) (Tokyo: JEIC, 1996).

Johnson, Chalmers, *MITI and the Japanese Miracle* (Stanford: Stanford University Press, 1982).

Kinzley, W. Dean, *Industrial Harmony in Modern Japan: The Invention of a Tradition* (London: Routledge, 1991).

Legge, James, *Confucian Analects, The Great Learning and The Doctrine of the* Mean (New York: Dover Publications, 1971).

Lockwood, William, *The Economic Development of Japan* (Princeton: Princeton University Press, 1954).

Lodge, George and Vogel, Ezra, *Ideology and National Competitiveness.* (Cambridge: Harvard Business School Press, 1987).

Mallaby, Sebastian, "Japan Survey," in *The Economist* (July 9, 1994), 1–18.

Marshall, Bryon, *Capitalism and Nationalism in Prewar Japan* (Stanford: Stanford University Press, 1987).

Ohkawa, Kazushi, and Rosovsky, Henry, *Japanese Economic Growth: Trend Acceleration in the Twentieth Century* (Stanford: Stanford University Press, 1976).

Ornatowski, Gregory, "Confucian Ethics and Economic Development: A Study of the Adaptation of Confucian Values to Modern Japanese Economic Ideology and Institutions," *Journal of Socio-Economics* 25, no. 5 (1996), 571–590.

Ornatowski, Gregory. "The End of Japanese-Style Human Resource Management?" *Sloan Management Review* 39, number 3 (1998), 73–84.

Pan, Lynn, "Playing the Identity Card," *Far Eastern Economic Review* (February 9, 1989), 30–37.

Prestowitz, Clyde, *Trading Places: How America Allowed Japan to Take the Lead* (Tokyo: Tuttle, 1988).

Redding, S. Gordon, *The Spirit of Chinese Capitalism* (Berlin: Walter de Gruyter, 1990).

Robinson, Michael, "Perceptions of Confucianism in Twentieth Century Korea," in *The East Asian Region: Confucian Heritage and Its Modern Adaptation*, ed., Gilbert Rozman (Princeton: Princeton University Press, 1991).

Rohlen, Thomas, *For Harmony and Strength: Japanese White-Collar Organization in Anthropological Perspective* (Berkeley: University of California Press, 1974).

Rozman, Gilbert, "Comparisons of Modern Confucian Values in China and Japan," in *The East Asian Region: Confucian Heritage and Its Modern Adaptation*, ed., Gilbert Rozman (Princeton: Princeton University Press, 1991).

Rozman, Gilbert, "The Confucian Faces of Capitalism," in *Pacific Century*, ed., Mark Borthwick (Boulder: Westview Press, 1992).

Sakai, Kuniyasu, "The Feudal World or Japanese Manufacturing," *Harvard Business Review* 68, no. 6 (1990), 38–49.

Saniel, Josefa, "The Mobilization of Traditional Values in the Modernization of Japan," in *Religion and Progress in Asia*, ed., Robert N. Bellah (New York: Free Press, 1965).

Shibusawa, Eiichi, *Rongo to Soroban* (The Analects and the Abacus) (Tokyo: Kokusho kankokai, 1992).

Smith, Thomas C., *Native Sources of Japanese Industrialization, 1750–1920.* (Berkeley: University of California Press, 1988).

Smith, Warren, *Confucianism in Modern Japan* (Tokyo: Hokuseido Press, 1973).

Tai, Kuo-hui, "Confucianism and Japanese Modernization: A Study of Shibusawa Eiichi," in *Confucianism and Economic Development: An Oriental Alternative?* Ed., Hung-chao Tai (Washington: Washington Institute, 1989).

Taka, Iwao, "Business Ethics: A Japanese View," *Business Ethics Quarterly* 4, no. 1 (1994), 53–78.

Takahashi, Akira, "Ethics in Developing Economies in Various Culture," in this volume.

Taylor, Alex, "Toyota's Boss Stands Out in a Crowd," *Fortune* 134 (November 25, 1996), 116–122.

Thurow, Lester, *Head to Head: The Coming Economic Battle Among Japan, Europe and America* (New York: Morrow, 1992).

Umezu, Mitsuhiro, "Ethics and the Japanese Miracle: Characteristics and Ethics of Japanese Business Practice," in this volume.

Vogel, Ezra, "Japan: Adaptive Communitarianism," in *Ideology and National Competitiveness*, eds.,. George Lodge and Ezra Vogel (Cambridge: Harvard Business School Press, 1987).

Vogel, Ezra, *The Four Little Dragons* (Cambridge: Harvard University Press, 1991).

Winckler, Edwin, "Statism and Familism on Taiwan," in *Ideology and National Competitiveness*, eds., George Lodge and Ezra Vogel (Cambridge: Harvard Business School Press, 1987).

Wokutch, Richard E., and Shepard, John M., "Corporate Social Responsibility, Moral Unity, and the Maturing of the Japanese Economy," in this volume.

World Bank, *The East Asian Miracle: Economic Growth and Public Policy* (Oxford: Oxford University Press, 1993).

Corporate Social Responsibility, Moral Unity, and the Maturing of the Japanese Economy[1]

Richard E. Wokutch and Jon M. Shepard

Abstract

This chapter examines corporate social responsibility in Japan today within the context of the paradigm of the moral unity of business. Under this paradigm, business is expected to operate under the same set of moral standards operative in other societal institutions. We suggest that a micro moral unity characterizes Japan, wherein business activity is linked to that society's moral values but only within carefully circumscribed communities of interest. Because of the strains brought on by the maturing of the Japanese economy, the negative consequences of this micro moral unity are now becoming apparent. A new paradigm will be required to address these challenges.

This chapter attempts to assess the implications of recent developments in the Japanese economy on the conceptualization and practice of corporate social responsibility (CSR). Drawing upon previous research, we attempt to show how a *micro moral unity* has existed in Japan, wherein business activity has been linked to society's values of morality within a carefully defined community of interests. It is argued that this approach worked very well for those within this community of interests and for Japan as a whole in its highly successful pursuit of economic development in the aftermath of World War II. However, those individuals who were outside this community did not reap the full benefits of this economic development, and a number of manifestations of the dark side of micro-moral unity cropped up on the periphery of mainstream economic life in Japan. These were, in many cases, easy to ignore as Japanese society focused on the real gains in economic standards of living made by the overwhelming majority of the population. However, with the economic, social, and political strains brought on by the maturing of the Japanese economy, the high yen, and the increasing internationalization of Japanese society and business, these manifestations are being brought into sharper focus and the apparent social consensus that supported this micro-moral-unity approach is being eroded.

In this chapter, we discuss first the business-society paradigm of moral unity. Then we describe two competing views of corporate social responsibility in Japan that are popular in the West, a positive view and a negative view, and we consider the societal underpinnings of the Japanese approach to corporate social responsibility. Subsequently, we consider the implications of changes in the Japanese economy as it matures, and the impacts these changes are having on the micro-moral-unity paradigm. We explain these impacts with respect to a number of different dimensions of CSR, including employment security, occupational safety and health, temporary and part-time workers, women's issues, relations with foreigners and ethnic minorities in Japan, consumer issues, environmental issues, philanthropic activities, and trade relations with South Africa. A closing thought regarding the development of business ethics thinking in Japan ends the chapter.

Business-Society Paradigms

Any business and society paradigm must necessarily define the relationship between business and the morality of the larger society. Without this connection, a business-society paradigm could neither explain the relationship between business and other social institutions nor the role of the individual in business.

Historically, two opposing paradigms have defined the relationship between business activity and morality in Western societies: the paradigm of moral unity and the amoral paradigm of business (Shepard et al. 1995; Steiner and Steiner 1991). The *paradigm of moral unity* in business rests on the assumption that only one set of moral standards exists within a society. Economic entities are denied the right to be considered "ethical sanctuaries" (Konrad 1982). Rather, economic relationships are held to be subject to the same standards as other social relationships. Business people are socially prohibited (deviance, of course, occurs) from practicing one set of ethical standards at church or at home and a more permissive set of ethical principles at work.

In contrast to the moral unity paradigm, the *amoral paradigm* of business holds that economic relations should be based entirely on the pursuit of exclusive self-interest, putting aside the requirement in most ethical theories that the interests of others affected by one's decisions are to be taken into account, though, of course, not always satisfied

(Rachels 1993). Milton Friedman's contention that, legal demands aside, the use of stockholders' money for nonprofit purposes is wrong epitomizes the amoral paradigm of business today (Friedman 1962, 1970, 1982). According to this paradigm, business relationships are not immoral; they are simply not subject to the moral constraints and practices covering other social relationships (see also Carr 1968). This compartmentalization of ethics permits business decisions to be based on moral considerations when it is convenient, but does not force ethical considerations on decisions if profits are to be negatively affected. The amoral paradigm provides a "moral free ride" for "good" people who make decisions sacrificing the common good for corporate good (De George 1986).

The micro moral unity paradigm we posit for Japan implies that there is indeed one set of moral standards that exist for corporations and the mainstream of Japanese society. This mainstream includes most Japanese people in Japan; it does not, however, include ethnic minorities, foreigners, and various individuals on the fringes of Japanese society. Our discussion of CSR in Japan will show how the interests of people on the outskirts of the corporate community are also frequently sacrificed for the interests of those at the core.

Global Cultures of Capitalism and Business-Society Paradigms

Although several variants of capitalism can be identified (Hampden-Turner and Trompenaars 1993), they can be collapsed into two basic types. "Industrialistic capitalism" is founded on the principles of self-interest, the free market, profit maximization, and the highest return possible on stockholder investment. This variant of capitalism dominated the world in the nineteenth century (Great Britain) as well as the twentieth century (the United States). Japanese capitalism of the late twentieth century, the example we wish to focus on, is known as "communitarian capitalism," the type of capitalism that emphasizes the interests of employees, customers, and society.

These two types of capitalism deserve the label "cultures of capitalism" because each is built on a distinctive business-society paradigm. Because communitarian capitalism links economic activities to other societal institutions, it is based on the business-society paradigm of moral unity. In contrast, individualistic capitalism, with its accent on the welfare of business over other institutions, is rooted in the amoral paradigm.

The cultural underpinnings are easy to observe in individualistic capitalism (Thurow 1992). Both individuals and separate firms have their own economic strategies for success. The individual wants to prosper and firms wish to satisfy their stockholders. Firms seek to maximize profits because shareholders invest to maximize profits. Customers and employees are the firm's means to reach the goal of higher shareholder return. Because higher wages cut into profits, firms try to keep them as low as possible and lay off employees whenever necessary. Short-term thinking in the name of profit maximization is the norm. Employees are expected to leave one job for another if they can get higher wages. Employees and employers have no mutual obligations outside the legal employment contract.

Within individualistic capitalism, government is not to interfere very much with the workings of the free market. Government is supposed to make minimal rules and act as an umpire to settle disputes (Friedman 1962). There is no place for government in investment funding or economic planning. So long as government protects private-property rights, the pursuit of profit maximization will insure the greatest prosperity.

Under communitarian capitalism in Japan, emphasis is placed on cooperation, interpersonal harmony, and the subordination of the individual to the community. Individuals in Japan attempt to select the best firm, and then work hard to be part of the company team; personal success or failure is identified with the fate of the company. Job switching is not widespread. In fact, in many Japanese firms, the person who voluntarily leaves a company has traditionally been viewed as a "traitor." At the same time, Japanese workers are less often laid off.

Japanese firms place the interests of individual shareholders far behind their employees and customers. Because employees are of first importance, job security, high wages, and comfortable working conditions are top priorities. Capturing market share to sustain these is emphasized over profit maximization and shareholders, in fact, earn relatively low returns. In Japan, the government is expected to play a significant role in economic funding, planning, and growth. There is cooperation between business and government as well as between labor and management.

Corporate Social Responsibility

One popular way of understanding CSR is through the stakeholder management model (Freeman 1984). According to one view of this model, managers attempt to balance the interests of the various stakeholders of the corporation with the intention of achieving the common good. Underlying this view is the notion that these stakeholders, including customers, suppliers, employees, stockholders, the local community, and interest groups are influenced by the corporation and can, in turn, influence the corporation. Because of this, firms find it to be in their "enlightened self-interest" to take account of the concerns of these stakeholders. Thus firms may undertake certain activities to benefit one or more of these stakeholders, that although costly in the short run, will benefit the firm financially in the long run.

But implicit, and in some cases explicit, in many Western notions of CSR is the idea that one should undertake certain actions above and beyond those that can be justified by bottom line considerations on the grounds that they are simply the right thing to do. Thus ethical motivations are often given for CSR. There also is an expectation that companies should adhere to certain standards of ethical behavior and maintain a concern for society at large even when there are no particular laws or regulations requiring such practices and when it is not in their economic self-interest to do so.

The practice and conceptualization of CSR in Japan (and in Japanese corporations operating overseas) are different in important ways from that in the West. There are what appear to be many contradictions in the practice of CSR that are confusing to outside observers. On many dimensions of CSR, Japanese companies are the world leaders, setting examples of performance that companies everywhere attempt to emulate. Yet on some dimensions of CSR (or in some situations), Japanese firms engage in activities that seem to violate generally accepted minimum standards of behavior. Outside observers focusing on one or the other of these sets of behaviors have constructed in some cases highly favorable and in other cases highly unfavorable stereotypes of Japanese corporations (Wokutch 1992a).

The Positive View of Japanese Corporate Social Responsibility

Japanese companies are on the cutting edge of international competition in providing quality goods and services. This has led to the customer satisfaction, loyalty, and repeat purchases that allowed Japanese companies to achieve great success in such industries as consumer electronics, cameras, computers, and automobiles. As a result of this success, Japanese productivity and quality management techniques have been studied the world over.

With respect to workers, Japanese participative management techniques, lifetime employment practices, extensive employee benefits, and workplace safety and health promotion activities are also the subject of high praise and intense scrutiny. These practices have been credited with giving advantages to Japanese companies in terms of worker productivity and loyalty, and product quality (Ouchi 1981; Pascale and Athos 1981; Schonberger 1982). In a detailed study of occupational safety and health in Japan, the first author found that these practices also contributed to extraordinarily low worker injury and illness rates (see Wokutch 1992b and Wokutch and McLaughlin 1992 for a complete discussion of Japanese injury and illness experience). Thus these labor practices have been credited with providing strategic advantages to Japanese firms and, consequently, many companies around the world have attempted to emulate them.

Even overseas, most notably in the United States, Japanese corporations have proven themselves to be model citizens on many dimensions of CSR. Their support of local community activities and other philanthropic endeavors has led to increased goodwill in the communities where they operate. They have become welcome guests and model corporate citizens in these communities and in the process they have won many important political allies who have helped them on a range of issues from local zoning questions to international trade disputes (*Economic World* 1992; Miller, Lee, and Tsiantar 1989).

Japanese firms have helped society, or important elements thereof, and have benefited themselves substantially as a result. Thus, along a great range of activities a harmony of interests between the corporation and society is achieved in Japan, thereby suggesting the dominance of the moral unity paradigm.

The Negative View of Japanese Corporate Social Responsibility

Despite this favorable image of Japanese corporations, there are a number of practices and activities of Japanese firms that are troublesome to outside observers and conflict with the moral unity paradigm. These are, for the most part, directed at individuals and groups who are at various distances outside the core of the carefully defined corporate community. It is for this reason that we contend it is a micro-moral-unity paradigm that explains the relationship between business and the morality of the larger society in Japan. Thus, while there is one set of moral standards that exists to govern interactions with people within these micro communities, a different set of standards exists for individuals outside these communities.

There are great discrepancies in working conditions within the Japanese economy such that working conditions are much more favorable for the most privileged workers, namely the regular employees of major employees, than they are for workers in subsidiary firms or for temporary or seasonal workers. Moreover, the favorable features of Japanese working conditions are often exaggerated even for these most privileged workers. For example, lifetime employment is something of a misnomer even for the regular workers in major firms since most face mandatory retirement from these firms in their mid to late 50s, a number of years before they are ready to retire from the labor market. Still, security of employment and other workplace benefits are much better for these workers than temporary or seasonal workers at these firms or for workers at smaller subsidiary firms (Kazuo1991; Shimada 1980).

With respect to workplace safety and health, small subsidiary firms have fewer resources devoted to injury and illness prevention, and many of the so called 3-K jobs – *kiken* (dangerous), *kitani* (dirty), and *kitsui* (demanding) jobs – are shifted to employees in these subsidiaries, resulting in safety and health problems. Small firms are likely to have higher injury and illness rates than large firms in any economy, but in Japan the small enterprise/large enterprise disparity is twice as great as it is in the United States (Wokutch 1992b, Wokutch and McLaughlin 1992).

Likewise, the lack of opportunities for women, foreigners, and certain minority groups in Japan violates the principle of equality of opportunity that is firmly espoused (although not always adhered to) in the United States. Despite the 1986 passage of the Equal Employment Opportunity Law, intended to promote equality of opportunity for women, most Japanese corporations maintain a separate non-career-oriented track for women employees. While over half of adult women work in Japan, women hold only 11.5% of managerial positions in Japan compared with 38.5% in the United States (Kazuo 1991). The use of the derogatory term *shomohin* (roughly translated as "consumables") to describe female workers is indicative of the low regard with which they are held by their male colleagues and their temporary status in the firm.

Discrimination against domestic minorities such as the indigenous Ainu, the Burakamin, and ethnic Koreans, as well as against foreigners, is widely practiced by businesses and individuals alike. Government requirements for alien registration, including the only recently discontinued practice of periodic fingerprinting, legitimize a certain degree of xenophobia directed at outsiders among the mainstream Japanese (Burgess 1986; *The Wall Street Journal* 1991; Williams 1992).

The homogeneity of management of Japanese firms even in their US subsidiaries (typically top managers are Japanese males and white males serve under them) has led to various problems in such areas as racial and sexual discrimination and sexual harassment in these US operations. Such companies as Mitsubishi, Sumitomo, Honda, Nissan, C. Itoh, and others have been the targets of legal action with respect to sexual and/or racial discrimination charges. After years of criticizing Japanese companies for discriminatory practices, civil rights activist Jesse Jackson began a boycott against selected Japanese firms to encourage them to change their culture of exclusivity (Reitman and Schuman 1996).

Notwithstanding the well-deserved reputation of Japanese corporations for consumer service, in many ways consumers have borne the burden of an economic system seemingly designed to promote the interests of employers. Because of the cumbersome distribution system and the remaining barriers to imports into Japan (both of which have the effect of maintaining employment levels), consumers must often pay exorbitantly high prices for goods and services. It is not uncommon to hear stories of Japanese who have purchased Japanese-made goods overseas for far less than they would have paid in Japan.

Japanese protection of domestic industry can have even more serious costs to consumers, as seems to be the case is the current scandal over the distribution of HIV-tainted blood products by the Japanese Green Cross Corporation. Critics allege that in the early 1980s, the Japanese Ministry of Health and Welfare prevented the importation of safer, heat-treated blood products from US firms in order to allow Japanese firms time to catch up on this new AIDS prevention technology. As a result, more than 1,800 Japanese hemophiliacs became infected with HIV from transfusions of tainted blood products (Hamilton 1996; *Japan Times* 1996).

In the post-war race for economic development, environmental concerns were frequently neglected in Japan. When environmental tragedies occurred, such as those related to Minamata disease and Itai Itai disease, the victims themselves have frequently been blamed for their problems and criticized for their efforts to seek redress of their grievances from the corporations deemed responsible (McKean 1981). Much of the environmental progress that has been achieved in recent years has come about in response to foreign criticism (Beck 1986); domestic critics have been largely ineffective (Hamilton and Kanabayashi 1994). In addition, Japan is routinely accused of environmental misdeeds in many of its offshore activities both publicly and privately funded (Gross 1989).

Philanthropic activities by Japanese corporations in the US have come under criticism from two directions. On the one hand, some in Japan complain that Japanese corporations are more generous towards American institutions than their Japanese counterparts. On the other hand, the use of philanthropic contributions to buy influence has been widely criticized in business and political writings (*Economic World* 1992; Holstein and Borruss 1988; Choate 1990; and Prestowitz 1989), and it has even provided the basis for the plot of the popular film and book, *Rising Sun* (Crichton 1992).

Relations with South Africa during the apartheid era brought international criticism to Japanese corporations, but little response from them. The fact that there is not a black constituency in Japan who enjoy membership in the micro communities of Japanese corporations made this a dimension of CSR that could be easily ignored. During the late 1980s this issue was probably the foremost CSR priority of the general public in the United States and many European countries, yet with Japanese companies stepping in to fill the gap created by US and European firms that left South Africa, Japan became that country's number one trading partner. Likewise the lack of black corporate stakeholders in Japan explains (in part) how Japanese firms could popularize the use of distorted caricatures of blacks in their advertising and in children's toys (Shapiro 1988).

Underpinnings of Corporate Social Responsibility in Japan

There are three primary characteristics of corporate social responsibility in Japan that distinguish Japanese thinking about the issue from that in the United States and Europe, and that help explain these apparently conflicting views of CSR there. These are the within-group/out-of-group distinction, the Confucian sense of duty to those with whom one has a specific relationship, and the strong emphasis placed on the value of loyalty.

In Japan, group membership is very important. One has a much greater sense of responsibility to those who are members of one's group, however that is defined. Although group membership plays a role in the definition of one's responsibilities in the United States and other Western countries as well, the differentiation is much more obvious in Japan. As noted with respect to occupational safety and health, clear distinctions are made in the corporate efforts to promote occupational safety and health for the full-time permanent employees compared to part-time or temporary workers. Likewise, secondary and tertiary subcontractors of major corporations are considered outside the normal corporate family, and safety and health considerations for them are frequently considered none of the business of the major employer. For example, one safety and health manager in a major Japanese automotive firm noted in response to a question of whether or not they collect injury and illness statistics from their subcontractors that they do not want to know about safety and health conditions in their subcontractors because the Ministry of Labor might then hold them responsible for improving these conditions (Wokutch 1992b). Still, many of the policies and practices of the major employer, such as subcontracting out the most hazardous operations, can have important safety and health implications for these subcontractors.

Other practices such as restricting of immigration into Japan, hiring and promotion practices that discriminate against women and minorities, and restricting foreign imports into Japan can all be understood better in the context of this within-group/out-of-group distinction. The crucial importance of this within-group/out-of-group distinction would then explain how the positive and negative stereotypes of CSR in Japan can both be valid depending on one's perspective. That is, whether one is considering activities related to parties within the corporate community or of those outside of it.

In Western societies, one motivation for corporate social responsibility is a generalized sense of altruism, the notion that one should help others in need, even those one does not know, without expectation of benefit or reward, simply because it is the right thing to do. Such a generalized sense of altruism is not an important motivation for CSR in Japan. Instead, arising from the Confucian influence in Japanese culture, there is a strong sense of duty to those with whom one has a relationship (e.g., father-child, husband-wife, oldest brother-sibling, and most importantly, master-servant). The closer one's relationship, the stronger is one's duties to the other party(ies) of the relationship. As a result, duties to those with whom one has a relationship dominate thinking about ethics in Japan. In modern terms, the employer-employee relationship embodies many of the characteristics of the master-servant relationship. Thus there are strong duties in both directions for employers and employees and this is reflected in CSR practices. However, duties to unknown others such as those who are outside the corporate community are given little attention or concern.

In Japanese culture, loyalty has long held a strong position of importance. In feudal days, Samurai held to a code of *Bushido* that entailed, among other things, unquestioned obedience and loyalty to one's lord. This loyalty was considered to be unconditional, and not in any way contingent on merit or righteousness. Elements of this way of thinking have survived to modern times, with employees acting with absolute obedience and loyalty towards their employer. This unbridled loyalty of employees seems to have been responsible at least in part for a number of scandals over the years, including the Lockheed/All Nippon Airways bribery case that led to the downfall of Prime Minister Kakuei Tanaka's government, Toshiba's sale of restricted defense technology to the former Soviet Union, and the more current Daiwa Bank trading scandal. The intention of loyally serving the interests of their employer, even though in violation of the law, exonerated the guilty employees in the eyes of many of their colleagues. Likewise, CEOs who have resigned to take responsibility for scandals have frequently been kept on as advisors or in other positions, receiving generous salary and perquisites. Beneficiaries of this Japanese version of a golden parachute include the chairman of Sumitomo Bank who resigned after a stock manipulation scandal, the chairman of Nomura Securities who admitted to dealings with the Japanese Mafia and illegally compensating large investors for stock market trading losses, the chairman of Fuji Bank who quit after a loan fraud incident, as well as executives at Daiwa Bank and Toshiba Corporation held to be responsible for the incidents noted above (Sapsford and Shirouzu 1995).

Moral Unity in Japan

In the past, given the nature of the Japanese economic and social system, it was easy to conclude that a moral unity existed in Japan. In the immediate post-war period, there was a strong consensus that economic development was the key to bringing about a better society. Actions which promoted this economic development were therefore seen as ethical. Placing the interests of employers and their employees above those of other corporate stakeholders was seen as consistent with economic development and therefore ethical. Protectionist trading policies that promoted the growth of jobs even at the expense of the living standards of consumers were in this sense understandable. Ignoring the concerns of stockholders for a better return on their investment or more say in decision making was also consistent. So, too, was ignoring the criticisms of environmentalists, consumer advocates, and minority and women's rights advocates. These practices were generally accepted by society as a whole even though some critics dissented loudly.

As the twentieth century draws to a close, the Japanese economy has achieved a high level of success and maturity, challenging the United States in many sectors for preeminence in the world. Precisely because it has matured, some of the contradictions between the micro approach to moral unity described here and a more macro approach have become more obvious and increasingly difficult to ignore.

The insularity of the Japanese economy that allowed the discriminatory within-group/out-of-group practices to go largely unnoticed has been undermined by the very success of Japan. In conquering foreign markets, Japanese corporations prompted overseas governments to erect retaliatory trade barriers. At the same time, the success of Japanese businesses produced huge trade surpluses that drove up the value of the yen and made it increasingly difficult and expensive to manufacture many products in Japan. Thus more and more of Japanese production was moved overseas. With this move abroad, practices that were widely accepted by the homogenous Japanese society have been the source of great controversy abroad. The employment of overseas nationals has brought out into stark relief the great difficulty Japanese have in accepting foreigners as full-fledged members of the corporate family. The serious difficulties Japanese employers have run into in the United States on such issues as product safety, corporate philanthropy, industrial espionage, and discrimination on the basis of race and sex have been noted above and elsewhere (Wokutch 1990).

It is telling that many of the problems Japanese companies have had abroad with respect to corporate social performance have begun to raise questions in Japan about the same issues. This is the case with the concealed financial trading losses of Daiwa Bank and Sumitomo Corporation. These losses, which were discovered overseas, have led to calls for tighter regulations and reporting requirements in Japan (Sapsford 1996). It is also the case for Mitsubishi Motors with respect to the embarrassing and controversial charges of sexual harassment at its Normal, Illinois plant. In the wake of the latter case, Mitsubishi and other Japanese corporations have been accused of essentially ignoring the problem of sexual harassment in their Japanese operations at the same time they have been taking aggressive measures to eradicate the behavior in their US facilities (Reitman 1996; Saito 1996). At Mitsubishi, these measures include the high profile hiring of former US Secretary of Labor Lynne Martin as a consultant on this issue. Indicative of perhaps a lack of appreciation of the problem, a recent survey of the Japan Overseas Enterprises Association revealed that over 50% of Japanese companies had written rules prohibiting sexual harassment in their US subsidiaries, but only 7% had undertaken the same measures in Japan (Saito 1996).

Similar pressures for change are occurring in other areas of Japanese society. The movement of jobs overseas (the so-called hollowing of the Japanese economy) has in many cases effectively shrunken the size of the corporate community. Fewer retiring workers in major corporations are being replaced by new college graduates. This has increased the number of individuals outside this community whose interests occasionally conflict with the interests of those inside, thereby exacerbating these conflicts. At the same time, the Japanese economy has attracted more and more immigrants, both legal and illegal, who fill jobs that many Japanese no longer find appealing. In 1990, nearly 38,000 foreigners entered Japan legally for work training – an increase from 14,000 in 1986 as a result of relaxation of immigration laws – and an estimated 300,000 were there illegally (Kanabayashi 1992; *The Wall Street Journal* 1990). Although these numbers are small by US standards, they are unsettling to the Japanese. Not surprisingly, workplace injuries and illnesses among these immigrant workers are becoming problematic (Yamagiwa 1996). Also with these foreigners increasingly visible in Japanese companies, prejudices that were formerly hidden become manifest. Likewise, foreign businesses that have attempted to enter the Japanese market to pursue opportunities have received a decidedly mixed reception.

Towards an Emerging New Paradigm

With the tensions brought on by the maturing of the Japanese economy, the apparent social consensus that supported the micro-moral-unity paradigm of business-society relations is being eroded. This raises some important questions. How will Japanese business and society respond? Will Japanese capitalism modify its existing micro-moral-unity paradigm? Will an entirely new paradigm emerge?

Academic interest in CSR and business ethics in Japan as well as practitioner commentary on the topics have historically trailed that of the United States and Western Europe. Recent developments, however, suggest that much more attention is being devoted to them and thus provide reason to be optimistic about the future evolution of the business-society paradigm in Japan.

The First World Congress on Business, Economics, and Ethics was held at Reitaku University in Tokyo in July 1996, and it brought together leading business ethics scholars and theologians from around the world as well as Japanese business and government leaders. This was an encouraging development as it demonstrated a far greater interest in Japanese business ethics than had previously been evident. It also revealed some promising trends with respect to the development of a new business-society paradigm in Japan.

The activities of Reitaku University and its Institute of Moralogy in advancing the thinking and practices on ethical issues in Japan are noteworthy. The Institute draws upon the thinking of ethical theory and the world's religions to resolve ethical issues in business. Principles of Moralogy include: benevolence, precedence of duties over rights, gratitude to one's benefactors, and renunciation of selfishness. In addition to sponsoring scholarship on these issues (see Dunfee and Nagayasu 1993), the Institute has an impact on business practice through relations with its over 6,000 corporate affiliates.

During this World Congress a relatively new Japanese conceptualization of business-society relationships was discussed at some length. This is the concept of *kyosei* (living and working together for the common good). Although it is not our purpose to fully consider this concept here, it is noteworthy that *kyosei* explicitly endorses a macro view of business ethics and corporate social responsibility that encompasses the local and regional communities, the nation, and the broader global community, in addition to the corporate community itself. It also includes concern for promotion of the common good, respect for diversity, and valuing community (de Bettignies et al. 1999; Goodpaster 1999; Yamaji 1999). Clearly this indicates a major departure from the thinking characterizing the micro-moral-unity paradigm described above. It will be interesting to monitor, however, how well the impressive executive speeches on *kyosei* will be translated into actual corporate practice.

Also, the 1993 formation of the Japan Society for Business Ethics Study (JABES) is another encouraging development. With approximately 150 academic and business members, annual meetings, a newsletter, monthly study meetings, special study groups, and a journal (*Journal of Japan Society for Business Ethics Study*), this organization should be able to advance the thinking on what is the most appropriate business-society paradigm for Japan. Such developments as these give reason for optimism and bear watching in the future.

Perhaps most encouraging of all is the stepping forward of several whistle-blowers in the HIV-tainted blood scandal. Whistle-blowing is extremely rare in Japan and it is anathema to the micro-moral-unity paradigm we have described. Perhaps (and hopefully) this action foreshadows a broadening of the moral unity paradigm in Japan.

Endnote

1. An earlier version of this paper was presented at the First World Congress of the International Society of Business, Economics, and Ethics in Tokyo, Japan, July 1996. Another version of this paper, under the title "The Maturing of the Japanese Economy: Corporate Social Responsibility Implications," is forthcoming at *Business Ethics Quarterly*.

References

Beck, J., *"Japan as a 'Rich Country'." (case) (Boston: Harvard Business School, 1986)*.

Burgess, J., "Japanese Proud of Their Homogeneous Society," *Washington Post* (September 27, 1986), A1.

Carr, A. Z., "Is Business Bluffing Ethical?" *Harvard Business Review* 46 (1968), 143–153.

Choate, P., *Agents of Influence* (New York: Alfred A. Knopf, 1990).

Chrichton, M., *Rising Sun* (New York: Alfred A. Knopf, 1992).

de Bettignies, H.-C., Goodpaster, K. E., and Matsuoka, T., "The Caux Roundtable Principles for Business: Presentation and Discussion," in this volume.

De George, R. T., *Business Ethics*, 2d ed. (New York: Macmillan, 1986).

Dunfee, T. W., and Nagayasu, Y., eds., *Business Ethics: Japan and the Global Economy* (Dordrecht: Kluwer, 1993).

Economic World, "Do Japanese Corporate Gifts Have Strings Attached?" (February 6–9, 1992).

Freeman, R.E., *Strategic Management: A Stakeholder Approach* (Boston: Pitman, 1984).

Friedman, M., *Capitalism and Freedom* (Chicago: University of Chicago Press, 1962).

Friedman, M., "The Social Responsibility of Business Is to Increase Its Profits," *New York Times* (September 3, 1970), 122–126.

Goodpaster, K. E., "Bridging East and West in Management Ethics: Kyosei and the Moral Point of View," in this volume.

Gross, N., "Charging Japan with Crimes against the Earth," *Business Week.* (October 9, 1989), 108–112.

Hamilton, D. P., "Blood Pact: In Japan AIDS Scandal, Many Wonder If Safety Came Second to Trade," *The Wall Street Journal* (October 9, 1996), A1, A6.

Hamilton, D. P., and Kanabayaski, M., "Belief Grows that Japan's Environment Has Been Sacrificed for the Economy," *Wall Street Journal* (May 13, 1994), A6.

Hampden-Turner, C., and Trompenaars, A., *The Seven Cultures of Capitalism* (New York: Currency Doubleday, 1993).

Holstein, W., and Borrus, A., "Japan's Clout in the US," *Business Week* (July 11, 1988), 64–66.

Japan Times, "Key Figures Deny HIV Blame" (July 24, 1996), 1, 3.

Kanabayaski, M., "Japan Becomes Major Importer of Asian Labor," *The Wall Street Journal* (March 9, 1992), 25A.

Kazuo, K., *The Economics of Work in Japan* (Tokyo: Toyo Keizai Inc., 1991).

Konrad, A. R., "Business Managers and Moral Sanctuaries," *Journal of Business Ethics* 1 (1982), 195–200.

McKean, M., *Environmental Protest and Citizen Politics in Japan* (Berkeley, Cal.: University of California Press, 1981).

Miller, A., Lee, C., and Tsiantar, D., "Charity Begins Abroad: Japan Uses Giving to Buy America's Good Will," *Newsweek* (August 21, 1989), 41.

Ouchi, W., *Theory Z: How Americans Can Meet the Japanese Challenge* (Reading, Mass.: Addison-Wesley, 1981).

Pascale, R., and Athos, A., *The Art of Japanese Management: Applications for American Executives* (New York: Warner Books, 1981).

Prestowitz, C., *Trading Places: How We Are Giving Our Future to Japan and How to Reclaim It* (New York: Basic Books, Inc., 1989).

Reitman, V., "Cramming for the Exotic US Workplace: Sex-Harassment Case Spurs Sensitivity Seminars in Japan," *The Wall Street Journal* (July 9, 1996), A15.

Reitman, V., and Schuman, M., "Men's Club: Japanese and Korean Companies Rarely Look Outside for People to Run Their Overseas Operations. Some Think It's Time to Change," *The Wall Street Journal* (September 26, 1996), A17.

Saito, R., "Sex Harassment in Japan Remains a Cloaked Issue," *The Japan Times* (July 30, 1996), 3.

Sapsford, J., "Sumitomo Debacle Reflects a Titanic Struggle" *The Wall Street Journal* (June 17, 1996), A11.

Sapsford, J., and Shirouzu, N., "Scandal-Ridden Executives in Japan May

Lose Face But Not Their Shirts," *The Wall Street Journal* (October 19, 1995), A19.

Schonberger, R., *Japanese Manufacturing Techniques* (New York: Free Press, 1982).

Shapiro, M., "Old Black Stereotypes Find New Lives in Japan," *Washington Post* (July 22, 1988), A18.

Shepard, J. M., Shepard, J., Wimbush, J. C., and Stephens, C. U., "The Place of Ethics in Business: Shifting Paradigms?" *Business Ethics Quarterly* 5 (1995), 577–601.

Shimada, H. *The Japanese Employment System*. Japan Industrial Relations Series 6 (Tokyo: Japan Institute of Labour, 1980).

Steiner, G. A., and Steiner, J. F., *Business, Government, and Society* (6th ed.) (New York: McGraw-Hill, 1991).

The Wall Street Journal, "Japan and Foreign Labor" (October 16, 1990), 23A.

The Wall Street Journal, "Foreign Residents of Japan" (December 17, 1991), 5A.

Thurow, L., *Head to Head* (New York: William Morrow, 1992).

Williams, J., "West Meets East," *The Washington Post Magazine* (January 5, 1992), 13–28.

Wokutch, R. E., "Corporate Social Responsibility Japanese Style," *Academy of Management Executive* 4 (1990), 56–74.

Wokutch, R. E., "Myths of the Japanese Factory" *Journal of Commerce* (August 26, 1992a), 10A.

Wokutch, R. E., *Worker Protection, Japanese Style: Occupational Safety and Health in the Auto Industry* (Ithaca, N.Y.: ILR Press, Cornell University, 1992b).

Wokutch, R., and McLaughlin, J., "The US and Japanese Work Injury and Illness Experience," *Monthly Labor Review* (April 1992), 3–11.

Wokutch, R., and Shepard, J. M., "The Maturing of the Japanese Economy: Corporate Social Responsibility Implications," *Business Ethics Quarterly* (1999). Forthcoming.

Yamagiwa, H., "Accidents Add to Illegals' Plight," *The Japan Times* (June 14, 1996), 3.

Yamaji, K., "A Global Perspective of Ethics in Business from a Japanese Viewpoint," in this volume.

A Global Perspective of Ethics in Business from a Japanese Viewpoint

Keizo Yamaji

Abstract

Business ethics should not just be a corporate code, but be implemented in the line of business as a corporate philosophy. As an example of the above, I would like to present corporate activities of Canon, Inc. based on the "Kyosei" Initiative which I directed, especially its global development. I would like to show what these activities are ahead of the times and result in great prosperity of a corporation, and to tell my dream to increase corporations which take the same types of actions based on the "Kyosei" Initiative.

Outline

Ladies and gentlemen, it is a great honor for me to have an opportunity to speak at this First World Congress of Business, Economics, and Ethics. I have been introduced to you as a company executive and businessman. I also graduated with a degree in physics and concentrated on the natural sciences but not on the humanities. As a result, I neither studied ethics systematically nor, indeed, even gave serious thought to this subject.

It is with some hesitation, therefore, that I speak today about a global perspective of ethics in business. Still, I shall try to present in my own way – simple but essential – my business ethics and their implementation in management, particularly in global operation.

Let me introduce to you the order of the topics I would like to discuss.

First, I will introduce my business ethics, "Kyosei", followed by how I have come to the conclusion that the Kyosei Initiative should make up the core of corporate philosophy.

Secondly, I will explain two management concepts derived from this corporate philosophy, namely Sensitivity Conscious Management (SCM) and Ecology Conscious Management (ECM), by introducing actual examples.

Following that, I will talk about actual implementation of the Kyosei Initiative in detail, from the viewpoint of globalization. I will then show how this implementation is structured within the corporate grand strategies. Finally I will introduce the degree of effect which the Kyosei Initiative actually produces on business performance, to provide you with an outlook for Kyosei Initiative in the future.

My Business Ethics

As a company executive, I naturally wish to help make mine a truly good company. It is my belief that a good company is one which is appreciated and respected by everyone throughout the world, and one that recognized its *raison d'être* because people around the world see that it brings the good to everyone. In other words, a good company, I would emphasize, is one which can become better together, and coexist for better future with the people of the world. In short, it is a Kyosei company.

Although my way of saying this may be very simple and even somewhat primitive, I recognize this is the origin of my business ethics.

Business Ethics and Corporate Philosophy

Business ethics will become meaningful only when they are implemented in the line of business, or within the principal business operation of a company. Activities conducted by a company to make cultural and social contributions are outside its main business operation and, thus, the implementation of business ethics can not be supplemented in these philanthropical events.

So business ethics should not just be a corporate code, but be implemented as the corporate philosophy.

There are two essential factors to corporate philosophy. One is that a company behaving in accordance with its philosophy be certainly successful, and the other is that the corporate philosophy create the mainstream of the times.

Concerning the first factor, how can we say that the Kyosei Initiative is the key for a successful corporation?

Here, Kyosei in business ethics requires two features to be effective; on the one hand, it must always be implemented; and on the other, it must not be exclusive.

Corresponding to these features, Kyosei as corporate philosophy has two conditions. One is prosperity through implementation of the philosophy; the other is prosperity through Kyosei with competitors.

Since any global enterprise will ultimately fail if hated by everyone worldwide, Kyosei is the necessary condition for the continuing prosperity and success of companies. Business competition stimulates progress, leading to the prosperity of all competing companies, and useless friction will be avoided through Kyosei among companies, which will help bring about efficient and practical use of limited resources, also leading to business success. Thus, the Kyosei Initiative is the key for a successful and prosperous business community.

What are the grounds for the second factor, that the Kyosei Initiative create the mainstream of the times?

Concerning this, let us consider the following points in turn. First, this is an age of mega-chaos, which needs to structure a new system. Second, studies on the return to the origins of politics, economy, and society, as well as on the return to the origins of industry and technology, will converge and reach a common conclusion that the new system should be based on the Kyosei Initiative. Hence, we can affirm that the mainstream of the times is heading for Kyosei.

Era of Mega-chaos

After the Cold War, the system maintained during the Cold War period collapsed, and the world is now in a chaos. Fierce economical conflicts exist between the developed countries, and developing countries are starting to participate in this conflict, which is growing to an economical war. This will soon result in a widening of the gaps between extremes, separating the strong and the weak, the rich and the poor. On the other hand, there is no sign to the end of the conflict between tribes, races, and different religious beliefs all over the world. These groups will see further division into smaller ones, each claiming the right of self-determination.

The other issue is ecology and natural resources. A very rapid economical growth is currently taking place in countries and areas which have large populations such as China. This may bring destruction to nature and a severe shortage of the world's natural resources. To stop such disaster, there is a risk of a new type of conflict, such as natural resources war or ecology war. On the other hand, poor countries are not in a situation to have concerns about environment or resources, and the destruction is out of people's hands. There are acceptable environmental limitations which should not be exceeded, but these threshold values are coming alarmingly near. The gap between the rich and poor will become more distinct.

In this era of mega-chaos, the lack of humanity is of the most serious concern. Egoism prevails, resulting in a lack of humanity at individual, corporate, regional, and national levels. A search for measures which will solve this problem is of the utmost importance.

Various attempts have been made to deal with this situation in society. One of the measures proposed and included in the agenda of this conference is the Ethics Officer system. Business ethics-related stipulations may be incorporated some day in ISO standards (i.e., the standards set up by the International Organization for Standardization based in Geneva). Having established product quality standards now, ISO's next step is the establishment of environmental standards. In both areas, inspection and registration systems play important roles carried out in accordance with stipulated standards. It is said that ISO's role will have to be further expanded to cover safety, hygiene, labor, and finance, and may eventually include business ethics as well.

While I believe these trends are quite necessary as a symptomatic treatment, what is required more fundamentally is the construction of a new system which replaces the one maintained during the Cold War period. Generally speaking, there is an experiential law which says anything in the world will progress spirally. So it is important to return to a starting point and to think of constructing a new system.

Structuring of a New System

Return to an Origin of Politics, Economy, and Society

The politics, the economies, and the society of this century was a confrontation between capitalist countries that pursue freedom and socialists that pursue equality. Countries that pursue free economy, mainly allies of the United States, have won a remarkable economical growth under the free economy and liberalized competition structure. What they have achieved in the free society was a harsh competitive society which has lead to a wide gap between the haves and have-nots. On the other hand, the socialist economical structure that was represented by the Soviet Union tried to create equality by force and as a result of this, they neglected humanity and the society became non efficient, and unnecessary equality was emphasized. The power of the party was strong and as a result, the difference between the haves and have-nots was also large.

In other words, the pursuit of freedom amongst the capitalist countries and the pursuit of equality amongst the socialist countries both did not seem to have succeeded.

On the other hand, China is introducing free market economy into the socialist structure and is trying to balance freedom and equality. As far as we see the Chinese situation today, there seems to be a very harsh competitive society similar to that of the United States, and the gap between the wealthy and the non-wealthy is widening.

One recalls the French Revolution when the idealism of freedom and equality was advocated. One more idealism there was fraternity. However, fraternity was not emphasized neither in capitalist countries nor in socialist countries. This seems to be the problem. This problem was not given so much attention, probably because the fraternity advocated in the French Revolution emphasized comradeship. In our new political, economical, and social structure, it is necessary to return to the starting point of the French Revolution. We have to re-construct a society where freedom and equality are engaged nicely; freedom, which is the basic human desire and motivator of progress, and equality, which is a fundamental human right and basic condition for progress are well engaged, and we should have a structure that the spirit of friendship works as a lubricant and a restraint and, in the process, build a heart-warming society of Kyosei.

Return to an Origin of Industry and Technology
The next area is industry and technology.

A new highly developed information age, or information society, is built on top of the very mature industrial society. This is what industry and technology are trying to achieve. We have definitely become affluent. However, human nature is that of greed and egoism, and people have a tendency that only they themselves want to be more rich, and they aim to stabilize their richness for themselves only. Therefore, the advancement of the industrial society ought to make reasons for conflict, and the weapons for such conflict, become more and more advanced. Also, wasteful use of resources happens and makes reasons for the destruction of nature. Therefore, as long as we continue today's character of industry and technology, so called sustainable civilization will not be achieved.

When one looks back at the time when humankind invented the primitive stage of agriculture, which is the starting point of industry and technology, it seemed that there was a simple hope for Kyosei to harmonize with the fluctuation of nature and still be able to supply food in a stable manner, so that there was no conflict on food shortage. Therefore, what I am advocating is nothing unusual. The only thing we need to achieve is to bring industry and technology back to its starting point. Industrialization and information-related technologies, so far, are those being used for competition. What we will need from now on are technologies for harmonization. We will not enjoy sustainable civilization or the new system for a Kyosei world until both technologies are fused.

Kyosei Initiative

Thus, my conclusion is that Kyosei creates the main stream of the times. It is also the key for corporate success, as seen before. This is why I have adopted the Kyosei Initiative as our corporate philosophy. To summarize, the Kyosei Initiative is the fusion of competition for progress and harmony for sustainable development. Competition based on freedom and equality is absolutely necessary for the progress of mankind, while harmony is indispensable for the continuous survival and prosperity of mankind. These two factors are fused into the Kyosei Initiative.

Now, I will move to a new managerial system for the effective implementation of the Kyosei Initiative. The underlying guideline for us is to choose the means to attain our goals. The Machiavellian statement "the end justifies the means" is outdated. The age of naive, blind pursuit of result is over. We are in the age of selecting means and measures, including states of mind, for attaining the end, in addition to the pursuit of result. Now, corporate performance is not only assessed by managerial indexes (figures and numbers) but also measures to take.

Following this guideline, corporate activity needs to be managed by a sensitivity conscious management, or management thoughtful of the other parties' position, when one aims at Kyosei between people and people. The corporate activity also needs to be managed by ecology-conscious management, or management with careful consideration of the environment and resources, when one aims at Kyosei of people and nature.

Implementation of SCM

Sensitivity Conscious Management (SCM) first requires observance of the rules of market competition.

Contenders will first observe rules to ensure that competition is fair and square. Comparatively weaker contenders will ask for measures that provide protection or support. Moreover, it is the duty of each contender to make some form of contribution to the infrastructures of the society or market, which form the arena for competition.

These rules for market competition may simply exist in the form of sound judgment or may appear as social rules, legislation, pacts, or guidelines. Within the arena of free market competition, Canon constantly looks for and adheres to such rules of competition.

In this regard, a basic approach for the understanding of profit is very important.

It is important for Canon to yield profits. For Canon, however, the pursuit of profits is not the ultimate corporate goal. Profits are one of the important motivating forces behind the materialization of our corporate goals. Nevertheless, they should be considered as an intermediate goal. As I have said many times before, Canon's ultimate goal is to "become a better corporation for the society and the earth." To achieve this ideal, Canon must at least refrain from "actions that damage the world and the society."

Even if investment of the infrastructures of competition does not immediately yield profits, Canon hopes to continue steadily building up these infrastructures, applying Canon's unique technologies. As investments in the infrastructures of competition, Canon:

- Supports new art activities using Canon's image-processing technologies;
- Participates in large national projects based on optical technologies;
- Provides processing machinery and measuring instruments that are central to integrated circuit production; and
- Offers clean sources of energy.

The above projects represent the themes that only Canon can handle; that is, that Canon regards as its mission projects.

Next, with SCM, it is necessary to avoid useless conflict or unnecessary competition.

What should one do to avoid useless conflict in the market place? First, stop copying others. For example, let us assume that there is a new product in the industry introduced by one company and the sale of the product is good. If another company copies this product or makes a small improvement, perhaps reducing the price and starts marketing the product, this company will take a certain portion of the market. This action seems to be a safe approach from the marketing point of view. However, a similar product will lead to competition of price reduction. In order to reduce price, people will rush to large capital investment to enable mass production. As a result of this, there will be an overproduction and a large inventory will be held. At the end, they will reach a mass write off. With the Kyosei Initiative, such pattern will not be repeated. Technologies and product categories that never existed in the past, in other words, an unexplored technology and an unexplored product category, will be the area for research and development. Business can be conducted where other companies have not entered. Business competition must be made always between heterogeneous products or business areas. In order to achieve this, it requires a long period of time and a large expense. It is, therefore, necessary to secure profit for the originator in order to collect the invested amount and to have the money available for the next investment. It is necessary to guard the business by intellectual property rights so that others may not easily copy the product. This means that the segmentation of business needs to be done through originality and intellectual property rights.

On the other hand, if other corporations similarly have technology and product in an unexplored business domain, and if we desire to have such product on our own shelf, we would discuss this with the other company so that we can sell their product through our channel. We will not choose to copy and make such product ourselves. This is the SCM way.

Furthermore, if that same company chooses to sell our original product, then they could sell our product and become good partners. By creating such partnership through segmentation of the business domain, wasteful duplication in using certain managerial resources can be avoided, and we can direct our own managerial resources where it is most needed. We can also utilize resources of the other party effectively.

Implementation of ECM

Under ECM (Ecology Conscious Management), product planning and business plan, which form the foundation of activity for manufacturing companies, changes greatly. For the product planning, rather than aiming at best sellers which only sell for a short period of time, like a firework display, we aim at a long seller that will steadily sell for a long period of time, the reason being long sellers require less investment for the manufacturing facility, the manufacturing can be conducted stably, and the sales can be stabilized. There will be no need to manufacture products that eventually will become an inventory and a target for write offs.

And there is also the subject of needs. Customers are human beings before being a user of the product. There are fundamental requirements for human to live in this world. The requirements as human are the will to maintain the beautiful earth and the natural environment. One is critical about wasteful use of natural resources. Viewing the customers as those who only enjoy the benefit of the machine is not sufficient. New products need to satisfy both of these two faces the customer has.

Therefore, thirdly, the existing products need to be replaced by environmentally friendly products "from the cradle to the grave." It does not use toxic material nor produce toxic emission. It also promotes more energy and material saving. Products using recycled material, or a product that is more easy to recycle, is what the new replaced product will be.

In business plan, too, there needs to be some self restriction. For example, one should choose "underproduction" over "overproduction." One should be more concerned about overproduction resulting in inventory increase and at the end write offs, rather than underproduction and missing sales opportunity.

On market share, one should aim at optimum market share rather than maximum market share. It is indeed an important strategy for a corporation to improve market share. However, these actions should not exceed the point that would stimulate the competitor and employ strategies to maintain optimum market share. If one exceeds this point, the competitor will feel threatened, and an endless price reduction war may start between the two. This could damage the market and it could also damage the business.

The three elements for competition so far were QCD (Quality, Cost, Delivery). However, now environment comes on top and the achievement of EQCD becomes the corporate target. The reason why we put the "E" at the top means Environment comes first. Any product that has a problem in "E" will not be made. Any factory that has problems in "E" will not be operated. The "E" at the top represents this firm commitment.

Two Types of Global Corporation

I hope I have defined the Kyosei Initiative together with the concepts of Sensitivity Conscious Management (SCM) and Ecology Conscious Management (ECM) clearly enough. Now I would like to proceed with some actual examples and results in implementing globalization based on the Kyosei Initiative.

In my opinion, there are two types of global corporations. The first type pursues globalization using power which, in this case, refers to the various capabilities possessed by a corporation such as management power, capital, technology, engineering expertise, production capacity, and sales power. Nearly all of the corporations in the world that are currently regarded as global corporations fit into this category. This first type of global corporation eagerly strives to localize operations. It pursues localization by allocating management resources such as personnel, goods, and capital to the area they launch. Concurrently, it deepens its relationship with the local community by participating in diverse events, donation to public facilities, taking part in volunteer activities, and so on. As a result, the presence of this type of corporation is also welcomed by local residents. In the final analysis, however, this corporation is only thinking about how it can facilitate its own work in the local community. When viewed from a broader perspective, this type of corporation may be contributing to the local community but is not always contributing to national development, or broader area development of its industries or culture.

In contrast, the second type of global corporation pursues globalization based on sensitivity. During its globalization process, this type of corporation strives for localization by giving top priority to the industry, national feelings, and culture of the other country or region. This type of corporation may be more moderate in direct investments or may decide against globalization of specific businesses. Consequently, its level of globalization may appear lower than that of the first type of corporation when judged by figures alone. Nevertheless, Canon believes that this second type represents a truly global corporation. Canon intends to become a truly global corporation and has actually started taking steps in that direction.

The following are actual examples of different aspects of Canon's globalization activities.

Implementation of SCM in Developed Countries

Launching When Invited

First, in globalization in developed countries, I have always had four guidelines based on Sensitivity Conscious Management.

First guideline is "Launching when invited." I will present three examples.

The first one was the launch of our factory and laboratory in France during the early 1980s. The French Government requested us to establish a factory for the production of personal copying machines, which were among the most advanced products of our company. The Government's intention must be, above all, to create new jobs, as well as to introduce this new industry to France. The general feeling toward France by Japanese companies at that time was not positive, causing reluctance to join in what was regarded as a somewhat difficult country including language difficulties. We, however, decided to launch the factory into France where other firms would not like to participate, considering this makes a special value for us. The company was treated quite well by the French Government because of the scarcity value. This led further to the production of other office machines as well as the establishment of a research center. This is an actual example of globalization carried out in close consideration of the local government's needs.

The second example is one of a decision made to withdraw from business, recognizing that it is not welcome. In 1988, the European Community announced the imposition of anti-dumping duties on made-in-Japan dot matrix printers being exported to EC countries. To avoid paying the duties, the Japanese manufacturers concerned suddenly moved to build plants in Europe. Canon's dot matrix printers were manufactured and yielded moderate profits, but Canon boldly decided to completely withdraw from the dot matrix printer business. In this case, would you say that a higher level of globalization was achieved by the Japanese manufacturers which built plants in Europe or by Canon which completely withdrew from the dot matrix printer business instead? On the basis of performance figures, the former will naturally be selected. Why did Canon choose to withdraw from this business? At a time when there were only three or four European manufacturers of dot matrix printers, more than ten Japanese manufacturers suddenly built a total of twelve printer plants in Europe.

Under these circumstances, Japan will inevitably be perceived as destroying European industries. Canon withdrew from this business by considering local industry.

The third example explains the transfer of the Electronic Typewriter (ETW) business to the United States. In 1990, Canon moved not only the production facilities of its ETW but the entire business function, including development and headquarters, to the USA. In both Europe and the USA, anti-dumping suits in the business machines category began with typewriters. Upon reflecting on why typewriters were the initial target, I realized that the West had been driven by necessity to invent the typewriter, which has since been used to set forth nearly all aspects of Western culture and civilization. The majority of prominent literary works as well as the famous scientific papers were created on typewriters. It occurred to me that typewriters may have been the first target of anti-dumping suits because Americans and Europeans have such a deep and traditional affection for them. I became aware of our conceit with technology to produce typewriters in Japan and export most of them merely because Japan was somehow advanced in technology. I then decided to immediately move all ETW operations to the USA, where all operations are handled by Americans. This move was the result of consideration for other cultures.

Minority Shareholder Policy

The second guideline for SCM-based globalization in a developed country is the minority investment system. The first example of this concerns the case of Olivetti-Canon Industriale.

In around 1980, the copier division of Olivetti had fallen technologically behind and was in a painful predicament, which generated a yearly deficit of 1,000 million yen. When Olivetti requested assistance of me, I resolved to help this prestigious Italian corporation out of its difficulties. We agreed to the separation of Olivetti's copier division and its restructuring into a new copier manufacturing joint-venture named OCI (Olivetti-Canon Industriale S.p.A.). When setting up OCI, however, we participated in its capitalization as a minority shareholder, entrusting the majority (over 50%) of voting stock and all management rights to Olivetti. We decided to concentrate on providing technical assistance. In this way, the copier division of Olivetti, a prestigious European corporation, could be restructured while remaining a European firm. It was concluded that this form of participation by Canon would be most acceptable to public sentiments in Italy as well as Europe. Canon provided full cooperation, enabling OCI to go into the black after just two years. This is an example of respecting the national sentiment of the target country. At the same time however, Canon's behavior helped encourage the morale of the joint-venture partner, which ultimately resulted in saving regarding Canon's personnel and investment.

The next example concerns minority participation in the capital of a new venture business. Canon invests in numerous business ventures around the world that are developing unique technologies. Canon is providing capital, technologies, and commercial support. Canon believes that technology should remain with local corporations in the country where the technology originated. Therefore, Canon never holds more than a minority stake in such business ventures, unless specifically requested to do so. This encourages the morale of the partner, leading to favorable results. For Canon, this will eventually save resources.

Segmentation, Partnership

The third guideline for SCM-based globalization in developed countries concerns segmentation and partnership. This subject was already touched upon when talking on competition in heterogeneity. Here, I will add some examples of our own experience.

In LBP business, we have been the first product developer and the first business creator. We were, therefore, able to form a partnership with companies that have strong capabilities in printer software and sales such as HP and Apple. By the OEM sales of our LBP products through these companies, we have achieved a 70% market share in this product category. On the other hand, we are marketing advanced personal computers and work stations that HP and Apple manufactures. In Japan, Canon is the largest distributor for Apple's Macintosh.

As such, the Kyosei Initiative brings benefits to both parties of these partnerships; both in Canon and in HP, printer business has grown tremendously, and has become the largest business sector within each company.

Idea of Balancing the Tripolar World

Now, I will talk on the fourth guideline for SCM-based operations, which is the balancing of the tripolar world.

We established full scale research facilities apart from our Japanese facility in the United States and Western Europe. There, we conduct research activities that are not taken up in Japan.

Technologies or research themes have regionality. For example, what Japan is strong at is hardware, particularly those that are based on electronic technology, and is aimed at consumer use or office use. This is the area Japan is good at.

In contrast, America is good at computer and software: technology and products that are system based, and also large scale industrial technology such as space technology or defense technology.

Western Europe has some specific technology areas in which it is strong.

Therefore, we will conduct research work in which the particular area has strength. By doing so, it is possible to hire skilled engineers and to be able to bring with them the achievement that they have already made.

Another important point is to commercialize and start up the business based on the achievement of each area's research facility locally. And from that area, the business will aim at the world market.

The ultimate picture is that the companies at three poles, Japan, Europe, and America, will grow to a similar scale, and they will work in such a way that the trade balance between them will be taken.

This plan is what I call " the tripolar balance plan."

Implementation of ECM in Developed Countries

Now, I will move to the company's ECM-based behavior in carrying out globalization in developed countries. In relation to this, I will take up the subject of material recycling.

In our LBP, the cartridges used in the LBP are collected in a global scale, disassembled, cleaned, and certain parts are reused, but most of the parts are returned to its original material level and reused.

In case of new product of cartridge, 3kgC of CO_2 are emitted during its life cycle. In contrast, in case of recycled cartridge, 2kgC of CO_2 are emitted. It means the emission of CO_2 is reduced by 1kgC, owing to recycling.

At present, the cost of producing a recycled cartridge is higher than the cost of producing a new cartridge. We simply accept and absorb this additional cost, considering as a necessary expense for eliminating 1kgC of CO_2, or making it harmless.

Implementation of SCM and ECM in Developing Countries

Optimum Support System

Now, I move to the presentation of actual cases of globalization in developing countries. We have had five viewpoints in order to implement the Kyosei Initiative in these countries. The first viewpoint is to offer an optimum support system. Here is an example case made in China.

Canon has set up production facilities in Dalian and Zhuhai as subsidiary companies 100% capitalized by Canon.

In earlier years, Canon formed two licensed-production projects and two joint-ventures with Chinese organizations. Whenever production was involved, however, Canon found the results to be unsatisfactory. For example, Canon was not satisfied with such points as:

- Factory management based on our production system.
- Attainment of quality and costs.
- Establishing parts factories and personnel training.

We realized that it could best benefit China by building our own ideal production facilities as models for Chinese industry.

We established four main objectives. The first objective is to perfect a Chinese version of our production system that has been modified to reflect Chinese culture and customs, and to firmly anchor this system at the production facilities. The second objective is to enable procurement in China of parts that satisfy international standards for quality and cost. At that time, China had a greater need to build a solid technical base for parts production than to acquire assembly technologies. The third objective is to produce products that meet international standards for quality and cost; that is, products that can compete as exports. The fourth objective is to foster capable Chinese personnel that genuinely agree with Canon's ideals and will work as team members toward common goals.

After these objectives are attained, our next step will be to form a joint-venture with a Chinese corporation. This joint-venture could get all of the expertise, capable personnel, and quality parts Canon subsidiary has gained.

This would enable Chinese consumers to also purchase products of the same high quality and low cost available in other industrialized nations.

The sequential process from a 100% subsidiary to a joint-venture may initially seem like a roundabout route, but it should turn out to be the most reliable way to genuinely contribute to China's development.

Support to Sustainable Development

The second viewpoint is that globalization must proceed with special consideration to the sustainable development of target regions. Factories being established in a developing country must embrace the same level of environmental standards as those of its home country. In some cases, globalization may increase energy demands as well as produce industrial waste, requiring the building of thermal power plants and waste disposal facilities. Thus, investing countries and corporations should be accordingly responsible for the costs of constructing and maintaining the pollution-free system of such local facilities.

Clean Production Process

As the third viewpoint, for globalization in developing countries, it is necessary to make production processes clean.

Let me give you two examples from our case. We develop optical glass which does not have a lead component, so that no sludge during the polishing process includes lead, therefore making it cleaner. The zoom-lens for our Single Lens Reflex camera has totally eliminated lead from all the elements used in this lens. Canon is one of the world's largest manufacturer of lenses, which has the manufacturing capacity of ten million pieces per year. We believe that it is our responsibility to complete a lead-free lenses.

BJ technology is the technology developed for computer output print. As an application of this technology, we are developing print on cloth.

In traditional process, screen print process and cleaning process can be reasons for pollution, and the new process can reduce such risk. The waste water after the cleaning process of the screen and printed cloth has been reduced to one tenth.

Joint Research of Sustainable Civilization

In the fourth viewpoint, it is necessary to conduct joint studies in cooperation with target countries for the realization of Sustainable Civilization (SC). Developed countries have a fully matured civilization today, but this maturity is structured on the basis of the notion that the earth is both a supplier of limitless resources and an assimilator/absorber of infinite discharge. Naturally, the prosperity of these developed countries puts a heavy load on the environment. Civilization attained in this way must really be regarded as non-sustainable. On the other hand, developing countries with large populations are eager for high economic growth in the pursuit of wealth, even if by means of simply careless introduction of this non-sustainable civilization. It is obvious that this would eventually cause environmental crises and exhaustion of natural resources early in the twenty-first century, if no measures were taken to prevent this. Thus, the developed countries are obligated to thoroughly reform their own non-sustainable civilizations, and not to export to developing countries their civilization as it currently is. We have to look for a new form of sustainable civilization through joint efforts between developed and developing countries, both sides offering their utmost wisdom. Joint studies must proceed quickly, with developing countries presenting their requirements and developed countries offering technologies. The future of the world depends on the outcome of these studies.

Such joint studies should have, as one of their central subjects, the system design of the infrastructure for creating and realizing SC in developing countries. Some important issues covered by this subject are:

    (1) Transportation System:

        The transportation mode must be a combination of electric railway (for long distance traffic) and electric vehicles (for short distance).

    (2) Communication System:

        Two-direction wireless multimedia systems.

    (3) Energy System:

        In low latitude areas near the equator, where it is very rich in solar energy, main energy resource should be renewable solar energy instead of fossil energy.

Particularly in clean energy, we are engaging in research of the amorphous solar cell technology. This technology has been derived from Canon's high speed plain paper copier technology which utilizes amorphous silicon drum. The condition that a solar cell can be commercialized for power purposes is that the cost is reduced to less than one watt per one US dollar, and our research work is aiming at this goal.

Solar generation is most effective near the equator and the desert area where there is plenty of sunshine. The advantage of amorphous silicon solar cell, contrary to crystalline cells, is that in these high temperature areas, the efficiency becomes higher.

It is possible that new sustainable civilization will realize first in the developing countries, not in the developed countries, because the developed countries have been heavily invested to their infrastructure in the past.

Relocating Industries

The fifth point is the relocation of industries. The ideal positioning of industries in the future would include manufacturing industries concentrated in lower latitude regions, with medium and higher latitude areas home to software and service industries (the latter including the research and development industry as an important sector). The above industry location concept aims at maximum utilization of solar energy which is abundantly available in lower latitude regions.

Management Based on the "Kyosei" Initiative

Five Principles of Management

So far, I have shown various actual examples of the implementation of our ideas. Now, I will present how we have incorporated such implementation in our management systems. In this regard, first I will talk about five management principles, followed by two guidelines set up based on these principles.

I have held five principles for my management.

1. Management must be led by ideology.
2. Management must create the main stream of the times.
3. Management must be easy to understand.
4. Management must not be trivial.
5. Management must be a beautiful system.

Out of these five principles, I have already touched upon the first and second. The other three concern the formation of management system. Management easy to understand is the key for successful implementation. Management which is not trivial provides its own *raison-d'être* and creates an advantage in competition. Finally, a truly good management should intuitively be recognized by all as beautiful.

Five Principles for R&D Activities

Based on these principles, we have established our five principles for R&D activities:

1. We reject research and development themes for military purposes.
2. We do not conduct R&D that is not desirable from an ecological point of view.
3. We create previously unexplored technologies and product categories.
4. We respect original technologies and/or product categories created by others.
5. We conduct R&D activities on a global scale and create new business activities in the country or territory of its findings.

These five principles are also the principles for our business operation. I am sure you will understand that the various actual examples already presented today comply with these principles.

Direction to Diversification

The other guideline is for business diversification.

First, the conclusion: The steps of the Kyosei Initiative are defined as "Kyosei between people and people, people and machine, people and nature." At these sequences, businesses will be diversified so the businesses will offer means to assist the Kyosei activities at each step.

The key Kyosei factor for people and people to coexist is communication, or dialogue.

The first business Canon took up was the camera business. Photograph overcomes the barrier of language, and helps people communicate with people.

Next, Canon entered the office equipment business. This is the area where people and people communicate deeper using the medium of various information.

The area that Canon needs to take up following the Kyosei between people and people is Kyosci between people and machine and, furthermore, people and nature. In these cases, what is necessary is the technology for harmony. From the technology of communication to the technology of harmony, it is necessary to make a break-through for Canon's technology.

For the Kyosei between people and machine, the necessary harmonizing technology is human interface. The most directly related business with human interface is peripheral equipment business. Especially, for printers, Canon has concentrated its research work on non-impact printers, and has created new technologies and product categories, such as the LBP and BJ printer. Both offer a noiseless office.

The next business direction is the businesses that will contribute to Kyosei between people and nature.

I have touched upon the cases of recycling, clean energy, and clean-process operations already. You have seen that the various examples meet these diversification guidelines.

Effects of the "Kyosei" Initiative

In the first part of this talk, I stated that the Kyosei Initiative is the key for a successful and prosperous business, and here is an actual example of effectiveness. Let us examine the transition which has taken place in the sales (non-consolidated) of six Japanese camera manufacturers over the past twenty-five years. While these six companies were at almost the same level twenty-five years ago, there are remarkable differences now. Canon has attained sales amounting over 1.2 trillion yen, double those of Company A which is in second place. We are ahead the other four companies by a margin of about 1 trillion yen.

This clearly shows the outcome of our implementation of SCM and ECM management based on the Kyosei Initiative, including competition in heterogeneity, segmentation, and partnership. I am strongly confident that these actual results have more than rewarded us for our joint efforts aimed at creating good companies which can become better together with all the people in the world.

Future of "Kyosei"

I am certain you agree with me in that the Kyosei Initiative is truly wonderful. So, I want to promote its recognition, approaches, and methods throughout the world. The very first step is to apply the Kyosei Initiative more and more to Canon, implementing it to bring about further Canon business success, making Canon a good model company for others and expanding its scale of business as well as its influence in the society.

The business partners we have are also partners in the Kyosei Initiative, and they have a good understanding of it. I wish to see this partner-link grow ever wider and larger. I would like to invite our present customers and future customers to join this chain of Kyosei partners, after recognizing Canon's ideal in our products.

I had the opportunity of speaking on this subject at CADAS conference of the French national academy, and IVA of the Swedish Royal Academy, as well as in the United States, and all were successful in increasing the number of supporters. I assumed the chairmanship of Nihon Tetra Pak K.K. in September last year, at the invitation of Dr. Gad Rausing, owner of Tetra Lavel Group, who appreciated and supported my views. These are some examples showing Kyosei partnership expanding on a global level, and I am more than grateful to see this ever-growing movement supporting our ideas.

Contributors

Tanri Abeng, former President Director and CEO of PT Bakrie & Brothers and PT Bakrie Nusantara Corporation in Indonesia, is now State Minister for State-owned Enterprises in Indonesia.

Norman E. Bowie is Elmer L. Andersen Chair in Corporate Responsibility in the Carlson School of Management, University of Minnesota, Minneapolis, Minnesota, USA. As of July 1, 1998: Executive Vice-President for Seminars, The Aspen Institute, USA.

S. K. Chakraborty is Professor and Founder-Convener, Management Centre for Human Values, Indian Institute of Management, Calcutta, India.

Elia V. Chepaitis is Associate Professor of Information Systems in the School of Business, Fairfield University, Fairfield, Connccticut, USA.

Joanne B. Ciulla is Coston Family Chair of Leadership and Ethics in the Jepson School of Leadership Studies, University of Richmond, USA.

Henri-Claude de Bettignies is Professor of Ethics at INSEAD, France, and Visiting Professor of International Business at the Graduate School of Business, Stanford University, USA.

Richard T. De George is University Distinguished Professor in the Department of Philosophy, and Director of the International Center for Ethics in Business, University of Kansas, Lawrence, Kansas, USA.

Georges Enderle is Arthur and Mary O'Neil Professor of International Business Ethics at the University of Notre Dame, Indiana, USA.

Carolyn B. Erdener is Associate Professor in the Department of Management, Hong Kong Baptist University, Hong Kong Special Administrative Region, China.

John M. Etheredge was Associate Professor in the Department of Management, Hong Kong Baptist University, Hong Kong Special Administrative Region, China (until 1998).

Kenneth E. Goodpaster is Koch Professor of Business Ethics at the University of St. Thomas, Minneapolis, Minnesota, USA.

Simon Grand is Associate Professor in the Institute of Management, University of Zurich, Switzerland.

Hans Küng is Professor Emeritus of Ecumenical Theology at the University of Tübingen, Germany, and President of the Global Ethic Foundation.

J. Coley Lamprecht is Professor of Educational Psychology at the Rand Afrikaans University, Johannesburg, South Africa.

Jegoo Lee was Lecturer at Chulalongkorn University, Bangkok, Thailand, and is now Instructor at Yonsei University, Seoul, Korea.

Jack Mahoney is Dixons Professor Emeritus in Business Ethics and Social Responsibility at London Business School, United Kingdom.

Toshio Matsuoka is Professor in the School of Business Administration, Kanagawa University, Japan.

Gregory K. Ornatowski Ph.D. is Lecturer in the Sloan School of Management, Massachussetts Institute of Technology, Cambridge, USA.

Hun-Joon Park is Associate Professor of Management in the Department of Business Administration, Yonsei University, Seoul, Korea, and Visiting Associate Professor in the Department of Management, College of Business Administration, Bowling Green State University, Ohio, USA.

Moses L. Pava is the Alvin H. Einbender Chair in Business Ethics in the Sy Syms School of Business, Yeshiva University, New York, USA.

Jacques Polet is Professor of Communication Ethics in the Department of Communication, Université Catholique de Louvain, Belgium.

Dr. *G. R. S. Rao* is the Director of the Centre for Public Policy and Social Development, Hyderabad, India.

Gedeon J. Rossouw is Professor of Philosophy at Rand Afrikaans University, Johannesburg, South Africa.

Stephan Rothlin is Professor of Business Ethics in the Institute of Physical Education, Beijing University, Beijing, China.

Eduardo Schmidt is Professor of Business Ethics at the Universidad del Pacífico, Lima, Peru.

Amartya Sen, Nobel laureate in Economics 1998, is Master of Trinity College, Cambridge, U.K., and Lamont Professor Emeritus, Harvard University, Cambridge, USA.

Jon M. Shepard is Pamplin Professor of Management, Pamplin College of Business, Virginia Tech, Blacksburg, Virginia, USA.

Alejo José Sison is Associate Professor of Philosophy at the University of Asia & the Pacific, Manila, The Philippines.

Ji-Hwan Song was Instructor at Yonsei University, Seoul, Korea.

Akira Takahashi is Professor Emeritus of Tokyo University and Director of the (governmental) Institute of Development Studies in Tokyo, Japan.

Mitsuhiro Umezu is Assistant Professor of Keio University, Tokyo, Japan.

Paul Vaaler is at the Fletcher School of Law and Diplomacy, Tufts University, Medford, USA.

Simon Webley is Director of the British-American Research Association, London, United Kingdom.

Judith White is Associate Professor of Organizational Behavior in the Insitute of Management and International Entrepreneurship, California State University Monterey Bay, USA.

Richard E. Wokutch is Pamplin Professor of Managment, Pamplin College of Business, Virginia Tech, Blacksburg, Virginia, USA.

Xinwen Wu Ph. D. is Lecturer of Ethics in the Philosophy Department and Research Fellow at the Centre for Applied Ethics, Fudan University, Shanghai, China.

Keizo Yamaji is Chairman of Nihon Tetra Pak K. K. and Honorary Adviser of Canon Inc. Japan.